VERÖFFENTLICHUNG DES VORGESCHICHTLICHEN SEMINARS MARBURG

VERÖFFENTLICHUNG DES VORGESCHICHTLICHEN SEMINARS MARBURG

Sonderband 2

Herausgegeben von

Otto-Herman Frey und Helmut Roth

Marburg 1984

VERÖFFENTLICHUNG DES VORGESCHICHTLICHEN SEMINARS MARBURG

Sonderband 2

LA TÈNE IN IRELAND

Problems of Origin and Chronology

by

BARRY RAFTERY

Marburg 1984

Publication of this book has been aided by a generous grant from the
ALEXANDER VON HUMBOLDT STIFTUNG, BONN

ISBN 3-924222-01-0

Typesetting: Nuala Raftery
Design and Layout: Barry and Nuala Raftery
Gesamtherstellung: Druckerei Kempkes, Offset + Buchdruck GmbH
D-3544 Gladenbach

Orders to: Wasmuth KG, Hardenbergstrasse 9a, D-1000 Berlin 12

FOR NUALA, SARA AND TILLY

TABLE OF CONTENTS

Contents

PREFACE

The present work was conceived and written as a commentary to accompany a catalogue of Irish Iron Age antiquities. The manuscript was submitted for publication early in 1980 and the book was due to appear in March 1982. Unfortunately, because of the business collapse of the publishing house, the book was returned to the writer when at page-proof stage. The catalogue subsequently appeared as an independent publication in October 1983, due to the timely and invaluable intervention of the Vorgeschichtliches Seminar of the Philipps-Universität, Marburg-Lahn and the exceptional dedication of the writer's wife who type-set the entire catalogue in record time. The catalogue is referred to throughout the text which follows as CIIAA.

A number of important works were not available to the writer when the book was in course of preparation. The most significant of these are two Festschrift volumes, one for Michael Duignan (Scott, ed., 1982), the other for R.B.K. Stevenson (O'Connor and Clarke, eds, 1983). Both of these contain papers of fundamental importance for Irish Iron Age studies. Some of the views expressed in the former volume have been incorporated into the text of the present work, but for technical reasons this could be done only on a limited scale. The Stevenson Festschrift appeared too late for consideration here and is merely referred to in the text. Some of the papers in that work, notably the contribution by R.B. Warner, are essential reading in any discussion of the Irish Iron Age.

The main aim of the present volume is to provide an extensive summary of the metalwork and related evidence relevant to a study of the La Tène phase in Ireland. Much of the discussion on this subject to date is dispersed throughout a wide range of journals, many of which are not readily accessible to foreign scholars. It has seemed thus worthwhile, even at the risk of repeating at times what has already been written, to bring together and review, in a single volume, the most important arguments and the available material evidence.

The basis of the work is a study of artifacts and no claim is made that the book represents anything more than this. A full study of the Irish Iron Age remains to be written. It is hoped, however, that by focussing in detail on one of the most important and most clearly recognisable aspects of Iron Age Ireland, a firmer foundation for future research on the Irish Iron Age as a whole will have been provided.

Barry Raftery,
Skerries,
Co. Dublin.

ACKNOWLEDGMENTS

It is with pleasure that I record here my indebtedness to the officers of the many museums and institutions who over the years facilitated in every way my examination of Irish La Tène material under their care

Firstly thanks are due to my father Dr. Joseph Raftery whose help and encouragement in his official capacity (first as Keeper of Irish Antiquities, later as Director, National Museum of Ireland) as well as in his capacity as colleague and friend, were inestimable. In the National Museum I would also like to thank Dr. A.T. Lucas, Mr. A.B. Ó Ríordáin (former and present directors respectively) and Mr. Michael Ryan, Keeper of Irish Antiquities, for facilitating my research on the Irish material. In the Ulster Museum, Belfast, thanks are due to Mr. L.N.W. Flanagan, Keeper of Antiquities, and also to Richard Warner, whose generosity, helpfulness and stimulating discussion have left me deeply in his debt. In the British Museum, London, I am indebted to Dr. Ian Longworth, Keeper of Prehistoric and Romano-British Antiquities, Miss Catherine Johns, Dr. Mansel Spratling and especially Dr. Ian Stead. In the National Museum of Antiquities of Scotland, I am indebted to the former Keeper of Antiquities, Mr. R.B.K. Stevenson and to Dr. Joanna Close-Brooks. In the National Museum of Wales, Cardiff, thanks are due to Mr. George Boon, Keeper of Numismatics and to Dr. Stephen Green. In the Deutsches Museum, Munich, I am indebted to Frau Menzel for facilitating my examination of the "Nice" horn and I must also express my gratitude to Dr. and Frau Franz Schubert who helped me greatly when I was in Munich. For help with material in Cork I am grateful to the late Professor M.J. O'Kelly. In the Free Public Museum Liverpool, I am grateful to Dr. Dorothy Downes for assistance. In the Cambridge Museum of Archaeology and Ethnology I received every assistance from Miss Mary

Cra'ster. In the Ashmolean Museum, Oxford, I was greatly helped by Mr. Humphrey Case and Dr. Andrew Sherratt. In Alnwick Castle I am grateful to His Grace the Duke of Northumberland for permission to examine and publish Irish objects in his collection and I am also indebted to Mr. J. Graham for help with the material in that museum. Mr. R.M. Weatherup of the Armagh County Museum was of great assistance and in the Armagh Public Library Dean S. Lillie afforded me every facility.

I am also indebted to a number of individuals who either drew unpublished material to my notice or who gave permission to include, or to refer to, unpublished material from their excavations. These are Dr. J. Raftery, Mr. D.M. Waterman, Mr. R.B. Warner, Mr. A.E.P. Collins, Professor Etienne Rynne, Professor B. Wailes, Mr. L.N.W. Flanagan, Mr. Peter Danaher and Mr. E.P. Kelly.

The drawings are in the main the work of Miss Ursula Mattenberger, Miss Freda O'Neill and above all Mr. Albert Siggins, whose sustained enthusiasm, industry and technical expertise contributed so much to the successful completion of this work. In the photographic studio of the National Museum of Ireland, a special word of thanks is due to Mr. Brendan Doyle and in the studio of the U.C.D. Archaeology Department I am grateful to Mr. Albert Glaholm for his endless patience with the illustrations.

I am happy to record my sincere thanks to the President of University College, Dublin, and its Governing Body for generous financial support during the preparation of this book and to the Royal Irish Academy for a research grant which enabled me to study Iron Age material in Brittany. To the Alexander von Humboldt Foundation my deep gratitude for moral support when the publication of this book was in jeopardy and for providing the financial support which finally made publication possible.

Lastly, thanks are due to my wife Nuala, without whose encouragement and help this work would not have been brought to fruition.

Acknowledgments of Plates

1. National Museum of Ireland, Dublin.
1; 2:1; 4; 5; 6; 7; 8; 9-13; 15-17; 22; 23; 24:2,3; 25; 29; 32; 33; 34; 35:1; 36; 39; 41-44; 46:2,3; 47-50; 51:1; 52; 53:1,2,4; 55:2; 56:1; 57-65; 67-69; 74:2; 75:1; 76-81; 83-87; 90-94; 96-99; 103; 111; 112.

2. Ulster Museum, Belfast.
21:2; 26-28; 32:2-5; 35:2; 51:2; 53:3; 54; 55:1; 56:2; 72; 73; 88; 100, 101.

3. British Museum, London.
14; 19; 21:1; 30; 31; 45; 46:1; 56:3; 70; 95.

4. National Museum of Antiquities of Scotland, Edinburgh.
2:2; 38; 74:1; 75:2; 89.

5. Cambridge University Museum of Archaeology and Ethnology.
18; 24:1,4.

6. Ashmolean Museum, Oxford.
66.

7. Free Public Museum, Liverpool.
82.

8. Colchester Museum, Essex.
71.

9. Department of Archaeology, University College, Dublin.
3.

10. Office of Public Works, Dublin.
102.

11. A.E.P. Collins.
106.

12. Barry Raftery.
104; 105; 107-110.

LIST OF FIGURES

LIST OF MAPS

INTRODUCTION

There can be little doubt that the archaeology of Iron Age Ireland is one of the most problematical fields of study in the whole of Irish prehistory. Because of the virtual absence of significant associations, the paucity of burials and clearly recognisable settlements and, indeed, the largely selective nature of the surviving remains, there are still immense areas of uncertainty confronting the archaeologist in almost every aspect of this extremely difficult period.

The Iron Age in Ireland is illumined, however dimly, by a not inconsiderable wealth of written material. This written record is of undeniable value to the archaeologist but arguably its existence has also had detrimental effects on the development of objective archaeology. This is so not only because the written sources have been misused but also because the complete and vivid picture of society in Iron Age Ireland apparently presented by the literature is at variance with, and obscures, the very real darkness which so often confronts the archaeologist in his study of the material remains of the period. As Powell has pointed out, the issue has been further confused by the incursions of specialists into each other's fields and by a lack of understanding of the real nature of the problem before them. He goes on, "in an endeavour to disentangle the truth about the Celts in Ireland, a practice has developed of picking and choosing passages from the manuscripts to bear out certain hypotheses; this has led to counter views and different quotations, each side claiming to have found the remnants of the true native tradition." (Powell, 1950, 175). O'Rahilly too, was trenchant in his criticisms of the misuse by archaeologists of the written evidence. "When archaeologists abandon their proper domain and indulge in linguistic speculations," he wrote "the precariousness of their theorizings is increased ten-fold" (1946, 440).

There can be no doubt that the society depicted in the Irish literature is a "Celtic" society closely comparable with that on the Continent as described by the classical authors. As such, it is an "Iron Age" society. Problems arise, however, owing to the long continuity of such a Celtic way of life in Ireland, untrammelled by Roman or barbarian invasion and overlain, but not substantially disturbed, by the coming of Christianity. Before the fifth century or so, the sources have little historical value and virtually all the extant source material dates to after 1000 A.D. so that the absolute chronological context of the documented descriptions and events is uncertain.

Pagan undertones are, of course, often clearly detectable and the Ulster Cycle, as Jackson has pointed out (1964), belongs to a period which predates the dismembering of the ancient kingdom of Ulster in the fifth century and presumably predates the coming of Christianity to Ireland. The *Táin* undeniably provides a "window on the Iron Age" (Jackson, 1964), however frosted that window may be, and strikingly the Ulster Connacht conflict in that saga and the geographical context of the events which take place in it correspond well with the distribution of material of La Tène type in the country.

But while the literary material establishes the former existence of a "Celtic" way of life here and while the oldest tales seem to imply close correspondence between society in Ireland and that in La Tène Europe in the last centuries B.C., with regard to many of the more specific questions which archaeology seeks to answer the written sources offer little assistance. The literature naturally tells us nothing of the chronology of Iron Age Ireland and, with regard to the origins of the Iron Age impulses which reached the country and their means of implantation here, the literature is largely a source of confusion. Invasions by specific groups are, of course, frequently referred to, notably in the *Lebor Gabála Éireann*, and folk movements across the country are mentioned such, for instance, as the westward retreating *Fir Bolg*. These, however, have little historical value and even if, as F.J. Byrne contended, such tales embody a dim folk memory of earlier population movements into Ireland (Byrne, 1967, 11), it is only by the witness of archaeology that such accounts can ever be finally shown to have a factual base. This is the kernel of the matter. Similarly, the presence of known Celtic tribes in various parts of the country is clearly indicated by documents such as the second-century map of Ptolemy. But it has not yet been possible to equate specific archaeological material with these alleged tribal areas. The early texts give tantalising glimpses of Iron Age society but only archaeology can confirm the veracity or otherwise of the details.

This is not to say, of course, that archaeology can or does provide all the answers to outstanding problems, for this is manifestly not so. The picture derived from archaeology, by its very nature, will always be incomplete but the potential for resolving the major problems lies with archaeology alone and it is in the field of archaeological research alone that significant new discoveries can always be expected. The literature can sometimes suggest rational explanations for features inexplicable in purely archaeological terms and can also amplify the picture based on the archaeological remains as well as supplying information on matters which leave no mark on the material record. The written sources can be viewed as providing a range of possibilities regarding cultural and social developments which can then be tested by archaeology. But, in the final analysis, for the prehistoric Iron Age in Ireland, it is by archaeological means that the answers to major problems must be sought.

As will become apparent, the difficulties encountered in the interpretation of the archaeological evidence are acute and not all the questions which must be posed can as yet be answered. From the very outset there are uncertainties. What do we mean by "Iron Age", for instance? The very term, basic to this study, is, in an Irish context, unclearly defined. Does it refer to the earliest contact with the world of iron or does it indicate a time when the earliest evidence for iron-working is detectable in the archaeological record? The two are not necessarily synonymous. Or should we regard the Iron Age as being best represented in the archaeological record by the material of La Tène aspect?

It is becoming increasingly clear that the concept of some homogeneous phase of Irish prehistory which can be conveniently labelled "Iron Age" is no longer tenable. The term covers a wide range of regional and chronological variations in the surviving material remains not all of which are as yet fully understood or clearly defined. In a sense it is almost possible to suggest that several "Iron Ages" existed in the country but because of the ambivalence and deficiency of the archaeological record it is difficult to be specific on this score, because nowhere is a complete cultural complex to be found.

In terms of what survives, there are hints of incipient iron-working, with Hallstatt undertones, occurring sporadically in the country perhaps before 500 B.C. but the material associated with this suggested phase is not extensive. The first clearly recognisable, positively identifiable phase of "Iron Age" culture in the country is represented by a substantial body of objects, mainly of metal, but including material of stone, bone, glass and even wood, which are spread across the northern two-thirds

of the country.   These exhibit a certain measure of unity by displaying
in their form and in their decoration contact with, and influence from,
the world of the La Tène Iron Age.

This group of La Tène material is, however, not representative of
an entire spectrum of cultural activity in the country and it may for
the most part represent only a very confined element of La Tène society
here.   The surviving remains clearly reflect only aspects of a far more
intricate cultural complex and the unbalanced picture which they present
is a product of the scattered and almost totally unassociated nature
of the La Tène objects.   Thus, the economic and social background to
this material is as yet in large measure unknown to us.

It can be seen, therefore, that the collection of artifacts which we
refer to as La Tène do not in themselves provide us with an "Iron Age".
They are, however, indicative of something new in the country. They
are indicative of a significant La Tène presence here even if the precise
nature of that presence, or the means of its introduction, remain to be
defined.   In terms of the physical survival of evidence, it is the La Tène
material alone which provides us with a sizable body of recognisably
"Iron Age" artifacts so that the La Tène complex is here being regarded
as the principal material witness to significant innovating influences
of "Iron Age" aspect in Ireland.

Undoubtedly, future research will enable us to identify material of
a non-La Tène character which may also be seen as "Iron Age" and in
the south of the country especially, where La Tène material is virtually
absent, it must be accepted as certain that an entire "Iron Age"
assemblage, devoid of La Tène influences, awaits full recognition.
Hillforts may well prove to have a significant role in such a recognition
(Raftery, B., 1976a, 194-5).   In the present light of our knowledge,
however, meagre though the evidence is, it is the culture represented
by the La Tène remains which provides the earliest clear indications
of an established Iron Age tradition in Ireland.

The problems relating to a study of the La Tène material in the country
are enormous, stemming, as they do, not only from the virtual absence
of significantly associated or stratified artifacts, but also from the high
proportion of objects which are devoid even of a provenance.   Lacking
independent fixed chronological points in Ireland, the only means of dating
our material is by comparing their form or their decoration with relevant
pieces from outside, the chronological position of which is more securely
established.   This process, as will be seen, is not without its drawbacks
for inevitable questions of timelag and archaism arise which are often
difficult to answer satisfactorily.   Furthermore, the use of an art style
as a dating criterion is at the best of times unreliable, but in an insular

context, where conservatism, individuality and long continuity are inevitable, the uncertainties are greatly magnified.

Divergences of scholarly opinion are even more evident when artistic criteria are used as a basis for determining the areas of origin of La Tène influences here. Thus, for instance, comparable ornamental techniques in Ireland and Britain can be taken to imply direct links between the two islands, but could equally be regarded as denoting a common origin for both on the European mainland. In addition, the very subjective nature of stylistic analysis diminishes its effectiveness for archaeological purposes. One commentator, indeed, has gone so far as to consider it as little more than a "game of chance" (Henry, 1965, 9). Nonetheless, whatever the hazards inherent in artistic appreciation, such must be attempted for there simply is no alternative basis for discussing the bulk of the stray La Tène artifacts from Ireland.

A consideration of this La Tène material in Ireland epitomizes one of the fundamental ambiguities of Irish prehistory as a whole. The material is at once exotic and local. Clearly, outside impulses are responsible for its presence and clearly the material represents an almost total break with what has gone before. Yet at the same time practically everything is of native manufacture. There is but a handful of recognisable imports. The art is for the most part treated in an entirely native manner. Many of the forms present are recognisably Irish and significant types present outside the country - notably distinctive Iron Age pottery - are not found here. Foreign and native, alien and indigenous - such are the hallmarks of the Irish La Tène presence here and such are the contradictions which render the proper interpretation of the available evidence so difficult.

As well as describing the La Tène material and attempting to set out some sort of broad chronological framework, the work which follows is also concerned with shedding some light on the means by which the innovating influences found their way to Ireland. Does the archaeological evidence indicate large-scale folk movements into the country, which supplanted the pre-existing societies - or was there merely a small-scale transfer of population, possibly chieftains and their retinues, which formed a thin cultural overlay on the indigenous groups? Could trade and commerce alone, along with a few refugees and a handful of stragglers, have been responsible for what emerges in the archaeological record as the La Tène "Iron Age"? Or, indeed, do the metal objects reflect specialised workshop activity carried out by a few immigrant craftsmen? As will become apparent, the crucial difficulty which these questions raise is the way in which an "invasion" may be recognised from the archaeological remains. What criteria are required for such a recognition and, indeed, to what extent can we expect the archaeological evidence to reflect accurately the actuality of historical events?   Such questions can only be considered when the factual evidence has been taken into account.

IRON AGE BEGINNINGS

The chronology of the Dowris Phase of the the Late Bronze Age, or more correctly, of its earlier stages, is well established and it seems clear that by the early seventh century B.C. a thriving and prosperous Late Bronze Age culture prevailed over much, if not most, of the country (Eogan, 1964). After this date, however, events become increasingly obscure in the archaeological record and the crucial centuries immediately after 500 B.C. enter what has rightly been referred to as a Dark Age (Scott, 1974; 1980). These are the centuries which are of vital importance for the beginning of Iron Age civilization in Ireland and it is here that the key to later cultural developments must lie.

The problems of when the Late Bronze Age ended and when the Iron Age began are complementary ones, which as yet defy solution. It is relevant, in this regard, to ponder again on the precise meaning of the terms Late Bronze Age and Early Iron Age. The terms, echoing the Three Age System of Thomsen and Worsaae, are based in each case entirely on a single aspect of what was a far more extensive cultural complex, though admittedly it is the one which in the archaeological record, best represents the material manifestation of the relevant era. The underlying, questionable assumption in the use of such terms is, however, that when the metal technology changes, so the culture changes. This need not be so and the ordinary life of the people is likely to continue without radical alteration even when a new technology has been mastered and become widespread.

The material representing the Late Bronze Age in Ireland is a clearly recognisable entity. The material which is taken to represent the Iron Age, however, is not as easily brought together. Whereas the Late Bronze Age remains form, in broad terms, an essentially homogeneous cultural unit, that material which may be described as representing the "Iron Age" spans a considerable length of time and appears to consist of several strands of cultural development not necessarily unified either in chronological or regional terms.

Again the question may be asked: what is meant by "Iron Age"? Does it mean simply the acquisition of the knowledge of iron by indigenous Late Bronze Age groups or does it mean a new culture - a "Celtic" culture - brought in with all the attendant trappings from outside? In Europe a clearly recognisable Iron Age culture, the Hallstatt culture, emerges around or shortly before 700 B.C. and by about 600 B.C. at latest the knowledge of iron-working had percolated to the west of Britain (Fox and Hyde, 1939; Savory, 1976, 46-7). What can we say about Ireland at this time?

Ireland was not unaffected by the momentum of cultural advances outside the country. Objects with Hallstatt affinities have been found scattered around the country, consisting mainly of swords and some chapes, but including also a few bracelets and pins and other miscellaneous items (Figs 2,5). A large iron spearhead from Castleconnell, Co. Limerick, with gold (or brass?) inlay on the socket, has also been claimed as a Hallstatt D import (Fig. 1; Rynne, 1979), although the grounds for this assertion are not entirely convincing. The spectacular flesh-hook from Dunaverney, Co. Antrim (Fig. 3:1; Megaw, 1970, 51-2), and the lost example from Lurgy, Co. Tyrone (Herity, 1969, 27, Pl. 14), probably belong to this era

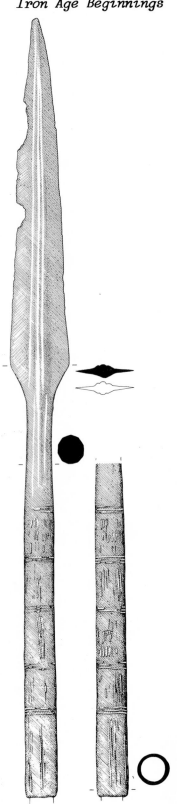

Fig. 1 Iron spearhead with inlaid socket. Castleconnell, Co. Limerick. - 2/5.

too and must surely be direct imports from Central Europe (Jockenhövel, 1974). A few Etruscan imports probably also found their way to Ireland round about this period (Fig. 3: 2,3). Most of the scattered Hallstatt material is without association, the principal exception being the penannular knob-ended bracelet from a hoard at Kilmurry, Co. Kerry (Fig. 2:3) which accompanied a deposit of Late Bronze Age bronzes (Eogan, 1964, 320).

It is not certain how this material should be interpreted. The distribution of the Hallstatt bronzes, especially the swords, is essentially riverine and coastal and this has been described by one commentator as representing a "classic raiding pattern" (Burgess, 1974, 213). The basically indigenous nature of the swords, however, all of which are of bronze, weakens this suggestion though there can be no doubt that the prototypes have a directly Hallstatt C background. It cannot be denied that the scattered material, however it is to be viewed, indicates contact with the world of iron.

The question of whether these objects represent merely trading contacts or actual Hallstatt immigrants is thus a vexed one, and the impact of this material on the native Dowris Phase industries has not yet been fully demonstrated. The absence of Hallstatt material in Late Bronze Age hoards (with the single exception of Kilmurry), especially the absence of swords, is notable. Does this suggest the cultural distinctiveness of Late Bronze Age and Hallstatt material, hostility between Hallstatt "intruders" and native peoples, or merely that the custom of placing swords in hoards - or, indeed, of depositing hoards at all - had ceased (Champion, 1971)? Some technological overlap has, however, been suggested by Eogan (1964) who viewed his Class VI swords as hybrids, incorporating native and Hallstatt features. Iron objects, too, such as the riveted, sheet cauldron from Drumlane, Co. Cavan (Fig. 4:3; Scott, 1974, 16 ; Raftery, B., 1980, 57, 61-2), or the looped, socketed axeheads from Lough Mourne and Toome, Co. Antrim (Fig. 4:1,2; Scott, 1974, 12-16; CIIAA 576, 577), might similarly be regarded as types demonstrating fusion between native techniques and innovating impulses.

Although it must be admitted that the dating of these iron objects is not as yet firmly established, they nonetheless raise the relevant question as to whether the Hallstatt influences, which are undoubtedly detectable in the archaeological material, were responsible for the earliest introduction of iron here: do the influences in fact represent the earliest Iron Age?

There are some indications that this might well be the case. The second level at Rathtinaun, Co. Sligo, crannog which followed immediately upon a purely Late Bronze Age Dowris Phase layer, contained material

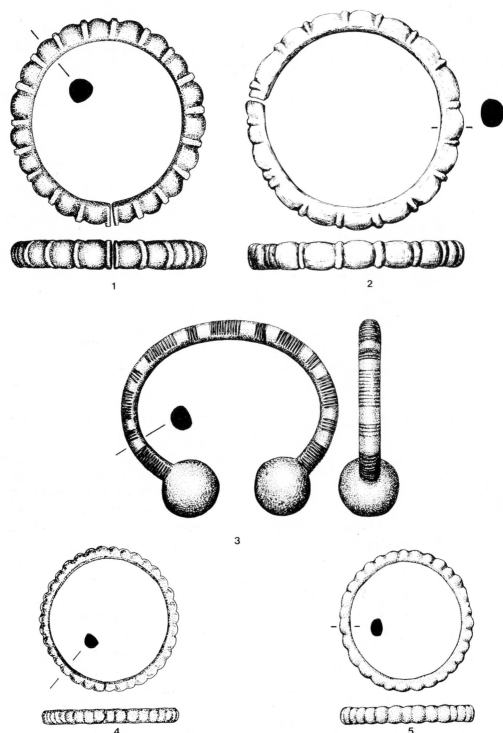

Fig. 2. Hallstatt bracelets of bronze in Ireland. 1,2,5 Co. Antrim.
3 Kilmurry, Co. Kerry. 4 no prov. - 3/4.

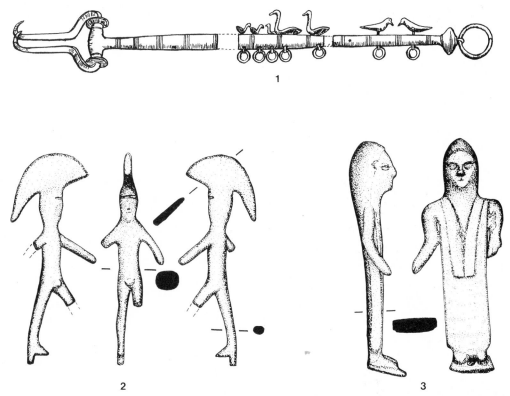

Fig. 3 European imports to Ireland. 1 flesh hook, Dunaverney, Co. Antrim.
2 no prov. 3 Co. Sligo. All bronze. 1:1/4. 2,3:3/4.

similar to the earlier level at the site but with the significant addition
of objects of iron (Raftery, J., 1972, 3).   These included a swan's-neck
pin (Fig. 5:3), a shafthole axehead forged of three separate pieces of
iron (Fig. 118:5) and a three-pronged flesh-hook.   Both the pin and the
axe denote an alien background for the presence of the iron-working.
The accompanying material, however, apart from these few exotic pieces
is entirely native, indistinguishable from the primary level at the site.
The crannóg thus shows that native, basically Bronze Age groups were
using iron objects.   More significant, however, is the axehead, the
workmanship of which seems strongly to suggest manufacture by someone
not yet well versed in the technique of iron-working - a native bronzesmith,
perhaps, gradually acquiring the new skill of iron-forging, and imitating
a new form of axehead (Scott, 1980, 195). Carbon 14 determinations
ascribing the early levels at Rathtinaun to the last centuries before
Christ are problematical as they seem hardly in keeping with the
archaeological evidence.   If they are to be accepted they indicate a
late survival for the Late Bronze Age in Ireland.   It seems more likely

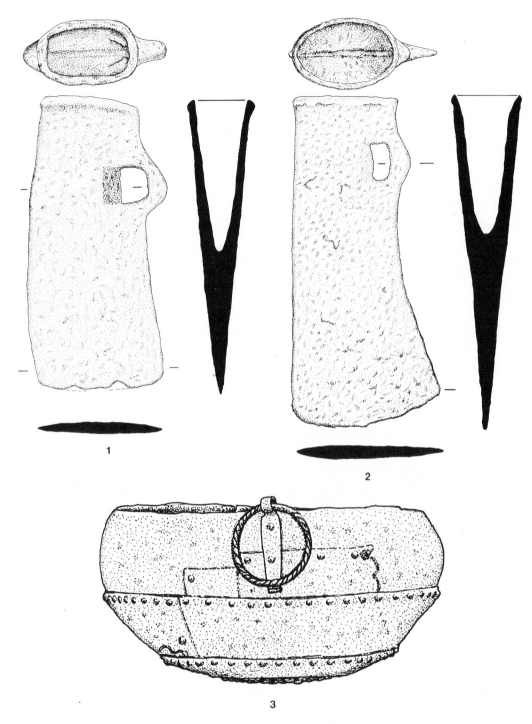

Fig. 4. Early iron objects from Ireland. 1 Toome Bar, Co. Antrim.
2 Lough Mourne, Co. Antrim. 3 Drumlane, Co. Cavan.
1,2:1/2. 3:1/4.

that the relevant levels are anything up to half a millennium older than the dates suggest.

Another site of considerable importance is Aughinish, Co. Limerick, where two ringforts have recently revealed a comparable picture. Here, material of native Dowris Phase aspect was found in association with an iron fragment which may be part of a horsebit (Kelly, 1974). Here, too, it seems, is a native settlement of early date already in the possession of iron. Further possibilities of early occupation sites with associated Hallstatt elements are represented by the bronze swan's-neck pin found around the middle of the last century at Ballyhoe, Co. Meath (Fig. 5:2), on the site of an alleged crannóg, and by the discovery of what appears to be an iron swan's-neck pin at "one of the Dunbell Raths" in Co. Kilkenny (Fig. 5:1). Unfortunately, no records survive regarding the contexts of these potentially very important pieces.

But even if an early iron-working phase is shown to be a phenomenon of some substance in the country, there still remains the problem of establishing how, and precisely when the Late Bronze Age ended. Many commentators have seen the Bronze Age as continuing until replaced by La Tène innovating influences (Eogan, 1964, 323; Raftery, J., 1972, 3), while Mahr regarded the Bronze Age as "a phenomenon of gradual extinction" (1937, 380). The question must be asked, however, whether a prehistoric metal industry would continue for centuries totally unchanged, with no detectable development and little apparent degeneration.

The problem would seem to revolve around the definition of Bronze Age and Iron Age and the confusion of "industry" with "culture". It seems possible to argue that for some reason around the middle of the last millennium B.C. Dowris Phase metal objects gradually ceased to be manufactured. This was a time when influences from the Hallstatt world were being felt in various parts of the country and the introduction of iron-working may have taken place sporadically. It was also a time, apparently, of climatic deterioration. Perhaps both factors played a part in the decline of the Dowris industry. The adoption of iron for weapons and implements of daily use would rapidly render the bronzes obsolete and might not, due to the poor preservative properties of the new metal, impinge radically on the archaeological record, not, at any rate, in terms of isolated finds in the countryside. Europe, by now increasingly a world of iron, would have less need to maintain her trading contacts with Bronze Age Ireland. An economic recession might have ensued with consequent cultural impoverishment (Hawkes and Clarke, 1963). But the way of life of the people at its essential subsistence level would continue for some considerable time without radical alteration

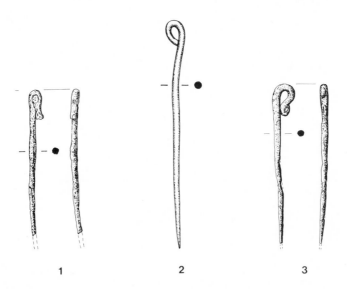

1   2   3

Fig. 5 Irish swan's neck-type pins. 1, Dunbell, Co. Kilkenny. 2, Ballyhoe, Co. Meath. 3, Rathtinaun, L. Gara, Co. Sligo. 1,3 iron. 2, bronze. 1/2.

and there are hints that such continuity is observable in the limited settlement and burial record. The basic ethnic substratum in Ireland during the last half millennium B.C. must have been one with a predominantly Bronze Age ancestry.

However the introduction of La Tène elements to Ireland is to be interpreted, and even if it can be demonstrated that these elements caused or contributed to the demise of the Late Bronze Age way of life, it is still clear that this can ever supply only part of the answer. For La Tène material is singularly lacking in the south of the country, and as the writer has elsewhere written (1976) an "Iron Age" of some sort devoid of La Tène influence must eventually have become established in southern Ireland. What was the nature of this shadowy "Iron Age"? Did it include Hallstatt elements as yet scarcely detectable in the archaeological record? Is it possible that the southern Irish concentration of major hillforts is in some way relevant to the nature of the changes which must have been taking place in this part of Ireland in the centuries after 500 B.C.?

The matter remains problematical and the question of the earliest "Iron Age" in Ireland is still unanswered. In the present light of our knowledge, however, it must be conceded that it is only with the appearance in the country of material of La Tène aspect that the concept of an Irish Iron Age becomes somewhat more of a tangible reality.

HORSE-TRAPPINGS

Horsebits

Horsebits and the associated Y-shaped objects ("pendants") together form the largest single group of La Tène-type bronzes from the country. Some 135 recorded examples of Irish horsebits are now known and several more examples may have existed; 96 complete or fragmentary "pendants" are recorded. Of the 231 items known a mere 97 are localised.

Significant typological study in modern times of the Irish Iron Age three-link snaffle bits has been undertaken by J. Raftery (1937, 409; 1951, 194, Figs 227-229), Fox (1946, 33), Ward-Perkins (1939, 182), Jope (1950, 56-60; 1955, 37-44), and most recently Haworth (1971). This last, the first attempt to list all known examples, remains a basic source work. It has, however, been possible to add a number of new items to Haworth's list and some corrections and modifications to it have also been necessary. All extant Irish horse-trappings are illustrated in CIIAA.

Typology

J. Raftery divided the Irish horsebits into three types on the basis of the developing form of the side-links. Haworth expanded this to include five groups, labelling each one alphabetically.

The principal details of the main types have been outlined by Haworth (1971) but for the sake of completeness these are being repeated here in summary form.

Overwhelmingly the bits are of bronze. There are two examples the rings of which are of forged iron (Fig. 7:1,2). A single fragmentary specimen entirely of iron is known (Fig. 25:3) and a possible horsebit

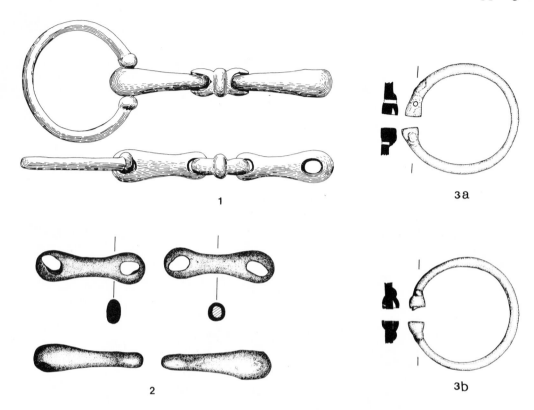

Fig. 6. Type A horsebits. 1 Llyn Cerrig Bach, Anglesey, Wales. Otherwise
no prov. (1 after Fox, 1946). – 2/5.

fragment from Aughinish Island, Co. Limerick, is also of this metal.
Practically all are of the three-link variety. The only exceptions are
three two-link bits and it may be that the two wholly iron bits were also
of two-link form.

Type A bits comprise six incomplete examples (Fig. 6). The side-
links are hollow, "symmetrical along a horizontal, longitudinal axis" and
devoid of any V-moulding at their inner ends. Only the specimen from
Llyn Cerrig Bach in Wales (Fig. 6:1) retains the central link. It is of
rather elongated form with a sub-spherical central moulding. The stop-
knops on the rings take the form of uniform bulges around the
circumference of the ring (Fig. 6:1,3).

Type B bits represent the largest of the sub-groups numerically. 56
examples are recorded. Within the group there is considerable variety
in detail but a clearly recognisable form can be determined. There
are, however, some examples which share features with bits of Type D
so that in several instances doubt exists as to the group into which a
specific bit should most appropriately be placed.

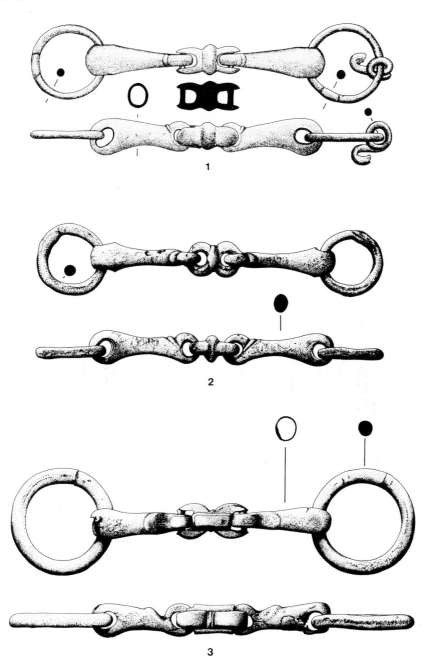

Fig. 7. Type B horsebits. 1 Ballynahinch, Co. Down.
2, 3 no prov. – 2/5.

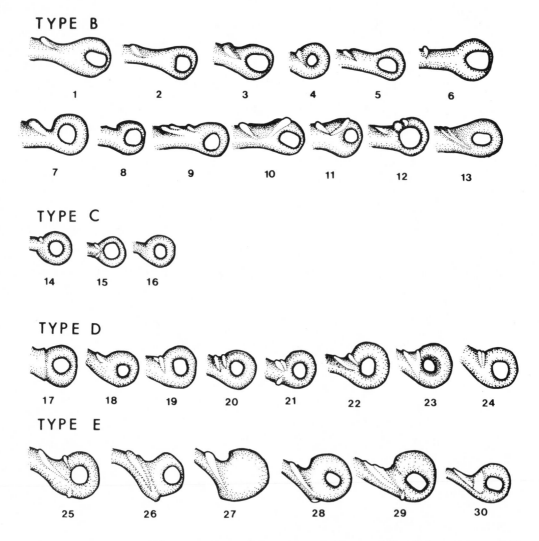

Fig. 8. Irish three-link horsebits. Selection of "V-moulding" features. – 1/2.

   The side-links of these bits, as Haworth pointed out, are more bowed
than those of Type A and while the majority are hollow some are solidly
cast.   Some of the hollow specimens retain their clay casting cores.
The V-moulding at the inner end of each side-link is almost always present
(Fig. 8:1-13).   It may be a short moulding confined to the immediate
concavity at the base of the inner loop of the side-link (e.g. Pl. 4:1) or
it may be an elongated moulding extending-one half to two-thirds the
length of the link-axis (e.g. Pl. 2:1). Sometimes more eleborate versions
such as doubled mouldings occur (Fig. 8:9-13), the most striking example
of such elaboration being the clearly ornithomorphic modelling on an

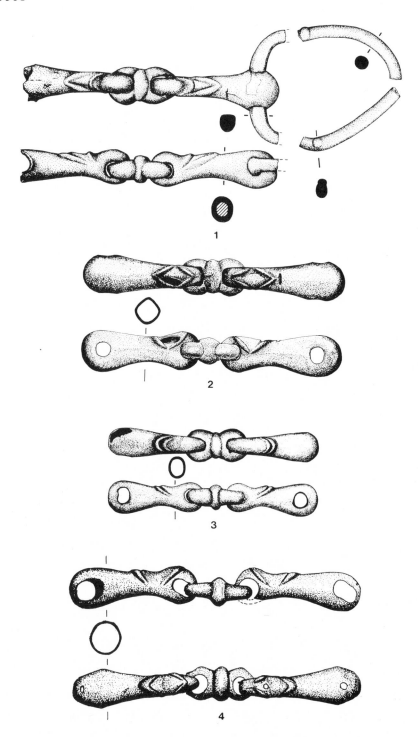

Fig. 9. Type B horsebits with elaborate "V-moulding". 2 Cotton, Co. Down.
3 Headfort, Co. Kerry. 1,4 no prov. - 2/5.

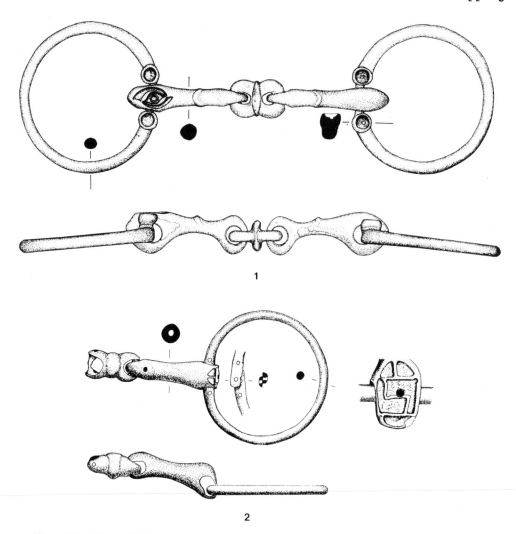

Fig. 10. Type B horsebits with champlevé ornament. 1 Lough Beg,
Co. Antrim. 2 no prov. - 2/5.

unprovenanced specimen in the National Museum (Fig. 11:1; Pl. 1). Only
one (Fig. 10:2), lacks any moulding; another from Armagh (Fig. 8:8)
preserves it only in the most vestigial form in the presence of slight
hollows at the base of the inner loops. Decoration is uncommon on the
links of Type B horsebits (Fig. 24). Apart from a few examples with
cast or incised lines extending along the link-axis, the only other
ornamented bits are two with champlevé panels (Fig. 10; Pl. 2), and two
exceptional bits (Fig. 11; Pls 1,3) with face motifs on the link-ends.

Aside from the two examples with iron rings (Fig 7:1,2), there is
only one other native bit the ring of which lacks stop-studs. Otherwise

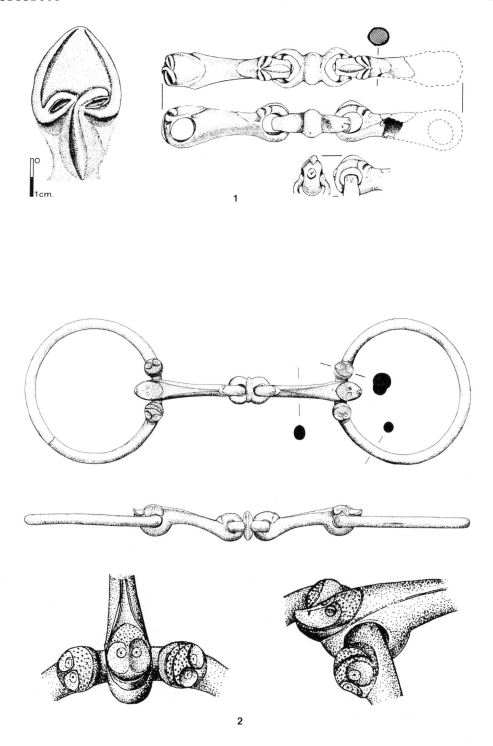

Fig. 11. Type B horsebits. No prov. – 2/5; details various scales.

the studs are always a prominent feature of the rings, the commonest form being domed. They are not infrequently decorated. Sometimes this consists of an incised S-motif dividing the surface of the stud (Fig. 12:2; Pl. 4:2) or a more elaborate series of cast trumpet curves may adorn it (Fig. 13:3). The Lough Beg, Co. Antrim example has traces of red enamel filling the hollows of the studs (Fig. 10:1; Pl. 2:1). The cast faces on the studs of a horsebit in the University College, Dublin, Archaeology Department teaching collection (Fig.11:2; Pl. 3) have no parallel on any other Irish bit. The relief sub-spiral form of the studs on another example, adorned on their surfaces with tiny, punched-circle motifs, represents another unique variation (Fig. 13:2; Pl. 5). The studs are normally cast with the ring but occasionally they are riveted or pegged into place. The rings are usually solidly cast and larger than is normal on other horsebit types. The rings of one, however (Fig. 7:3, that without studs), appear to have been hammered to circular shape from a cylindrical bar of bronze. In the case of three others the rings are penannular with the overlapping ends originally held together by bronze rivets.

While it can be argued that the iron rings present on two examples (Fig. 7:1,2) are secondary, even recent, additions (Wilde, 1861, 608-9), they give every appearance of being ancient. In addition, the loop of bronze wire linked around one of the rings of the Ballynahinch example (Fig. 7:1) hardly indicates modern usage for this piece.

An incomplete Irish bit in the British Museum (Fig. 9:1) is the only example in which the ring does not articulate in the loop of the side-link, but it is not a solid casting with the side-link as is the case with some of the British bits. It is, however, interesting that this is the only example in the whole of the Irish series where the studs, set on the rings well away from the side-links, are wholly non-functional. The shape of the surviving ring too seems different from that of any other Irish bit. It is now broken in three pieces and distorted but it appears to have been originally of decidedly flattened oval form.

Type C bits (of which there are now 6) seem to embody elements of Type B and Type D and are the simplest and least elaborate examples in the Irish series (Fig. 14). They are characterised by having solidly-cast, extremely slender side-links. The rings, where present, are reminiscent of those of Type B while the link form has more in common with Type D. Thus, for instance, there are grounds for including the Gortgole specimen (Fig. 14:2) in B rather than C as here, while the elaborate University College, Dublin, bit already referred to (Fig.11:2), regarded here as belonging to Type B, could with equal facility be moved into category C. The type seems clearly to be a hybrid, sharing features with bits of Types B and D. Decoration is always absent on these horsebits and little attention is paid to the V-moulding.

Twenty-nine examples of Type D are recorded to date. These are normally solidly cast with sharply bowed links of angular, gabled cross-section. The outer link-ends are sometimes rather pointed. In virtually every case the V-moulding is present in some shape or form (Fig 8:17-24).

It may be merely suggested by a faint ridge or a lightly incised line or it may be more prominently cast. In whatever form it occurs, however, it is always a "short" moulding at the base of the inner loop. There are no examples of "elongated" mouldings on any bits of this group. Such mouldings are confined to Type B bits.

There is a fair degree of uniformity amongst the central-links of Type D bits for these tend generally to a squat, waisted form with a central, oval moulding dividing the two loops.

Eighteen of the twenty-nine bits of this group bear decoration on their side-links (Fig. 24:8-25; Pls 7,9,10). In several cases stop-studs also bear decoration. The ornament may be cast or lightly incised. An isolated side-link (Fig. 15; Pl. 7) bears a series of panels for champlevé enamel. The ornate ring in the Ulster Museum (Fig. 16) may also belong to this group. The designs on the link-ends may take the form of a pair of simple circles which sometimes acquire a vaguely zoomorphic effect (e.g. Fig. 24:14,16,21,22). On more elaborate pieces combinations of scrolls, S-curves and peltae occur.

The rings of these bits are not quite circular in shape and are somewhat smaller in internal diameter than are those of Type B. In section, too, Type D rings are thicker than Type B rings and this is most often oval or pointed-oval rather than round. The commonest form of stop-stud is domed and the majority are cast. A small proportion are pegged or riveted into place but in a number of instances such studs may be secondary additions.

Type E bits are the most developed Irish group (Figs 19,20; Pl. 11). Twenty-nine examples exist and they display a high degree of uniformity. The side-links are markedly curved. They expand in width considerably towards their outer extremities and have a pronounced central spine extending along the axis of the link; this provides a sharply gabled cross-section. The ends normally project some distance into the plane of the ring. The thickness of the links decreases considerably towards their inner ends where the inner loops acquire a virtual disc-like appearance. The V-moulding is prominent and this, in conjunction with the flat inner loop, gives to the link-end a distinctly ornithomorphic appearance (Fig. 8:25-30). Sometimes on the underside of the link, at the base of the V-moulding, there may be a pair of tiny, cast lentoid bosses.

The central-links are always narrow and parallel-sided. The rings

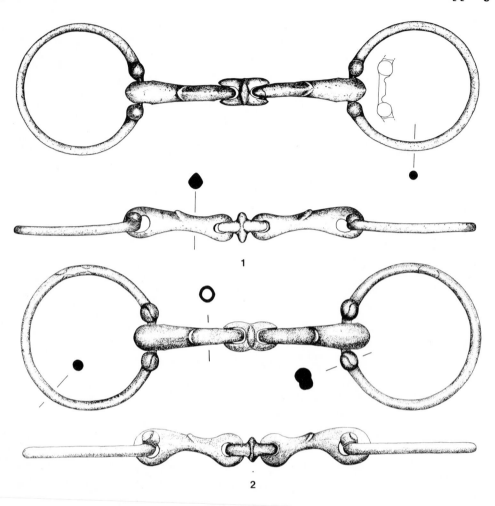

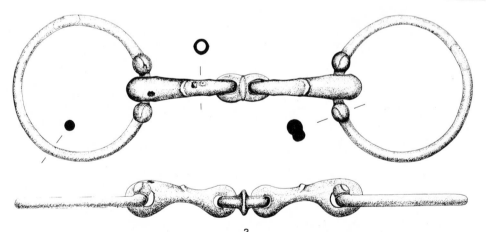

Fig. 12. Type B horsebits. 1 Urraghry, Aughrim, Co. Galway.
2, 3 Abbeyshrule, Co. Longford. – 2/5.

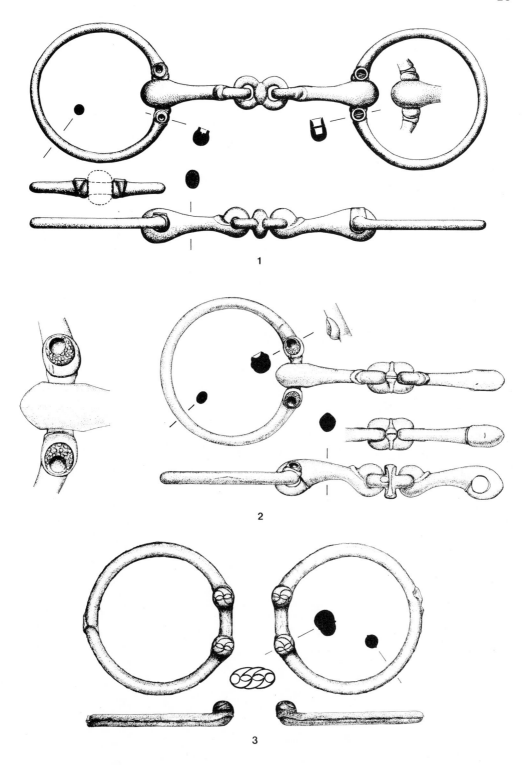

Fig. 13. Type B horsebits. No prov. – 2/5.

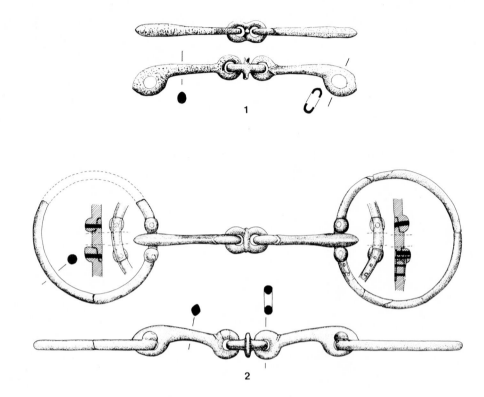

Fig. 14 Type C horsebits. 1, no prov. 2, Gortgole, Co. Antrim. 2/5.

are always of flattened, sub-triangular section with rounded edges. The
stop-studs are always cast with the ring and are consistently of sub-
conical shape.   Decoration cast in low relief on the side-links occurs
on four examples (Fig. 24:26-28).

An unfinished horsebit fragment belonging to this group (Fig. 20:1;
Pl. 11:1) is an interesting piece from the point of view of technique.
In this instance the ring has been cast into the outer opening of the side-
link, but the inner extremity of the side-link is imperforate.   Clearly
the next stage in the process of manufacture would have been to drill
the inner loop of the link before casting on the central-link and the other
elements of the bit.

Most of the Irish horsebits exhibit evidence of extensive wear. In
several instances repairs were effected and areas of weakness strengthened
to retain the particular horsebit in use and at times the Iron Age
bronzesmiths went to surprising lengths to achieve this (Raftery, B.,
1977; Figs 14:2; 17:2,3; Pl. 8).   The skill and ingenuity of these early
repairs contrast sharply with the crude, botched modern repair attempts
which took place in three instances.

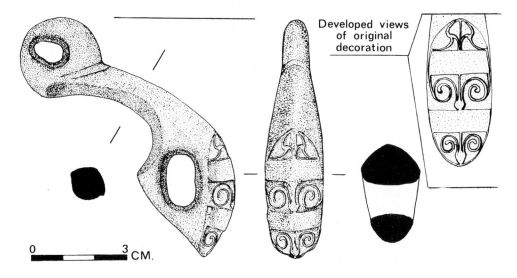

Developed views
of original
decoration

Fig. 15. Type D horsebit link. No prov. – 2/5.

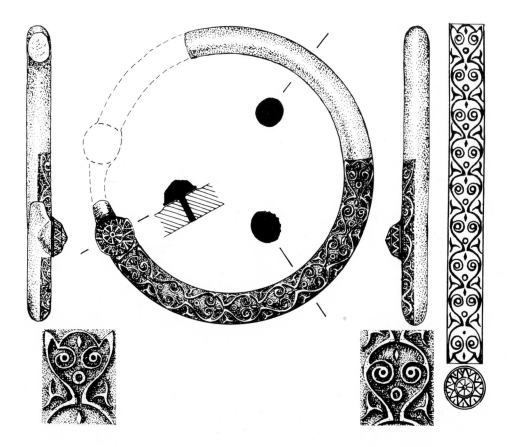

Fig. 16. Type D (?) horsebit rings. No prov. – 1/1.

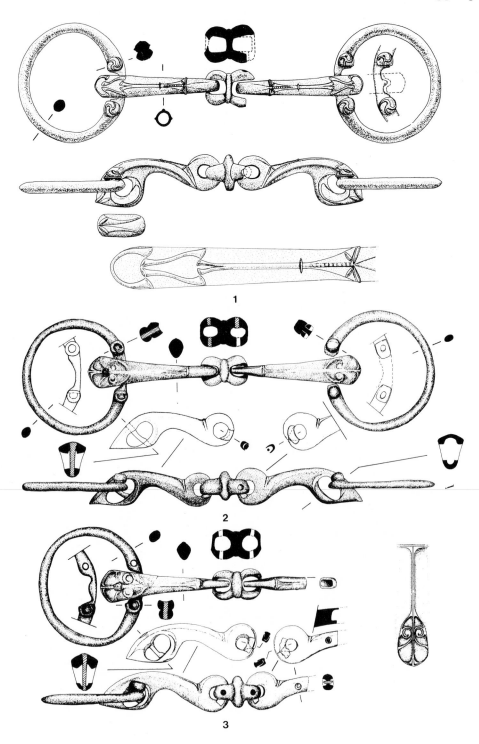

Fig. 17. Type D horsebits. 1 no prov. (based on drawing provided by
R.B. Warner). 2, 3 Streamstown, Co. Westmeath. - 2/5.

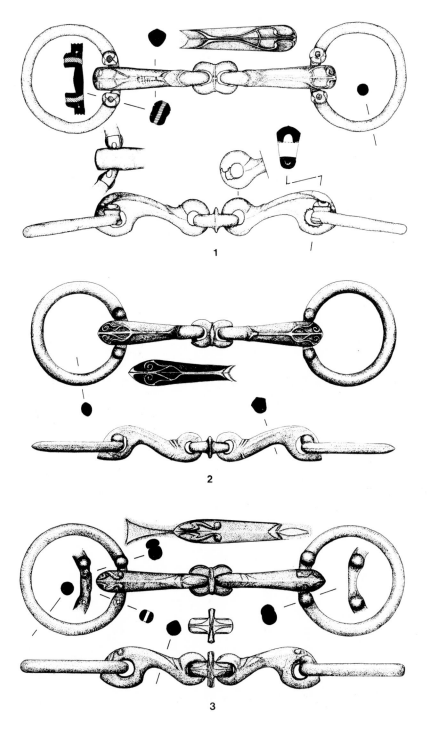

Fig. 18. Type D horsebits. 1,2 no prov. 3 Clongill, Co. Meath. – 2/5.

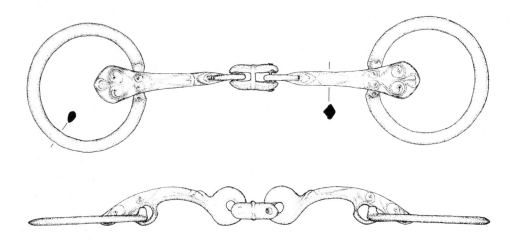

Fig. 19. Type E horsebit. Attymon, Co. Galway. - 2/5.

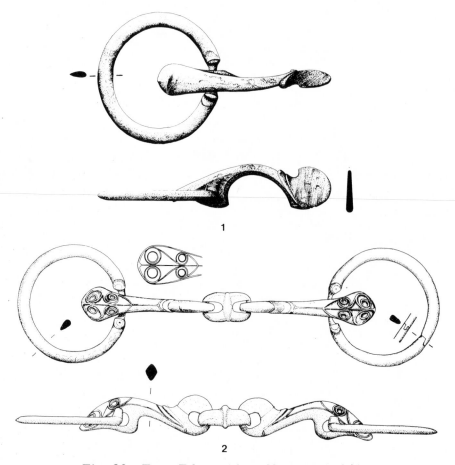

1

2

Fig. 20. Type E horsebits. No prov. - 2/5.

Affinities and Chronology

Because of the absence of significantly associated material the dating of the Irish horsebits rests on no very firm ground and the question of their ultimate origins and cultural affinities is still not certainly resolved.

The typological sequence originally set out by J. Raftery remains acceptable today. In terms of relative chronology it is reasonable to suppose that within Type A/B are the earliest bits while those of Types D and E include later specimens. It is, however, at all times possible that a bit of typologically "early" form can continue alongside bits held to be typologically "later" for it is as yet impossible to determine with any precision the longevity of any single type.

Bits of Types D and E are clearly native developments, notwithstanding the fact that elements of their decoration may be closely compared with patterns outside the country. A discussion of the origins of horse-bit manufacture within the country thus rests essentially on a consideration of the Type A/B pieces. Because of the almost total lack of internal evidence the only clue as to the affinities and chronology of these Irish bits is provided by an examination of relevant, foreign parallels. But even this, because of the basic insularity of the Irish material, gives no very clear picture of their dating and cultural background. It is still possible to maintain sharply opposing views as to their source.

Type A/B

Outside the country, the two horsebit groups of possible relevance to the genesis of the Irish Type A/B series are the bits of Arras type in eastern and southern England (Figs 21, 22:1), and the small number of bronze, three-link bits from Early La Tène graves in the Marne region of France (Fig. 22:2,3). Both groups have in the past been postulated as providing the ancestry of the Irish bits (Ward-Perkins, 1939; Jope, 1954a, 88) and Piggott has gone so far as to suggest that the Irish bits, along with the decorated scabbards, indicate the "plantation of Ulster by Yorkshire charioteers" (1950, 16).

In fact, neither of the two external horsebit groups provides precise prototypes for the Irish series though in each area some elements present on the Irish examples are detectable. The common use of stop-studs in England and Ireland and some superficial similarities of link-form may suggest overlap of some sort between bits in the two areas but the differing planes of the perforations through the side-links in the two islands (parallel in Ireland and at right angles to one another in Britain) is a significant point of distinction between the insular groups. There

is not one example of a Type A/B bit in Ireland which can justifiably
be seen as an import from Britain.   The Marnian bits of bronze do have
the perforations through the side-links parallel to one another as in Ireland
but otherwise the similarities are not close.   The present writer has
already commented upon the ornament on an unlocalised Irish horsebit
fragment (Fig. 11:1; Pl. 1) and has pondered on the possibility that
Continental Early La Tène influence may be detectable in the treatment
of the decoration on this unique specimen (Raftery, B., 1974).   Indeed,
the combination of human and bird-head representations on this Irish
horsebit calls forcibly to mind similar combinations on Continental Early
La Tène *Maskenfibeln* (e.g. Jacobsthal, 1944, 303, 304, 307). The bird-
head designs on this horsebit can, however, be compared equally to the
ornithomorphic renderings on the Ballymoney mirror handle, which probably
dates around, or just after, the birth of Christ (below, p.208; Figs 104:1;
111:12,13) so that an early date for the bit in question can hardly be
regarded as firmly established.

The truth of the matter is that we simply have not yet enough
information to determine with any degree of confidence or objectivity
the source or sources which inspired the development of the Irish horsebit
series nor can we date the introduction of the type.

Outside Ireland there are some chronological fixed points.   The French
bits already adverted to cannot be dated much later than about 400 B.C.
and in Britain the majority of the surviving bits date to the second and
first century B.C.   Stead has, however, argued that the British series
may well have begun earlier than this, possibly even as early as the period
of use of the Marnian three-link specimens (1965, 42) and Harding too
felt that "there is no reason why the three-link bits should not have been
introduced into Britain at any time from 400 B.C. onwards" (1972, 91).
He accepts, however, that none of the surviving examples is earlier than
the second century B.C. For Spratling, on the other hand, there is "not
a scrap of evidence" that the British bits (and indeed the Irish also) were
made any earlier than the second century B.C. (1973, 123).

If we are to assume that the idea at least of the three-link bit of
bronze was introduced into Ireland from outside then it is somewhere
within this chronological range that the introduction took place.   But
since both the Continent and Britain may equally be claimed as the
progenitors of the Irish group then the dating of the latter on external
grounds remains open.

Internal evidence within Ireland provides little positive advance in
our knowledge of the dating and origins of these Irish bits.   Two early
references to alleged associations exist, which must, however, be regarded
as of doubtful authenticity.   The first is in the manuscript catalogue

of the Brackstone collection, where it is stated that a Type B horsebit was found at Toomyvara, Co. Tipperary, in 1850 along with a bronze socketed spearhead and a trunnion chisel (Raftery, J and Ryan M. 1971, 212, 219). A now-lost horsebit of unspecified type is similarly stated, in a catalogue issued about 1900 by Hugh Kirk of Newtownards, to have been found at Ballyblack Moss, Co. Down, in c.1810 under a tree trunk with a bronze razor (Jope, 1950, 60).

The acceptance or rejection of these alleged associations must now be a matter of individual preference. If genuine, these would clearly strengthen the notion of an early beginning for the manufacture of three-link horsebits in Ireland, though Haworth, conversely, has taken the Toomyvara "association" to suggest a late dating for the Late Bronze Age bronzes (1971, 40).

The present writer is, however, unconvinced of the reliability of these supposed "associations". It is worth bearing in mind the case of the Hagbourne Hill hoard in which a pair of undoubtedly first century B.C. bits was found in association with Late Bronze Age, and even Middle Bronze Age, bronzes. This led Hawkes to conclude that the find represented a founder's hoard of Iron Age date. At all events there was no question of the bronzes dating the bits (Harding, 1972, 91-92)!

The presence in the Llyn Cerrig Bach hoard in Wales of an Irish bit of Type A (Fig. 6:1) does not give a precise indication of the date of the Irish piece (Fox, 1946, 21, 26-27, 62; Savory, 1976, 32-3). The material from the hoard spans a number of centuries, certainly as late as the first Christian century and possibly back as far as the second century B.C. Fox dated the bit to the first century B.C. (along with the Irish trumpet fragment from the site) but offered no very good reason for this assertion. The Irish bit could quite easily be amongst the earliest of the objects in the deposit so that a second century B.C. date is just as possible as a first century B.C. date for this piece. If it was old when deposited it could even be earlier but in the last analysis Llyn Cerrig Bach shows only that one bit of this type was in use somewhere in the period around the birth of Christ and was exported from Ireland to the island of Anglesey.

The sparse ornamentation which occurs on bits of Type B equally sheds little light on their dating or cultural affinities. Apart from the interesting renderings on the face-adorned specimen already referred to (Fig. 11:1; Pl.1), there is only one other example the decoration of which may give some indication of its dating. This is the horsebit from the University College, Dublin, Archaeology Department teaching collection (Figs 11:2; 23:1,2; Pl. 3). The ornament on this object is difficult to parallel exactly. The dotted decoration which occurs on it is a mode

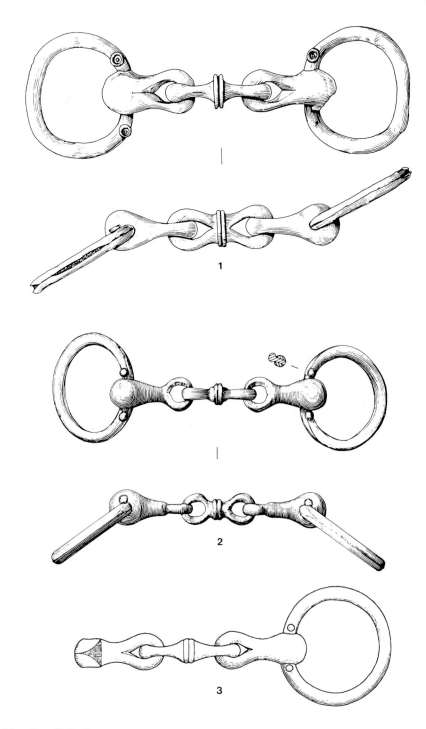

Fig. 21. English Arras-type horsebits. 1 King's Barrow, Arras, Yorkshire.
2 Lady's Barrow, Arras, Yorkshire. 3 Hagbourne Hill, Berkshire -2/5.
(1, 2 after Stead, 1979. 3 after Harding, 1972).

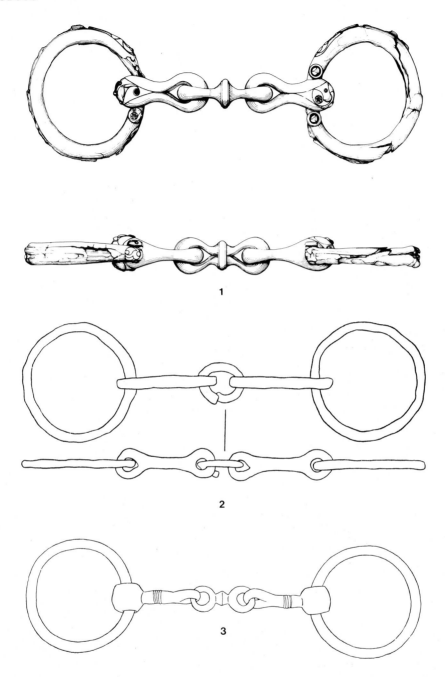

Fig. 22. English and French three-link horsebits. 1 Ringstead, Norfolk. 2 Ciry-Salsogne, Marne. 3 Somme-Tourbe ("La Gorge-Meillet"), Marne. 2/5. (1 after Spratling, 1979. 2, 3 after Stead, 1965).

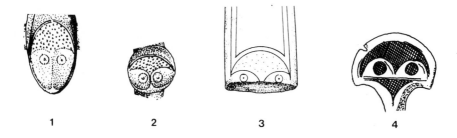

Fig. 23. Face and pseudo-face motifs. 1,2 unlocalised horsebit.
3 Lough Crew, bone flake. 4 Seven Sisters, Glamorganshire,
Wales, terminal of harness-loop.

of ornamentation not infrequently encountered on Irish objects for which
a date just before or just after the birth of Christ can be argued but
it cannot on its own be taken as an infallible index of such a date, for
outside the country it occurs in Early La Tène, even Hallstatt, contexts
and, indeed, it is known to continue into the Christian period in Ireland.
Relevant comparisons for the faces on the link-ends of the horsebit in
question might, however, be forthcoming in the strange faces with upturned
snouts which are present on brooches from Birdlip, Gloucestershire and
Ham Hill, Somerset, in England.   These date to the late first century
B.C. or the early first century A.D. (Fox, 1958, 93, Fig. 59).   The faces
on the stop-studs can be compared with patterns on one of the Lough
Crew flakes (Fig. 23:3) where dot-filled peltae occur, each combined
with a pair of tiny dot-in-circle motifs, which give to the design a clear
face-like appearance.   Such could well have provided the inspiration
behind the dotted faces of the horsebit.   Closely similar too is the
ornament on a pair of bronze "pendant-hooks" from the hoard discovered
at Seven Sisters, Glamorganshire, Wales (Davies and Spratling, 1976,
129, Fig. 5; Savory, 1976, Fig. 39:5).   Here the pelta is again present,
also combined in each case with a pair of small, circular elements, but
in this instance inlaid with red opaque glass (Fig. 23:4).   A date in the
first century A.D. is argued below (p. 261) for the Lough Crew flakes and
such a date is indicated for the Seven Sisters material by the presence
in the hoard of datable Roman bronzes.   It seems likely that the Irish
horsebit probably belongs to the same chronological horizon and it is
thus entirely appropriate that the bit should in form be typologically
intermediate between Type B and Type D.   The University College,
Dublin bit probably belongs to the end of the development of the Type
B series.

Types D and E

The introduction of the La Tène-type horsebit to Ireland is hardly later than the second or first century B.C. and a date even earlier than this is not ruled out. Whatever the source, it is clear that once the bit was introduced it proceeded along its own insular lines, little affected by external developments. Lacking outside parallels for the later Irish bits, and in the absence of clear associations within the country, the dating of these bits is based almost entirely on the art which adorns them. In terms of form and decoration there are broad areas of hybridisation between bits of the two groups and it would seem that Type D and Type E horsebits may to a very large extent be coeval.

The ornament on these objects (Fig. 24:8-28) along with the decoration on the associated "pendants" (see below p. 56) points consistently to a dating in the early centuries A.D. Jope, for instance, compared the design on the Curran Collection ring (Fig. 16), with that on Romano-British bronzes (1955, 42-4). Close analogies for the ornament on it are also to be found on a third century Roman, openwork bracelet of gold from Tunis in north Africa (Higgins, 1961, Pl. 60B). The champlevé design on this ring has much in common with the ornamentation on horsebits of Types D and E (especially Fig. 15) and it may well once have had a mouthpiece of Type D. Designs on many of the Romano-British fantail brooches are also forcibly reminiscent of recurring patterns on the Irish specimens (e.g. Collingwood, 1930, Fig. 6). "Slender trumpet" designs on north British objects such as the massive armlets (MacGregor, 1976, Nos 231-250), on the Culbin Sands tankard handle (ibid., No. 289), and especially on the spiral armlet also from Culbin Sands (ibid., No. 214), provide good first century parallels for the ornament on some of the more elaborate Irish specimens (e.g. Fig. 17:1). In purely native terms, too, of course, comparable patterns can be detected on spear ferrules (Pl. 34:2), on the Cork Horns (Fig. 132), on the Petrie Crown (Fig. 133) and elsewhere.

A measure of support for dating these horsebits to the early centuries A.D. is supplied by the find circumstances of a fragment of a Type E bit at Newgrange, Co. Meath (CIIAA 107). This object was not clearly stratified, but it seems that the area of the excavation from which it came produced exclusively a mass of Roman and sub-Roman material of the first to fourth centuries A.D. (Carson and O'Kelly, 1977, 52, Pl. IX). It may be, therefore, that the horsebit fragment belongs somewhere within this period of activity. A further oblique hint at an early centuries A.D. date for the Type E horsebits is provided by the discovery of a copy of an Irish bit in Romania in the area of ancient Dacia (Hampel, 1886,

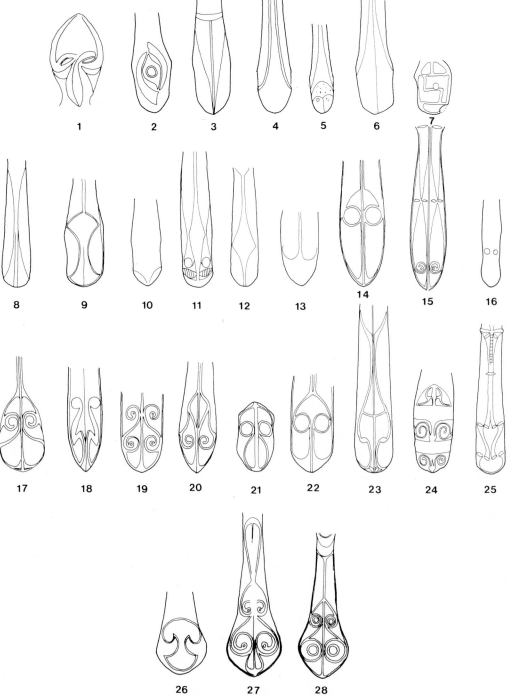

Fig. 24.   Decoration of Irish horsebits. 2 Lough Beg, Co. Antrim. 8
Bushmills, Co. Antrim. 12 Killucan, Co. Westmeath. 13 Co. Roscommon.
15 River Bann, Co. Antrim (sketch based on photograph). 16 Ballymoney,
Co. Antrim. 17 Streamstown, Co. Westmeath. 18 Clongill, Co. Meath.
22 Tara-Skreen, Co. Meath. 27 Attymon, Co. Galway.
Otherwise no prov. - 1/2.

Pl. LX:3; Roska, 1944, 56, Abb. 12; Haworth, 1971, 29; Zirra, 1981, 143, Abb. 10:2). Warner has pointed out that the Legion II Adiutrix, originally from Pannonia (the western Hungarian Plain), was stationed in Britain in the 70's and 80's A.D. and was recalled around the year 88 to take part in the successful Dacian campaign. He goes on to state that numerous "British" auxiliaries were serving in Dacia in the second century (1976, 281). It is possible that this is the context by which knowledge of an undoubtedly Irish bit-type was transmitted to eastern Europe.

The solid circular section of the fragmentary ring, Fig. 25:1 and Pl. 12, suggests that it may belong to a horsebit of Type B or Type D. The raised trumpet motif which curves outwards from each ornamental stop-stud is reminiscent of the repoussé trumpet curve on the decorated Somerset "box" (Fig. 140:2; Pl. 98) and also calls to mind trumpet curves on some of the Monasterevin-type discs (Figs 136-7; Pl. 90). The same element is also, perhaps, detectable, again in repoussé, on the Broighter collar, especially on the cylindrical portions immediately adjacent to the terminals. A date around, or just after, the birth of Christ for this horsebit ring may thus be suggested.

Miscellaneous horsebits

There is in the National Collection a small number of bits which fall outside the main native series. An unlocalised three-link bit (Fig. 25:2), is one of only three examples in Ireland which have the perforations through the side-links at right angles to one another in the English manner. This bit is of the "ring-and-muff" form, as Stead put it, and may be compared to bits Nos 47-49, especially the last, from Llyn Cerrig Bach (Fox, 1946, Pls VIII, IX; 1958, 19, 20, 23, 60-61). Bits of this type are found not only in the Anglesey hoard, but also in the south-west of Britain at Glastonbury (Bulleid and Gray, 1917, Pl. LXII, I 12B, I 12 A) and Bredon Hill (Hencken, 1938, 72, Fig. 5:1, 2, 3) and, in fact, the Llyn Cerrig Bach examples are arguably of south-west British manufacture. These British bits probably belong to the last century B.C. and into the first Christian century (Lynch, 1970, 268; Fox, 1946, 24).

The formal similarity between the western British bits and the Irish bit is evident but there are some differences in detail. The British bits are iron coated with bronze and it is not certain if the Llyn Cerrig Bach bit, No. 49, ever had stop-studs. On the Continent, comparable Early La Tène bits from Somme Tourbe in France, are wholly of bronze and are also of "ring-and-muff" form, close in shape to the Irish specimen (Fig. 22:3). These French bits, which have already been referred to above, have the perforations through the side-links parallel to one another

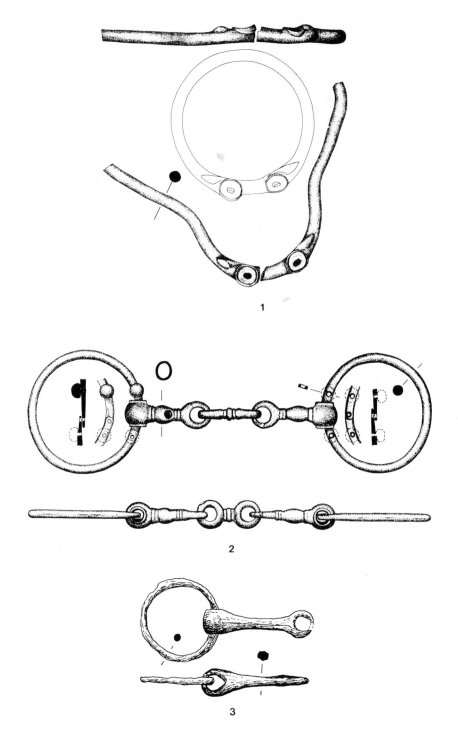

Fig. 25. Miscellaneous Irish horsebits. No prov. 1, 2 bronze.
3 iron. – 2/5.

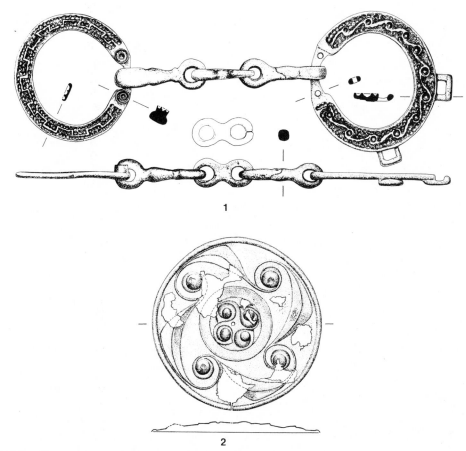

Fig. 26. Horsebit and bronze disc. Killeevan, Anlore, Co. Monaghan. - 2/5.

as is otherwise normal in Ireland. They never have stop-studs. Stead mooted the possibility that the Llyn Cerrig Bach "ring-and-muff" bits are late survivals of now lost early examples introduced directly from France to Britain in the fourth century B.C. (1965, 42). Whatever the truth of this hypothesis, it can hardly apply to the Irish bit. Notwithstanding its totally bronze manufacture, the plane of the perforations clearly links it with the late British examples for, as already stated, a genuine late survival in Ireland would have had parallel perforations as on all the other native pieces. The domed studs which adorn the Irish specimen compare also with the studs on Llyn Cerrig Bach 47 and 48 and the Irish horsebit may be regarded as an import from western or south-western Britain, dating probably to the last century B.C. or the beginning of the Christian era.

Apart from the fragment of a possible horsebit of iron from Aughinish

Fig. 27. "Whirligig" comparisons. 1 Killeevan, Co. Monaghan, 2 Lisnacrogher, Co. Antrim. 3 Mortonhall, Midlothian, Scotland.

Island, Co. Limerick, the only instance of an iron horsebit from Ireland is a single, fragmentary, unlocalised specimen (Fig. 25:3). Its cultural context is probably the same as that of the British-type horsebit just referred to and it too may be an import from the neighbouring island. It is best compared to the Bredon Hill and Llyn Cerrig Bach examples (Nos 47 and 48; Fox, 1946, Pl. VIII), though the rings on the Welsh specimens are bigger than on the Irish piece and differ also by the possession of stop-studs.

The only other bit of British type from Ireland is the unique example from Killeevan, Anlore, Co. Monaghan (Fig. 26:1; Pl. 13). This was found in association with a circular bronze disc decorated in repoussé style (Fig. 26:2; Jope, 1955, 44). Though the general form of the links is broadly comparable to the southwest British group just referred to, the Killeevan bit is essentially sui generis, particularly in the form and decoration of the rings and in the presence of rectangular loops soldered on to one ring.

Neither the sequence of interlocking S-scrolls on one ring of this specimen, nor the key pattern on the other is precisely datable on its own. The former, however, can be compared to the pattern which is present in cast relief around the central moulding of one of the bronze spearbutts from Lisnacrogher (Fig. 60:2; Pl. 34:1), and it is suggested below (p. 125) that such objects belong to the end of the last pre-Christian century or more likely to the beginning of the Christian era. There is, moreover, a hint of the north British boss style on the art of this spearbutt which is also detectable on the repoussé disc accompanying the Killeevan bit. In addition, the moulded pattern which adorns the basal expansion of the same Lisnacrogher butt is reminiscent of the design which fills the outer surround of the Killeevan disc. It is also worth noting that the central area of this disc (Fig. 27:1) has an interesting ornamental pattern which can be paralleled closely on a pair of thin,

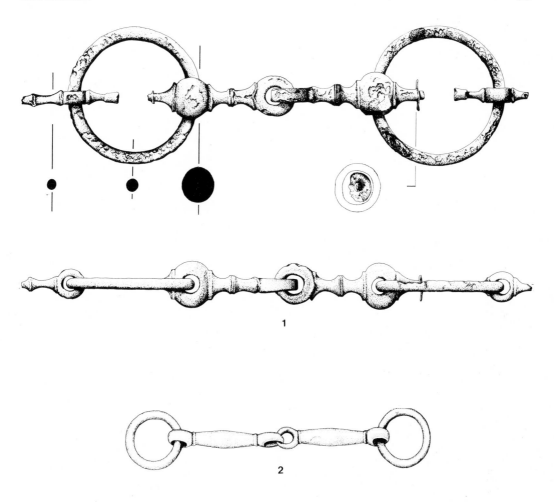

Fig. 28. Irish two-link bronze horsebits. 1 no prov. 2 River Bann.
(after photo supplied by A.E.P. Collins). - 2/5.

bronze mounts, also from Lisnacrogher (Fig. 27:2). Indeed, in the four
sub-circular expansions which dominate the central area of the Killeevan
disc there is more than a suggestion of the predominantly north British,
first century A.D., petal loop design which occurs on at least one Irish
horse "pendant" (Pl. 15:4). A similar first century A.D. north British
context is also suggested when it is realised that the central motif on
the Co. Monaghan disc is but a squashed version of the elegant four-
armed design on the scabbard from Mortonhall Estate in Midlothian
(Fig. 27:3; MacGregor, 1976, No. 150).

The most recent discussion of the Killeevan disc is by Lloyd-Morgan
(1976, 217-222), who compared it, along with several other insular sheet-
bronze discs, to a small group of similar, decorated bronzes in the Lower

Rhine area of north-west Europe. Relevant associations for the Continental representatives of the group point to a dating range from mid-first into the second century A.D. and such a chronological context for the Killeevan disc is in accord with what has been tentatively suggested above. Lloyd-Morgan wondered whether the Co. Monaghan object could be a direct import, from Britain or even direct from the Continent (op. cit. 221) and this possibility must indeed be entertained, for the art on it is by no means so obviously native as is clearly the case with the majority of the Irish La Tène bronzes.

It is likely, therefore, that the Killeevan horsebit and its associated disc date to the first or early second century of the Christian era and the other two Irish bits of British type considered above probably also belong in this chronological context. The link-form of the Killeevan bit is not typical of the Irish series and it might be seen as of British manufacture, but it is so different from anything in Britain that even this must be regarded as not certain and it could be an Irish copy of a British type.

The unlocalised pair of two-link bits (Fig. 28:1), allegedly from Ireland, is difficult to parallel outside the country. Though one of the Llyn Cerrig Bach bits (Fox, 1946, Pl. XI) has a projecting disc at the tip of one link-end as on the two Irish specimens, the Welsh object, which is a three-link horsebit, is otherwise quite unlike the two Irish bits. The latter also, significantly, lack stop-studs. A comparable two-link bit was found during the excavations at the late Celtic oppidum of Manching in southern Germany (Jacobi, 1974, Tafel 49:774) and an Early La Tène example in the Nyiregyháza Museum, from Szikszo in Hungary (Hunyady, 1942, Taf. LIII:3) is also closely similar to the two from Ireland. We do not know, however, if the Irish bits are ancient or modern imports.

A bronze two-link horsebit from the River Bann, now in private possession (Fig. 28:2), has no ready parallels in these islands. A specimen of iron, strikingly similar to the Irish example is, however, recorded from the Marne region of France and may well be from an Early La Tène burial (Joffroy et Bretz-Mahler, 1959, Fig. 19:8).

"Pendants"

Apart from the unique Killeevan association, the only object reliably found to accompany a horsebit in Ireland is the Y-shaped artifact of bronze (a single iron example is known), which seems certainly to have been an intrinsic element of Irish horse furniture. Its function is, however, quite unknown. It has been variously interpreted as a plume-holder, a curb, a yoke-saddle, a leading-piece, a handle and a pendant. Its most likely function, or perhaps its least unlikely function, is that in some way it was suspended below the bridle and it is here being referred to as a "pendant" partly for this reason and partly because the term is less cumbrous to use than the admittedly more objective "Y-shaped object". Moreover, the term "pendant" does have a certain currency in the literature, having been used by Wilde more than a century ago (1861, 609), and thus has as much right to retention as do such terms as "Food Vessel", "ring money" or "sleeve-fastener".

The number of extant or recorded pendants is now 96. Two broad classes have been isolated, based on the nature of the attachment loop on the extremities of the prongs (Fig. 29; Haworth, 1971), but these classes can be further subdivided (CIIAA, pp. 52, 69-70).

"Pendants" of Type 1 are of bronze and are rarely decorated. In most instances the stem- and prong-terminals are separately cast units and the main distinguishing feature of the group is the presence of a pair of small, D-shaped loops projecting inwards towards each other from the prong-terminals. The form of the prong-terminals usually corresponds closely with that of the stem-terminal but most frequently the prong-terminals are hollow along their inner surface. For ease of description five groups are here suggested but clearly, each group could be further subdivided, for there are substantial variations in basic form within the sub-groups and several quite unique examples exist. Type 1a (Fig. 30:1-4) is represented by pendants with terminals of almond or acorn shape or related form. A rounded expansion usually occurs on that part of the terminal which joins directly with prong and stems. On the prong-terminals the D-shaped loop usually extends from the concave inner face of this expansion. The prong-ends are generally tapered to fit neatly into the terminals. Sometimes the almond shape of the terminals expands almost to spherical form. Type 1b (Fig. 30:5-8) consists of pendants the terminals of which are ribbed. The ribbing may be very fine, little more than parallel, transverse grooving, or it may take the form of quite prominent spherical or sub-spherical mouldings. In some instances the moulding on the extremity of the stem-terminal may be

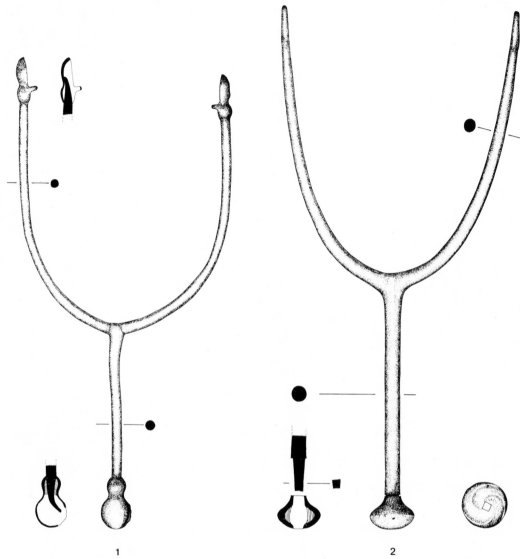

Fig. 29. Bronze pendants. 1 (Type 1) no prov. 2 (Type 2) Drumanone,
Co. Roscommon. - 2/5.

a knob-like expansion.   Type 1c (Fig. 32:1,2; Pl. 15:4) includes three
specimens which have large circular or sub-circular loops at their
extremities.   Type 1d   (Figs 31; 32:3,4;   Pls 14; 15:1, 17:2) represents
a small group of very elaborate pendants, which, though their terminals
vary, seem to be unified by having very short stems and by the extremely
developed nature of their terminals.   The form and proportions of their
forks are also factors which link the pendants of this group.   Type 1e
(Fig. 32:5-7) includes three examples the terminals of which are flattened

and have decorative panels for the retention of enamel inlays. The terminals tend towards a hook-like form.

Pendants of Type 2 exhibit rather more uniformity than do the specimens of Type 1. The main distinguishing feature is the absence of the inward-projecting loops at the prong-ends which characterise Type 1. Instead, there is a perforation through the expanded prong-ends. Two sub-types can be isolated. Type 2a (Fig. 33:1-3) has a heavy, hemispherical knob attached to the end of the stem. The knob is hollow and the stem-end usually has a square-sectioned tang which fits into the knob (Fig. 29:2). Decoration may occur both on stem and on prong-terminals (Figs 34, 35; Pls 15:3, 16, 17:1). The expanded prong-ends of pendants of this group are circular and flattened almost to disc-like proportions. These are pierced centrally by an opening which is always circular. There may be an inverted V-moulding at the junction of stem and prongs, usually on both faces.

Type 2b pendants (Fig. 33:4-8) are normally more slender pieces and are usually cast as a single unit. The stem-ends are far less prominently expanded than in the case of Type 2a. The prong-ends are also less prominently expanded, and the form of the opening is more varied, being pelta-shaped (Pl. 15:2), D-shaped or oval, but never circular. Curvilinear decoration may occur at the prong-ends, but it is rare at the extremity of the stem.

Affinities and Chronology

The pendants represent a distinctively Irish development and do not appear to have any definite parallels outside the country. Jope has compared them to vaguely similar objects from La Tène (1954a, 89), while Haworth (1971, 39) wondered whether north European "Kehlbergen", (U-shaped metal bars), might in some way be related to the Irish pendants. These are thought of sometimes as "throat protectors", which are commonly found with horse-burials and bog offerings in the Germanic world of northern Europe in the early centuries A.D. A further possibility is that the Y-shaped objects (Zügelhälter), such as those found at the Late La Tène oppidum of Manching, may have served a similar function. These have loop-ended prongs as on the Irish Type 2 pendants (Jacobi, 1974, 205-209; Tafel 53:821-823). A group of iron artifacts of Early La Tène date from the Marne region in France (pièces d'articulation en fer), probably chariot or harness fittings, also bear some resemblance to the Irish Y-shaped objects (Joffroy et Bretz-Mahler, 1959, Fig. 17) and could conceivably have played a role in their genesis. None of these possibilities, however, appears at present very convincing so that it seems,

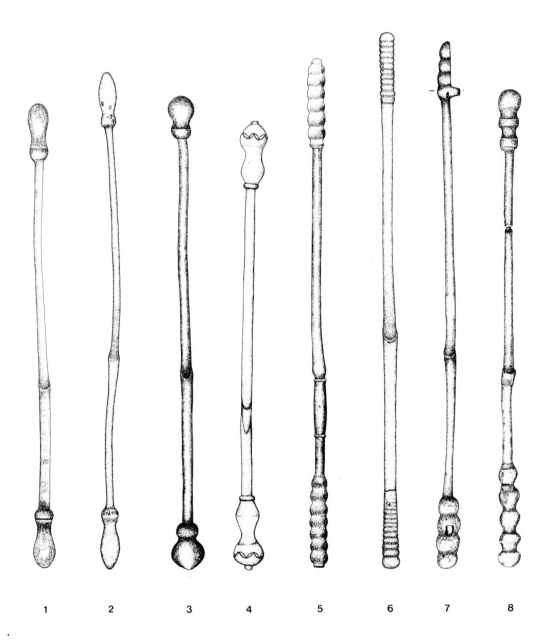

Fig. 30. Type 1 pendant sub-groups. 1–4 Type 1a. 5–8 Type 1b. 1 Aughrim,
Co. Galway. 2 Ballina-Costello, Co. Mayo. 4 Knockmany, Co. Tyrone.
Otherwise no prov. – 2/5.

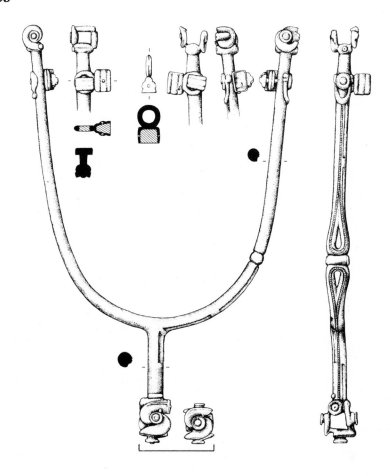

Fig. 31. Elaborate Type 1d pendant. No prov. - 2/5.

for the moment at least, that these objects must be considered an entirely native invention.

As with the horsebits the majority of pendants are stray finds and more than half the known examples are unprovenanced. The few recorded associations are hardly illuminating and much of the dating of these bronzes is entirely dependent on the dating of the horsebits. It is thus necessary to guard against the hazards of circular argument.

There are thirteen recorded cases in which a pendant was found together with another object. Potentially the most important of these are the two associations of pendants with Type B bits. These are both from the west of the country. Ballina-Costello, Co. Mayo (CIIAA 24, 145), and Aughrim, Co. Galway (Raftery, J., and Ryan, 1972, 196-197; Fig. 6). In each case the pendant is of Type 1a; both are identical pieces

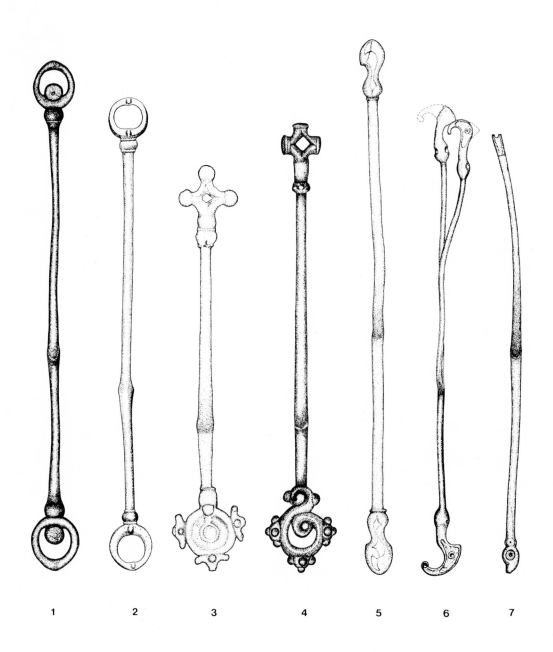

Fig. 32. Type 1 pendant sub-groups. 1-2 Type 1c. 3-4 Type 1d. 5-7 Type 1e.
7 Co. Monaghan(?). Otherwise no prov. - 2/5.

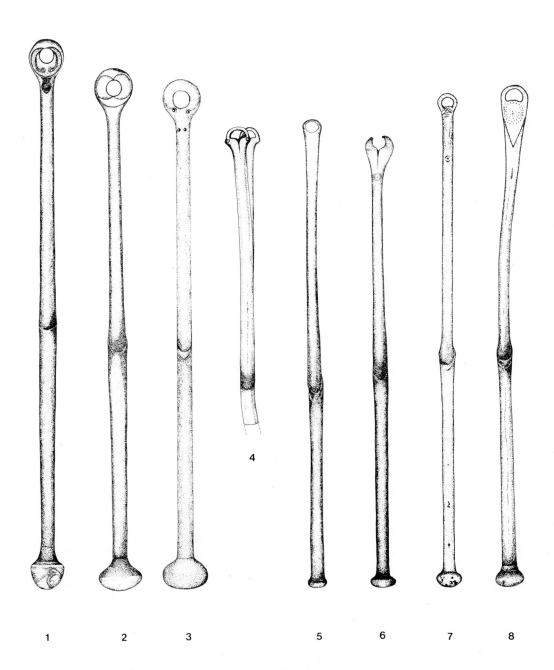

Fig. 33. Type 2 pendant sub-groups. 1-3 Type 2a. 4-8 Type 2b.
2 Drumanone, Co. Roscommon. 3 Cormongan, Co. Leitrim.
7 Clongill, Co. Meath. Otherwise no prov. - 2/5.

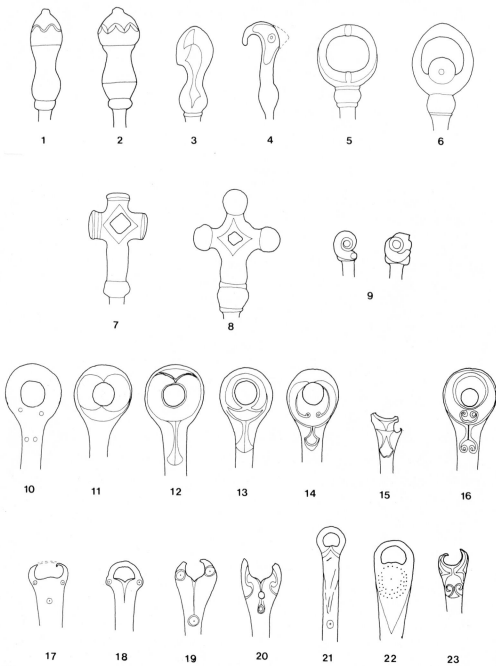

Fig. 34. Decoration on Irish pendant prong-terminals. 2 Portnelligan,
Co. Armagh. 10 Cormongan, Co. Leitrim. 11 Drumanone, Co. Roscommon.
12 Tara-Skreen, Co. Meath. 13 Co. Roscommon. 15 Ballyalla, Co. Clare.
16 Attymon, Co. Galway. 17 Coleraine, Co. Derry. 20 Derlangan, Co.
Meath. 21 Clongill, Co. Meath. 23 Emly, Co. Roscommon. Otherwise
no prov. - 1/2.

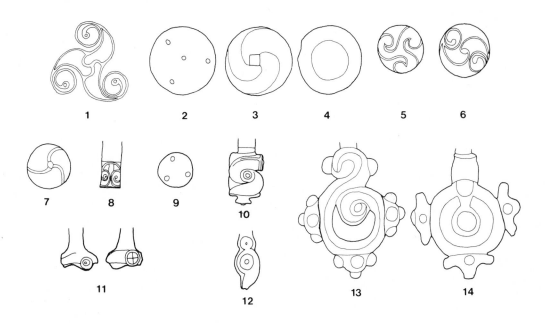

Fig. 35. Decoration on Irish pendant stem-terminals. 1 Attymon, Co. Galway. 2 Cormongan, Co. Leitrim. 3 Drumanone, Co. Roscommon. 4 Tara-Skreen, Co. Meath. 5 Co. Roscommon. 8 Emly, Co. Roscommon. 12 Co. Monaghan (?). Otherwise no prov.

with tapering, acorn-shaped terminals. Neither of the bits, however, has any notable distinguishing features, so that apart from a possible dating to the last centuries B.C. these two associations remain of limited assistance in establishing an absolute chronology for the pendants. It might tentatively be implied, however, on the basis of these two associations, that the pendants with almond-shaped or acorn-shaped terminals are amongst the earliest of the group as they are the only type associated with the presumed earliest class of horsebit.

As against this, a pendant assigned to Type 1a was found at Mullingar, Co. Westmeath, with a pendant of Type 2b, suggesting no great chronological gap between the two groups. The pendant in question, however, has stunted prong-terminals cast to a solid D-shaped section rather than the normal concave-sided, C-shaped section and is conceivably late in a typological series. There are two other instances where Type 1 pendants have been found associated. At Kilbeg, Co. Westmeath, a pendant with ribbed terminals of Type 1b was found along with a corroded iron example and three shafthole axeheads (Fig. 118:1-3). Rynne dated the axeheads on the basis of the association with the bronze pendant, which he stated to be "third or fourth century A.D." (1958, 149), though no attempt is made by him to substantiate this dating. Axeheads of this type are notoriously difficult to date closely and while a Late La Tène or sub-Roman background to them is inherently likely (e.g. Jacobi, 1977, 21-23, Taf. 14-17), there are no precise external parallels for their method of manufacture (see below p. 240). Thus, in terms of absolute dating, the Kilbeg association must be used with caution. It may be, however, that the axes date after, rather than before the birth of Christ.

The Kishawanny hoard from Co. Kildare (Pl. 18; CIIAA 169, 592-3, 861-2) is of greater help. Here another ribbed-terminal pendant was found with a hook, a bell and two hollow rings, all of bronze. The bell, with its small handle, is a Roman type and first century A.D. parallels can be found at Wroxeter (Atkinson, 1942, 210) and elsewhere. The hook also can be compared to several from the Carlingwark hoard, especially C57 (Piggott, 1952-3, Fig. 10), which may reasonably be assigned to the first century A.D. If the Kishawanny material represents a genuine hoard such a date is likely for the pendant from it. The alleged association of a "brass" pin with a pendant of Type 1b (both lost) at Glenbuck, Co. Antrim, as suggested by a MS. drawing in the Royal Irish Academy (CIIAA 167), is not illuminating in terms of dating for, even if the association is acceptable the drawing of the pin in the RIA manuscript is unclear so that its precise nature cannot be determined.

The rest of the pendants are associated with bits of Type D (four times) and Type E (three times). With the exception of Clongill, Co. Meath (Raftery, J., 1966, 13 and Figs 2,3; CIIAA 78, 217), where a pendant of Type 2b is present, the other six associations involve the heavy, knob-ended Type 2a pendants. It has been tentatively postulated above, mainly on the basis of their decoration, that bits of Types D and E may belong to the early centuries A.D. and where decoration occurs on the pendants it clearly derives from precisely the same source as that which inspired the ornament on the bits.

Limited though the information is regarding chronology based on these meagre, at times unhelpful, associations, the weight seems to be towards a generally late date for many, if not most, of the pendants. Type 2 especially seems firmly rooted in a post-Christian context. The Kishawanny and Mullingar associations point to a similarly late date for some Type 1 pendants, and even Kilbeg, if a Late La Tène or sub-Roman context for the axes could be more firmly demonstrated, would fit into such a pattern of lateness. Only the pendants from Ballina-Costello and Aughrim found in association with Type B bits leave the possibility of a pre-Christian date for the pendants with acorn-shaped

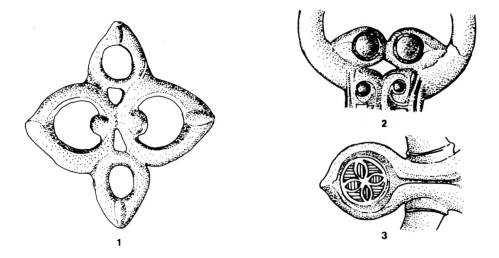

Fig. 36. Examples of north British "petal-loop" design. 1 Corbridge, Northumberland, England. 2 Stanhope, Peeblshire, Scotland. 3 Rise, Holderness, Yorkshire, England. - 3/4. (After MacGregor, 1976).

Fig. 37. Bronze bracelet. Egglfing, Ldkr. Griesbach, Bavaria. Approx. 2/3. (After Torbrügge and Uenze, 1968).

terminals open. But even here it must be admitted that there is no inherent reason why such bits could not have continued in use into the early Christian centuries.

Decorative details where such occur (Figs 34, 35) seem also to indicate a late date for many of the pendants, especially those of Type 2. Numerous parallels for many of the motifs are to be found on British metalwork objects of the early centuries after Christ. The "petal" design on one of the pendants (Fig. 32:1; Pl. 15:4) is particularly important for it is a typically north British development of the first centuries A.D. (Fig. 36). MacGregor noted this Irish example and regarded its presence in Ireland as representing "a true communion of decorative spirit" between Ireland and north Britain (1976, 185).

Not all the ornamentation on the pendants, however, points so unequivocally to a post-Christian dating. The elaborate cast terminals of two Type 1d pendants (Figs 32:3,4; 35:13,14; Pl. 17:2) echo far earlier designs. The arrangement of small bosses in cruciform pattern around a larger boss can, for instance, be closely paralleled on a Middle La Tène bracelet from Egglfing, Kr. Griesbach, Bavaria in Germany (Fig. 37; Torbrügge and Uenze, 1968, 284, Fig. 263); some of the Irish Type 2 ringheaded pins are similarly ornamented (Fig. 83:1-6: Pl. 54).

The possibility of an early date for pendants such as these two exceptional specimens cannot, therefore, be wholly dismissed. Lacking corroborative evidence, however, the question must remain open.

Summary

Horsebits and pendants together comprise nearly 240 surviving or recorded items. They thus constitute more than one quarter of the known metal objects referred to as of La Tène type from Ireland. Fixed chronological points are pitifully few for either category but the indications are that both types of horse-trappings were in use in the early centuries A.D. The date of the beginning of horsebit manufacture in Ireland is as yet unclear, but there are some grounds for dating the earliest bits at least to the second century B.C. and perhaps even before this. It is not as yet possible with any confidence to place the pendants as early as this and it may be that they came to be made only at some date subsequent to the introduction of the horsebit into Ireland.

The problem of the origins and the mechanism of their implantation remains unresolved. All the bits are Irish (with the few exceptions referred to above) so that there are no exact parallels for any of them outside the country. The earliest bits share some features with examples in various parts of England, especially Yorkshire, and a link of some

Fig. 41. S-motifs. 1 Lough Gur, Co. Limerick. 2 Somerset, Co. Galway.

referring to the Lough Gur mounts he expressed support for Piggott's contention (1969, 378-381) that they were mounted on the ends of a yoke. This, indeed, seems the most likely explanation for them.

Fox places the Lough Gur specimens in the late first or early second century A.D., a dating based on their alleged devolved form and the decoration which adorns them. The simple S-motif which occurs on the end of each (Fig. 41:1) is found, though in more plastic form, on the elaborate pendant in the British Museum (Fig. 31; Pl. 14), but far closer to the Lough Gur designs is the S-motif on one of the Somerset, Co. Galway, mounts (Fig. 41:2). The pendant is an extraordinary piece completely without parallel and is hardly susceptible to close dating. The Somerset mount, however, is likely to date within the first century A.D. (below p. 286) and such a dating for the Lough Gur mounts does not conflict with the view of Fox based on grounds of typology.

Finally, a number of wooden yokes of possible Iron Age date may be referred to (Rees, 1979, 72-75 and Fig. 72). One from Northern Ireland (Pl. 19) with side perforations and clearly intended for use by two animals, was discussed by Piggott (1949) who compared it to yokes from La Tène (Piggott, 1969, Fig. 12) and elsewhere in Europe. The structural similarity between the Irish yoke and the European examples is readily apparent (Mariën, 1961, Fig. 66) and the Irish object may fall within the dating range of the Continental pieces. It is, however, unwise to be dogmatic on this point for yoke-forms need not have changed in Ireland over many centuries. Haworth (1971, 44) refers to a number of other wooden yokes from Ireland of conceivably Iron Age date but again, being totally devoid of context, their chronological position is uncertain.

WEAPONS

In Ireland weapons and objects associated with warfare which can be dated to the Iron Age are of relatively infrequent occurrence. There are less than two dozen swords certainly of La Tène type from the country, eight complete or fragmentary scabbards and a few isolated chapes. There is a single complete shield and a few fragments which may be portions of similar implements. Remains of a possible helmet exist from Cork but this was certainly never meant to be worn in battle. Spears were probably widespread in Iron Age Ireland but individual spearheads are difficult to date in most cases so that the number of examples which may be ascribed with certainty to the Iron Age is limited. The importance of the spear in Ireland is, however, suggested by the use of the word *gaisced* for the set of weapons formally presented to a youth on reaching manhood, for this is an old compound meaning originally "spear and shield" and *gaiscedach* "a warrior" was "one bearing a spear and shield" (Jackson, 1964, 16-17). Spearbutts which may be regarded as firmly Iron Age in date are fairly numerous (over 60 examples) and there are also several contemporary mounts and ferrules which have been discovered still attached to their original wooden spearshafts.

Swords

At the time of writing 22 complete or fragmentary swords, certainly or probably of La Tène or sub-La Tène type, are known from the country. Fourteen of these may with confidence be regarded as of firmly La Tène aspect because of the characteristic bell-shaped metal hilt-guard mount (Type 1), while seven others belong to a group characterised by curved quillons of organic material (Type 2) and may represent a local

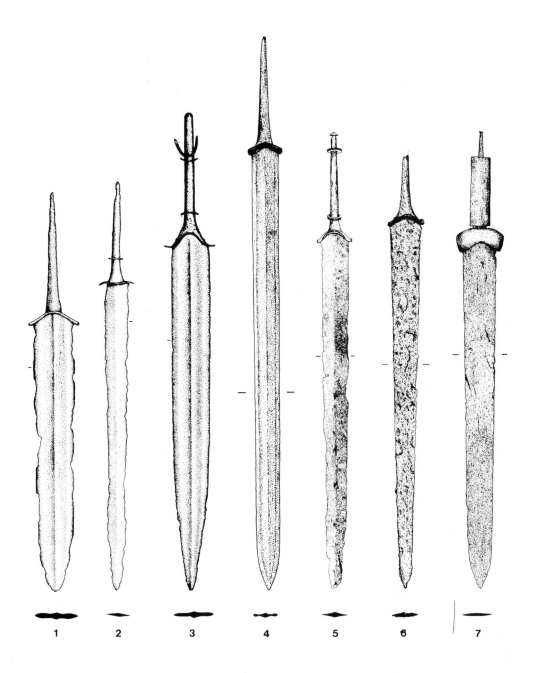

Fig. 42. Selection of La Tène-type swords from Ireland. 1, 2 Edenderry,
Co. Offaly. 3 Lisnacrogher, Co. Antrim. 4 Ballinderry, Co. Westmeath.
5 Cashel, Co. Sligo. 6 Dún Ailinne, Co. Kildare (included courtesy
Prof. Bernard Wailes). 7 no prov. - 1/4.

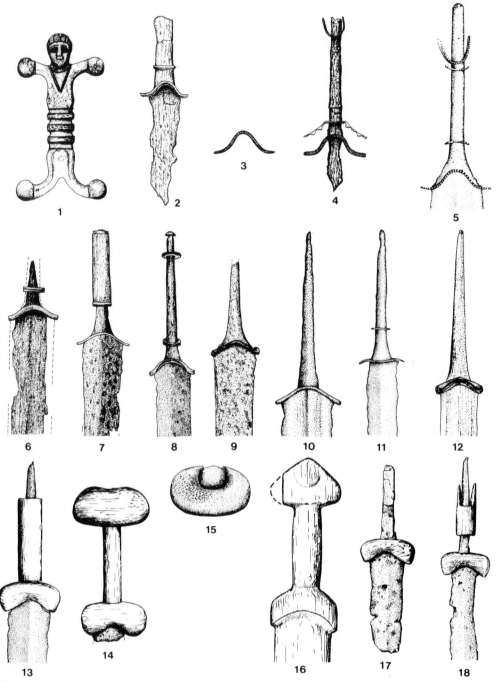

Fig. 43. Irish Iron Age sword-hilt types. 1 Ballyshannon, Co. Donegal.
2 River Bann, Toome, Co. Antrim. 3-5 Lisnacrogher, Co. Antrim.
6 Killaloe, Co. Clare. 7 Lough Gur, Co. Limerick. 8 Cashel, Co. Sligo.
9 Dún Ailinne, Co. Kildare. 10-11, 13-14 Edenderry, Co. Offaly. 12 Ballinderry, Co. Westmeath. 15 Dungarvan, Co. Waterford. 16 Ballykilmurry,
Co. Wicklow. 17-18 River Shannon, Banagher, Co. Offaly. - 1/3.

development of the La Tène form. There is one other example of uncertain type. In addition, there are other iron swords in the National Museum from the River Shannon and elsewhere which could conceivably date to the Iron Age but, lacking distinctive features, this cannot be demonstrated. A short iron sword with straight bronze hilt-guard from the River Boyne at Russelswood, Co. Kildare has been regarded by Rynne as of Late La Tène date (1982, 93). A date considerably later than this is also possible.

Because of the extensive corrosion which many of the swords have suffered, it is difficult in many cases to establish the original shape or size of the blade. It is clear, however, even allowing for the small sample available, that the normal Iron Age sword in Ireland had a surprisingly short blade, making it a weapon of questionable effectiveness. Some variety is detectable in blade form.

The bulk of the swords (and this may also be deduced from the surviving scabbards) appear to have blades parallel-sided for most of their length or tapering gently towards the point. The most complete Lisnacrogher, Co. Antrim sword (Fig. 42:3; Pl. 21:1) has a leaf-shaped blade. The Dún Ailinne, Co. Kildare, piece (Fig. 42:6) has edges which converge sharply towards the point, giving a narrow triangular shape.

The blade may be pointed-oval or lozenge-shaped in cross-section. The Ballinderry, Co. Westmeath, sword (Fig. 42:4) and one from Edenderry, Co. Offaly (Fig. 42:1) stand out from the rest in having a shallow groove extending along the length of the blade on either side of the mid-rib. Traces of such grooves may perhaps also be detectable on the sword from Lough Gur, Co. Limerick (Pl. 22:1).

The largest surviving sword, and one of the best preserved, is the fine Ballinderry example, the total length of which is 57.9 cm. The length of the blade is just over 46 cm. Where blade-lengths can be established on other swords they average from c. 44 cm to the smallest examples from Dún Ailinne (included here by courtesy of the excavator, Prof. Bernard Wailes, University of Pennsylvania) and Cashel, Co. Sligo (Rynne, 1960a; Figs 42:5; 43:8), each of which has a length of around 37 cm, making it in effect little more than a dirk. Blade-widths range from 1.6 cm to 3.4 cm.

The most distinctive feature of the Irish Type 1 La Tène swords is, of course, the hilt-guard mount (Fig. 43) which is almost always a separately-made unit of bronze. On one sword, that from Dún Ailinne, Co. Kildare, the hilt-guard mount may be of iron. It is usually oval or almond-shaped and has a bell-shaped profile ("campanulate" - see de Navarro, 1972, 23, Fig. 3), in the normal Early to Middle La Tène manner. It may be a thin strip of perforated bronze, hammered to shape as in the case of one of the Edenderry swords (Fig. 43:11), but it is usually cast.   Decoration occurs sometimes on the hilt-guard mount.   Three from Lisnacrogher (Figs 42; 43:3-5), for instance, bear incised hatching along one of the narrow edges (the edge presumably on view when the sword was worn).   In two other instances, Ballinderry (Fig. 43:12) and Cashel (Fig. 43:8; Pl. 22:2) cast relief trumpet curves are present.   The former is the more elaborate, having a background of irregular punched dotting to the raised curves

On five Irish swords the original organic grip survives and in each case it is a simple cylinder of bone or horn identified in the case of the Lough Gur specimen (Fig. 43:7; Pl. 22:1) as being made from a sheep's metatarsal.   The mounts which held the organic hilt elements in place frequently survive, being usually small, oval discs of bronze.   More elaborate mounts, some with finely-milled edges, occur on two of the Lisnacrogher swords (Fig. 43:4; Pl. 21).

It is impossible to determine with certainty the nature of the pommels which might once have been affixed to the ends of the tangs of Type 1 swords.   Prominent, sub-spherical pommels of bone are, however, a feature of the Type 2 swords (Fig. 43:14-16; Pl. 24:2-4).   The C-shaped mounts remaining on the tang-ends of two Lisnacrogher swords (Fig. 43:4,5; Pl. 21) may have been so shaped to support comparable sub-spherical pommels (see Rynne, 1982, 95, Fig. 3).

The Ballyshannon sword is unlike anything else in Ireland and may well be an import (see below).   None of the remaining swords, however, need be viewed as other than of native manufacture.   In this regard it seems likely that an armoury existed somewhere in the Antrim area, for the swords from this region differ in detail from those elsewhere in the country, and it is here too that the decorated scabbards are concentrated.   Significantly, perhaps, it is in Antrim alone that hilt-guard mounts and scabbard mouths of steeply bell-shaped profile (de Navarro's Type A2, "high campanulate" group) are found.

Affinities and Chronology

Type 1

The campanulate hilt-guard mount, both in its steeply-curving and in its shallowly-curving form, is a feature of Early and Middle La Tène swords on the Continent and is also found, though less frequently, on swords of Late La Tène date.   There is, however, no way of knowing what weight if any, should be placed on the shape of the hilt-guard mount in Ireland as an indicator of absolute dating.   Nonetheless it is evident

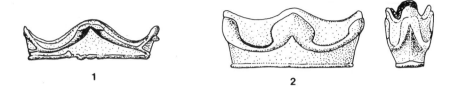

Fig. 44. Bronze sword-quillons from Scotland. 1 Newstead, Roxburghshire. 2 Middlebie, Dumfriesshire. - 3/4.

that the Ulster swords as a group, differing from those elsewhere in the country, are closest in the shape of their hilt-guard mounts to the classic Middle La Tène swords of Europe and it may be that these are the earliest of the Irish group.

Some support for the early dating of the Lisnacrogher swords is provided by the leaf-shaped blade of one specimen from that site (Fig. 42:3; Pl. 21:1), for this is one of the characteristic blade types of Early La Tène swords on the Continent (e.g. de Navarro, 1972, Pls II, III). These early European swords are also by far the shortest of the Continental La Tène series and in this regard are thus closest to the Lisnacrogher and the other Irish examples (see Stead, 1983, 504 and Fig. 5).

The only other Irish sword blades which offer any chronological clues are those with longitudinal grooves flanking the mid-rib, the finest example of which is that from Ballinderry, Co. Westmeath (Fig. 42:4). Such grooves are often called "blood channels" but, as Wyss has pointed out (1968, 673-4), the grooving is more likely to reflect considerations of blade elasticity, stability and balance; aesthetic considerations may also have played a part in the fashioning of such blades.

Although grooved blades of Early La Tène date are known from Europe (e.g. de Navarro, op. cit. No. 6), they are extremely rare, not only at this early date, but during the Middle La Tène period as well (de Navarro, op. cit. 361). During the Late La Tène period, however, and continuing in use into early Roman times, such blade types are relatively common. Close Continental parallels for the Ballinderry sword blade are readily forthcoming. These are, of course, always considerably longer than the Irish specimen but resemble closely not only its grooving but also its shape. Good examples, for instance, may be cited from the Late La Tène river deposit at Port, Kt. Bern in Switzerland (Wyss, op. cit., Taf. I:5,6)

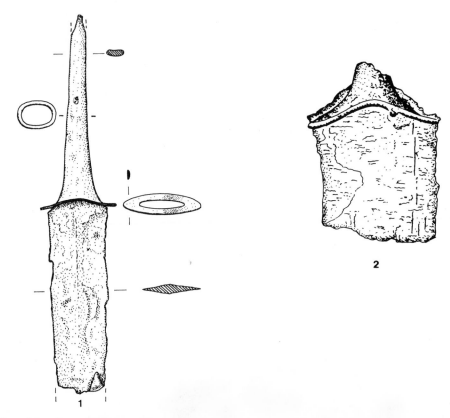

Fig. 45. Sword fragments possibly of Irish manufacture. 1 Llyn Cerrig
Bach, Anglesey, Wales. 2 Stevenston Sands, Ayrshire, Scotland.
1:1/2. 2:3/4. (2 after MacGregor, 1976).

and from the Late La Tène/Early Roman-period cemetery at Großromstedt
in eastern Germany (Eichhorn, 1927, 139, Fig. p. 140). Similar grooved
blades of Late La Tène date are known from as far east as Jugoslavia
(Todorovic, 1968, Sl. 24:6), but do not appear to be known from Britain.

The distinctive blade of the Ballinderry sword is likely, therefore,
to indicate for it a date around the birth of Christ. The cast trumpet
and lentoid ornament on its hilt-guard mount does not conflict with this
dating. Comparable decoration also occurs on the hilt-guard mount
of a sword from Cashel, Co. Sligo (Fig. 43:8; Pl. 22:2). The decoration
is plainly insular and, as is suggested below, such trumpet curves are
hardly earlier in date than the last century B.C. They become one of
the dominant motifs of the early centuries of Christianity. Rynne (1960,
13) compared the form and decoration on the Cashel hilt-guard mount
with those English swords from Bugthorpe (Fig. 54:5; Harding, 1974,
Fig. 61) and Amerden (Piggott, 1950, Fig. 3, No. 4A) and on this basis
postulated a first century B.C. date for the Co. Sligo specimen. Perhaps

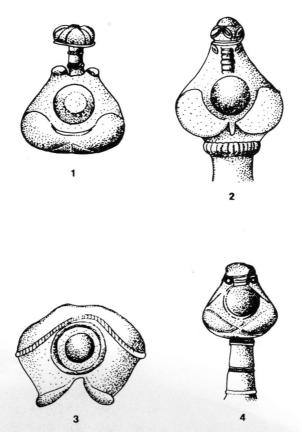

Fig. 46. British sword pommels. 1 Brough-under-Stainmore, Westmoreland. 2 Worton, Lancashire. 3 Embleton, Cumberland. 4 Caerleon, Monmouth-shire. 1-3:3/4. 4:1/2. (1-3 after MacGregor, 1976. 4 after Savory, 1976).

more relevant is the quillon from Newstead, Roxburghshire, Scotland (MacGregor, 1976, No. 151), which though differing in form from either of the Irish examples, bears comparable cast relief, trumpet lobes ending in tiny lentoid bosses as on the Ballinderry weapon (Fig. 44:1). The Newstead piece was found in a pit in the upper levels of which a Flavian coin was found and a date at the end of the first century A.D. is probable for it. The ornament on a broadly contemporary hilt-guard from Middlebie, Dumfriesshire, Scotland, may also be comparable with the two Irish swords in question (Fig. 44:2).

Tentative support for a date around the beginning of the Christian era for some, a least, of these southern Irish swords is supplied by the context of the only Irish La Tène sword to come from a controlled excavation, that from Dún Ailinne, Co. Kildare (Fig. 42:6). The excavator, Dr. Bernard Wailes, in a personal communication, has kindly informed the writer that the sword came from deep in the fill of one of the two trenches outlining the Phase 3 structure, one of the complex series of circular palisade trenches uncovered on the hilltop (Wailes, 1976, 231-9). According to the excavator, it could not be stated with absolute certainty whether it was in the primary or the secondary fill, but from its position - almost against the side of the trench and fairly well down - Dr. Wailes feels that it is likely to be primary. Three recently published Carbon 14 determinations for samples taken from the fill of the Phase 3 trench are consistent with a first century A.D. dating for the sword. The dates are: A.D. 50±85; A.D. 20±85; A.D. 195±90 (Wailes, 1976, 338).

Outside Ireland several swords occur which may conceivably be of Irish origin. One is the fragment from Stevenston Sands, Ayrshire, in Scotland (Fig. 45:2), which has a distinctly Irish appearance (MacGregor, 1976, No. 139) and MacGregor, in fact, wondered whether it might not be included in Piggott's so-called Group IIIa, his Irish group (op. cit., 79). The possibility of Irish origin for this specimen is interesting in view of the Irish-type scabbard (Bargany) from the same part of south-west Scotland (see below). One of the swords from Llyn Cerrig Bach (Fig. 45:1) could well also be from Ireland (Savory, 1976, Fig. 30:2).

The Ballyshannon sword (Fig. 43:1; Pls 23,112:2), with its distinctive cast bronze hilt belongs to the well known group with anthropoid hilts, which were studied definitively by Hawkes more than twenty years ago (Clarke and Hawkes, 1955; see also Petres, 1979; Bulard, 1980). The Irish example is an outlier of his Class G, a Gaulish type "with classical influence manifest in its style of modelling" (1955, 213). Southern and south-western Gaul seem to be the source of these objects and two examples are recorded from north-eastern England, probably native imitations of the type (Map 5). Hawkes has referred to the Ballyshannon example as "the most typical example outside France" but allows for the possibility that it was, in fact, made in Ireland. Jacobsthal (1944, 14, Fig. 4) compared the leaf pattern on the heads of the Pfalzfeld pillar with the arrangement of the hair on the forehead of the Ballyshannon hilt but the analogy is obscure.

Such sword-hilts are a phenomenon of the European later La Tène and Hawkes has suggested that the Co. Donegal sword may with confidence be dated to about or just before 100 B.C. It is likely to be a direct import to Ireland and through it, movement along the western seaways directly between western Europe and the west coast of Ireland is strongly implied.

Type 2

As Rynne has recently pointed out the swords here referred to as Type 2 are subject to further subdivision on the basis of the presence

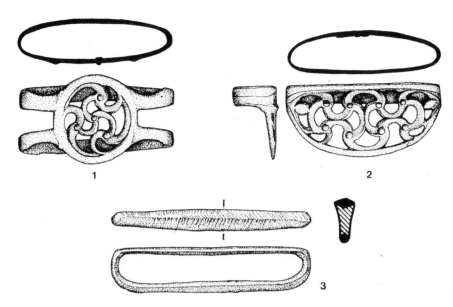

Fig. 47. Bronze scabbard-mounts. Lambay, Co. Dublin. - 3/4.

or absence of skeuomorphic representations of metal elements (Rynne, 1983)[1]. Type 2a comprises of two examples, the wooden Ballykilmurry, Co. Wicklow specimen (Fig. 43:16; Pl. 24:3) and the deerhorn pommel from Dungarvan, Co. Waterford (Fig. 43:15; Pl. 24:2). The function of the Ballykilmurry sword with its projecting, half-cylindrical element on the blade is uncertain but it seems clearly to represent a complete sword of the type under discussion. The hilt-guard retains the memory of the curved metal hilt-guard plate of the normal La Tène sword and Rynne's suggestion that the sub-spherical feature carved on the Ballykilmurry and Dungarvan pommels is also ultimately a skeuomorph of a spherical organic pommel clasped within a curved metal mount (as is preserved on the tang of two of the Lisnacrogher swords (Fig. 43:4,5; Pl. 22) carries conviction. The other five swords of the group (Type 2b) are obviously related to the two just discussed but lack any skeuomorphic elements.

The precise dating of these swords has been a subject of some debate. Raftery (1939, 172) took the curved quillons to suggest for the group a local development of the normal La Tène type and he wondered on this basis if such weapons could date to the early centuries of Christianity. Hencken (1950, 88) compared the bone pommel from Dungarvan to Roman

---

[1] I am indebted to Professor Rynne for allowing me to read his paper in typescript prior to its eventual publication.

and Romano-British swords of the first century A.D. and cited such possible English parallels for the Irish Type 2 swords as weapons from Embleton, Cumberland (Fig. 46:3; MacGregor, 1976, No. 145) and Worton, Lancashire (Fig. 46:2; MacGregor, 1976, No. 158). He considered the possibility that the Irish swords may be a simplified version of the Roman and late La Tène examples.

Most recently Rynne has treated these swords as a group and has drawn attention to parallels for the distinctive pommel-type outside the country. He stressed the skeuomorphic hilt-guard mount on the Ballykilmurry specimen which indicates the La Tène context of these swords and this suggestion derives support from the discovery of a bone pommel of Dungarvan-type at the late La Tène oppidum of Stradonice in Czechoslovakia. Similar pommels (unfortunately unstratified) are also known from two Scottish brochs - Burrian on North Ronaldsway, Orkney, and North Uist in the Hebrides. A hilt-guard of bone similar to the Irish Type 2 examples (though somewhat larger) comes from a Scottish wheelhouse at A'Cheardach, South Uist. Rynne finally drew attention to the representation of a sword with comparable hilt-fittings on a Celto-Roman grave-marker in Mainz, Germany, and concluded, while admitting the obvious dating difficulties, that these Irish swords belong to a type "which developed in the Celtic non-Roman parts of these islands during the early Roman period of England, Wales and Lowland Scotland, and might thus be referred to as of Ultimate La Tène type". He suggested a date during the second and third centuries A.D. for them.

A further parallel for the distinctive Dungarvan pommel-type appears to be represented by the bronze sword-hilt of "Worton-type" from the Roman legionary fort of Caerleon in Monmouthshire, Wales (Fig. 46:4; Boon, 1974, 205-206 and Pl. XX). The object, with characteristic late Celtic trumpet and zig-zag ornament, is compared to similar pieces from Brough in Westmoreland (Fig. 46:1) and the eponymous Worton specimen, and its presence in a Roman legionary fortress is taken by Boon to suggest that it may have been "a trophy of some engagement....in the early years of the Roman conquest of Britain."

A final example possibly relevant to the chronological position of these Irish swords is the early second century A.D. carving from Adamklissi in Bulgaria, of a Roman soldier fighting Dacians. The sword being used by the soldier has a pommel and hilt-guard strikingly reminiscent of the swords of our Type 2 (Dixon, 1976, frontispiece).

There appears, thus, to be a considerable measure of agreement regarding the dating of Type 2 Irish swords. All the indications are that they were in use in the period shortly after the birth of Christ and their immediate background seems to be a Romano-British one perhaps centred in the northern part of the neighbouring island. It may be that influence comes ultimately from central Europe.

Miscellaneous

The surviving fragments of the Lambay sword in the National Museum are so corroded and amorphous as to allow of little comment. The sword-blade seems to have been parallel-sided for most of its length and, assuming that the bronze mounts (Fig. 47; Pl. 25) are from the scabbard which held it, then a date about the middle of the first century A.D. is indicated (Rynne, 1976, 231-244). The bulk of the Lambay material has well-established north British affinities and represents a clearly intrusive complex. Piggott included the sword in his Group V (Battersea type) and attributes these swords to Belgic influence (1950, 21-22). It seems, however, in view of the north British connections for the Lambay material, that the sword could more readily be included in his Group IV.

Summary

It can be seen from the above that, on their own, the La Tène-type swords of Ireland can, for the most part, be considered only in their broad cultural context and closer details of chronology and, indeed, of precise affinities are by no means firmly established. With the probable exceptions of Ballyshannon and Lambay the La Tène swords here represent a local development, their Irish character emphasised by the extreme shortness of the blades. Their Middle La Tène background is evident but it is not yet clear how long this tradition of sword-making continued in Ireland. It seems unlikely to have had a long life, however, and a span between the third or second century B.C. and the first century A.D. probably covers the floruit of the genuine La Tène sword in this country. Type 2 swords probably developed from this and they may have continued in use for a few centuries after the true La Tène sword became obsolete here.

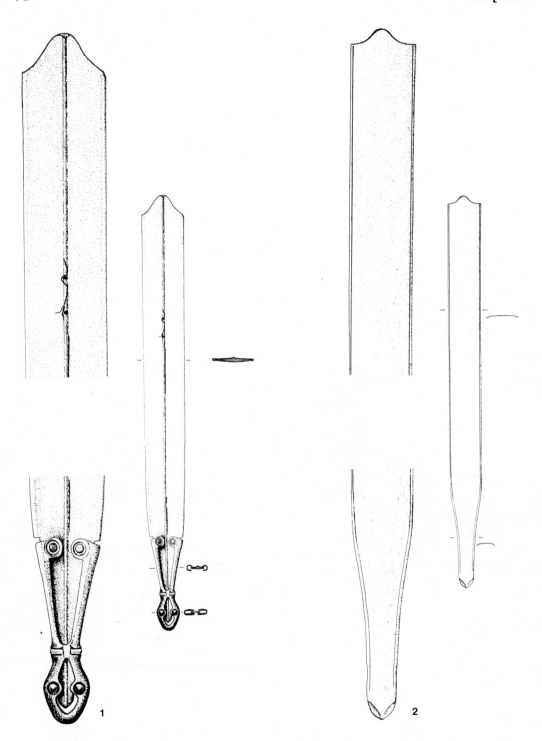

Fig. 48. Bronze scabbard-plates. 1 Lisnacrogher, Co. Antrim.
2 Toome, Co. Antrim. - 1/4; details 1/2.

Scabbards

One substantially complete bronze scabbard of Iron Age date survives from Ireland and there are seven single scabbard-plates. Six openwork bronze chapes exist (three still attached to their scabbards) and two figure-of-eight shaped bronze loops from Lisnacrogher may be unfinished portions of such objects.

The scabbard-plates (Figs 48-51; Pls 26-31) are well-known because of the fine engraved decoration which adorns six examples. A seventh specimen, from Toome, Co. Antrim, bears a pair of very slight, leaf-shaped facets at the tip but is otherwise undecorated, while the eighth, the only complete scabbard, comes from Lisnacrogher and is plain.

There are also three bronze mounts from the first century A.D. Lambay burials which are usually deemed to have been scabbard-mounts (Fig. 47; Pl. 25).

For ease of description the following conventions, some already current in the literature, are used here: Lisnacrogher 1 (Fig. 49:1) is the scabbard with a broken tip in the Ulster Museum (B. 5); Lisnacrogher 2 (Fig. 49:2) is the British Museum specimen (BM 80.8-2.115); Lisnacrogher 3 (Fig. 50:1) is the Ulster Museum example with gridded basketry (B. 4). Lisnacrogher 4 (Fig. 48:1) is the complete, plain scabbard (UM B.3). Toome 1 (Fig. 50:2) is that with overall decoration (UM 113-1951). Toome 2 (Fig. 48:2) is undecorated apart from the two hammered leafy elements at its tip. Toome 3 (Fig. 51:1)[1] is in the National Museum of Ireland (NMI 1937:3634) while Bann 1 (possibly from near Coleraine; Fig. 51:2) is now in the British Museum.

The scabbard-plates consist of thin sheets of bronze beaten to gently curved, "cambered" section with folded edges (overlaps). The complete example from Lisnacrogher (No. 4), shows how the two plates were held together; the edges of one plate were folded over the edges of the other plate, clamping the two firmly together. On Lisnacrogher 2 (Fig. 49:2) wear was such that the folded-over flange broke away along part of each edge and was painstakingly replaced by narrow, riveted-on strips of U-shaped cross-section.

The sides of the plates are usually parallel for most of their length, curving slightly inwards in several instances towards the sharply narrowed tongue at the lower end. The latter was a technical necessity in order

---

1. This scabbard has hitherto been regarded in the literature as coming from the river Bann at Coleraine, Co. Derry. Its correct findspot "from near the river Bann at Toome" has been established by Kelly (IK 1983, No. 34).

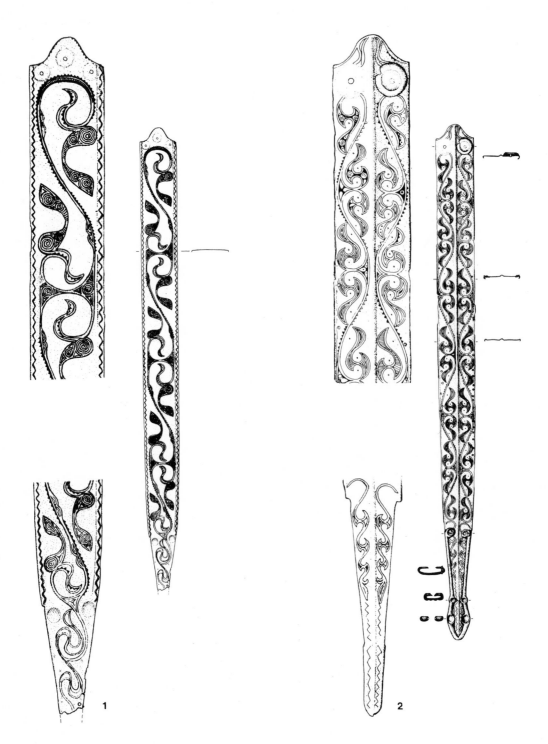

Fig. 49. Bronze scabbards plates, Lisnacrogher, Co. Antrim.
Scale 1/4; details 1/2.

to facilitate the fitting-on of the openwork chape. The tongue either curves inwards from the main portion of the plate in converging, concave sweeps towards the narrow tip or is a separate element, cut back and sharply rebated from the edge of the scabbard. The width of the tongue varies from 1.5 cm on Toome 2 (Fig. 48:2) to as little as 7 mm on Toome 1 (Fig. 50:2) and on Bann 1 (Fig. 51:2). The tip of the tongue is either rounded or triangular. The tongue of Lisnacrogher 3 snapped off in antiquity (Fig. 50:1) and was repaired by riveting a metal strip across the break at the back of the plate. Two tiny perforations, set one above the other, occur near the tip of Toome 3 (Fig. 51:1). This feature is not found on any of the other scabbards and the purpose of these perforations is uncertain.

A hammered mid-rib is present on one of the plates of the complete Lisnacrogher scabbard (Fig. 48:1). Two other plates, also from Lisnacrogher (Nos 2 and 3), have hammered mid-ribs (Figs 49:2, 50:1).

Five at least of the six decorated scabbards appear to have had decorative settings riveted to the plate near the bell-shaped mouth. Lisnacrogher 2 and 3 had each a circular bronze mount riveted opposite one another on either side of the mid-rib. On No. 2 (Fig. 49:2) one of these is missing but the circular impression left by it is clear. On this specimen the size of the mark does not correspond exactly with the size of the surviving mount so that the latter may be a secondary (though ancient) addition. On the other plate (Fig. 50:1; Pl. 28) it seems that the craftsman originally bored the rivet-holes too close to the mouth of the plate, for he had to bore a second pair and the mounts now cut across the initial incorrectly-placed perforations.

The other four plates had an arrangement of three circular mounts, set in triangular formation to mirror the curve of the ogee mouth. On Toome 1 (Fig. 50:2) and Lisnacrogher 1 (Fig. 49:1; Pl. 26) the circular outline of the original mounts is evident. On Toome 3 (Fig. 51:1) there is no detectable trace of any mounts. Indeed, if such ever existed they must have been of extremely thin metal, for the surviving rivet-heads have been filed almost flush with the surface of the bronze plate so that there scarcely seems room to accommodate any bronze fittings.

On Bann 1 (Fig. 51:2; Pl. 31) three rivet-holes under the mouth presumably indicate the former presence of some sort of decorative mounts here but no trace of these can be detected on the object.

In the case of the four Lisnacrogher examples the shape of the mouth is of steeply bell-shaped, "high campanulate" profile (de Navarro, 1972, 23). Toome 1 has a similarly-shaped mouth but there is a slight concavity at the apex of the curve on this example; in the case of Toome 2 the mouth is somewhat less sharply curved. Toome 3 and Bann 1 have more

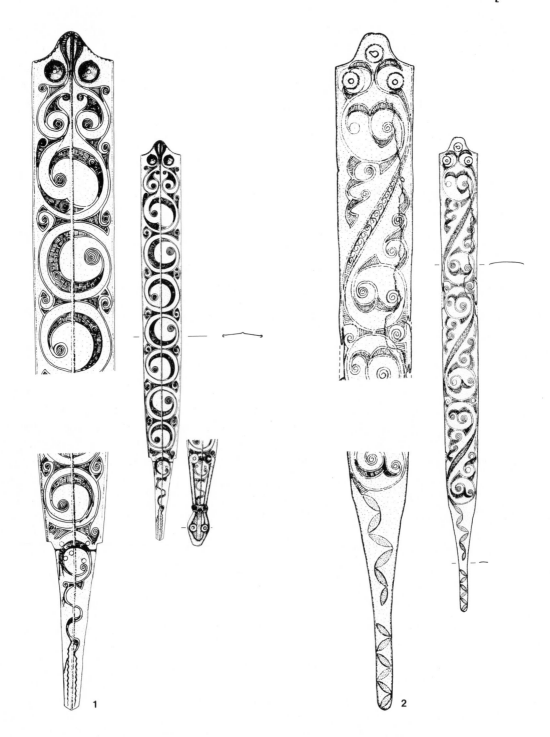

Fig. 50. Bronze scabbard-plates. 1 Lisnacrogher, Co. Antrim. 2 R. Bann,
Toome, Co. Antrim. – 1/4; details 1/2.

shallowly-curved (sub-campanulate) mouths, one especially (Fig. 51:2), forming a barely perceptible bell shape. The decoration at the mouth of Toome 3 (Fig. 51:1) appears to have been severely truncated by the cutting of the mouth. There can be little doubt that this is a two-period piece and this probability is emphasised by the row of small punched bosses along the edges and under the mouth. These ignore the decoration, and project from the undecorated face which in the final phase of use formed the front of the plate. A central groove, obviously caused by the sword point, cuts across the ornament which is also obscured by oblique hammer marks. It would seem that initially the plate was longer than it now is and had engraved ornament along the front. Then the plate was shortened and was hammered to reverse the concavity and turn the decoration inwards. The surface finally on view was thus plain, but for the row of low hemispherical bosses which decorated the edges. Indistinct traces of worn decoration are also discernible on the inner, concave, face of Bann 1 (Figs 51:2; Pl. 31).

In length the scabbard-plates range from 41.1 cm to 55.4 cm; six of the eight are less than 50 cm long.

Decoration

Six of the eight Irish plates bear engraved decoration along their length. The technique of ornamentation is unclear on Toome 1 because of corrosion; on the other scabbards rocked-graver in various forms is used throughout. On Lisnacrogher 2 the implement employed has been recognised as a fine, round-nosed graver (Lowry et al., 1971, 180, Pl. XIVa,b) and on Toome 3 and Bann 1, a similar tool was probably also used. The decoration is for the most part executed free-hand, the compass being used only sparingly. On Lisnacrogher 2 alone, where some of the smaller curves appear to have been partially laid out with a compass, can such an implement be recognised with confidence. In one instance at least (Toome 1), traces of a marking-out line have been recognised (Jope, 1954, 81).

The standard of workmanship varies somewhat from scabbard to scabbard. On Lisnacrogher 3, for example, small but unsightly scratches are clearly visible at a number of points, especially near the bottom, where the graver slipped in the hands of the craftsman. The entire composition of Toome 3 is clumsy, having seemingly been produced by a learner or by an artificer of indifferent skill.

Lateral bands of decoration, flanking the long edges of the scabbard-plate, are present in three instances. On Lisnacrogher 1 each border is defined by a zig-zag line. Along each edge of the decorated surface

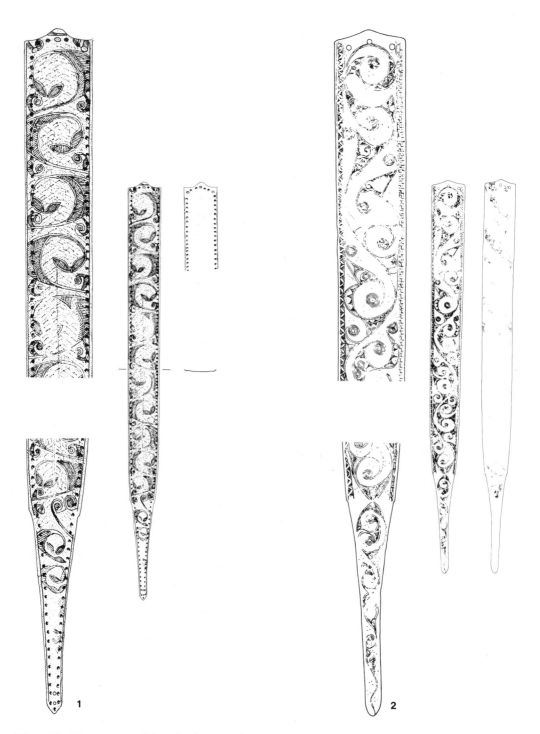

Fig. 51. Bronze scabbard-plates. 1 R. Bann, Toome, Co. Antrim. 2 R. Bann. - 1/4; details 1/2. (2 drawing supplied by Dr. I.M. Stead, British Museum).

of Toome 3 there are fine, rocked-graver lines. On the same specimen, in its final phase of use, when the faces had been reversed the edges of the plain surface were adorned by a row of small, punched bosses. One edge of Bann 1 is decorated with a narrow band of somewhat unevenly produced step-pattern. The other edge of the same plate has a band of continuous, leafy zig-zag, the angle between the leaves being filled with simple hatching.

The three decorated Lisnacrogher scabbards have traces of zig-zag or punched triangle motifs defining the curved edges of the mouth. This feature is absent on the other scabbards.

The curvilinear ornament on the scabbards can best be described by considering it in its three main aspects. Firstly, there are the major, curved elements which provide the overall pattern of the design. Next, there are the lesser devices, the appendages, as it were, which are joined to, or spring from, the major decorative units and which fill the blank areas provided by the major curves. Finally, there are the lesser designs, the often tiny motifs which fill the bodies of the main units or which are occasionally found tucked in amongst the principal curved elements (Fig. 55).

S-motifs and running curves form the dominant themes in the overall designs of the Irish scabbards. On Lisnacrogher 1 and Toome 1 the major pattern comprises a continuous series of large S-figures, each one touching the next, while on Bann 1 the pattern which dominates is that of a continuous, sinuously curving wave. On Lisnacrogher 2 both decorative concepts are present according to how the design is "read". On this specimen a mid-rib is present so that the S-figures on either side of it combine to provide a series of elegant lyre designs. If the S-idea is allowed to recede into the background the ornament on either side of the mid-rib becomes a continuous, slender, tendril wave. On Lisnacrogher 3 the design is based on a series of touching spirals which extend rather awkwardly across the mid-rib, touching one another on their longitudinal axis in a manner closely similar to the way in which the ends of the S-figures of Toome 1 touch (the junctions have been described by Jope, following Jacobsthal, as "hour-glass" junctions, 1954, 81). The sixth scabbard, Toome 3, bears a series of crude C-shaped patterns, each an independent unit open to alternate edges of the plate. It may be that the original intention was to produce spiral motifs comparable, perhaps, with those on Lisnacrogher 3; but if this was so the attempt has been largely unsuccessful.

On two scabbards (Lisnacrogher 1 and 2), alternate edges of the slender, tendril bodies of the main figures are defined by rows of tiny, sub-triangular "teeth" (see Frey with Megaw, 1976, 56).

The voids formed by the main decorative pattern have been filled in different ways on each scabbard. On Lisnacrogher 1 a single comma-shaped motif is repeated eight times in identical form, touching in each case each of the curled ends of the main S-figures. On Lisnacrogher 2 the areas enclosed by the "waves" are filled with combined peltate and "sickle"- or "crescent"-shaped designs which can be "read" either as individual units terminating each of the S-figures or taken together to provide a form of flattened-palmette motif. Toome 1 has varying S-shaped and "wavy" designs filling the voids, while Bann 1 uses a bewildering variety of pelta-, "sickle"- and S-motifs to complete the pattern. On Lisnacrogher 3, apart from the principal spiral units already referred to above, the only other designs on the main area of the plate are the small, hair-spring spirals which occur along each edge of the plate in the concavities formed by the "hour-glass" junctions of the main spiral units. On Toome 3 the incompetence in design is matched by the limited imagination displayed; for the only attempt to fill the voids produced by the main curves, apart from a single, roughly engraved double spiral (Fig. 55:E11), is in the form of a repetitive series of crude, comma-spirals which project awkwardly from various parts of the main figures (Fig. 55:E1).

The craftsmen naturally paid particular attention to the extremities of the decorated areas, that is, they concentrated on the most effective means of beginning and ending the ornamental composition at the top and the bottom of the plate. The narrowed tip was especially challenging and various devices were employed to finish off the designs here. On that portion which survives of Lisnacrogher 1 a squashed "running-dog" was used. On Lisnacrogher 2 a variant of the "running-dog" occurs with the interlocking heads of the individual S-scrolls taking the form of opposed pelta designs. This "running-dog" device halts a short distance from the scabbard-tip to be replaced, on either side of the mid-rib, by a simple zig-zag line. On Lisnacrogher 3 a short, wavy line extends two-thirds of the way along the narrowed tip ignoring the mid-rib as it goes. The last few centimetres of the scabbard-plate are decorated by a parallel pair of "zig-zag" lines one on either side of the mid-rib as on Lisnacrogher 2. These "grow" uncomfortably from the wavy line and it may not be a coincidence that the awkward junction of zig-zags and wavy line was concealed by the transverse moulding of the chape.

On Toome 1 the narrowed tip is simply adorned with a leafy zig-zag (reminiscent of the leafy border on Bann 1) which is left blank for a short distance at that point where part of the chape would have extended across the scabbard end. The artificer of Bann 1 was, perhaps, the most successful at embellishing the scabbard-tip, for he succeeded in continuing, almost to the end, the same pattern as on the main portion of the plate, though in attenuated form. Only at the very end did he have recourse to a short wavy line. Apart from a few indistinct areas of tooling and two stunted, deformed "spirals", further attempts to adorn the narrow end of Toome 3 were dispensed with.

The means of commencing the ornament at the upper end of the scabbard-plate differs on each of the specimens. On Lisnacrogher 1 no special elaboration occurs, apart from hatching the upper body of the first S-figure. On Lisnacrogher 2 the main design ends at two circular settings which occur a short distance from the scabbard-mouth. "Growing" out of each of these settings and extending on either side of the mid-rib towards the peak of the bell-shaped mouth is an odd "sickle"-shaped motif. In the same position on Lisnacrogher 3 a pair of comparable "sickle"- or "crescent"-shaped elements face one another on either side of the mid-rib. Unlike Lisnacrogher 2, however, these are not independent units but form the ends of a pair of elegant trumpet finials which, uniquely on this scabbard, effectively exploit the mid-rib. The same trumpet finial motif is precisely matched on only one other Irish scabbard, Bann 1, near its tip. On Toome 1 the head of the first S-figure divides at its peak and the ends thus formed curve upwards and outwards to form a pair of crescentic "eyebrows" above the lower two circular settings which formerly existed there. On Bann 1, distinct in so many ways from the other scabbards, the ornament terminates below the mouth of the scabbard in a unique and clever manner, for here the flowing wave contracts and curls upon itself to provide what can best be described as a cunningly-conceived yin-yang motif (Duval, 1977, 282) without appreciably breaking the rhythm of the wavy design.

The minor motifs filling out the main decorative figures on the scabbards are of considerable interest, emphasising as they do in their variety the imagination and ingenuity of the Irish artificers (Fig. 55). In some instances a number of basic themes are repeated along the length of the plate, while on others a quite extraordinary profusion of ornamental devices is evident. The most limited repertoire of filler motifs occurs. on Lisnacrogher 3 and Toome 3. On the former all the main units are filled with gridded basketry (Fig. 55:C2, 13) within each one of which (with one exception) a single, tightly-coiled, hair-spring spiral occurs, perhaps in an effort to break the monotony of unrelieved basketry. Apart from the spirals and the basketry the only other filling device on this specimen is simple hatching. Toome 3, as already emphasised, is an inferior piece. Filling designs are restricted to awkward hatching which, centrally divided on the bodies of the main C-figures, acquires the appearance of rough herring-bone ornament (Fig. 55:E7/8).

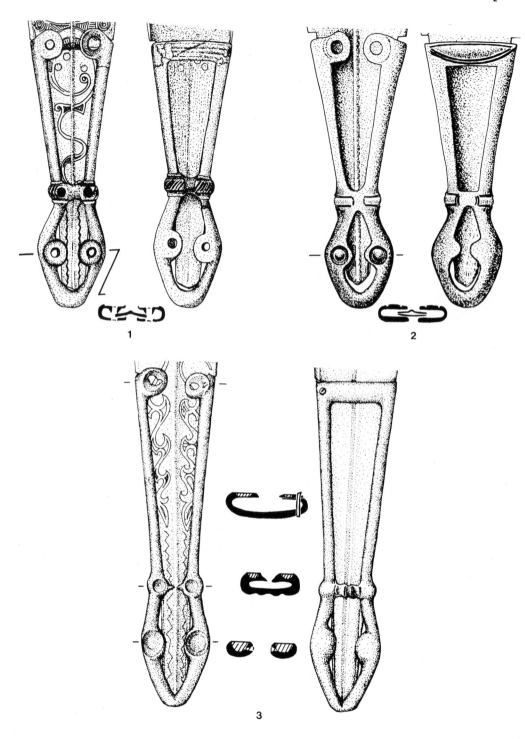

Fig. 52. Bronze scabbard-chapes. Lisnacrogher, Co. Antrim. – 3/4.

The principal filler designs on Lisnacrogher 1 are tight, carefully executed hair-spring spirals, either single or double, combined with open triangles or hatching (Fig. 55:A1,2). The single spiral, centrally placed within a triangular field and enclosed by three tiny triangles, is a recurring theme on this scabbard (Fig. 55:A2); only on Bann 1 can a comparable motif be recognised (Fig. 55:F2). The "sickle"- or S-shaped units which form the ends of the main S-figures are blank apart from a row of tiny punched triangles which cling to the inner, concave edge of each "crescent" (Fig. 55:A5). Precisely the same motif occurs on Lisnacrogher 2 (Fig. 55:B5) and variants of it can also be found on Bann 1 (Fig. 55:F5-7). A filler design unique to Lisnacrogher 1 is the tiny, equal-armed Y-motif enclosed within a triangular frame (Fig. 55:A3) which is encountered five times on this scabbard. Finally, of note on Lisnacrogher 1, and elsewhere absent, are the strange "oculus" or "M" swellings which project from the tendril stems of each of the four principal S-figures (Fig. 55:A15).

The bodies of the three large S-figures on Toome 1 are filled in two principal ways – by simple hatching (which predominates) and tight hair-spring spirals. The manner in which the bodies of these figures swell to be filled with rows of tiny, hair-spring spirals (Fig. 55:D11) has no parallel in Ireland. The two indistinct motifs which occur near one edge of the scabbard, which Jope interpreted as stylised flowers (1954, 83), are also otherwise unknown in Ireland (Fig. 55:D15). One final filling device is employed on this specimen; this is the fine stippling which fills each of the leafy elements at the tip of the plate (Fig. 55:D18). Stippling, though not precisely in the same form, is otherwise on the Irish scabbards encountered only on Bann 1 (Fig. 55:F6,9,14).

The variety and disposition of the filler motifs on Lisnacrogher 2 are especially interesting. Close inspection of the piece shows that on the upper 15 cm or so of the scabbard (the total length of which is some 55.4 cm) at least twelve separate filling devices are used whereas on the rest of the scabbard only three filler motifs are repeated. A number of the fillers on this scabbard have been encountered already above (Fig. 55:B5,8,10) but none of the others such as the trefoil in a triangle (Fig. 55:B3), the circle in a triangle (Fig. 55:B2) and the tiny spiral-and-leaf combinations (Fig. 55:B12) is precisely matched on the other scabbards.

The variety of filler designs encountered on the upper portion of this scabbard contrasts with the plainness and repetitiveness of filler designs on the remainder. Here, apart from the trefoil-in-triangle (Fig. 55:B3), which recurs along the length of the scabbard at the junctions of the S-figures, the only filler devices present are simple hatching, which is confined to one longitudinal half of the scabbard (Fig. 55:B8,13),

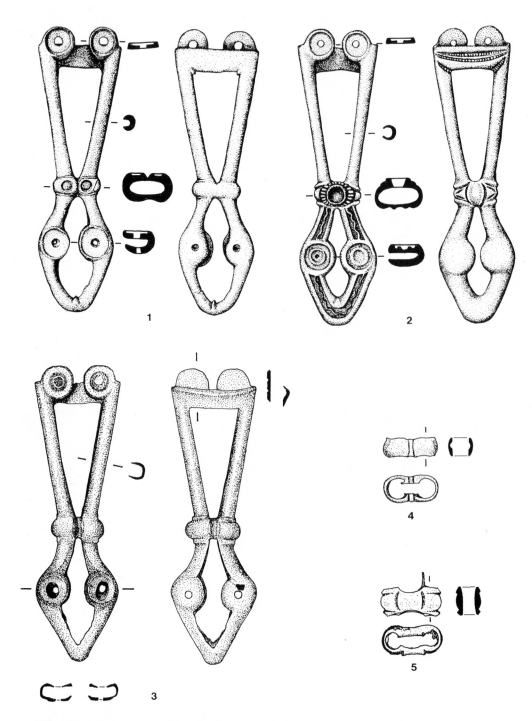

Fig. 53. Bronze scabbard-chapes. 1 Athenry, Co. Galway. 2 Northern
Ireland. 3 Roscrea, Co. Tipperary. 4, 5 Lisnacrogher,
Antrim. - 3/4.

and the pelta, "crescent" and "sickle" motifs, set "concentrically" within one another, which are found on the opposite half of the plate (Fig. 55:B7,14). The reasons for the contrast between the profusion of design on the upper portion of the scabbard and the relative plainness of the lower area are unclear. It could indicate no more than a loss of patience by the craftsman.

Bann 1 displays in its ornamentation the greatest variety and imagination of any of the six decorated Irish scabbards. A small number of the filler motifs on this specimen are matched elsewhere in the Irish series (e.g. Fig. 55:F2,5,6) but in the main this scabbard stands apart from the other Irish examples. There appears to be no order or preconceived planning in the overall disposition of the filler designs. In his choice of filler devices the artist has, it seems, cast aside all discipline and restraint and given himself over almost entirely to impulse and whim. Tiny spirals and minute, leafy shapes, hatching and stippling, rows of little triangles, even an occasional trumpet or pseudo-trumpet motif – significant, perhaps, in view of later insular developments (Fig. 55:F8,14) – are encountered along the length of the plate, in ever-changing combinations and forms. Most important of all, however, is the tiny triple-dot motif which repeats itself along the entire length of the scabbard in the blank areas between the main curvilinear elements of the design (Fig. 55:F4). The same triple-dot design is present elsewhere on the Irish scabbards only once, but not in the same way, on Lisnacrogher 2, where it is used as a filler design within a sub-peltate frame (Fig. 55:B4).

Indistinct traces of rocked-graver ornament are visible on the back of Bann 1. As far as can be detected this ornament has little in common with the decoration on the front. Some spiral or concentric-circle designs seem to be present near the upper edge of the plate, below which are some vague shapes, somewhat leaf-like in appearance, which extend obliquely from one of the long edges of the scabbard to the other. These, as far as can be determined, are confined to the upper half of the scabbard and to its lower extremity.

Chapes

The six surviving bronze chapes from Ireland (Figs 52,3; Pl. 27) exhibit general uniformity in shape and manufacture. Each is an openwork casting. The end has a lozenge-shaped outline, resembling somewhat the form of a stylised serpent's head, from which extend the two metal bindings which terminate at the top in a pair of circular clamps on the front and a straight bridge at the back (see de Navarro, 1972, 28). The "eyes" of the "serpent" consist of a pair of circular settings, which in most instances probably once held enamel studs or inlays; the chape clamps were similarly adorned, but no enamel remains today. At the narrowest portion of the chape there is a rounded moulding sometimes with a further pair of small circular settings. This moulding may be a skeuomorph of an original binding element.

The chape in the British Museum from "Northern Ireland" (Fig. 53:2) is the most elaborate of the group. The single, large, oval setting, enclosed by a band of rope moulding at the front of the constricted portion of the object, is unparalleled and the panel of "reserved zig-zag" ornament around the front of the chape-end is also without parallel on the other Irish chapes.

The two figure-of-eight loops from Lisnacrogher are jagged-edged, incomplete castings (Fig. 53:4,5). Their shape is forcibly reminiscent of the "skeuomorphic" mouldings at the narrowed parts of the complete chapes so that they may represent unfinished chape fragments.

Affinities and Chronology

The Irish scabbards are critical in a consideration of the origins and chronology of the La Tène Iron Age in the country and have at all times figured prominently in discussions on such topics. They lack clear associations, but their decoration has been subjected to detailed scrutiny and far-reaching conclusions have been arrived at as a result of this study. British influence on the scabbard ornament has been stressed repeatedly and several commentators have gone so far as to postulate a population incursion into north-east Ireland from Britain, the scabbards providing one of the chief witnesses to this alleged event. A direct Continental background for the Ulster scabbards has also been put forward.

An issue which is not in doubt, however, is the indigenous nature of the Irish pieces. It is clear that they were made by native craftsmen working on Irish soil, craftsmen obviously in close touch with contemporary artistic and technological developments outside the country. The extent to which foreign influences emanated from Britain or directly from the Continent is, of course, a matter for discussion as are the means by which they reached Ireland.

Earlier Views

As stated above, up to relatively recently most scholars have viewed Britain as being the main source of inspiration for the development of the Irish scabbard series. Leeds, for instance, in 1933, included the scabbards in his Witham-Wandsworth-Torrs group of objects which included material classed by him as amongst the earliest of the native La Tène school of craftsmen and the splendid decoration of which bears unmistakable traces of Continental Waldalgesheim motifs. Leeds had no doubt that the Irish Scabbard Style was derived from Britain. He wrote ".....when the analogous objects on both sides of the Irish Channel are compared, both quantitatively and typologically the Irish group will be found to lag behind." (1933, 15). Ward-Perkins also saw the Irish scabbards as deriving from Yorkshire in England. He felt that this was demonstrated by the existence of the basketwork motif in Ireland, believing it apparently to be present on more than one scabbard (1939, 182, fn. 2). Piggott, in an important paper on insular swords and scabbards (1950), recognised the Continental elements in form and ornamentation of the Irish scabbards and wondered whether this implied an early context for the Irish objects or merely archaic survivals of earlier motifs. He was, however, inclined to the latter view and he called on the horsebit evidence, as he understood it, to demonstrate this, since "the Irish horsebits .... must derive from the north-east English series" and goes on to refer to " ... the plantation of Ulster by Yorkshire charioteers", stating that "with this event should surely be taken the introduction of swords in decorated scabbards" (1950, 16). He thus saw the Irish scabbards as derived from his Group III Bugthorpe class in north-east England, and dated them to the last century B.C.

This view is also put forward by de Navarro in his analysis of insular Iron Age art styles (1952, 77) and three years later Atkinson and Piggott repeat this thesis during their discussion on the Torrs "chamfrein", where the Irish scabbards and other decorated material in this island are classed as being ultimately derived from their "Torrs school" of craftsmanship (Atkinson and Piggott, 1955, 231-2). In 1954, however, Jope published a newly discovered, decorated scabbard from Toome (1954a, 81-91) and in a detailed analysis of the decoration of the scabbards, as well as using the allied evidence of chape form, he postulated direct Continental inspiration for the Irish objects. In contrast to Piggott, he saw the horsebit evidence as supporting such a view. Rynne, at the Hamburg Conference in 1958, disagreed with Jope's view; while accepting Waldalgesheim elements in the art on the Irish scabbards he dismisses them as being merely an archaic survival, for "the art on these objects is not really like any of the Continental art styles" (1961, 708). Like Piggott, however, he accepts the essentially Continental Early/Middle La Tène chape form on the Irish scabbards. In his earlier paper Piggott had already stated in this regard "their development in the Group IIIA series can hardly be related to direct contacts with La Tène cultures on the Rhine or the Marne" because "the chronological difficulties would be insuperable" (1950, 15).

Jope, also in 1958, reiterated the theory of direct Continental influences on the Irish scabbards in a conference on the problems of the Iron Age in Southern Britain (1958, 79). In the same year, too, Fox's major work on Celtic art in Britain was published but in it he pays little attention to the Ulster scabbards. He refers to the decorated Toome scabbard only in passing (erroneously describing it as being from "Lisnacroghera") but states, significantly perhaps, that " it retains 'Marnian' motifs, which British art has now lost". He nonetheless sees the Irish material as deriving from England and dates the scabbards to the first century B.C. (1958, 43). More recently, Megaw has considered the art of the Irish scabbards and, while also recognising the Continental features, he is largely dismissive of them as being "no more than a series of archaic elements such as are commonly found on insular art" (1970, 148). He is more inclined to stress the dependence of the Irish craftsmen on their counterparts in Britain, seeing the Torrs-Witham-Wandsworth group as providing the immediate inspiration for the Irish material.

Savory, in a number of contributions on the Iron Age in Wales, has stressed his belief in the importance of native Welsh craft centres, particularly north-western ones, in the development of insular metalworking traditions (1964; 1971, 74; 1973, 685-709). He has at all times argued in favour of influence of immediately European origin on the development of the earliest La Tène material in Wales. With respect to Ireland, he wrote that ".......we have to consider the possibility that Wales was the immediate source of those influences, which alongside direct continental influences, created the distinctive Irish metalwork groups, particularly that of the Ulster scabbards, from the end of the 3rd century B.C. onwards" (1973, 705-7).

Spratling commenting on the discovery of a decorated bronze shield-boss fragment during the excavation of the hillfort at South Cadbury, Somerset, England (1970a,b,c), argued for a down-dating of the "Torrs school" bronzes and, by implication, a down-dating of the Irish scabbards which he saw as derivatives of that "school".

In his volume on the Iron Age in Lowland Britain, Harding, en passant, supported Jope's view regarding the direct Continental contribution to the Irish scabbard tradition. He wrote: "there can be no doubt that Jope was right to emphasise the Continental, and not British, La Tène tradition" (1974, 181).

Frey, with Megaw, in the latest scrutiny of earliest insular La Tène metalwork, has stressed the clearly local nature of the Irish Scabbard Style while pointing out detailed stylistic links with Continental designs,

particularly as represented on examples of "Hungarian" Scabbard Style
pieces (1976, 55-60). The Irish scabbards are compared by him to the
Torrs-Witham-Wandsworth group of objects, not in a derivative role,
but rather as belonging to one of "an interrelated group of 'schools' of
early Celtic art in the British Isles" (loc. cit., 59). Frey admits the
vagueness of the absolute chronology of the Irish scabbards but concludes
that the Lisnacrogher scabbards cannot be dated "any earlier than a
post-Waldalgesheim period or sometime in the 3rd or even 2nd century
B.C." (loc. cit., 57).

Lisnacrogher and Bugthorpe

Piggott (1950, 12-14) brought together six items to form his Bugthorpe
Group (Fig. 54). These included two swords and their scabbards from
warrior burials in Yorkshire (Bugthorpe and Grimthorpe, Stead, 1979,
60-64); two cast bronze chapes from south-east Scotland (Glencotho
and Hounslow, MacGregor, 1976, 78-9), a bronze scabbard from near
the River Tweed at Carham on the English/Scottish border (MacGregor,
1976, op. cit., No. 136) and a bronze scabbard-plate from Sutton Reach
in Lincolnshire (Fox, 1958, 32, Pl. 21).

A cursory glance at this small scattered group of artifacts shows
that the principal element linking them is the distinctive chape form
which has in each case (where it survives) a characteristic lip-like division
at its lower extremity. Otherwise there is considerable diversity, varying
from undecorated scabbard-plates to the lavish overall decoration on
the Bugthorpe specimen and the loose tendrils on the Sutton Reach piece.

The "manifest analogies" (Piggott, 1950, 14) of the Irish scabbards
to this group are not perhaps as close as is often assumed. Indeed, when
the British objects in question are examined critically it is the differences
rather than the similarities between the Irish "Group IIIA" and the British
Group III scabbards which become manifest.

In the first place, the Bugthorpe-type chapes are utterly distinct
from those in Ireland. The British examples with their lipped features,
their heart-shape and the ornament which some of them bear have nothing
whatever in common with the slender, clinging Irish chapes where never
so much as a hint of a lip occurs. The scabbard from Carham is also
unrelated to the Ulster Group. It has a simple, shallowly curved mouth
which differs from the mouths on the Irish scabbards and the raised central
spine which extends longitudinally from the tip, ending near the mouth
in a pelta-shaped element, has no parallel in the Irish series. Its
fragmentary heart-shaped chape also differs fundamentally from those
in Ireland (Fig. 54: 1a,b).

Similarly, the Grimthorpe scabbard (Fig. 54:3) differs from the Irish scabbards not only in the form of the chape but also in the shape of the hilt-guard of the sword within it.   It is also considerably longer than the longest Irish specimen.   The almost triangular mouth of the Sutton Reach scabbard contrasts with the shape of the mouths on the Irish scabbards while the loose, tendril-like ornament, though sharing elements of decoration with some of the Irish scabbards, clearly differs from them in the treatment and layout of the design.   Significantly, however, the Sutton Reach scabbard is included by de Navarro in the group of scabbards "copied from or influenced by Swiss models" (1972, 310-311), i.e. those closest to the ultimate prototypes on the Continent.

The fine scabbard from Bugthorpe (Fig. 54:5) stands out from the other examples of this group in its heavy, decorated chape and in its tightly-ordered overall decoration.   This is the scabbard which has given its name to the group and which has been most closely and frequently identified with the Irish series.

Piggott in his 1950 paper made the statement that ".... incised ornament running the length of the scabbard, and not only confined to the mouth and chape, is characteristically British ...." (1950, 2).   In fact, apart from the atypical example from Sutton Reach, Bugthorpe stands out as the *only* scabbard in Britain with ornament along its entire length. Such overall decoration is not common on the Continent, but does occur. In Ireland, of the eight recorded scabbards, six have overall decoration.

The very presence of such lavish ornament could by itself be regarded as a factor linking the Irish group with the one British example with this feature.   There are, however, major areas of dissimilarity between Bugthorpe and Ireland.   The Yorkshire scabbard is considerably longer and wider than any Irish example and similarly the sword within it is certainly a more massive and effective weapon than any of the preserved Irish specimens.   The bronze hilt-guard mount of the Bugthorpe sword has been compared to the hilt-guard mount on a sword from Cashel, Co. Sligo (Rynne, 1960, 13; Fig. 43:8; Pl. 22:2) but the comparison is of the most generalised kind only.   Most conclusively, the Bugthorpe chape is that one of the whole British group which is most distant from the slender Irish examples.

Thus, the only feature which might conceivably be seen as linking the Irish group with the scabbard from Bugthorpe is the overall decoration. In concept, layout and design, however, the Irish and British pieces are quite different.   The only Irish scabbards which may even remotely be compared, in their overall decorative arrangement, to the Yorkshire one are Lisnacrogher 2 and Bann 1, the only ones of the Irish series which have continuous wave designs rather than a series of S-motifs (Figs 49:2;

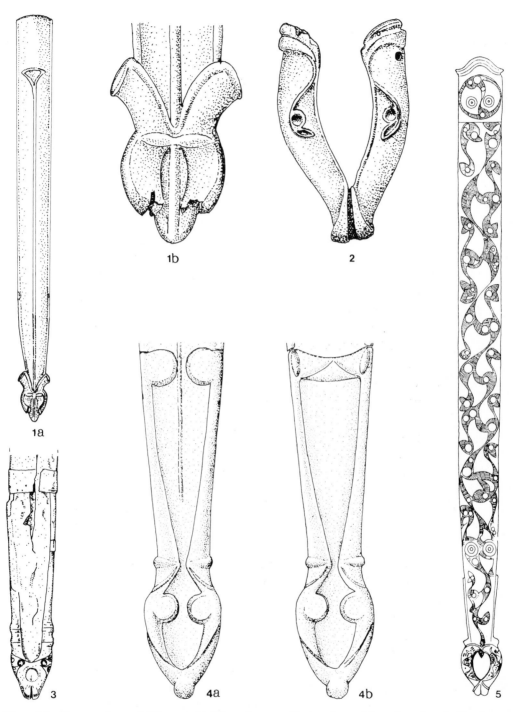

Fig. 54. Examples of Piggott's "Bugthorpe Group" scabbards. 1a, b Carham, Berwickshire, Scotland. 2 Glencotho Farm, Peebleshire, Scotland. 3 Grimthorpe, Yorkshire, England. 4a, b Bargany House, Ayrshire, Scotland. 5 Bugthorpe, Yorkshire, England. Various scales. (1,2,4 after MacGregor, 1976. 3 after Stead, 1979. 5 after Harding, 1974).

51:2). But even here the treatment and feeling are totally different. There is a certain monotony in the stereotyped layout of the Bugthorpe ornament, especially in the almost exclusive use of basketry to fill the bodies of the curves, a feature found on one only of the Irish examples. None of the characteristic minor elements which adorn the majority of the Irish scabbards is present: the hair-spring spirals, the dot-filled leaves, the triangular teeth, the "concentric" peltae and many others (Fig. 55). The "fish-tail" endings to many of the curves are reminiscent, perhaps, of the pairs of leaves set at an angle to one another as, for instance, on Toome 3 (Fig. 51:1), but now they are in an advanced state of development (degeneration?). The repetition of small, blank, circular motifs on the Bugthorpe scabbard, from which the hatched curves extend, finds no parallel on the Irish scabbards but is rather a feature of the Mirror Style and comparable ornament of the last century B.C. and the beginning of the Christian era in Britain. Most significant, perhaps, is the attention which has been paid to the voids on the Bugthorpe scabbard, something which differs totally from the arrangement on the Irish scabbards and points Bugthorpe again in the direction of British Mirror Style ornament.

Thus, on almost every point of detail the Yorkshire scabbard can be seen to contrast sharply with its Ulster counterparts. Only the custom of overall decoration, and the use of basketry on one Irish scabbard (Lisnacrogher 3, Fig. 50:1, Pls 27,28), serve as possible links. The presence of basketry on one Irish scabbard may well reflect some contact with British metalworking traditions. It should not be forgotten, however, that regular gridded basketry is known on objects of Early La Tène date on the Continent, notably on the bow of a fibula from Panenský Týnec in Bohemia (Megaw, 1970, No. 65; Kruta, 1975, Fig. 7:1), and on the handle of a flagon from the river Aue at Borsch, Kr. Bad Salzungen in eastern Germany (Megaw, 1970, No. 66; Schlette, 1980, Bild 41). Gridded basketry in Ireland cannot, therefore, be taken as certain evidence of late date, nor should it be regarded as unequivocally of English origin.

The development of the Irish scabbard series therefore, is here regarded as having been independent of, and uninfluenced by, the Bugthorpe group or any of the other British scabbard types. Indeed, it could just as easily be argued that the idea of overall decoration on the Bugthorpe specimen was adopted by the Yorkshire scabbard engraver through the sight of a lavishly adorned Irish specimen. This is, of course, mere speculation but the discovery of a scabbard of Irish-type at Bargany House, Ayrshire in the south-west of Scotland (Fig. 54:4; MacGregor, 1976, No. 140), indicates clearly that influence from Irish craft centres did in fact move eastwards across the North Channel. The Bargany specimen is unlikely to be of Irish manufacture (Stevenson, 1967, 24); it is more likely to have been made by an Irish craftsman working in Scotland or by a local metalworker strongly influenced by Irish methods of scabbard manufacture. The sword fragment from Stevenston Sands, in Ayrshire, discovered not far from the findspot of the scabbard, if it is an Irish piece (above p.70), provides additional evidence of a contemporary Irish presence in south-west Scotland. Furthermore, as is suggested below, there are grounds for believing that the engraved ornament on the horns of the "chamfrein" from Torrs, Kircudbrightshire in south-west Scotland (Atkinson and Piggott, 1955), may reflect influence from Irish craft traditions.

Lisnacrogher and the "Torrs School"

In consisdering British analogies for the art on the Irish scabbards, decorated bronzes of the so-called Torrs-Witham-Wandsworth group are of far greater relevance than are the Type III scabbards. This body of artifacts, first isolated by Leeds (1933, 6-15), includes some of the finest, and perhaps also some of the earliest, examples of insular La Tène metalwork and objects of this group are frequently seen as supplying the source from which the Irish Scabbard Style developed. One commentator has gone so far as to suggest that the Irish scabbards were actually made in southern England, their route to Ireland marked by the findspot of the Torrs "chamfrein" (de Navarro, 1952, 77). However, though the origins of the Irish Scabbard Style continue to be a matter for debate, their Irish manufacture is no longer in question. There can be no doubt that the scabbards were made and embellished on Irish soil, and one at least of the centres of specialist scabbard engraving must have been at or near the bog deposit of Lisnacrogher, Co. Antrim.

There are, of course, obvious similarities between the art on the British bronzes and that on the Irish scabbards. For the most part, however, these are only of a generalised kind; significant and extensive stylistic overlaps between Irish and British material are found only on the Torrs "chamfrein". Otherwise it is the differences between the two insular traditions of metalworking, which are manifest. In particular, the emphasis on filler designs on the Irish scabbards, and the at times almost bewildering variety of the tiny details (notably on Bann 1), contrast with the greater simplicity of the southern English bronzes. Closest in concept to the Irish Scabbard Style are the engraved roundels of the Witham shield (Megaw, 1970, No. 252; Jope, 1971), but here again, apart from a number of features such as the common preoccupation with hair-spring spirals, there are distinct differences of detail and of ornamental construction between Witham and the scabbards (see especially von Jenny, 1935, Taf. 10:2 where the design on the shield roundels is reproduced as a straight band). It may, however, be significant that it is this piece, often taken as one of the earliest objects of the southern English group and that deemed by Jope to be closest in its decoration to the art of its Continental progenitors, which has most in common with the Irish Scabbard Style. It might thus be argued that the resemblances in decoration between the Irish and southern English bronzes reflect their common respective roots in European Waldalgesheim traditions.

Such an interpretation for the relationship between the scabbards and the Torrs "chamfrein" is not so easily sustained. The technical and stylistic similarities between the ornament on the horns of the Scottish object and that on the scabbards are so close that direct contact between them seems certain. On the horns, for instance, especially on the repair piece of Horn A, there is exactly the same proliferation and variety of "filler" motifs as occurs on the scabbards, and in many tiny details there is an almost precise parallelism. Indeed, some details on the horns, which are otherwise absent on contemporary British bronzes, can only be paralleled in Ireland. The axially-dotted leaves, for example, common to the horns, to Lisnacrogher 2 and to Bann 1 (Fig. 55:B10;F3,9,10,13) are not present in southern England. Piggott noted this absence (1955, 221) and suggested, not very convincingly, that this motif was derived from the dotted ornament of British La Tène fibulae. Fine stippling is also common to the horns and the scabbards and apparently absent on the major southern British pieces, while the poor quality step-pattern along one edge of Bann 1 is also reminiscent of the angular designs on one of the horns of the Torrs "chamfrein". There are other details in the decoration of the horns which are matched in Ireland but which are also found in southern England and, finally, there are motifs, such as the "fan" and "batwing" designs, which are closely paralleled on southern English bronzes but absent in Ireland.

In significant details, therefore, it is evident that the art on the horns has more in common with that on the Irish scabbards than with that on any of the southern English bronzes. Piggott recognised this fact and explained it by deriving the Irish Scabbard Style from his "Torrs school". He adverted to the possibility of a reverse movement of influence but stated that "one could not on any reasonable showing derive the Torrs Style from the known Ulster pieces which, if the combined evidence of the bridle-bits and of the sword scabbards be accepted, can hardly be earlier than the first century B.C." (1955, 233). However, if the possibility, indeed the liklihood, of a date earlier than the first century B.C. for the bits and the scabbards is allowed, then the reasons for

Piggott's dismissal of movement of influence from Ireland across the North Channel are removed. It is thus an entirely valid hypothesis to postulate Irish inspiration on the engraved art of the Torrs horns. It is even possible that an Irish scabbard engraver was working in Scotland, for the horns could hardly have been engraved in Ulster because of the presence on them of decorative details absent from the repertoire of the Irish Scabbard Style. Working in Britain, the putative Irish craftsman could have incorporated local designs into his "grammar" of ornament.

The discovery in south-west Scotland of a number of objects of likely or possible Irish origin or influence (the Bargany House scabbard and perhaps the Stevenston Sands sword) supports the theory of an Irish presence in that part of Scotland in the last centuries B.C. Most important of all, however, is the general recognition that the engraved decoration on the horns reflects the traditions of a scabbard engraver. The abrupt vertical break in the design has, in fact, been taken as deriving from the break which sometimes occurs in the designs of Continental scabbard ornament to accommodate the scabbard binding-band, as seen for instance on one of the scabbards from Bölckse-Madocsahegy, Kom. Tolna, in Hungary (Jope, 1958, 80, Pl. VIb; but see Frey, 1974, 144, Abb. 2). Megaw wrote that the decoration on the horns was "probably the nearest thing to the conception of the engraved ornament of the Swiss sword-makers" (1970, 146).

The combined picture is, therefore, that the horns were found in an area, not far distant from Ulster, where independent evidence of a broadly contemporary Irish presence exists; the ornament on the horns shares much with that on the Irish scabbards and, in some details, can only be matched in Ireland; the general technique of ornamentation is that of a scabbard engraver. It seems reasonable, therefore, to argue that eastward-moving influences from the Ulster scabbard-engraving schools, themselves but a generation or two removed from their Continental ancestry, contributed significantly to the design and ornamentation of the Torrs horns.

Absolute dating for the "Torrs style" bronzes and the Irish scabbards is problematical. The generally held belief in the early dating for the British objects has been called into question by Spratling (1970c) who correctly drew attention to the Late La Tène form of the Wandsworth round shield-boss. He also took the presence of the decorated shield-boss fragment in a first century B.C. metalworker's hoard at South Cadbury, Somerset, England as further confirmation of a late date for "Torrs" metalwork. Whereas it is possible to question whether the South Cadbury fragment must be as late as the material found with it (the piece was clearly scrap and could thus be considerably older than the rest of the

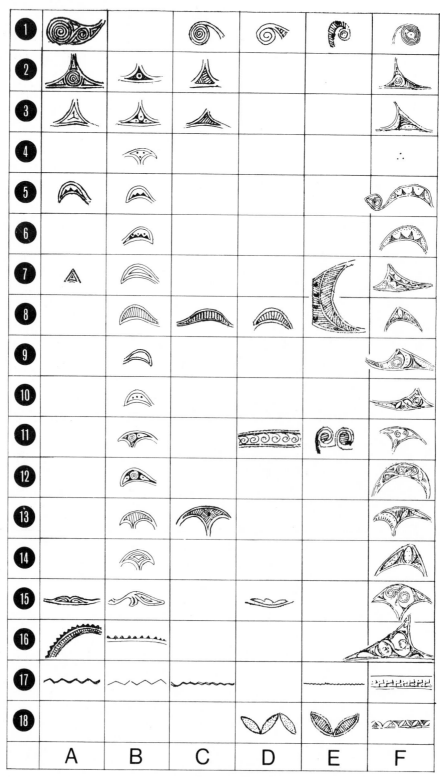

Fig. 55. Filler motifs on Irish scabbards. A,B,C = Lisnacrogher 1, 2 and 3.
D = Toome 1. E,F = Bann 1 and 2. – 1/1.

hoard), Spratling's arguments are otherwise sound and it seems likely that some of the objects of the so-called Torrs-Witham-Wandsworth group are as late as the last century B.C. But it remains probable that the earliest of them are a century or two older.

As argued above there is no need to regard the Irish scabbards as later than the earliest development of the British schools and a direct Continental ingredient in the genesis of the local Scabbard Style is postulated below. Thus it seems likely that scabbard-making centres were already established in Ulster in the second century B.C. The earliest of them could even date to the preceding century.

Lisnacrogher and the Continental Sword Styles

There can be no doubt that the custom of decorating bronze scabbard-plates in Ireland with engraved ornament of ultimately Waldalgesheim ancestry can be traced, in the last analysis, to the heartland of La Tène Europe. As is clear from the foregoing discussion, the extent to which this European tradition affected Ireland either directly from the Continent or via British craft centres has been vigorously debated. Implicit in what has been written above is the writer's belief that impulses directly from Europe are detectable on the Irish scabbards.

The ornamental conception on the Irish scabbards, the ordered symmetry of the decoration, and the preference for overall patterning clearly emphasise their local character. Evident too are the substantial differences in many decorative details which distinguish the Irish scabbards from their European counterparts. On the other hand, however, there are also details in Ireland which can only have come from Europe, some, indeed, which can be traced as far as the Middle Danubian Sword Style. Megaw, writing on the Irish scabbards, queried such postulated links when he wrote "much has been made of the influence of the Continental sword 'style' without there ever being any concrete suggestion as to how such an influence might have been transmitted" (1970, 148). Surely, however, ignorance of the means of transmission is not in itself proof that transmission did not take place? More recently Frey (with Megaw) seems less dismissive of the possibility of direct Continental elements in the decorative repertoire of the Irish scabbards, though it is pointed out again that the means by which such influence was introduced to the west is "still one of the major and as yet unanswered questions of British Iron Age art" (1976, 59). In this, Frey is echoing a statement made almost forty years earlier by Jacobsthal who, when describing the unaxial character of the ornament on the River Witham scabbard locket stated that "this feature, like others of Celtic art in the British Isles, has its roots on the Continent, not in France, but in Hungary and Switzerland, a remarkable fact which I can only state here, but not try to explain" (1939, 28).

The matter is, however, no longer as obscure as it once was and a number of recent finds is beginning to mark the route westwards of eastern European traditions. The Dürrnberg cemetery at Hallein in Upper Austria has produced its first scabbard with "Hungarian" Sword Style ornament (Gibson and Megaw, 1982). A scabbard of Middle Danubian origin has been dredged from the River Sâone in France (Bonnamour et Bulard, 1976), while two magnificent iron fibulae from Conflans in the Marne have also been identified as products of eastern manufacture (Kruta, 1975). The famous scabbard from Cernon-sur-Coole, Marne, too, is now established as an eastern piece (Megaw, 1973). Most striking of all, perhaps, is the virtual identity in the treatment of dragon pairs on three European scabbards, one from France, one from Bavaria and the third from Hungary (Bulard, 1979, Fig. 2). The mechanism of movement remains uncertain but direct links between the Danube and the west of Europe are now established beyond question. Any elements of Middle Danubian Sword Style ornament detectable in Britain or Ireland are, therefore, likely to have been transmitted through Gaul.

Though the scabbards in Ireland are of recognisably native character there are numerous details in their decoration which are closely matched on the Continent, as Jope (1954) and Frey with Megaw (1976) have shown. Comparisons with elements of the Swiss and Middle Danubian Sword Styles can be made and on the Irish scabbards archaic Waldalgesheim, even Early Style, features are recognisable. We do not yet know how the presence on Irish scabbards of such varied influences is best to be interpreted, and caution is necessary when engaged in the "seductive sin of trait-chasing" (Megaw, 1975, 17). The cumulative evidence seems, however, sufficient to indicate direct links between Ireland and the major scabbard-engraving traditions of Europe.

The emphasis on overall decoration is, of course, essentially Irish. A few early examples of this feature, Weiskirchen in south-west Germany and Fillotrano in north Italy (Megaw, 1970, Nos 109, 137), have little to do with the Irish development. Wavy decoration which extends partly along the length of several Swiss scabbards from La Tène (e.g. Nos 63 and 71; de Navarro, 1972, Pls XXX:1, XXXIII:2) may be more relevant. The design on No. 63 in particular compares well with the arrangement of the ornament on Bann 1.

The zig-zags, or punched triangles, which define the mouths of each of the three decorated scabbards from Lisnacrogher (Pl. 28) are readily paralleled on both Swiss and Middle Danubian Sword Style pieces (e.g.

de Navarro, op. cit., Pls CXLIX:1a, CXXXVII:1a; Gustin, 1982, Abb. 5:2). Nearer home, a version of this motif is present on the early dagger sheath from Wisbech (Frey with Megaw, 1976, 10:2; May, 1976, Fig. 67) and it may also be present on the scabbard of a late, anthropoid-hilted dagger (now lost) from Lincolnshire (Hawkes, 1955, Pl. XXVI:2). A background in the Swiss Sword Style for the serrations along the tendril-stems of two of the Lisnacrogher scabbards has also been suggested (Jope, 1954, 85; cf. de Navarro, op. cit., Pls LXXXII:1,2; XC; CLVIII:I). Frey, with Megaw (op. cit., 56, Fig. 10), however, regard these serrations as the remains of the leaves of stylised palmettes as are present in more recognisable form on such early insular bronzes as the Wisbech dagger sheath and the fragmentary Cerrig y Drudion bowl.

The tight hair-spring spirals so typical of the Scabbard Style and the contemporary British bronzes are sometimes regarded as a diagnostically insular element, distinguishing the island "schools" from those on the Continent. Such spirals are, however, known on European scabbards. On examples from Halimba and Tapolca in Hungary, for instance, tiny spiral designs, used as filler motifs as on the Irish scabbards, are present (Frey with Megaw, op. cit., Figs 6; 8:2; Szabo, 1982, Figs 8, 10). The scabbard from Cernon-sur-Coole in the Marne, undoubtedly a Hungarian piece, displays a magnificently constructed, hair-spring spiral, precisely as on the Irish scabbards, at the tip of the beak of the crested bird's head which embellishes the top of the scabbard. This scabbard, adorned also with fine stippling, axially-dotted leaves, and triple-dot motifs (see below) is critical in considering the origins of the Irish Scabbard Style.

A further detail linking the Irish bronzes with European scabbard-engraving traditions is the M or "oculus" motif which occurs a number of times on the S-stems of Lisnacrogher 1 (Fig. 55:A15). Both Jope (1954, 85) and de Navarro (1972, 294) have drawn attention to the significance of this detail, the latter hinting at a possible Hungarian source for it. Good European examples of the design can be found on scabbards from Sremska-Mitrovica, Jugoslavia (Jacobsthal, 1944, No. 126; Todorovic, 1968, Sl. 15:1), Ritopek, Jugoslavia (Todorovic, 1973-4, Fig. 1), La Tène (de Navarro, 1972, Pls XCII:Ib; XCIV:6) and Sanzeno, north Italy (Jacobsthal, op.cit. No. 104; Nothdurfter, 1979, Tafel 75:1266).

Of the six decorated scabbards from Ireland the most varied and interesting is one from the River Bann, possibly Coleraine, Co. Derry, here designated Bann 1 (Figs 51:2,55; Pls 30, 31). This scabbard, in private possession and unavailable for study for almost a quarter of a century, has lately come into the custodianship of the British Museum in London. Hitherto unnoticed details have come to light which emphasise the exceptional nature of this object.

The scabbard, as already noted, bears decoration laid out as a continuous wave design, a feature compared above with the design on one of the scabbards from La Tène in Switzerland. The lateral bands framing the main ornament distinguish this scabbard further from the other Irish examples but call to mind such early Continental scabbards as Moroux (alias "Bavilliers") in France, which has a lateral band of leaf zig-zag (Megaw, 1968a; Osterhaus, 1969, 138k, Abb. 2:1; Rilliot, 1975), and the famous La Tène scabbard from Hallstatt which has bands of step ornament (Megaw, 1970, No. 30). A decorated spearhead, probably from the River Broye at Joressant in Switzerland, combining curvilinear and angular ornament as on Bann 1, seems also in ornamental conception to have much in common with that of the Irish specimen (de Navarro, 1972, 282, Fig. 35; Degen, 1977, Fig. p. 116).

There are other details on this Irish scabbard for which close Continental comparisons may be cited. The most striking feature of its decoration, however, and that which points most convincingly to direct inspiration from the European Sword Styles, is the recurring triple-dot motif, disposed without any obvious order in the blank spaces left by the curvilinear pattern (Fig. 55:F4). At least 32 of these motifs are recognisable, each comprising of three minute, pin-prick impressions arranged in triangular formation.

The triple-dot motif, as it occurs on the Bann scabbard, is otherwise absent on contemporary Irish work. In Britain, apart from a single instance of the design on Horn A from Torrs in Scotland (already noted for its close relationship with the Irish scabbards), the triple-dot is thus far known only on the Cerrig y Drudion bronzes the decoration of which is either Gaulish or Gaulish inspired (Stead, 1982). There can be little doubt that the origins of the recurrent triple-dots on the Bann scabbard are to be sought in the Celtic heartlands of Europe.

Already in Early Style contexts a version of the triple-dot design occurs as, for instance, on the Etruscan flagon now in Besançon, the surface of which was engraved by a Celtic craftsman (Frey, 1955, Tafel VIII). On this object, the triple-dots are appended to the pointed tips of leafy motifs, just as they are on the Cerrig y Drudion fragments. Triple-dots are treated in a comparable manner on several early, decorated pots from Brittany (Schwappach, 1969, Abb. 6:59,60; Duval, 1977, 247, No. 262), and also on a number of Waldalgesheim-style plaques of bronze said to be from Commachio in north Italy (Jacobsthal, 1934; 1944, No. 401). The blade of an iron spearhead from Hungary, decorated with elaborate Waldalgesheim ornament, provides an important eastern example of the use of the triple-dot device (Schwappach, 1971, Abb. 10:6; Szabo,

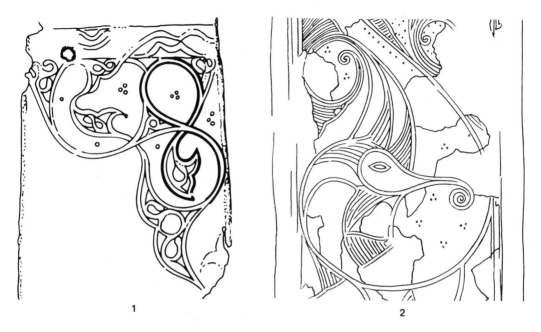

Fig. 56. Examples of triple-dot design. 1 Cernon-sur-Coole, France.
2 Bölcske-Madocsahegy, Hungary. - Various scales.
(1 after Frey, 1976, 2 after Duval, 1974).

1976, I tábla; 1977, Fig. 1).

The triple-dot design is also known on scabbards of the Middle Danubian Sword Style and the importance of this for Ireland cannot be underestimated. On two fragmentary examples from Bölcske-Madocsahegy in Hungary and on the well-known specimen from Cernon-sur-Coole in the Marne, the triple-dot is employed in precisely the same way as on the relevant Bann scabbard, dispersed arbitrarily among the tendrils of the curvilinear ornament. Cernon-sur-Coole is of likely eastern manufacture (Megaw, 1973) and it may be that it was in an eastern workshop that the use of this motif on scabbards originated. The way in which a number of the triple dots "cling" to the pointed ends of some of the curvilinear motifs on one of the Bölcske scabbards (Szabo, 1982, Fig. 18), seems to indicate a derivation for the design from those earlier pieces on which the triple-dot is exclusively placed at the pointed tips of vegetal figures. An immediate background for the triple-dot on Hungarian soil is supplied by the unlocalised spearhead with Waldalgesheim ornament already noted (p. 102), for this is likely to be of local fabrication rather than an import from the west.

It should be remembered that the majority of European scabbards are of iron and many are badly corroded. Thus a device as small and unobtrusive as the triple-dot could, in many instances, easily escape detection by modern scholars. It might have been more widespread across La Tène Europe than at present seems the case. There can be little doubt, however, that the presence of the triple-dots on the scabbard from the Bann (allied especially to the M-designs on Lisnacrogher 1) indicates direct and intimate links with European scabbard engraving traditions stretching as far as the Middle Danube. The unaxial layout of the indistinct ornament on the back of Bann 1, and its apparent arrangement on upper and lower ends of the scabbard, seem also to point in the direction of the Middle Danubian Sword Style. There seems even to be a strong resemblance between the odd forms which extend obliquely across the Irish scabbard on this face and the elongated, roughly pointed-oval elements which are arranged in a similar manner on the scabbard from Halimba (?), Veszprem in Hungary (de Navarro, 1972, Pl. CXXXI; Frey, with Megaw, 1976, Fig. 6).

The Cernon-sur-Coole scabbard has been commented upon as there are a number of details on it, apart from the triple-dots, which are paralleled in northern Ireland. It may be that it is this fine object which indicates the route westwards of decorative concepts of ultimately eastern European origin. A date for the French scabbard early in the European Middle La Tène phase is probable (Megaw, 1973, 130-1). The absolute dating of the commencement of La Tène C in Europe is by no means certainly established. Recent dendrochronological dates, however, suggest a beginning for the phase sometime in the first half of the third century B.C. (de Navarro, 1972, addendum p. 354; Haffner, 1979). A date in the same century for the beginning of the Irish Scabbard Style is thus possible.

The evidence of the chapes favours an early date for the establishment of the scabbard tradition in Ireland. These, as most commentators have noted, are in their form closely related to Continental types which date to the end of the Early La Tène period and the beginning of the Middle La Tène period. Their Continental pedigree is, indeed, hardly in question (see Jope, 1974, 2-7) and this cannot legitimately be ignored when chronology and origins are discussed. Close comparisons for the Irish chape form are numerous. Jope, for instance, has drawn attention to specific examples from Mirabel (Aisne) and Prosne (Marne) in France, and from Kund in Hungary (1954a, 88). At La Tène in Switzerland (de Navarro, op. cit., Pls II:2, III:I), St-Étienne-au-Temple (Marne) and Wieselburg in Upper Austria (idem, Pls CXIV:1, CXXVII) parallels for the Irish chape form are evident. Most appropriate of all for the Irish series, however, are the chapes on recently unearthed scabbards of La Tène Ic (=B2) date from north-east France, especially those from

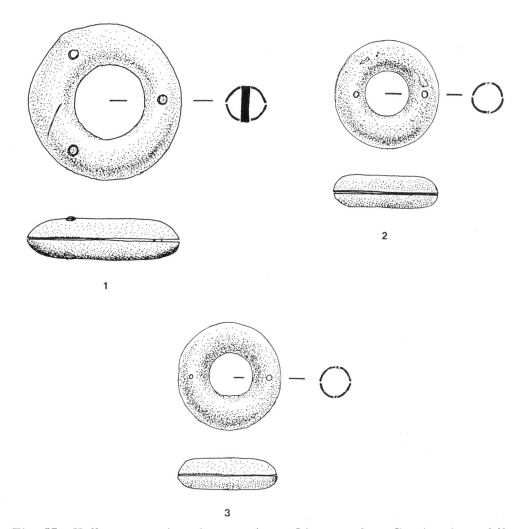

Fig. 57. Hollow, two-piece bronze rings. Lisnacrogher, Co. Antrim. - 1/1.

cemeteries at Montigny-Lancoup, Villeperrot, Pontoux and elsewhere (Bulard, 1979, Figs 6:1; 7:1; 8:1,3). It is likely that it is this region which supplied the prototypes for the Irish chapes.

Hollow, two-piece bronze rings

Three hollow bronze rings of two-piece construction from Lisnacrogher, Co. Antrim (Fig. 57), provide further evidence for an early, directly Continental presence at that site. These rings are pointed-oval in section and are of hammered sheet bronze. Their external diameters vary from

2.85 cm to 4.15 cm. The halves, meeting along a horizontal seam, were originally held together by either two or three tiny rivets of bronze. One ring contains the remains of a clay core.

Such rings are found widely across La Tène Europe. Two main groups may be recognised: those in which rivets are used to hold the ring halves together and those devoid of rivets. The earliest examples, concentrated mainly in south-west Germany, western Switzerland and western Austria, belong to the La Tène A phase of the European Iron Age and are almost exclusively of the riveted type (e.g. Haffner, 1976, 198, Taf. 7:4; Kromer, 1959, 50, Taf. 5:16; Hodson, 1968, 42, 76, Pl. 2:677). In the later phases of the European Early La Tène, especially in La Tène B2, rings of the type under discussion become more widespread, reflecting, perhaps, the migrations of the Celts in the fourth and early third centuries B.C. While riveted rings continue to be used (e.g. Scherer et Mordant, 1972, 367, Fig. 6; Licka, 1968, 353-6, Obr. 2:1a-c; Waldhauser, 1978, 88-9, Taf. 33.9050-1), the unriveted form becomes dominant (e.g. Bulard, 1979, 40, 44, Figs 6:2b; 7:3b). After the earlier part of La Tène C the rings become increasingly rare in Europe and, with one or two exceptions, are all but absent in the Late La Tène period (e.g. Mariën, 1961, 177, Fig. 68:6; Vannacci-Lunezzi, 1977, 26, 58-9, Pls XXVII; XXX:8; XXXVI:1-4). The later examples are all unriveted.

There can be no doubt that the Irish rings belong to this Continental La Tène group. They are, indeed, so close in size, form and method of manufacture to their European counterparts that a strong case exists for regarding them as actual imports from mainland Europe. Rings from eastern France provide parallels of most immediate relevance for the Irish rings (e.g. Scherer and Mordant, op. cit.; C. et D. Mordant, 1970, 95, Fig. 44:4). The French examples date to the Early/Middle La Tène transition (LT Ic/II or, in Reinecke's terminology, LTB2/C1). It is surely significant that it is precisely in this chronological horizon, and in the same eastern French region, that the best comparisons for the Irish chapes are also to be found.

Hollow rings of the type here considered are in Europe frequently found in graves where their association is often with the belt. In many cases their function can clearly be seen as having been related to the suspension of the scabbard from the belt (Haffner, 1977/8, 49-54, Abb. 8; Waldhauser, 1978, 121-2, Abb. 49; Roualet et al., 1982, 35-8, Pl. VI). The presence of three hollow rings at Lisnacrogher, a site which also produced four scabbards, thus allows the speculation that the rings and the scabbards there could be related. If this could be substantiated, independent support for the concept of an early contribution to the Irish scabbard development, directly from the Continent, would be forthcoming.

Summary

From the foregoing remarks it is evident that the absence of a precise chronology for the Irish scabbards is a major obstacle in the task of establishing the relationships between the Irish Scabbard Style and comparable traditions outside the country. The means by which this style, with its intricate hybridisation of widely scattered foreign elements, was introduced into Ireland, are also unknown to us. There can be no doubt, however, that in north-east Ireland, in the last centuries before Christ, there existed a significant centre of skilled scabbard-engravers who were closely in touch with contemporary developments outside the country and highly receptive to new ideas, but at the same time, inventive and imaginative in pursuing a vigorously individual style. Decorative details such as the triple-dot and the M-motif indicate direct links with Middle La Tène workshops in Europe and these links need not be late in the phase, as is suggested by the La Tène B2/C1 background to the chapes and the hollow rings. The evidence of the chapes, the rings and the Cernon-sur-Coole scabbard combine to suggest eastern France as the immediate source of the Irish Scabbard Style, and it is through Gaul that influences of ultimately Middle Danubian origin are likely to have reached Ireland. The contemporary Irish and British schools of early La Tène craftsmanship are best interpreted as representing parallel developments of Continental ancestry. Interaction between British and Irish workshops in spheres of art and technology would have blurred the distinctiveness of each of the two metalwork traditions as together they grew increasingly distant from that in the areas of their ultimate genesis.

Spearheads

A discussion of spearheads in Iron Age Ireland is severely handicapped by the virtual impossibility of dating isolated examples. Spearheads of iron need not have changed radically over many centuries and unless clearly associated or unless there is some obvious decorative detail which assists dating, individual specimens in museum collections must be disregarded. Thus, the eight iron spearheads from the Murray Collection, now in Cambridge and said to be from Edenderry, might include some Iron Age examples, or such leaf-shaped specimens as that from Ballykeaghra, Co. Galway (Raftery, J., 1970, 156, Fig. 2:c), could conceivably belong to the Iron Age. An iron spearhead with incised linear decoration in the Ulster Museum, from Aghaloughan, Co. Antrim, could also be Iron Age but is more likely to be later than this. There are many other examples possibly, but not demonstrably, of Iron Age date.

The number of spearheads for which an Iron Age date may with confidence be suggested is, therefore, small. A Hallstatt D date has been claimed for a spearhead from Castleconnell, Co. Limerick (above p. 8, Fig. 1; Rynne, 1979). Suggestions that this piece might be a modern import from Africa should, however, be borne in mind. The Roodstown example, the leaf-shaped blade of which is pierced by a single circular hole (Fig. 58:2), may well be of Early or Middle La Tène date on the basis of comparison with a spearhead with similarly perforated blade from a probable warrior burial at Villevenard in the Marne (Brisson, 1935, 79-80 and Fig.). The Corrofin spearhead (Fig. 58:3) is certainly of Iron Age date. The perforations through the blade are reminiscent, perhaps, of the perforated blades of some later Bronze Age spearheads, but the angular pattern discernible on the shaft is best compared to the designs on some of the Lisnacrogher ferrules (Fig. 59; Pl. 32). The unique bronze spearhead from Boho, Co. Fermanagh (Fig. 58:1; Pl. 32:1) is also a probable Iron Age piece. The design on the octagonal socket and on the blade bears close comparison with designs on the ornate "north of Ireland" ring in the Ulster Museum (Fig. 142; Pl. 100) and is also not far removed from some of the designs on the Lisnacrogher ferrules referred to above. The concentric circle motifs on this spearhead also recall the frequent presence of such designs on North European spearheads of the Early Imperial Period (Eggers et al., 1964, 68, Pl. p. 69). A date in the first or second century A.D. might, perhaps, be appropriate for this piece. The large Lisnacrogher spearhead with irregular, haphazard rocked-tracer designs on its forged blade (Fig. 58:4) is also certainly Iron Age in date but its precise chronological position is uncertain. Although allegedly attached to the wooden shaft which had a spearbutt and a decorative

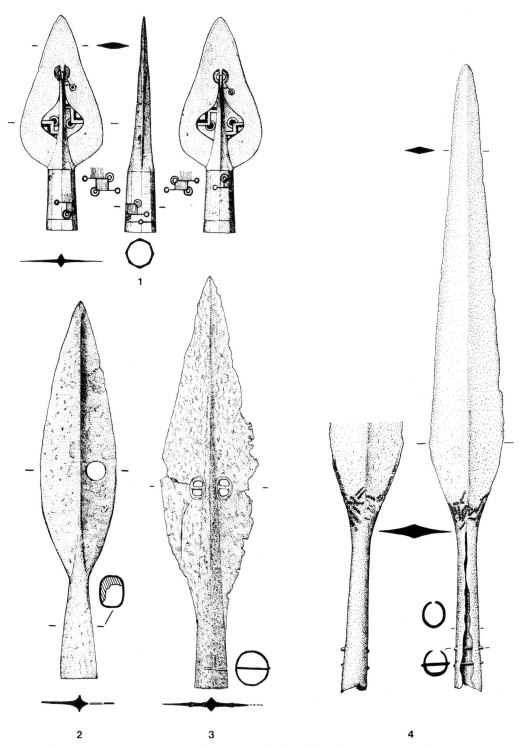

Fig. 58. Irish Iron Age spearheads. 1 Boho, Co. Fermanagh. 2 Roodstown, Co. Louth. 3 Corrofin, Co. Clare. 4 Lisnacrogher, Co. Antrim. - 1/2.

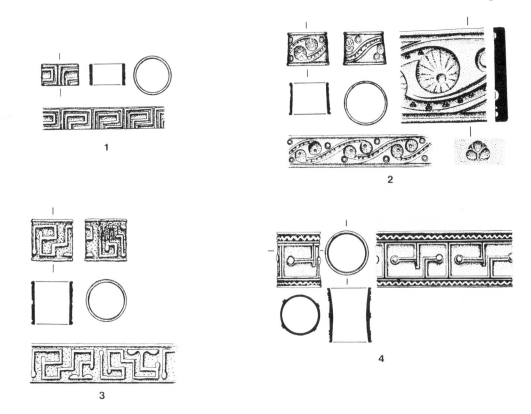

Fig. 59. Decorated bronze spear ferrules. Lisnacrogher, Co. Antrim. – 1/2.

ferrule at its other end (Wakeman, 1883-4, 390), this has not in fact been clearly demonstrated. Its date must, however, lie within the range suggested for the swords, scabbards and spearbutts from that site. A very large plain spearhead from the same Co. Antrim site in the Ulster Museum, Belfast (CIIAA No. 282) is less certainly to be dated to the Iron Age. In size and form, however, it is strikingly similar to one from Llyn Cerrig Bach (Fox, 1946, Pl. V:14) so that a dating to the Iron Age is not too unlikely.

Spearbutts

There are sixty-five or sixty-six bronze spearbutts of probable Iron Age date from the country, and three tanged iron examples are recorded which might also belong to the Iron Age. These objects thus constitute, after horse-trappings, the second largest single body of identifiable Iron Age metalwork from Ireland (Raftery, 1982).

Typology

Bronze spearbutts of the Irish Iron Age may be divided into four main groups as follows – 1: Lisnacrogher type; 2: doorknob type; 3: tubular type; 4: conical type.

1. *Lisnacrogher type*

Nineteen examples from Ireland are included in this group. Their name derives from the fact that all but two of the Irish examples come from the Co. Antrim site and it is indeed possible that all are products of a single workshop, possibly even one situated in the area of Lisnacrogher itself. Two sub-groups may be discerned: 1a, the Lisnacrogher type proper (Fig. 60:1-7) and 1b, three examples (Fig. 60:8-9) which may share some elements with the doorknob variety (Type 2) and which may be regarded as transitional between the two main groups.

All the Lisnacrogher-type butts are hollow with circular sockets and all are single castings. Spearbutts of Type 1a are smaller and of more delicate manufacture than the doorknob type. Their maximum height can be as little as 2.9 cm and in no case is it greater than 6.7 cm. The butt-end is flattened-spherical in form and considerably less prominent than the knobs of Type 2. A convex moulding encircles the socket a short distance below the mouth and in every example the segment between this moulding and the mouth, and between the moulding and the expanded butt-end, is sharply waisted. Ten of the Type 1a butts possess a pair of opposed circular rivet-holes, either immediately below the rim or through the convex moulding. A narrow rectangular slot, surrounded by small, incised, concentric, circles, pierces the convex base of one example (Fig. 60:7).

Decoration is, with one exception, simple. It comprises either continuous or hyphenated lines outlining the rims and expanded portions, or simple concentric-circle motifs on the underside of the base. One example (Fig. 60:2; Pl. 34:1) has a band of relief, cast, curvilinear ornament encircling its base, which in this instance tends towards a polygonal shape.

The three butts of Type 1b (Figs 60:8,9; Pl. 33:1) have been set apart as a separate sub-group because they are larger and more massive than the rest of the Type 1 butts. In each case the knob-end is well within the range of the knobs on Type 2 butts but they are distinguished from the latter group by the possession of the prominent convex rib and the sharply waisted portions above and below this as on the other Type 1 butts. The proportions are thus closer to Type 2 but the shape is clearly of Type 1 so that these three specimens might be regarded as hybrid

Fig. 60. Knobbed bronze spearbutts. 1-7 Type 1a. 8-9 Type 1b. 10-13
Type 2. 1-7,9 Lisnacrogher, Co. Antrim. 8 Coleraine, Co. Derry. 10-11
no prov. 12 Derrymore Island, L. Gara, Co. Sligo. 13 Roscommon. - 1/2.

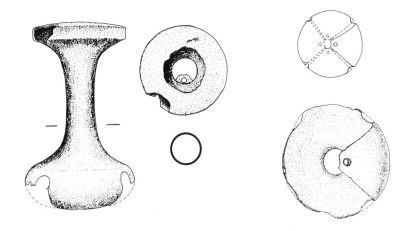

Fig. 61. Type 2 spearbutt. Lisnacrogher, Co. Antrim. - 1/2.

between the two groups. Two of the examples have tiny, rectangular slots on their bases, a feature which occurs on one of the Type 1a butts referred to above. The example from Coleraine, Co. Derry (Fig. 60:8; Pl. 33:1), stands out from the rest with its sharp edges, prominent step and exaggerated expansions. Its closest parallel is, however, to be found in the Type 2 group (e.g. Fig. 60:10).

2. Doorknob type

There are twenty examples of this type known from Ireland. Though varying somewhat in size, doorknob spearbutts display a considerable degree of uniformity in form (Figs 60:10-13, 61; Pl. 33:2). The typical butt of this group has a short cylindrical or funnel-shaped socket, projecting from a large, rounded knob which is also hollow and normally in the form of a flattened sphere. The socket is usually circular in section, but there are four instances where it is square internally with rounded corners. Where the socket joins the knob a slight ridge occurs; in one instance (Fig. 60:10) this is a pronounced step.

All the butts of this group, with one exception, were formed originally as a single casting. The unique example from Lisnacrogher (Fig. 61), had the knob-end formed by hammering four triangular tongues of bronze together at the base of the socket so that their apices touched to form the hollow sphere. This example further differs from the others in possessing a flat, expanded collar around the mouth. Such a feature

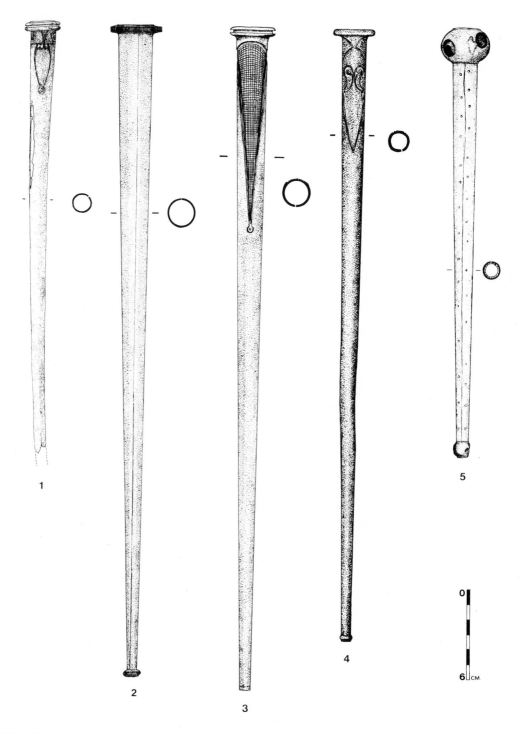

Fig. 62. Type 3a tubular spearbutts. 1 R. Shannon. 2 R. Shannon, Carrick-
on-Shannon, Co. Leitrim. 3-4 no prov. 5 R. Shannon, Banagher, Co. Offaly.

is reminiscent of the tubular and conical types (Types 3 and 4), and also invites comparison with the three butts of Type 1b.

The base of the knob on these butts may be flat or occasionally somewhat concave. Frequently, wear is noticeable on the underside of the knob. In three instances the centre of the base is pierced by a circular rivet-hole. On one butt three small, circular depressions form a straight line across the centre of the base.

Decoration is infrequent on doorknob spearbutts and is generally confined to a small number of closely-spaced, finely-incised lines encircling the mouth of the socket. On one slightly more elaborate example (Fig. 60:11; Pl. 33:2), there is a zig-zag band on the socket, each angle of which is filled by a single dot.

3. *Tubular type*

This group comprises seventeen examples. Though broadly linked by their elongated, tapering, tubular form there is considerable variation in size, shape, decoration and method of manufacture. Out of this variety three main forms may be distinguished.

Type 3a: Five butts stand out from the series (Fig. 62), because they are of hammered sheet bronze. They include the longest specimens in the country (up to 43 cm) and each one is decorated. They taper markedly from one end to the other. As with all the butts of Type 3 (and indeed Type 4) they are open at both ends.

In each case the specially-prepared bronze sheet has been folded so that the long edges touch. To keep the tube closed a separately-cast bronze ring was fitted around it at each end. On several examples a transverse, enamel-filled groove embellishes the edges of the rings. In one unusual example (Fig. 62:5) the bronze sheet has been hammered around a tube of iron. Where the edges of the folded-over bronze sheet meet, a metal sealing-strip, held in place by rivets, once existed. This is now lost. This butt is further distinct from its fellows by the presence at each end of prominent expansions which take the form of hollow, flattened spheres, each one of which has a series of circular depressions on its surface which once held inlays of red enamel or some other substance.

Engraved decoration, consisting either of curvilinear patterns, cross-hatching or herring-bone design is present on the other butts of the group (e.g. Pl. 34:2).

Type 3b: These butts, six in all, are cast (Figs 63:2, 67:2; Pl. 35:1). In three cases the remains of the original wooden shaft are present.

Type 3c: These butts, again six in number, are also cast (Fig. 63:3-

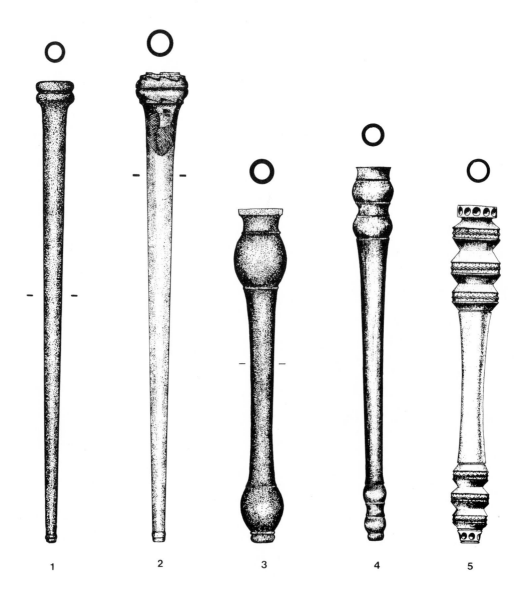

Fig. 63. Tubular spearbutts. 1-2 Type 3b. 3-5 Type 3c. 1 no prov. 2 Clondalee, Co. Meath. 3-5 River Bann, Toome, Co. Antrim. - 1/2.

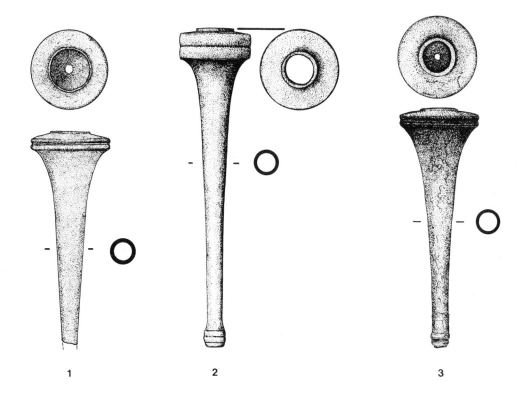

Fig. 64. Type 4, conical spearbutts. 1 Ballybrit, Co. Galway. 2 River Shannon, Banagher, Co. Offaly. 3 River Shannon. - 1/2.

5; Pl. 35:2). They are more solid in appearance than 3b butts and they tend to taper rather less than is the case with the other butts of Type 3. Their principal distinguishing feature is the occurrence of prominent, hemispherical knops at each extremity. In four examples there are two such protuberances at each end. In the fifth instance there are three knops at each end and on the sixth butt of the group there is but a single knop at each end. The only decorated example is the elaborate piece from the River Bann at Toome (Jope, 1951; Fig. 63:5; Pl. 35:2), adorned by reserved zig-zags and circular depressions which retain traces of red enamel inlays.

4. Conical type

Ten examples of this type are known (Fig. 64; Pl. 36). All are single castings, four of which are of rather poor-quality workmanship. There is a very marked decrease in width from one end to the other, giving the cone shape. At the wide end there is a prominent moulding around the mouth which is usually divided by a cast, transverse groove around its edge. The opening of the mouth is considerably less than the total diameter of the moulding so that the latter is thus in the form of a flat collar. The edge of the opening is defined by a low raised flange. At the narrow end of the butt a less prominent moulding is present.

Tanged Spearbutts

Three recorded examples of this type (two iron, one bronze), all from Co. Meath, are known. Only one, that from Lagore (Hencken, 1950, 98, Fig. 32; CIIAA No. 360) survives. While these were in use throughout the La Tène period on the Continent, their date in this country is uncertain. They could postdate the Iron Age in Ireland.

Function

Although it could be argued that the use of these objects, especially the knobbed specimens, as protective adjuncts to the ends of spearshafts has not been demonstrated, there seems sufficient cumulative evidence available to indicate that this was so. At Lisnacrogher in at least two instances the bronze butts remained in position on the ends of wooden shafts. In one case the shaft, now shrunken and fragmentary, was allegedly 2.40 m in length and as well as the butt it was also decorated with an ornamented cylindrical ferrule (Wood-Martin, 1886, 64). The other shaft fragment which was formerly attached to a butt is now lost (Knowles, 1897, 115, Fig. 3). In England, MacGregor has drawn attention to a butt said to have been discovered attached to a spearshaft in Jubilee Cave, Settle, Yorkshire, but this object too is now missing (Raistrick, 1939, 141).

Further apparent confirmation of the use of such objects as decorative attachments to the bases of spearshafts is provided by some north British iconic representations. A carving from Maryport in Cumberland (Pl. 40:1) figures a horned warrior/god with a shield in one hand and a spear in the other (Ross, 1967, Pl. 49a). At the extremity of the spear there is a rounded protuberance which must surely be a knobbed butt. A silver plaque from Bewcastle, Cumberland, also shows a figure, named as the god Cocidius, holding a spear at the lower extremity of which there is a definite rounded expansion (Pl. 37). This too may legitimately be regarded as a knobbed spearbutt (Gillam, 1958, Pl. 7).

In the writings of the eleventh century Byzantine scholar Xiphilinus there is a passage which has been regarded as relevant in the present context. Xiphilinus epitomised some of the historical works of the third century Dio Cassius and through him is preserved the latter's account of the Emperor Severus' campaigns in Britain. Dio Cassius, speaking of the Kaledonioi and the Maiatai as the two greatest tribes of the Britons beyond the wall (the Maeatae nearest the Wall, the Caledonians beyond them to the north) writes: "They go to war in chariots with small but swift horses; they are also very swift at running themselves and very steadfast in holding their ground when they fight on foot. Their weapons consist of a shield and a short spear, which has a bronze apple on the tip of its spike which rattles when shaken and so terrifies the enemy; they also have daggers." It is possible that the "bronze apple" may refer to a spearbutt of doorknob type, though the nature of the "terrifying rattle" is unclear. MacGregor (1976, 85) wondered whether this "may have been an unintentional side effect of trimming the weapon's balance by variation of the ballast in the hollow terminal" but this does not seem likely.

The use of these objects as spearbutts is thus probable. It should, however, be pointed out that, in the doorknob variety especially, the diameter of the socket is extremely small being at times barely over 1 cm so that with any sort of robust handling the heavy butts of this type at least would have caused the shaft-end to snap off at the mouth of the socket. This, of course, raises the question as to the extent to which these objects were for actual use in battle or merely for parade purposes.

Jope 1957a, 87) compared the "knob-type butts" to iron "standard heads" from a Romano-British burial at Brough in Yorkshire and wondered whether a similar function could be ascribed to some of the Irish pieces. In Europe too, objects of varying date, comparable in shape to the Irish knobbed butts are known. From tumulus 54 at Kaschenbach, Kr. Bittburg in Germany, for example, a hollow, ferrule with convex mouldings was found in a cremation of probable Early La Tène date (Dehn, 1949, 278, 281, Abb. 6). Professor Dehn, in a personal communication, suggests the object might have been the head of a sceptre. Mid-second century A.D. knobbed ferrules from Bohemia (Breidel, 1930, 199, Abb. 219) and Germany (Stimming, 1912, Taf. XLIV:1k,l) are seen as possible drinking horn mounts. None of these interpretations, however, seem appropriate to the Irish specimens. Equally, superficial similarities between the form of some of the Lisnacrogher butts (e.g. Fig. 60:1) and some British linch-pin heads of the early centuries A.D. (e.g. from Westhall: Clarke, 1939, Pl. XVIII:4) may have some relevance for the dating of the Irish objects but the comparison can have no bearing on their function. Iron objects from Newstead referred to as "part of the framework of a seat" also resemble somewhat the Lisnacrogher butts (Curle, 1911, Pls 1;2,4,5) but this too must be largely coincidental.

Affinities and Chronology

Spearbutts of Doorknob and Lisnacrogher type

There is no single instance in Ireland of a clearly associated or stratified spearbutt[1]. All are isolated, chance finds with the exception of those from Lisnacrogher and here there can be no certainty as to their exact context. Iron Age material at that site, as already stated, can be as early as the third or early second century B.C. and an Iron Age presence seems certainly to continue there into the first century A.D. at least and possibly even later. It is interesting that some doorknob butts (Type 2) were found there as well as the numerous Type 1 specimens, but none of the other forms. It is also perhaps, significant, that two of the "hybrid" examples (Type 1b) came from the same site and it thus appears likely that spearbutts of Types 1 and 2 overlap with one another in time and probable cultural context. It seems, therefore, that they may legitimately be discussed together.

The knobbed spearbutt is an insular phenomenon and the majority of extant examples come from Ireland. Clear prototypes for these butts are not readily forthcoming. In Late Bronze Age contexts there are some superficially comparable castings which have from time to time been put forward as possible progenitors of the type. For instance, there is a pair from Fulbourn in Cambridgeshire with circular, perforated sockets and expanded ends. In each case, however, the expanded end is a disc rather than a knob, and is sharply concave on its underside (Clarke, 1821, 56-61). A specimen similar to these examples is said to have been found in 1726 in a cairn in Midlothian in Scotland with two portions of a bronze spearhead (Anon., 1893-4, 237). Somewhat closer to the Irish specimens than these examples are the ferrules found occasionally in Late Bronze Age hoards in England (Evans, 1881, 341, Fig. 427) and France (Mortillet, 1881, Pl. 83:952; Pl. 82:924,925). These objects have a cylindrical or slightly flared socket, a small spherical knob at the base, incised lines around the mouth and perforations through the socket near the mouth. They are smaller than the doorknob butts, however, and sometimes have parallel bands of convex ribbing around the lower end of the socket which is not found on any of the Irish castings. It is

---

1. The recent discovery of a doorknob butt from a Medieval level at Carrickfergus, Co. Antrim (information courtesy Ms. Lesley Simpson), can have no significance for the chronology of the type.

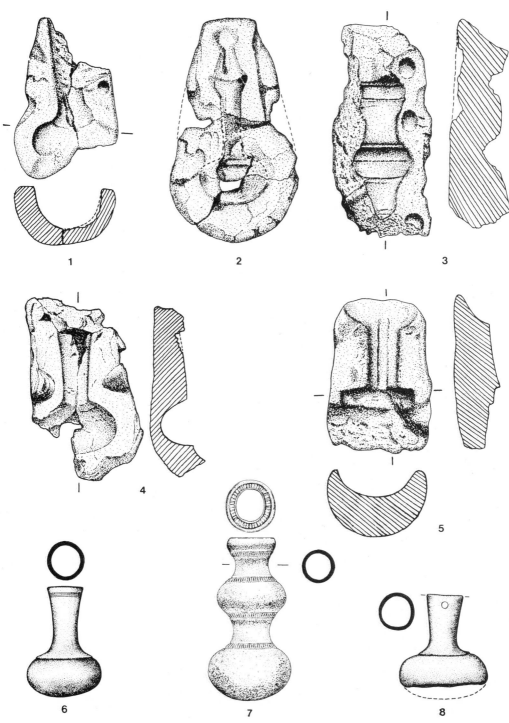

Fig. 65. British knobbed spearbutts and spearbutt mould fragments.
1,4 Traprain Law, East Lothian, Scotland. 2 Dun Mor Vaul, Tiree, Scotland.
3,5 Dunagoil, Scotland. 6 Inverurrie, Crichie, Aberdeenshire, Scotland.
7 Broch of Harray, Orkney, Scotland. 8 Rushall Down, Wiltshire, England.
- 1/2.

nonetheless possible that in these bronzes is to be seen the ultimate background for the insular specimens. The parallels are not precise, however, and, as will emerge below, there is as yet no evidence to suggest that any of the insular Type 1 or 2 butts are as early as the Late Bronze Age types, nor is there any indication that the latter continued late. It should also be borne in mind that these English and French objects are not certainly spearbutts. Otherwise, the only possible parallels in Europe for the Irish butts are the few examples earlier noted (p. 120), and these may have had a function quite different to that of the Irish bronzes.

Spearbutts of Types 1 and 2 closely comparable to the Irish examples are found sporadically in various parts of Britain, particularly the north, and their contexts shed some light on the dating of the Irish specimens. From Inverurrie, Crichie in Aberdeenshire comes a doorknob butt of bronze which is indistinguishable from the normal Irish Type 2 butts (Fig. 65:6). This is said to have been found in association with a terret of the type referred to by Kilbride-Jones as "Donside-type" (1934-5), "Massive-type" by MacGregor (1976, 47) and "Don-type" by Livens (1976, 149), along with seven pierced shale balls, which are usually interpreted as the heads of pins.

Terrets of this type are confined largely to northern England and the north-eastern part of Scotland and the majority of commentators would agree that they were "devised by British craftsmen, working under Continental influence some time between the late first and the mid-third centuries A.D." (MacGregor, 1976, 47); Livens has concluded (1976, 151) that such terrets "probably developed in north-eastern Scotland, perhaps during the first or second century A.D." He allows, however, for the possibility that the type may have enjoyed a long vogue.

If it could be accepted that the terret and the spearbutt were in fact genuinely associated a date in the early centuries A.D. would be indicated for the latter object. Doubt exists, however, as to the the integrity of the Crichie hoard so that for the moment this alleged association must be regarded with caution in a consideration of the dating evidence for the doorknob spearbutts (Callander, 1926-7, 243-6; Livens, op. cit., 161, fn. 25).

From the broch of Harray in the Orkneys comes a bronze butt, of Lisnacrogher type (Farrer, 1866-7, 103), but of the more massive variety which shares with examples of Type 1b some elements of the doorknob form (Fig. 65:7; Pl. 38:1). The exact context of this object is unknown but a dating range from the first century B.C. to the second or third centuries A.D. has been suggested for other material from the site, though admittedly on no very secure grounds (MacGregor, 1976, 86).

Four Scottish sites have produced mould fragments for the manufacture of spearbutts of the type under discussion. At Traprain Law two almost complete halves of clay moulds were found (Fig. 65:1,4; Pl. 38:3,5), the matrices in which clearly indicate that the objects to be cast were normal doorknob type butts (MacGregor, 1976, Nos. 182, 3 and references). There are several other smaller fragments of moulds from the site and in every case, where recognisable forms exist, they appear to be from moulds for casting doorknob butts. Exact dating at Traprain is rather uncertain and one of the large fragments (CVM 561a) has been variously interpreted as from first/second and fourth century A.D. levels. The other large piece (CVM 563) appears to have been associated with coins of the late first and second centuries A.D. The remaining mould fragments are even less certainly stratified. Burley, in considering the Traprain metalwork, suggested a last century B.C./first century A.D. context for these moulds, but her attempt to extend their range back before the birth of Christ is influenced, it seems, by an incorrectly-founded belief that these objects are of Late Bronze Age date in Ireland (1955-6, 203). It is likely, however, that the Traprain moulds fall in with the mass of material from the site and may in all probability be seen as belonging to the period between the first and at latest the fourth century A.D.

Apart from a composite bronze and iron spearbutt from Traprain (Fig. 66:1) which is not directly related to the Irish series (MacGregor, 1976, No. 185), the only surviving metal example from this Scottish site which might be compared to the Irish bronzes is a small casting (GVM 407; MacGregor, 1976, No. 196; Fig. 66:2). The relationship is however, tenuous and the object differs in most details from the butts under discussion. It is not even certain that it was in fact a spearbutt. None of the other bronze objects which MacGregor suggests could have been spearbutts seem related to the Irish material.

One of the two clay mould fragments from the Dunagoil vitrified hillfort in Buteshire (Mann, 1925, Pl. 40) is clearly for the manufacture of a butt of the heavier Lisnacrogher type (Fig. 65:3; Pl. 38:2) similar to that from Harray. The form which is represented on the matrix of the other fragment from the same site (Fig. 65:5; Pl. 38:4) may be that of a doorknob butt with everted collar around the mouth. The exact context of the fragments from Dunagoil is also unknown but recent work on the material by Leechman, referred to by MacGregor (1976, 85), has enabled her to suggest that the site was occupied from the first century B.C. to the first century A.D., but there were "conceivable expansions in both directions". Thus Dunagoil is also of limited assistance in establishing the precise dating range of these objects. Mould fragments

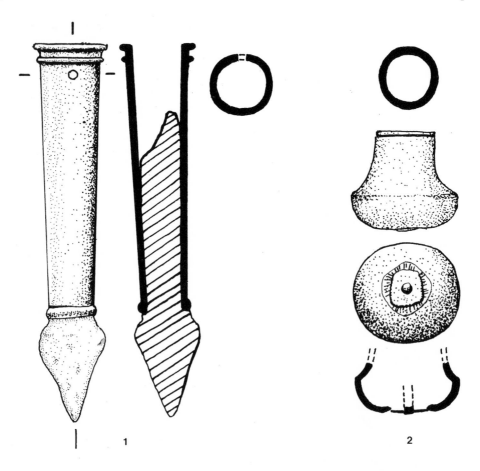

Fig. 66. Spear (?) ferrules. Traprain Law, East Lothian, Scotland. - 1/1.

from a broch at Gurness came from the fill of the inner ditch around
the broch.   From the same ditch came fragments of moulds for ringheaded pins but it is unclear if all are of the same date.

The only piece from a controlled excavation is the mould fragment
from the broch of Dun Mor Vaul on the island of Tiree off the west coast
of Scotland (MacKie, 1974, 152-3; Fig. 65:2).   The spearbutt represented
by the reconstructed mould from this site is again a hybrid Lisnacrogher
type (1b), possessing the heavy knob of Type 2 and the waisted socket
of Type 1.   There are other fragments from the site which could be
for casting similar objects.   The recognisable piece is recorded as coming
from "near the top of the primary broch floor" (MacKie, 1974, 153).   The
initial use of the broch (period 3a) began "between 70 and 40 B.C." and
this primary phase appears to have ended about 200 or 250 A.D. (ibid,

94). A fragment of a glass bowl of Roman type, datable to between 160 and 250 A.D., came, it seems, from the same upper level of the primary floor as the mould, so that a date not later than about 200 A.D. is suggested for the Dun Mor Vaul spearbutt mould.

The only other surviving example of a doorknob spearbutt in Britain is from a habitation site at Rushall Down, Wiltshire, in southern England (Fig. 65:8). It is almost indistinguishable in form from many of the Irish examples. Rushall Down was excavated in 1897-9 but the results were never published. A large quantity of material came from the site, ranging in date from Neolithic, through Bronze Age to Iron Age and into the Roman and Romano-British periods. The dominant presence at Rushall Down, as far as the surviving remains indicate, seems to be Romano-British. It may well be that the spearbutt was related to this phase of activity but an earlier, pre-Roman Iron Age context for it is not ruled out. Close dating for the Rushall Down specimen is thus again not possible.

Notwithstanding the vagueness of the chronology in several instances, the cumulative picture indicated by the British evidence for the dating of these butts, though far from overwhelming, suggests a date for the doorknob and Lisnacrogher types in the first century or two of Christianity. A date back into the first century B.C. is not entirely excluded in one or two instances but is nowhere proven and the weight of evidence is towards the early post-Christian dating. The classical reference of Xiphilinus quoted above (if the "bronze apples" are in fact knobbed butts) strengthens this contention and further support is given to this dating if the Romano-British carving at Maryport and the silver Bewcastle plaque do in fact portray spears with doorknob butts attached.

The dating of the Irish specimens thus rests almost entirely on the dates of the British examples. All that can be said in a purely Irish context is that the cast relief decoration on the knob of one of the Lisnacrogher butts (Fig. 60:2; Pl. 34:1) is in keeping with an early centuries A.D. dating and, indeed, appears to have in the treatment of the pattern elements of the Scottish boss style.

There can be little doubt that the distribution of doorknob and Lisnacrogher type spearbutts (Map 10) indicates clear evidence for contact between Ireland and north Britain in the centuries around, or just after, the birth of Christ. Virtually identical forms occur on both sides of the North Channel. Mould fragments in Scotland demonstrate that butts were made in that country but the overwhelming numerical dominance of extant examples in Ireland (39 specimens now recorded), as well as their wide spread in the country, argue strongly in favour of Ireland as having also been an area of spearbutt manufacture. We cannot say which country had chronological priority in the casting of knobbed spearbutts but there are grounds for suggesting that the type developed in Ireland, possibly even the north-east, and spread thence to Scotland (Raftery, 1982, 78). The isolated example in southern England is likely to be an export from Ireland.

Spearbutts of Tubular and Conical type

Spearbutts of Types 3 and 4 are even more difficult to date than are the smaller butts of Types 1 and 2. Not only are they entirely without context within Ireland, but they also appear to be without wholly convincing parallels outside. Comparisons can be made between the tubular type and the cylindrical ferrules of Late Bronze Age date such as that from Toome Bar, Co. Antrim (Eogan, 1964, 269, Fig. 1:8). The latter, however, differ in general proportions, tending more towards a parallel-sided outline, they are always cast and are closed at one end. They never have decorative mouldings and are frequently perforated halfway down their length. There is no convincing reason to regard the Iron Age examples as influenced by them. Closer, perhaps, both in form and in time to the Irish tubular butts are some metal ferrules which occasionally occur in Continental Early La Tène burials (Schaaff, 1973, Abb. 8-10). These may be of bronze or iron and, though considerably smaller than the Irish specimens, they share with the latter the prominent convex mouldings at the ends. In addition, both ends are open, cast and hammered examples are known, the latter having metal rings encircling the extremities of the hammered tube, as is the case with the Irish Type 3a ferrules. The function of these Continental objects as spearbutts has not been clearly established but some still contain wooden shaft fragments within the sockets so that this is possible.

It is tempting to regard these Early La Tène objects as having played a part in the genesis of the Irish tubular spearbutts, and indeed, it is even possible to invoke appropriately early parallels for the ornament on some of the Irish specimens (compare, for instance the design on Pl. 34:2 with motifs on the Waldenbuch pillar (Jacobsthal, 1944, No. 11). Equally close comparisons for the decoration are, however, forthcoming on far later insular metalwork (e.g. Figs 16; 18:2; 130:1; 132). Compare also hatched, leafy motifs on a tubular (Type 3b) spearbutt from Clondalee, Co. Meath (Fig. 67:2), to a similar repoussé design on a fragment of bronze foil from a first century A.D. level at Newstead, Roxburghshire, Scotland (MacGregor, 1976, No. 340; Fig. 67:1). The reserved zig-zag bands on a Type 3c butt from the River Bann (Jope, 1951; Fig. 63:5; Pl. 35:2) are also, perhaps, best compared with a whole range of insular bronzes the date of which in most cases seems to centre on the birth of Christ.

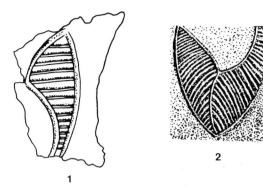

Fig. 67. Leaf design. 1 Newstead, Roxburghshire, Scotland. 2 Clondalee, Co. Meath.

Nonetheless the exclusively western Irish distribution of all the localised Type 3a butts (the folded-over, sheet bronze examples) should not be forgotten and it is these which are closest in method of manufacture to the Continental pieces.

If the Type 3 butts are considered in purely insular terms it is possible to suggest a hypothetical sequence of development for them (Fig. 68). Such a sequence envisages the cast mouldings with transverse grooves which adorn the ends of Type 3b butts as skeuomorphic representations of the functional rings with enamelled grooves of Type 3a. From this the elaborate castings of Type 3c develop. Such a typology is wholly theoretical since it is unbuttressed by fixed chronological points, but it is interesting to observe that all the localised Type 3a butts (three out of five) are from the River Shannon and that three of the four localised Type 3b specimens are also from the same river (the last coming from Co. Meath). Type 3c is the only group which includes examples in Ulster. Three are from the River Bann in Co. Antrim; there is also an example from Co. Galway and one from the River Shannon (Map 8).

While the dating of Type 3 butts is uncertain it can be said that the dating of Type 4 butts is entirely unknown. The only one from a controlled excavation is the Ballybrit example (Fig. 64:1; Pl. 36; Waddell, 1966-71), but this came from an unstratified position in the bank of a ringfort. The find is thus not illuminating. The only observations which can be made are that butts of this type are unknown either in Late Bronze Age or Early Historic contexts and that their general form bears superficial comparison with some of the Type 3 castings. It may be that their period of use overlaps with that of Type 3 butts.

Finally, the frequency of rivers as the source of butts of Types 3 and 4 is perhaps worthy of comment. Of the nineteen provenanced

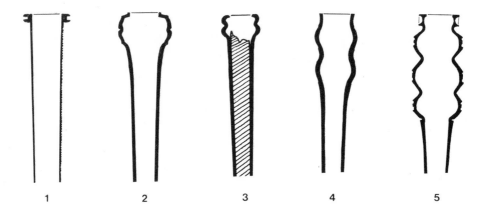

Fig. 68. Hypothetical development of the Irish tubular spearbutt.

examples ten come from the Shannon, three from the Bann and one from the Erne. The concentration at sites deemed to be ancient fords (e.g. Banagher on the Shannon, Toome Bar on the Bann, Portora on the Erne) has been variously interpreted as reflecting accidental loss by people traversing the shallows, or combat at strategic routeway crossings. Deliberate deposition in rivers as offerings to the supernatural inhabitants of the watery depths is also possible as there is ample evidence for this practice amongst Celtic peoples outside this country. Neither possibility can, however, either be proven or disproved and it should be borne in mind that the riverine concentration of these objects may well be exaggerated, reflecting little more than the intensity of drainage activity during the late nineteenth and early twentieth centuries.

The predominantly riverine context of spearbutts of Types 3 and 4 contrasts with the find circumstances of butts of Types 1 and 2, only one of which (in fact an atypical example, CIIAA No. 306), has as yet come from a river. There is no ready explanation for this difference.

Shields

There are only two certain occurrences of Iron Age shields from Ireland. An L-shaped binding strip from the Athlone, Co. Westmeath, "box", (below p. 284; Fig. 140:9; CIIAA No. 878) and a similar, as yet unpublished fragment recovered during the recent excavations at Navan Fort, Co. Armagh, are comparable to binding strips from South Cadbury and

Spettisbury in England, where they are regarded as mounts from shields of Roman type (Alcock, 1972b, Pl. 10; Gresham, 1939, 120, Fig. 4). Such binding-strips of Roman and sub-Roman date are also known from the Continent where their function as edge-bindings for shields is clearly demonstrated (e.g. AuhV V, 1911, 110, Taf. 21:365; Eichhorn, 1927, Figs p. 102, 104, 121). While this interpretation is possible for the Irish pieces, they appear a trifle too slender to have served such a purpose.

From one of the destroyed burials at Lambay, Co. Dublin, came an object of bronze which can only be interpreted as a shield boss (Fig. 69). This is a hollow casting, made up of two elements. It is sub-conical in form with the remains of a mounting-flange projecting laterally from the edges at the open end. There is a circular, disc-like projection at the front. The shield presumably comes from a warrior's grave and its date, assuming it to be contemporary with the openwork scabbard mounts (Fig. 47; Pl. 25) and the other objects from the cemetery, must lie in the middle or second half of the first century A.D. Strangely, however, there seem to be no close parallels for the disc-ended boss at this time in north Britain – the area to which most of the influences detectable in the Lambay material can be traced (Rynne, 1976, 236ff.). Indeed, it seems that it is only in Anglo-Saxon contexts that such shield bosses (of iron) become common (e.g. Alcock, 1971, 330, Fig. 29:b,d).

The final member of the Irish shield group is the most interesting. This is a complete specimen found at Littleton Bog, Clonoura, Co. Tipperary (Ó Ríordáin et al., 1962, 152, Pl. XVII). It is a small rectangular shield, 57 cm by 35 cm, composed of alderwood planks covered on both surfaces with sheets of leather. These sheets are held in place by stitching strips of leather around the edges of the object. The grip consists of a straight length of oakwood skilfully secured across an oval opening in the centre of the shield. This opening was covered at the front by a separately-made, more or less hemispherical wooden boss which was held in place by stitching a leather cover across it (Fig. 70; Pl. 39).

Although a considerable number of shield fittings is known from both Britain and the Continent, including a number of complete, magnificently decorated examples, none of the extant pieces is directly comparable with the Clonoura specimen. It is likely that the great masterpieces of British Iron Age art, such as the Witham, Wandsworth or Battersea shields, were for parade purposes only and it is to the humble but effective implements such as that from Clonoura that the Celtic warrior would actually have entrusted his life in battle; such would, of course, rarely survive.

Most of the surviving British and Continental Iron Age shields vary in shape from rectangular to oval and are on the whole larger than the

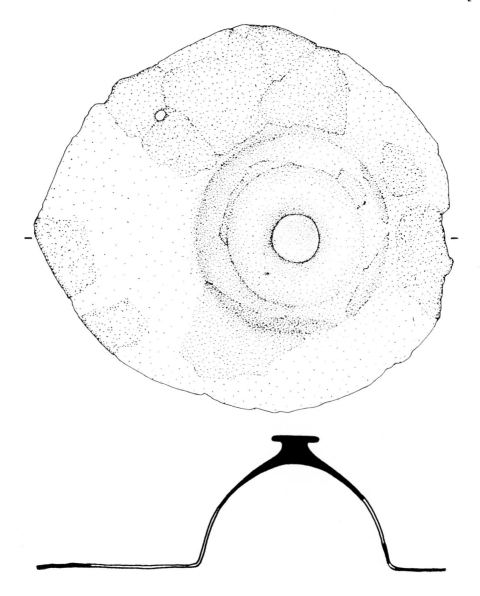

Fig. 69. Bronze shield boss. Lambay, Co. Dublin. - 3/4.

Irish piece. The method of attaching the umbo to the shield board is
usually more elaborate than is the case on the Clonoura specimen. Of
the three boss-types outlined by Ritchie (1969, 31) - wooden midrib with
hollow, circular expansion, the same with extra protecting bronze strip
and, lastly, a circular boss nailed to the shield by means of a side-flange
- it is only the third which is here of concern. Possible shield fragments
of iron come from the Carlingwark and Blackburn Mill hoards and both

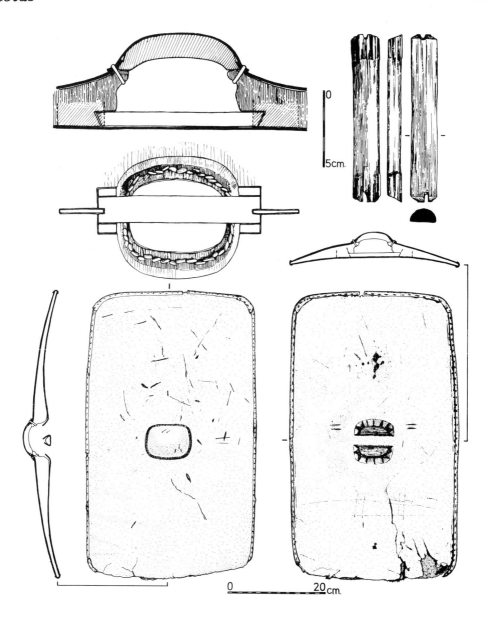

Fig. 70 Leather-covered wooden shield. Clonoura, Co. Tipperary.

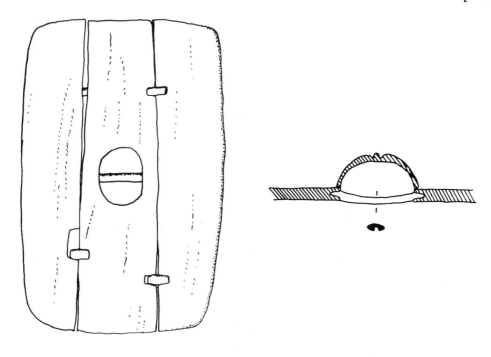

Fig. 71. Wooden shield with detail of handle attachment. Hjortspring,
Denmark. – (After Rosenberg, 1937–43).

Piggott and Ritchie consider it is not unlikely that native armourers
could have adapted Roman techniques of shield manufacture (Ritchie,
1969, 34).

The closest parallels for the Clonoura shield are, however, to be found
on representations in stone and metal in the north of Britain.   Two
rectangular shields with central, circular boss are shown on an Antonine
Wall distance slab at Bridgeness in West Lothian (Pl. 40:2; Gillam, 1958,
Pl. 6).   A similar milestone at Summerston, Lanarkshire, depicts a
comparable shield (MacDonald, 1934, Pl. 64).   Both these Antonine Wall
stones are dated to the middle of the second century A.D.   A further
similar shield is held in the left hand of the horned figure already referred
to above (p. 118), carved on a slab from Maryport in Cumberland (Pl. 40:1).
In his right hand he holds a spear which appears to be shod with a doorknob
butt.   The carving is on one of a group of altars and reliefs of
Romano-British date (Ross, 1967, 156, Pl. 49a).

A wheel god (Taranis?) on a pottery mould from Corbridge in
Northumberland also bears a small rectangular shield with central circular
boss.   This, too, belongs to the early centuries A.D. (MacGregor, 1976,
87).

The majority of examples mentioned above date within the early centuries of the Christian era and such a dating is possible for the Irish shield also. Rynne has, however, suggested a date in the second or first century B.C. for the Clonoura shield on the basis of the similarity of its shape and the method of fixing its hand grip to shields found in the deposit at Hjortspring on the Danish island of Als (Fig. 71; referred to in Ritchie, 1969, 37). Ritchie points out, however, that most of the Hjortspring shields (Rosenberg, 1937-43, 48-55) appear to have had spindle-shaped rather than rounded bosses as is the case on the Irish and Scottish examples, but the parallelism in handle form between the Irish and Danish shields is not lightly to be ignored.

The precise dating cf the Clonoura shield and its cultural affinities are thus uncertain. The Hjortspring evidence may suggest a date in the last centuries B.C. (Krämer, 1949-50), but the close similarities with north British representations may favour a date in the early centuries of Christianity.

WIND INSTRUMENTS

Horns

Three complete or fragmentary horns of hammered sheet bronze survive from Ireland and a fourth fragment of presumed Irish origin has been discovered in the Llyn Cerrig Bach deposit on the island of Anglesey, Wales (Figs 72, 73, 75; Pls 41-44). Several wooden examples, one at least of possible Iron Age date, are also preserved from Ireland (Fig. 76). A number of lost horns of bronze is referred in the literature. The latter include three which formerly accompanied the Loughnashade, Co. Armagh, specimen (Stuart, 1819, 608-9; Petrie, 1833-4, 29-30), and a pair from Bushmills, Co. Antrim, found in 1827 and subsequently sent to England. In referring to these last, Petrie states specifically that they were similar to those from Loughnashade and it seems not unreasonable to regard them as having been of Iron Age type (1833-4, 29). The possibility of the former existence of portion of an Iron Age horn from Loughbrickland, Co. Down, has been referred to though without further elaboration or documentation (A.S.D. 1966, 54, fn. 199).

The bronze horns are all made in the same way by hammering prepared bronze sheets to tubular form and sealing the junction by means of a thin strip of the same metal, riveted either to the inner or outer surface, or sometimes both. In each instance the horn has been made of two or (in the case of that shown in Fig. 72:2) three segments, joined by inserting opposing ends of the tubes into hollow biconical bosses. One segment of the Loughnashade trumpet was repaired several times in antiquity, and on it there are several interesting patches. Ardbrin is technically the finest example and indeed it can still be blown. Its method of manufacture has been described in detail (Norreys, 1876-8; A.S.D., 1966, 56; Tylecote, 1962, 144-5), though strangely, no published account

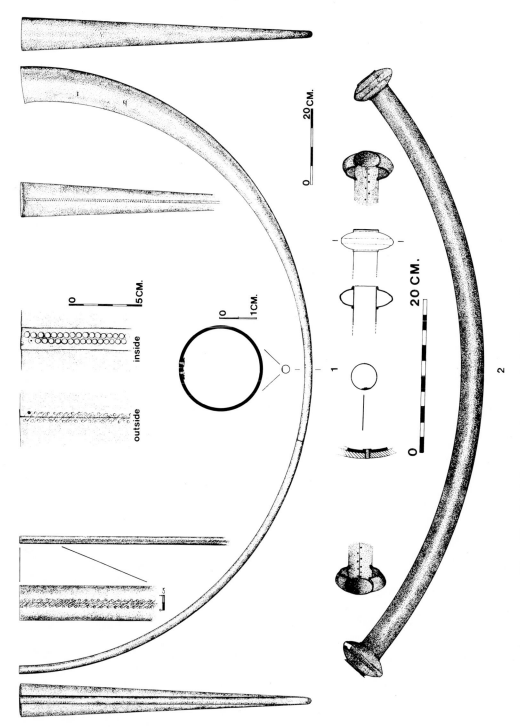

Fig. 72. Irish bronze horns. 1 Ardbrin, Co. Down. 2 no prov.

has given the correct number of rivets used on it, which is 1094.   A repair on the Llyn Cerrig Bach fragment bears engraved decoration (Fig. 75) and the disc attached to the bell of the Loughnashade specimen is elaborately decorated with repoussé curves (Fig. 73, Pls 42, 43).

Of the wooden specimens, that from Killyfaddy Bog, near Clogher, Co. Tyrone, is most likely to be of Iron Age date (Fig. 76:1).   It is a large curved piece made of four segments joined to form a unit by alternately inserting the end of one unit into the end of the next.   The four wooden segments were hollowed by first splitting them longitudinally, hollowing out each half, then rejoining the pieces.   Originally the junctions were sealed by pinning on strips of what must have been copper or bronze (Wilde describes them as "brass"), but of these the pins alone remain.   According to Wilde (1857, 245) the metal strips were present when the object was found in 1837 and they are said to have been ornamented. Unfortunately, no details survive as to the nature of this ornament.

Another wooden horn of even more uncertain date is housed in the National Museum.   It comes from Diamond Hill, Killeshandra, Co. Cavan (Wilde, 1857, 245; Fig. 76:2).   This example is made from a single length of wood, bent to C-shape and hollowed skilfully without splitting the wood.   To assist the work of hollowing, a long rectangular opening was cut along the concave curve.   There are no traces on the wood to indicate that this opening was ever sealed so that it is now unclear how the object functioned in its original state.

There is no way of dating this specimen.   As stated, it could belong to the Iron Age but this is merely a guess.   A somewhat generalised resemblance to the cast bronze horns of the Late Bronze Age (e.g. Eogan, 1964, 308, Fig. 17) allows for the possibility of an even earlier date but who is to say that the object is not considerably later than this?

Affinities and Chronology

Discussion of the Irish horns has to a large extent been dominated by the very fine repoussé design on the Loughnashade disc and there has been disagreement regarding the position of this piece in the development of insular decorated metalwork.   By far the closest parallel to the ornament of the Loughnashade disc is to be found on the Torrs "chamfrein", an object which has been considered at some length above (pp. 96-99)   in relation to the Lisnacrogher type scabbards.   In the definitive study of the Scottish object the relationship between Torrs and Loughnashade is clearly acknowledged (Atkinson and Piggott, 1955, 216), although the Armagh disc is dismissed as "the Torrs style in uncomfortable decline" (ibid., 231).   Megaw, in comparing the art on

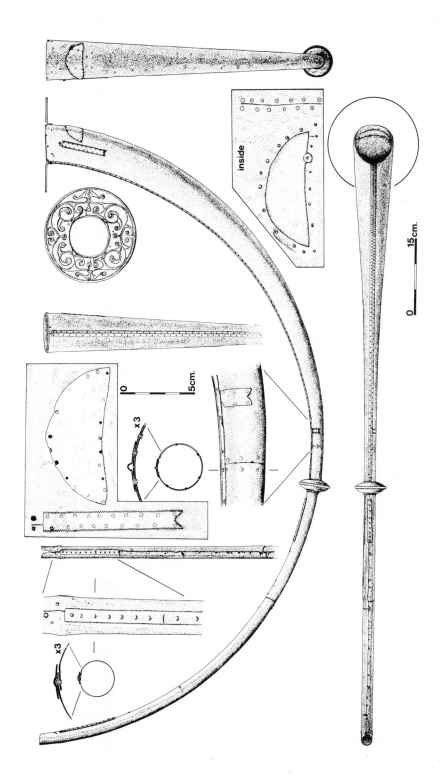

Fig. 73. Bronze horn. Loughnashade, Co. Armagh.

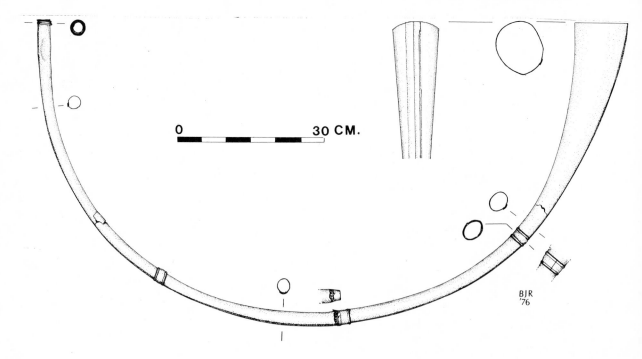

Fig. 74. Bronze horn. "Nice", France.

Torrs to Loughnashade, goes so far as to suggest that these horns are not Irish at all but rather imports into this country from Britain (1970, 147), a view with little to commend it. He is inclined to date the disc to the second or first century B.C. on stylistic grounds.

In discussing the relationship of the Torrs "chamfrein" to early Irish metalwork it has been argued above that the grounds for deriving the best of the Irish metalwork from a "Torrs School" are not firmly established. The eastward movement of influences from Ireland to Scotland cannot be ruled out. At any rate, the ornament on the Loughnashade disc cannot be far removed in time from the repoussé art on the Torrs object, though this need not necessarily be as early as the earliest of the scabbards. Megaw (1970, 147) drew attention to similarities in layout and design between Loughnashade and the Battersea shield (Brailsford, 1975, 2531), which could point to a date close to the birth of Christ for the art of the Loughnashade disc (assuming the conventional dating of the British shield is accepted). In this regard, it is interesting to compare a D-shaped patch on the horn with those on cauldrons of probable first century A.D. date (see below). If such patches have any chronological significance, a late dating for the horn

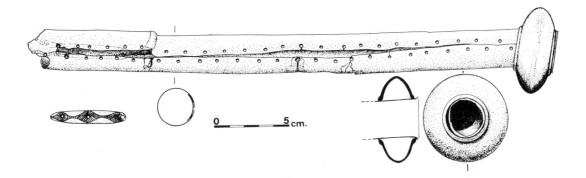

Fig. 75. Bronze horn fragment and decorative repair patch.
Llyn Cerrig Bach, Anglesey, Wales.

might be inferred. Similarity in technique of manufacture between the horns here under discussion and "horns" on the "Petrie Crown" and from Cork (below pp. 270-275) could also imply a late dating for the Irish wind instruments. We have, however, no way of knowing how long the relevant techniques were practised in the country so that their chronological importance must be regarded as uncertain. Internal evidence, therefore, indicates only that the likely span within which the horns could have been used is between about the second century B.C. and the first century A.D.

The only example of an Iron Age horn from any sort of an archaeological context is the fragment from Llyn Cerrig Bach in Wales (Fig. 75; Fox, 1946, 44, 86, Pl. XXXI; Savory, 1976, 58, Fig. 23). This has a repair strip bearing matted ornament which is unlike anything in Ireland and suggests that the horn may have been used and repaired after it had arrived in Britain. The matting would perhaps indicate a last century B.C. or early first century A.D. date for the repair, but clearly the horn itself was made and used for some time before repair became necessary. Thus again the evidence from the Welsh site gives only a very general terminus ante quem for the period of manufacture of the Irish horns.

Outside Ireland there are few close parallels for the Irish horns. Representations of somewhat comparable instruments are present on the famous Dying Gaul carving, a Roman copy of a bronze casting, one of a group erected at Pergamon in about 230 B.C. at the behest of King Attalus I to commemorate his victory over the Galatians (Bienkowski, 1908, 2-4, Nr. 1, Abb. 1-4; Özgan, 1981, Abb. 1,3). A small bronze anthropomorphic casting from the Late La Tène oppidum of Stradonice in Bohemia (Megaw, 1970, 134, Pl. 213) carries on its shoulder an object which may be a horn such as the one from Loughnashade.

Actual surviving Iron Age horns from the Continent are few in number and examples of direct relevance to a discussion of the curved Irish specimens are limited indeed. Fragments of a bronze horn have come to light at Stenstugan in Sweden; this shares a number of technical features with the Irish specimens (Oldeberg, 1947, 76-9). The horn was made of hammered sheet bronze, the junction being sealed internally by a narrow strip of bronze, riveted into place in the Irish manner. Unlike the Irish examples, however, it seems that the Swedish trumpet fragments were originally attached to an animal horn. Another point of difference, too is the presence, along the length of the surviving bronze tube and on the bell portion, of a series of closely spaced bronze rings, separately made and soldered to the outer surface of the horn. These form a succession of thin, projecting ribs along the length of the horn.

The Stenstugan horn is taken as dating to the Early Roman Iron Age "as near as possible the second century A.D." (Oldeberg, op. cit., 79).

While the Swedish horn does share some details of manufacture with the Irish specimens it is unique in Europe and need not be directly related to the Irish group. The only really close parallel to the Irish specimens on the Continent is a fine, bronze example in the Deutsches Museum in Munich (Behn, 1954, 143, Abb. 186). This is a large horn of hammered sheet bronze, curved in precisely the manner of the Irish pieces. Its size, method of manufacture and general outline bear close comparison with the complete Irish specimens.

The object (Fig. 74), which was allegedly found in Nice in southern France at the beginning of this century, is composed of four tubular elements each fitted into the next in a manner reminiscent of the wooden Clogher specimen (Fig. 76:1). The junctions are now sealed by cylindrical ferrules, each consisting of a strip of beaten metal (which seems to be brass) wrapped around the tube. The antiquity of these ferrules is questionable. At the narrow end of the trumpet, however, there is a circular mount of cast bronze around the tube which is more likely to be an original piece.

In contrast with the Irish horns, the two edges of the folded bronze sheet of the Nice example meet along the convex rather than the concave curve of the object. The junction is sealed externally by a thin bronze strip which is not, however, riveted into place as in the insular specimens, but is apparently soldered in position. This strip replaces an earlier, somewhat wider strip, the marks of which are clearly visible.

For most of its length, the horn from Nice is some 2.5 cm in internal

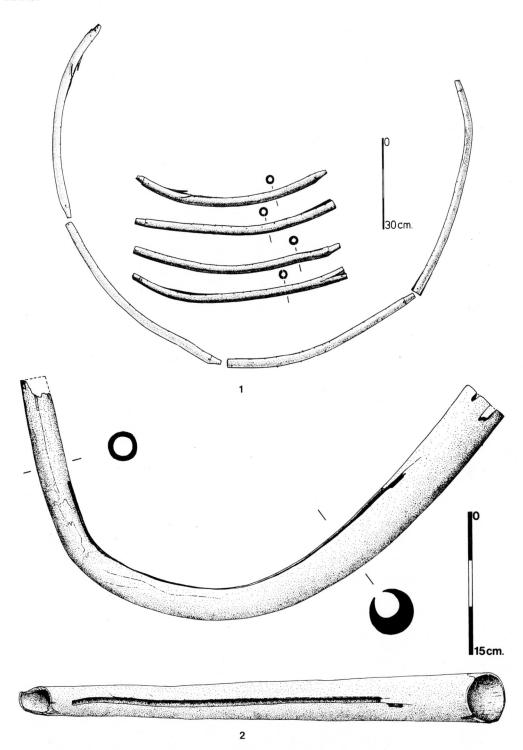

Fig. 76. Wooden horns. 1 Killyfaddy Bog, Clogher, Co. Tyrone.
2 Diamond Hill, Killeshandra, Co. Cavan. – Various scales.

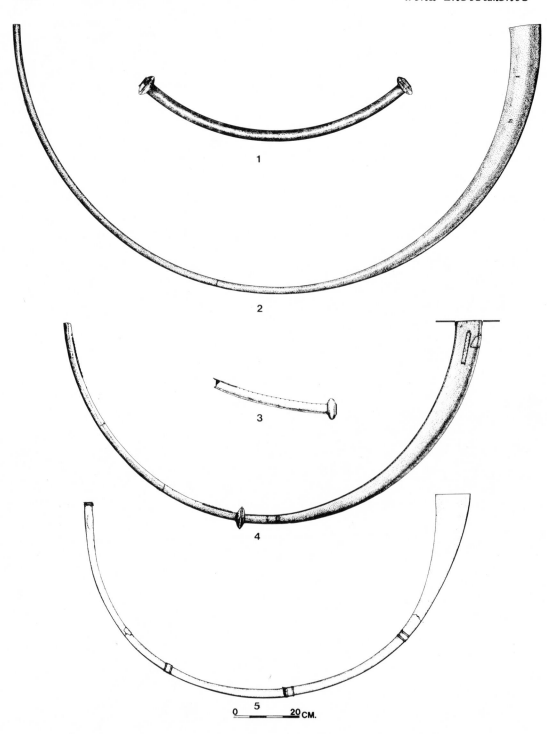

Fig. 77. Bronze horns, comparative diagram. 1 No prov. 2 Ardbrin,
Co. Down. 3 Llyn Cerrig Bach, Anglesey, Wales. 4 Loughnashade, Co.
Armagh. 5 "Nice", France.

diameter; at the bell (which is now somewhat misshapen) the internal axes are 10.5 cm by 9.5 cm. The chord length from the bell to the narrow end is 118.7 cm.

It can be seen, therefore, that close similarities exist between the horn just described and the sheet bronze examples from Ireland. There are, however, significant distinctions in the position of the sealing-strip on the convex surface of the tube of the Nice object and in the means of attaching it to the horn. The nature of the surviving ferrule (or ferrules) is also different on the Nice specimen and the use of four units contrasts with the two-fold composition of the Loughnashade and Ardbrin horns. The unlocalised Irish fragment (Fig. 72:2; Pl. 44) has, however, a boss at each end and in this case the horn of which it was a part was, when complete, formed of at least three units. The wooden horn from Clogher is composed of four sections as in the case of the specimen from Nice. Notwithstanding the technical differences between the horn from Nice and those from Ireland there seem, therefore, to be grounds for suggesting a relationship of some sort between the French piece and the Irish horns.

Unfortunately, the details of the find circumstances of the Nice trumpet are unknown. It was acquired by the Munich museum in 1910 from a dealer and the museum records simply refer to it as a "Gaulish horn from Nizza". The reason for referring to it as "Gaulish" is thus obscure but perhaps in view of the similarity which now emerges between it and the Irish examples it is possible that the "Gaulish" appellation is not spurious but rather indicates for it an Iron Age context. Its date must for the moment, however, be regarded as uncertain, but it remains possible that in horns such as that from Nice can be seen evidence for a direct Continental contribution to the development of the insular series.

PERSONAL ORNAMENT

Safety-pin fibulae

Brooches of Iron Age date are infrequent in Ireland. We can point to only about twenty-six examples of La Tène type and the preceeding Hallstatt period is represented by scarcely half a dozen specimens, most of which could be recent imports to the country (Fig. 78). Only one of these, a Hallstatt D piece, is localised; it is said to be from "somewhere in Co. Dublin" (Fig. 78:3). Otherwise there are no preserved details of provenance or find circumstances. They are thus of uncertain significance in a consideration of the earliest Iron Age in Ireland.

Similarly, there are doubts concerning the only Early La Tène fibula from Ireland, which is recorded as having been found "near Galway" Fig. 79:1). The object is certainly an import, its ultimate homeland being in the northern Alpine regions (cf. Zambotti, 1938, Fig. 236a,b; Jacobsthal, 1944, No. 323; Krämer, 1961, 305-322; Tanner, 1980, Taf. 11:1, 23:17, 24:21, 22). There are no intermediate examples in western Europe, however, so that the integrity of the Galway fibula as a genuine ancient import must be seriously questioned. The western findspot is, however, interesting in view of the presence in the west of the country of other La Tène objects of Continental origin.

Almost all the fibulae from Ireland are of obviously local character so that the increasingly refined typological subdivisions of the La Tène fibula in Europe have only the most generalised relevance for the study of the fibula in Ireland. A few of the Irish examples display features characteristic of Middle or even Early La Tène brooches on the Continent, but it is not certain if the absolute chronology of such fibulae is, of necessity, correspondingly early. The majority of the Irish specimens

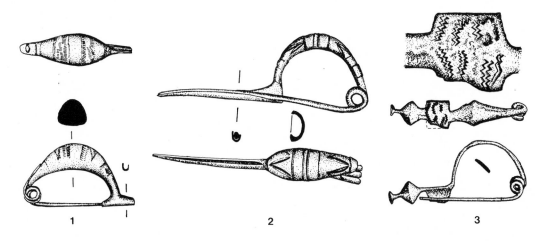

Fig. 78. Irish Hallstatt fibulae. 1,2 no prov. 3 possibly Co. Dublin. - 3/4.

may be considerably later than this. Two principal types occur in the country, those with rod-bows and those with leaf-bows.

There are at least ten fibulae from Ireland with rod-bows and three further examples exist which are too fragmentary for the original nature of the bow to be determined. Bows, where preserved, are flattened or gently curved in profile with the single exception of that of the Clogher Co. Tyrone fibula (Fig. 79:8; Pl. 45) which is pronouncedly arched. All are of bronze, apart from one iron specimen, from Feerwore, Co. Galway (Fig. 79:3); the presence of an internal chord on this example further distinguishes it from the other Irish rod-bow fibulae, all of which have external chords. The Navan Fort, Co. Armagh, piece with its "Middle La Tène" construction and its simple, looped spring (Fig. 79:2), also stands apart from the rest of the Irish series. The fibula from Clogher, Co. Tyrone is an exceptional piece. Apart from its arched bow and elaborate openwork foot, it has elegantly cast, relief trumpet-and-lentoid curves in combination with three circular settings on the bow (presumably for enamel insets), which are also without parallel on any other Irish specimen. Aside from fine milling along the bow of several Irish rod-bow brooches, decoration is otherwise confined to the foot which is sometimes cast, in the form of a bird's head with varying degrees of naturalism. An especially fine example of modelling on a minute scale is the tiny bird's head clearly recognisable on the foot of the Lecarrow, Co. Sligo fibula (Fig. 79:9; Pl. 47:2). On this specimen, on the end of the bow nearest the spring, there are three small, spherical expansions (the "vestigial moulding", see Jope, 1961-2, 30). In three cases, Navan Fort, Co. Armagh

(Fig. 79:2), Aran, Co. Galway (Fig. 79:7) and Lough Gur, Co. Limerick (Fig. 79:6; Ó Ríordáin, 1954, 340) the spring broke away from the bow in antiquity and a new one was riveted in its place.

Eight leaf-bow brooches are known from Ireland (Fig. 80). In profile, the bows of these fibulae tend to flattened or gently curved outline, a feature they share with the rod-bow class; only the Modeenagh piece (Fig. 80:2) has a noticeably arched bow. Bows both hammered and cast are known and these vary in shape from those which are a fairly regular, pointed-oval to those which taper markedly to an almost pointed foot. The leaf-bow of one example (Fig. 80:1) is attenuated, comprising of a small oval element near the spring, the remainder being more or less rod-shaped. Where the two elements of the bow meet on this specimen there are three fine mouldings similar to those already noted on the Lecarrow specimen. This brooch is also interesting in having a secondary spring riveted to the underside of the bow in a manner reminiscent of the repairs on a number of the rod-bow fibulae.

Six of the eight Irish leaf-bow brooches have an external chord with two loose coils. Two unlocalised examples, which resemble each other closely in other details, have an internal chord with five tight twists of the spring (Fig. 80:3,6).

Decoration of some sort occurs on the bow in each instance and it can be seen that there is a considerable amount of uniformity in its treatment. The simplest ornament is a dividing line which runs centrally along the bow of three of the brooches. A slightly more elaborate version of this is a brooch from Navan Fort (Fig. 80:4), in which the central spine expands at each end to form a pair of arcs set back to back, the hourglass-shaped area between being filled with hatching. On the fibula from Bondville, Co. Armgh (Fig. 80:7; Pl. 46:1), the two arcs are disposed in such a way as to form what Jope interpreted as a representation of the wings folded on a bird's back (1961-2, 30, Fig. 6), and the arrangement of the ornament on the Modeenagh brooch (Fig. 80:2; Pl. 46:2) is closely comparable to this, though more stylised and more elaborate. The lines on this specimen are doubled and there is a compass-drawn circle at the end nearest the spring. The Kiltierney, Co. Fermanagh brooch (Fig. 80:8) is unique among the Irish fibulae. Its bow is pierced along its axis by a pointed-oval opening flanked on either side by relief, cast, trumpet curves. The design, however, is evidently a developed version of the simpler engraved and cast ornament on the other leaf bow brooches. There is no decoration on the truncated bow of the unlocalised fibula (Fig. 80:1) already alluded to.

In every instance the foot is cast with the bow and is open apart from the solid catchplate of the Bondville brooch. On one example at least

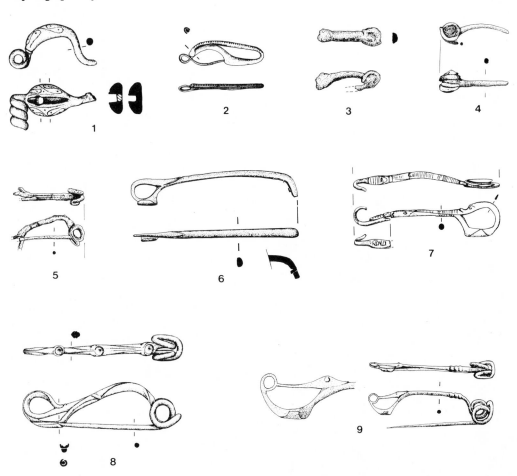

Fig. 79. Irish La Tène Fibulae. 1 near Galway. 2 Navan Fort, Co. Armagh.
3 Feerwore, Co. Galway. 4 Dundrum Sandhills, Co. Down. 5 Grannagh,
Co. Galway. 6 Lough Gur, Co. Limerick. 7 Dun Aengus, Aran, Co. Galway.
8 Clogher, Co. Tyrone. 9 Lecarrow, Co. Sligo. - 1/2.

(Fig. 80:6; Pl. 48:1), a clear bird's-head motif is present and in the case
of an otherwise very similar brooch the foot is cast in what can only
be described as serpentine form (Fig. 80:3; Pl. 48:2). There are three
instances in which the returned foot of the brooch is defective but where
raised, angular elements survive at the original point of junction of foot
and bow (Fig. 80:4,5,8); these could indicate the former presence of stylised
bird- or serpent-head forms.

There are two Irish examples of the late, Nauheim-derivative form
of brooch, one from Derrybeg, Lough Gara, Co. Sligo (Raftery, J., 1973,
204; Fig. 81:1), the other from "Loughey", Co. Down (Jope and Wilson,
1957, 73-95; Fig. 81:2). A fragment from Castleskreen, Co. Down, may

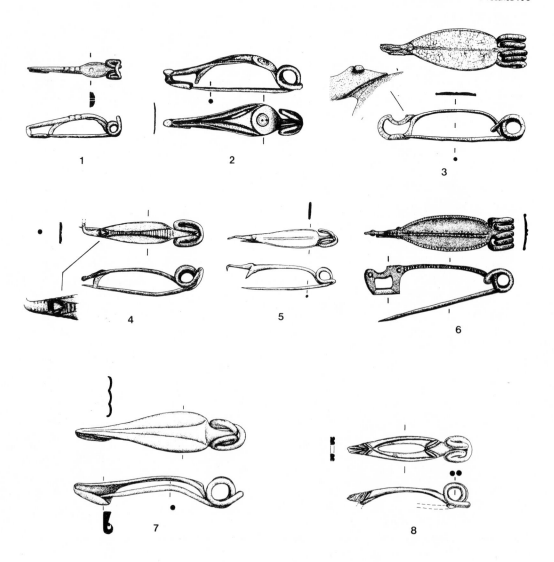

Fig. 80. Irish La Tène leaf-bow fibulae. 1,3,6 no prov. 2 Modeenagh,
Co. Fermanagh. 4 Navan Fort, Co. Armagh. 5 Kells, Co. Meath.
7 Bondville, Co. Armagh. 8 Kiltierney, Co. Fermanagh. - 1/2.

be, but is not certainly, a third example (Dickinson and Waterman, 1960,
71, Fig. 5:4). Finally, there is one brooch of "Colchester" type recorded
from Ireland (Fig. 81:3), a typical specimen with openwork catchplate
and separately-made spring hooked to the front of the bow. The bow
is hexagonal in section, with a series of incised transverse lines on its
underside.

Affinities and chronology

A recurring feature of many of the surviving Irish fibulae (both of rod-bow and leaf-bow form) is their flattened profile, brought about by bows which are more or less parallel to the pin. Flattened-bow brooches are also known in Britain. Those closest in appearance to the Irish examples are found in Wessex for this is the only area in Britain where such fibulae, in common with those in Ireland, lack foot-discs. Both Jope (1961-2, 26) and Hawkes (1982, 53) regarded the flattened-bow brooches of south-west Britain as providing prototypes for the Irish group. Hawkes, in fact, considered these fibulae as representing a Belgic invasion of Ireland, one which "succeeded .... in implanting the culture of La Tène" in the country (op. cit., 71). The latter view is difficult to sustain, especially when the small number and the exclusively native character of the Irish fibulae are taken into account. Influence from the south-west of England on the development of the Irish fibula is, however, likely, although this can only be taken as demonstrated fact when the Irish fibulae are shown by independent dating evidence to postdate the relevant series in Britain. There is, however, other evidence to indicate contact between the two areas (below p. 333). Hawkes too has drawn attention to a fibula from Somerset (op. cit., Fig. 6:4) which might, in fact, be of Irish manufacture and south-west English elements seem also detectable on some of the Irish ringheaded pins (below p. 167).

Hawkes, in a detailed reassessment of the chronolgy of the flattened bow brooches in Britain (op. cit., 53-7), has pointed to the Middle La Tène influences in their composition and, in keeping with the current back-dating of this phase in Europe, has suggested a date in the third century B.C. for the earliest flattened-bow brooches in Britain. With regard to the appearance of the flattened-bow brooch in Ireland, he noted the absence in that country of the involuted brooch, an exclusively English variant which developed from the flattened-bow group. Thus he concluded that the flattened-bow must have been adopted in Ireland before the invention of the involuted version, and accordingly he postulated a date for the commencement of the Irish series within the third century B.C.

Hawkes' arguments are plausibly put but confirmation of such an early dating for the Irish fibulae must await the discovery of significantly associated examples. There are, however, other features of the Irish fibulae which may reflect early traditions. Both Jope and Hawkes recognised the ultimately Early La Tène background to the leaf-bow brooch in Ireland. For Jope this indicated archaism, a feature "introduced early, while .... in current practise on the Continent" demonstrating in Ireland "a long-lived continuity of craft tradition" (op. cit., 31). Hawkes stressed the horizontal foot of the Irish leaf-bow brooches as a factor distinguishing the Irish from the Continental pieces, and preferred British leaf-bows with comparable horizontal feet as the immediate prototypes for the Irish series.

But if an early date for the Irish fibulae is regarded as not unreasonable, then the possibility of directly Continental influence on the native development must be seriously taken into account. Two brooches in particular are important in this context, both unfortunately without provenance (Fig. 80:3,6).   These seem especially close in many details to fibulae of the European La Tène B1/B2 Dux horizon (Kruta, 1971; 1979) which are found across Europe from Bohemia to the Marne (e.g. Viollier, 1916, Pl. 4:160-165; Filip, 1956, Obr. 26:11,13,15; Hodson, 1968, Pl. 27:830; Bretz-Mahler, 1971, Pl. 15:4,5; Kruta, 1979, Figs 16:2, 17:1). Particularly significant is the internal chord which these two fibulae possess for this is absent on the British leaf-bow specimens but well represented on the Continental fibulae of Dux type. Hawkes noted this feature but took the horizontal foot of the Irish examples, as significant concluding that ".... an Irish internal chord need not have been borrowed directly from the Continent: but if it was, then the leaf-bow and foot that it was mated with were British" (op. cit., 53). An early Continental element in the Irish leaf-bow brooches remains, however, possible.

The bird's head foot, not infrequent both on rod and leaf-bow brooches in Ireland, is a further detail which calls to mind Early La Tène, Continental parallels (e.g. Jacobsthal, 1944, Nos. 289, 292, 298) and it should not be forgotten that, of the two potentially early examples with internal chords just referred to, one has a cast bird's head foot (Pl. 48:1); the other appears to have a snake's head foot. We do not know, however, to what extent the bird's head foot in Ireland is indicative of early influences, for this motif is found on undoubtedly late metalwork. Moreover, the bird's head on the Lecarrow brooch (Pl. 47:2) can hardly date to the Early La Tène period for Jope is surely right in regarding the vestigial moulding on the bow as a relic of the Middle La Tène binding of the foot to the bow. The Lecarrow specimen can thus hardly date earlier than an advanced stage of the Middle La Tène phase. The moulding on it, indeed, can be exactly paralleled on fibulae of Late La Tène date such as those from Grave 14, Hoppstädten, Kr. Birkenfeld in Germany (Werner, 1955, Abb. 7).

While in most cases the dating of Irish fibulae is wholly dependent on typological considerations a number has been found in contexts which allow the possibility of independent dating. A ring-barrow at Grannagh, Co. Galway, for example, yielded the remains of at least three rod-bow brooches as well as a range of beads of bone and glass and some other

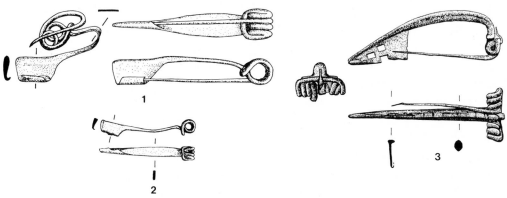

Fig. 81. Irish imported fibulae. 1 Derrybeg, Co. Sligo. 2 "Loughey",
Co. Down. 3 no prov. - 1/2.

items (below p. 200; Raftery, 1982, 195-7; Hawkes, op.cit., 60-61). The
date of deposition seems to have been the last century B.C. or the
beginning of the Christian era. The splendid specimen from Kiltierney,
Co. Fermanagh (Fig. 80:8) was found with glass beads for which a date
in the last century or so B.C. could be argued (below p. 202; Raftery,
op. cit., 196; Hawkes, op. cit., 63-64). The Co. Fermanagh specimen
is especially important in discussing the Irish Navan-type brooches, for
there can be no doubt that it is intimately related to them in form and
ornament (see below p.155). The iron fibula from Feerwore, Co. Galway
(Fig.79:3) came from an occupation level which also contained an iron
axehead with rectangular-sectioned socket (Fig. 118:4). The excavator
suggested a date in the first century B.C. for the fibula (Raftery, J.,
1944, 41-2), and this does not conflict with the likely dating of the axehead
(below p. 240). Both objects could well be of Continental manufacture.
Finally, from a probable cremation grave at "Loughey", Co. Down (the
correct locality is unknown), comes a fibula of the well-known Nauheim-
derivative type, found in association with a necklace of glass beads,
two bracelets of the same material and a number of personal items of
bronze (below p. 201 ; Jope and Wilson, 1957; Hawkes, op. cit., 59; Raftery,
op. cit., 195). The assemblage is foreign and Jope and Wilson have argued
convincingly in favour of a southern English origin for the lady buried
at the Co. Down site. It is possible, however, that the first century
A.D. dating put forward by them should be revised slightly due to the
back-dating of the Nauheim fibula on the Continent (Müller-Beck and
Ettlinger, 1962-3, 43-4; Radford in Bersu, 1977, 63, fn. 2; see also Hawkes,
op. cit., 59), but the date of the Loughey burial need not be substantially
older than that suggested a quarter of a century ago by Jope and Wilson.
The Derrybeg specimen (Fig. 81:1), larger and more robust than that
from Loughey, belongs to the same family as the Co. Down fibula and

it too is likely to be an import.

Finally, there is a small number of unassociated fibulae which stand apart from the main Irish series. That from Navan Fort, Co. Armagh (an old find), is the only Irish example displaying true Middle La Tène construction with foot wrapped around bow (Fig. 79:2). In absolute date, however, the object may substantially postdate the classic Middle La Tène of Europe for it belongs to a class of brooches sometimes referred to as "pseudo La Tène II" (Fauduet, 1979, 239), which date to the last century B.C. and the first Christian century (Thomas, 1968, 464; Maier, 1973, 473). Jope sought Scottish parallels for the Irish object (1961-2, 26), a good comparison coming from Craig's Quarry fort (Piggott, 1958, 61-77). A date just after or shortly before the birth of Christ is likely for the Navan fibula. The object is probably of local manufacture.

Another fibula, perhaps the masterpiece of the Irish brooch-makers, is the example from Clogher, Co. Tyrone (Fig. 79:8; Pl. 45) for which there are, unfortunately, no recorded details of find circumstances. This dress-fastener is obviously unaffected by the insular, flattened-bow tradition and in its arched profile and sloping foot could well reflect Continental inspiration (e.g. Viollier, 1916, Pl. 1:34; Hodson, 1968, Pl. 55:428). Indeed, the elaborate foot arrangement of the object looks for all the world like an Early La Tène fibula with attached loop. The three circular settings on the bow can also be paralleled in Europe (e.g. Filip, 1956, Abb. 33:4,6). The trumpet-and-lentoid ornament on the bow, however, indicates its native character and the Clogher ornament might most appropriately be compared with that on the gold collar from Broighter, Co. Derry (Fig. 96; below p. 187). The collar dates to the last century B.C. and the fibula might also date to the same century. Hawkes has, however, suggested a somewhat earlier date for it (op. cit., 56).

The unlocalised "Colchester-type" fibula is of great potential importance for it is a Belgic type dating to the end of the last century B.C., and found widely in both Britain and the Continent (e.g. Wheeler, 1943, 258, Fig. 83:14; Haffner, 1971, 106, Fig. 2:5,6). However, in the absence of information concerning find circumstances, the significance of the object for the Irish Iron Age must be considered with caution.

Summary

The number of safety-pin fibulae in Ireland is small and the earliest dating for the introduction of the type to the country is uncertain. This could have been in the third century B.C. and some might reflect influences of Early La Tène, Continental derivation. Flattened-bow brooches have their closest counterparts in the south-west of England, however, and influences from there could have inspired the Irish development. Apart from a few late examples, the great majority of Irish fibulae are of native manufacture.

Navan-type Brooches

There are five dress-fasteners of so-called Navan-type recorded from Ireland. The name derives from the fact that two of the five (not three, as both Jope and Hawkes state), including the finest example, come from Navan Fort, Co. Armagh.

These brooches are a uniquely Irish development characterised by open-work bows bearing raised, finely-cast trumpet and lentoid-boss decoration (Fig. 82; Pls 49-52). On one of the Navan Fort specimens delicate stippling sets off the raised trumpet curves (Fig. 82:2; Pls 49, 50). The same brooch possesses at the centre of the bow a shallow, empty setting from the centre of which a knob-headed rivet projects; this must once have held a stud of red enamel. On a brooch from the metalworker's hoard at Somerset, Co. Galway (Fig. 82:1; Pl. 51:1), a comparable circular setting adorns the centre of the bow, but in this instance the enamel was applied in the champlevé technique. The Somerset brooch resembles closely the Navan brooch in general shape but differs from it, and from the other Navan-type specimens, in having a circular, enamelled disc similar to the one which decorates the bow, at each of the three extremities.

These two are the most elaborate of the Navan-type brooches. The smaller of the two from Navan Fort (Fig. 82:5; Pl. 52:1) and one from the sandhills at Dunfanaghy, Co. Donegal (Fig. 82:4; Pl. 52:1), resemble each other closely and represent simpler versions of the type. There is somewhat less emphasis on the trumpet patterns on these examples and the oval opening which in each instance longitudinally pierces the bow, is without the circular decorative setting present on the two larger brooches. The fifth example of the group is unlocalised. The object (Fig. 82:3; Pl. 52:2), with its openwork bow, its raised trumpet curves and its snout-like end clearly belongs to the class in question. In one important detail, however, it differs from the other four Navan-type brooches. These last had the pin attached to the back of the bow by means of a ball-socket mechanism. The present unlocalised piece does not have this feature. Instead a hollow, imitation spring, through which a narrow rod of bronze was inserted, has been cast at the wider end of the brooch. This rod passes through the expanded, perforated head of the functional pin which is thus attached to the rear of the brooch at a point midway along the pseudo-spring.

In the form of these brooches it is possible, perhaps, to recognise a stylised bovine representation. The smaller of the Navan Fort brooches in particular (Fig. 82:5; Pl. 52:1), with its upturned "snout" and prominent "ears", could be construed in such a manner. The suggestion of a possible zoomorphic content in the shape of these brooches is, of course, entirely subjective, but it seems preferable to the alleged sexual symbolism with which Duval imbued the distinctive form of these Irish objects (1977, 228).

Affinities and Chronology

Of the five extant examples only the Somerset, Co. Galway, specimen comes from a reliable context. The two brooches said to have come from Navan Fort were found in the last century and no details of find circumstances are recorded. At Somerset, however, the associated objects are of great importance in establishing the cultural and chronological context of the Navan-type brooches.

Along with the brooch at Somerset were found five decorative bronze mounts, a cake and an ingot of bronze, a finely-cast, bird's-head cup-handle of the same material and a ribbon torc of hammered gold (Raftery, J., 1960, 2-5; 1961, 93, Fig. 24). A number of other objects of bronze and iron from the hoard unfortunately never found their way to the National Museum.

The most useful chronological indicator from the hoard is the bird's-head cup-handle (Fig. 107:2), for its affinities with the handle on the much-discussed Keshcarrigan, Co. Leitrim, cup (Fig. 107:1; Pl. 69) are obvious and it must surely be contemporary with it. The Keshcarrigan cup belongs to a small but significant group of Irish bronze containers which are considered at some length below (p. 214). Though displaying technical and stylistic affinities with comparable vessels in southern and northern parts of Britain, the Irish examples of the group are here regarded as essentially a native version of the type. A date for them in the last century B.C. and in the first century A.D. is likely. Such a dating range is appropriate for the Somerset brooch with its profusion of trumpet and lentoid-boss motifs and this is the context in which the Navan-type brooches as a class may be placed.

Brooches of Navan-type are clearly a tightly-knit group, products of closely related, contemporary workshops. The larger of the Navan Fort brooches, though geographically distant from the Somerset example, is closely similar to the Galway piece in details of form and decoration and the interrelationship is further emphasised by comparing the fine

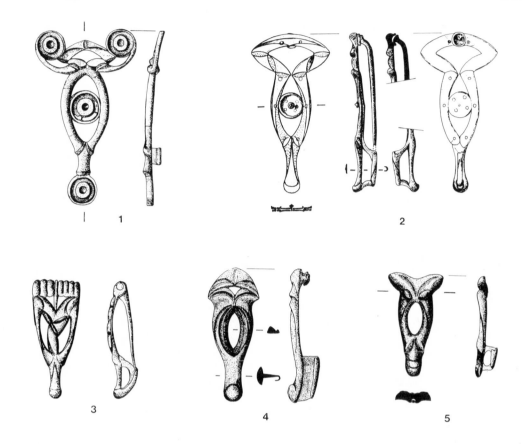

Fig. 82. Navan-type brooches. 1 Somerset, Co. Galway. 2,5 Navan Fort,
Co. Armagh. 3 no prov. 4 Dunfanaghy, Co. Donegal. - 1/2.

stippling on the same Navan brooch with that again encountered on one
of the mounts from the Somerset hoard (Fig. 140:2). It is also interesting
that Navan Fort itself produced a cylindrical mount of the same type
(Fig. 140:7)as are present at Somerset (unfortunately again an old find),
and it may be that at Navan, as at Somerset, the brooches and the mount
were associated.

These dress-fasteners are a distinctly Irish development emphasising
the ingenuity and inventiveness of native bronzesmiths. Underlining
this originality is the ball-socket mechanism present on four examples
of the group, for this technique seems unknown elsewhere at this period.
The workshops did not practise in isolation. Stippled decoration and
trumpet-and-lentoid-boss ornament are features shared with a wide range
of contemporary native bronzes. Of these, the most striking is the
Kiltierney fibula (Fig. 80:8; above, p. 151), which, in form and ornament,
demonstrates clear overlap between the centres producing Navan-type

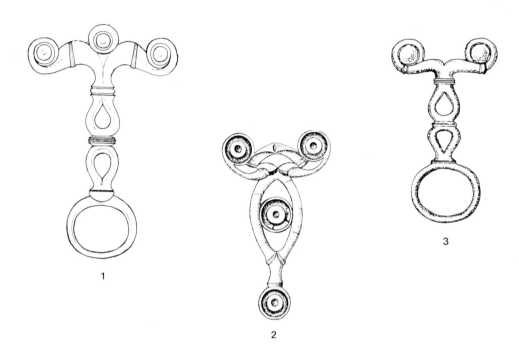

Fig. 83. Somerset brooch (2) and comparisons. 1 bronze mirror handle, Great Chesterford, Essex, England. 3 bronze mirror handle, Colchester, Essex, England. - Various scales.

brooches and those responsible for the leaf-bow fibulae. Indeed, the distinctive form of the Navan-type brooches may have been influenced by fibulae, such as that from Kiltierney.

Jope, however, sought a different source for the shape and ornament of the Navan-type brooches (1961-2, 36). He pointed to the similarity in form between them and the divided-bow brooches of provincial Rome and he also drew attention to the numerous openwork bronze buckles, mounts and clasps which are characterised by profuse trumpet ornamentation and which are widely scattered throughout the far-flung Roman empire in the early centuries of Christianity. Superficial similarities are indeed evident between the Irish and the Roman bronzes but the chronological relationship between the two groups is not, perhaps, entirely clear and the likelihood that the Irish brooches are earlier than the Roman bronzes must be taken into consideration. It is important also to bear in mind that the trumpet-ornamented openwork bronzes of provincial Rome are themselves, in all probability, products of Celtic workmanship (von Jenny, 1935; Oldenstein, 1976, 203-7; MacGregor, 1976, 186-9), so that the similarities between them and the Irish bronzes need be no more than a reflection of common roots.

Hawkes too, in his recent discussion of the fibula in Ireland, rejects any influence from the Roman bronzes on the development of the Navan-type brooch and dates these objects to the last half century B.C. and the first century A.D. (1982, 62-3).

Another possible source of external influence on the form of the Irish brooches is conceivably to be sought in the openwork arrangement of some of the southern English mirror handles. Examples from Great Chesterford (Fox, 1960, 207-210, Fig. 1) and Colchester (Fox, 1958, Fig. 66:1) for instance, possess handles the form of which resembles closely that of the Somerset brooch (Fig. 83). Though the objects differ substantially in size, the analogy seems clear and it may be significant that the Colchester mirror came from a burial which produced a handled bronze bowl (Fig. 110:4; Pl. 71; Fox, ibid., Fig. 58), the closest insular parallel for which is the Keshcarrigan cup (below p. 218). The Keshcarrigan cup, of course, leads directly to the Somerset bird's-head handle. Thus, it is possible that the Colchester-type mirror handles may supply one element in the genesis of the Irish Navan-type brooches and the suggested dating for the Colchester burial early in the first century A.D. (Fox, ibid., 92-93) does not conflict with what has been suggested above regarding the chronology of these brooches.

Ringheaded pins

There are at least 36 recorded ringheaded pins from Ireland and several other specimens exist which may belong to, or be related to, the ringheaded pin group. Several additional pins found in Britain may legitimately be regarded as exports to that country from Ireland (see below). Three pins of the earlier swan's-neck type are also known from Ireland (Fig. 5).

It is possible to isolate, for the purposes of discussion, four main groups of Irish ringheaded pins. Dividing lines between the types are not, however, always rigid, as there are substantial areas of typological and technological overlap between the various categories.

Type 1: Some 13 examples are grouped together here to form a somewhat heterogeneous collection of pins (Fig. 84; Pl. 53:1,2). There is no reason to believe that all are necessarily contemporary. The main criterion for inclusion in this group is the presence of a simple, circular head – usually annular – and a long, straight shank tapering to a sharp point. The pin is normally cast. One example from Co. Antrim, now in the United States, is of bent wire (Fig. 84:6). Another specimen, the whereabouts of which are now unknown (Fig. 84:5), may also be of bent wire.

Included in this group is a pin from Co. Antrim (whereabouts also unknown), which has a decidedly S-shaped shank (Fig. 84:7). The unique Bawnboy, Co. Cavan pin with cast, penannular head (Fig. 84:4) is also included here.

Internal ring diameters vary from as little as 3 mm to as much as 4.9 cm. On this account it is possible that the four pins with ringheads greater than 3.5 cm in internal diameter could be set apart as a separate sub-group. Rings are most often undecorated but ribbing, hatching or dotting occurs. In two instances the ring is adorned with three cast, spherical knobs (Fig. 84:3; Pl. 53:1) and the Bawnboy piece has a variation of this in the form of cylindrical elements which project from the front and side of the ringhead. The convex outer surface of the shoulder of these pins is usually unadorned apart from minor projecting elements, which occur in three instances, and a shallow concavity which occurs on the shoulder of one specimen. The surviving rivet in the shoulder of an example from Co. Antrim (Fig. 84:1) suggests the former presence of a setting of some sort here and this may also have been the case on another unlocalised pin.

Type 2: Seven specimens are included in this group (Fig. 85:1-6; Pls 53:4; 54; 56:1). The distinctive feature is the cast relief decoration on the ringhead; it consists of spiral bosses joined by curved lines. The opening of the ring is quite small, being generally 5 mm to 8 mm in internal diameter. Sometimes the raised ornament on the head gives the impression of a grotesque animal head (Fig. 85:4) or even a bird head (Fig. 85:6), but it is unclear if this is deliberate or accidental. A setting for a red enamel inlay, or a decorative bronze stud, was riveted in each case to the convex surface of the shoulder, which is usually worked to a flat plane to receive the attachment. The shank is straight and usually tapers to a sharp point.

Type 3: This group comprises 10 specimens (Fig. 86; Pls 55; 56: 2,3). Although some variety is present they are clearly linked by the decoration on the ringhead. This expands to the front of the pin as it curves towards the shoulder, gradually acquiring a U-shaped or V-shaped section. This provides a setting to which an enamel stud was originally riveted. Such studs are preserved in two instances (Fig. 86:3,4; Pl. 55). The shoulder at the front of these pins also held a decorative setting. This is sometimes a separate unit independent of the setting on the ring (e.g. Fig. 86:3,5), but sometimes the settings coalesce to form a single "keyhole-shaped" inset for the enamel studs (e.g. Fig. 86:2,8). The shank of the pin is either straight or curved gently to the front and usually bears several convex

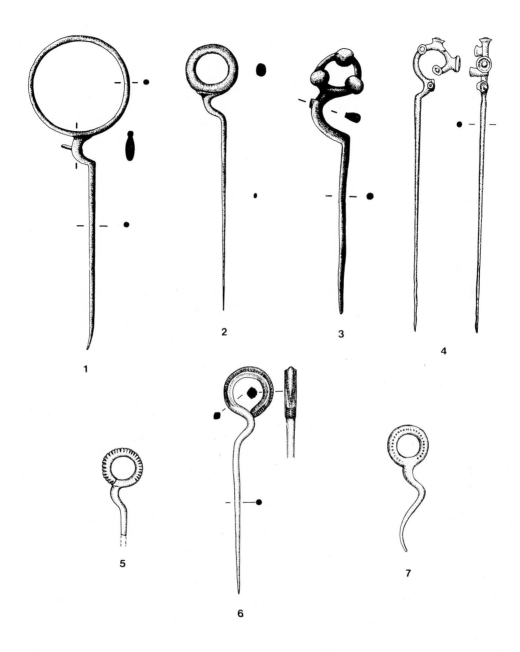

Fig. 84. Irish Type 1 ringheaded pins. 1, 5-7 Co. Antrim. 2,3 no prov.
4 Bawnboy, Co. Cavan. - 1/2.

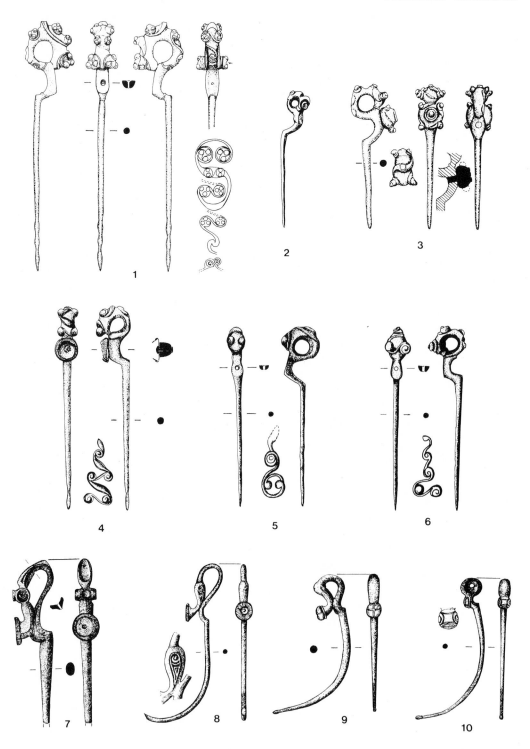

Fig. 85. Ringheaded pins. 1-6 Type 2. 7-10 Type 4. 1,3,5 no prov. 2 Coll,
Scotland. 4 Grange, Co. Sligo. 6 Athlone, Co. Westmeath. 7 no prov.
8-10 River Shannon. - 1/2.

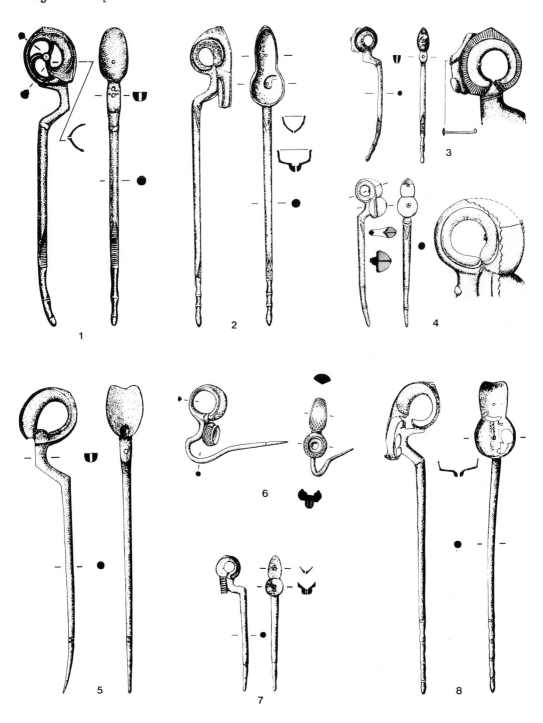

Fig. 86. Irish Type 3 ringheaded pins. 1,5,7,8 no prov. 2 Roscavey, Co. Tyrone. 3,4 Lisnacrogher, Co. Antrim. 6 Clough, Co. Antrim. – 1/2.

mouldings near the tip; the latter is, in most instances, rounded to a somewhat bulbous point. Triangular areas of hatching may occur below the shoulder, above the mouldings at the end of the pin-shank or at the back of the head. The head of the Clough, Co. Antrim, pin (Fig. 86:6; Pl. 56:3) has a distinctly skeuomorphic appearance. Its form is undoubtedly based on the appearance of a ringhead with its original setting in situ. The fragmentary example (Fig. 85:7) shares with Type 3 the concave ringhead but is included in Type 4 because of the S-shaped curve of the head. This piece, however, indicates clear interaction between Types 2 and 4.

Type 4: Seven pins are included in this group (Fig. 85:7-10; Pls 57, 58). The main features are the extreme forward curvature of the pin and the generally S-shaped or swan's-neck head joining with a sharp shoulder. Two of the four complete pins have rounded, bulbous points (Fig. 85:9, 10), a detail linking them, perhaps, to Type 3 pins; the other two have deliberately blunted tips. In three examples where a definite bird's-head form can be detected (Fig. 85:7-9; Pl. 57), the end of the "beak" is adorned with a circular disc. The fourth pin (Fig. 85:10), which has a simple, narrow ring and a cast bronze hemispherical setting on its shoulder, would be included in Type 1 but for the curvature of the pin and the moulding at its end. The concave setting on the ring of an unlocalised pin (Fig. 85:7) has been compared above to the pins of Type 3 and the cylindrical projections on the same pin are reminiscent of similar elements on the Type 1 Bawnboy pin (Fig. 84:4). Again, technical overlap between the various types is indicated.

The Beaghmore pin is quite distinct from the other six examples in this group but is included here because of the S-shaped head and the sharply curved shank (Pl. 58). A sixth example, in the Armagh Museum (CIIAA No. 431), has a straight shank but its cruciform projection seems most closely compared to the Beaghmore object, and it is possible to detect in the profile of the head and the position of the cruciform casting an echo of the bird's-head form typical of the other pins of this group. Its inclusion here is, however, somewhat arbitrary as is the inclusion of a superficially similar pin from Co. Waterford (CIIAA No. 429).

Affinities and Chronology

Ringheaded pins have been recognised as a well-known Iron Age type since they were first studied systematically by Smith in the early part of the twentieth century (Smith, 1913). Later, a more detailed typological study by Dunning (1934) brought together most of the insular pins then known and his paper remains basic to a study of the British and Irish

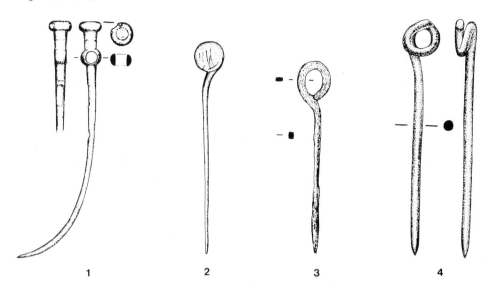

Fig. 87. Miscellaneous Irish pins. 1 Tullamore, Co. Offaly. 2 Newtown-ards, Co. Down. 3 Dunbell, Co. Kilkenny. 4 Drumbo, Co. Monaghan. - 1/2.

groups.

Dunning viewed the ringheaded pins as an insular development deriving ultimately from the iron Continental swan's-neck pin of Hallstatt origin. A handful of swan's-neck pins in Britain was considered by him as providing the immediate stimulus and his earliest ringheaded pins, those with penannular heads bent from iron or bronze wire, were seen as deriving from these in the fourth century B.C. They then developed in the third century, according to Dunning, into cast ringheads after which a series of local variants followed in succeeding centuries. Stead, however, pointed to possible Continental Early La Tène prototypes for the insular series, and wondered whether one element in the genesis of the type might not be sought there (1965, 57-9). Duval pondered on the possibility that in form the insular ringheaded pins could owe something to the safety-pin fibulae (1977, 228-30). In this context, the unique pin from Drumbo, Co. Monaghan (Fig. 87:4) could be taken to represent a hybrid transitional piece between the springed fibula and the true ringheaded pin. The date of this Monaghan specimen is, however, unknown.

There can be no doubt, at any rate, that close similarities exist between a number of the pins in Ireland and their counterparts in Britain, and it is evident that the workshops which produced them in the two islands were in close contact with one another. It is possible, as Dunning suggested, that the earliest ringheaded pins in Ireland were inspired by

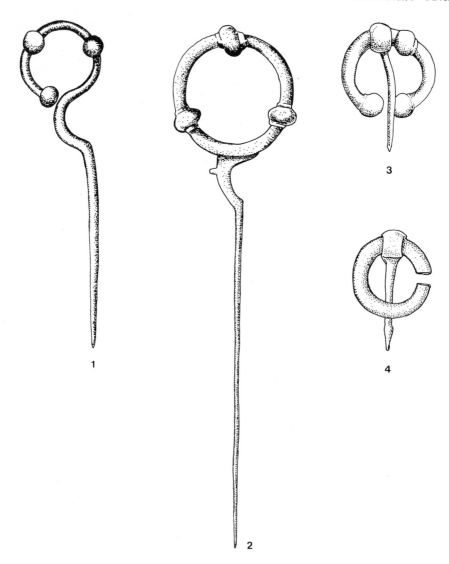

Fig. 88. English pins and brooches. 1,3 Sawdon, Yorkshire. 2 Ham hill,
Somerset. 4 Bridlington, Yorkshire. - 1/1.

prototypes from the neighbouring island but the matter of origins is
complicated, inevitably, by the absence of a precise chronology.

We cannot say when ringheaded pins first came to be made in Ireland.
A number of earlier Hallstatt-type pins have already been adverted to
(Fig. 5) though it cannot be stated if these had any influence on the native
development of the ringheaded series. There is, too, a straight-shanked
pin of iron from Dunbell, Co. Kilkenny (Fig. 87:3) and a similar one of
bronze from Lough Ravel, Co. Antrim (Knowles, 1904,52, Fig. 2; CIIAA

No. 432), which have been bent to provide, in each case, a simple, circular head.   These could conceivably constitute an early form of ringheaded pin in the country but they lack the distinctive shoulder which is a characteristic of the type, so that the typological position of these examples is unclear.   Their date is unknown and the form is simple. Nonetheless, it is perhaps worth drawing attention to the almost identical pins of iron from eastern Germany which date between the fifth and the third centuries B.C. (Heiligendorf and Paulus, 1965, 40, 65, Taf. 29:143; Schwantes, 1911, 110, Taf. 18:4).

A number of pins of our Irish Type 1 are closely matched by pins in Britain and some, indeed, could have been imported from that country to Ireland.   The chronology of the relevant British examples thus has important implications for Ireland where objective dating evidence is virtually non-existent.

The most obvious instance of contact with Britain is represented by the two Irish knob-ringed specimens (Fig. 84:3; Pl. 53:1).   These are clearly related to a similar pin from Sawdon in Yorkshire (Fig. 88:2; Stead, 1965, Fig. 32; 1979, Fig. 30:2) which, though larger than the Irish examples, not only has the three cast spheres on the ring, but also the small, projecting cylindrical element on the shoulder as on the Irish pins. In addition, there is a moulding at the junction of ring and shoulder on the Sawdon pin, which is a standard feature on the majority of Irish pins. In Dunning's typology, the Sawdon pin is a development of the bent wire pin from Ham Hill in Somerset, the penannular head of which is also adorned with three distinctive bosses (Fig. 88:1; Dunning, 1934, 275, Fig. 3:7).   If his typological progression is correct (as seems the case, since most of the cast pins retain in the form of the head the memory of a wire bent on itself) then the British bent-wire specimen from Ham Hill should indeed be the earliest, with Sawdon and the Irish variants a development from it.

The precise chronological position of the Sawdon pin is not securely established for Dunning's dates are, to a large extent, arbitrary. He included it in his third century B.C. development (deriving from the allegedly fourth century B.C. Ham Hill type).   Hawkes was more specific in viewing it as belonging to his "East Second B" horizon, i.e. second half of the third century to first half of the second century B.C. (Hawkes, 1958, 13-14).   Stead regarded the Sawdon pin (which is an old find coming, perhaps, from a destroyed cart burial) as being contemporary with the flattened-bow brooch from the same parish and he included it in his chronological phase "Arras/Danes Graves/Eastburn". This, he says, "is unlikely to be earlier than the second and much of it probably belongs to the first century B.C."   He admits, however, that any date for this

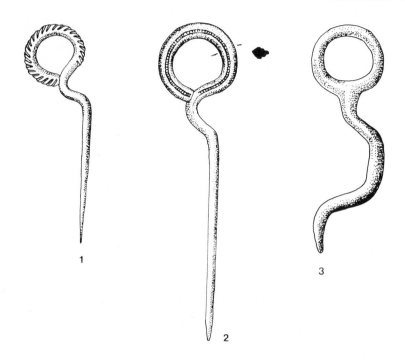

Fig. 89. English ringheaded pins. 1 River Thames. 2 Little Solsbury, Somerset. 3 Cold Kitchen Hill, Wiltshire. - 1/1.

phase must be "extremely vague" (1965, 82).

From the Sawdon parish comes a penannular brooch which bears the same triple boss decoration on its ring as occurs on the pins under discussion (Fig. 88:3). Fowler, in her consideration of the British penannular brooches (1960, 155), suggests that this Sawdon example may be associated with the La Tène II brooch (referred to above) which she says "can be put somewhere after 250 B.C." Such an association is, of course, entirely hypothetical. She does, however, compare the Sawdon brooch to one from Bridlington (Fig. 88:4; ibid., 155), one of a pair which were found in a burial associated with a La Tène II fibula. The moulded tip of the Bridlington brooch is also compared by her to the moulded ends of some British ringheaded pins of "involuted" type (see below). She concludes that these penannular brooches developed in Britain in the second quarter of the third century B.C. and accepts Dunning's third century date for the Sawdon ringheaded pin. She writes that ".... the remarkably close correspondence between the Sawdon ring-head pin and the unassociated Sawdon penannular seems more than a coincidence" (op. cit., 156). The involuted ringheaded pins (see below) are also taken by her as belonging to the third century B.C.

There are, therefore, some grounds for regarding the Sawdon ringheaded pin as a product of the third or early second century B.C. and its immediate background is likely to be in southern England. The Irish knob-ringed pins cannot be far removed in time from those in Britain and must be seen as either imports from that country or local imitations of the British type.

There are several other pins of the Irish Type 1 which have close parallels in Britain. The fragmentary example with the penannular, ribbed ring from Co. Antrim (Fig. 84:5) is strongly reminiscent of one of the pins from the River Thames at Hammersmith (Fig. 89:1; Dunning, 1934, Fig. 3:5; Brailsford, 1953, 64 and Fig. 24:7), while the hatching on the returned end of the penannular ring of another Co. Antrim specimen (Fig. 84:6), calls forcibly to mind such British wire examples as one from Meare in Somerset (Dunning, 1934, Fig. 3:4 and Fig. 4:11). This same Irish pin is also very like a pin from Little Solsbury Hill in Somerset (Fig. 89:2; Dunning, 1934, Fig. 3:6). The resemblance is striking not only in size and overall shape, but also in the sub-trapezoidal section of its penannular ring and the fine beading on it which is clearly echoed on the Irish piece by the disposition of the dotting on each face.

A further Irish pin of undoubted British type is the Co. Antrim piece with the S-shaped shank (Fig. 84:7). This seems to be a version of a small group of pins found mainly in the Oxfordshire/Somerset region of Britain but occurring also in Dorset (e.g. Maiden Castle: Wheeler, 1943, 270, Fig. 87:7) "which show a tendency for the bent shoulder to move down the stem of the pin, the better to secure it in the clothes" (Dunning, 1934, 276). Closest to the Irish example is the cast bronze pin from Cold Kitchen Hill, Wiltshire (Fig. 89:3; Dunning, 1934, Fig. 4:13). This development is considered by Dunning to be a third/second century B.C. phenomenon but the Maiden Castle pin was found in a pit with bead-rim pottery of a type which suggested to the excavator a date in the "first quarter of the first century A.D." for the pin (Wheeler, 1943, 270). The life span of these pins could thus have covered centuries so that the chronological position of the Irish example is uncertain. Its presence in Ireland seems, however, to indicate further links with south-west England.

The other pins of our Type 1 represent for the most part a more obviously native development. Those with exceptionally large rings and examples such as those from Bawnboy and Carnfinton, Co. Antrim, (CIIAA No. 394; Wood-Martin, 1904, 13, Fig. 3:6), have no close parallel outside the country. The unlocalised pin illustrated as Pl. 53:2 is unlike anything abroad apart from the comparable hourglass-shaped ring perforation in such Scottish examples as a pin from Dunagoil (Dunning,

1934, Fig. 7:6) or, in imperforate form, on a pin from Traprain Law (ibid., Fig. 7:8).

Precise dating for the Irish Type 1 pins is thus vague. They could begin in the third or early second century B.C. but it is quite possible that some pins of the group were being made even after the birth of Christ. Their predominantly Antrim distribution is interesting and there can be little doubt that an important manufacturing centre existed somewhere in that county.

The whereabouts of the pin from Newtownards, Co. Down, are now unknown (Fig. 87:2). The only record of its original appearance is the photograph and sketch in the files of the National Museum of Ireland, and in neither instance is the nature of the alleged "La Tène decoration", stated to have been on the head, visible. It may, however, be worthwhile in this context to draw attention in passing to the disc-head on one of the involuted pins from Meare in Somerset (Fig. 90:1; Dunning, 1934, Fig. 5:3), but for the moment the chronological and typological position of this Irish object remain unknown.

Type 2 pins are undoubtedly a wholly independent Irish development. The only example found outside the country is a now lost pin from the island of Coll on the extreme western coast of Scotland (Fig. 85:2), and this cannot be viewed other than as an export from Ireland. It was recovered from a sandhill deposit on the island; its find circumstances are thus uninformative.

These pins form a coherent and uniform group and are clearly the product of a single workshop tradition. It is thus interesting to note, notwithstanding the small number of extant specimens, the wide spread of the type from Sligo, in the west of the country, through Athlone and Armagh to western Scotland (Map 15). The chronology of these objects depends on a consideration of the cast ornament which adorns them and their dating is in consequence uncertain. The only one to come from an excavation is that from Navan Fort, Co. Armagh, but its stratigraphical position cannot be discussed until the excavation report appears.

The raised spiral and boss decoration which characterises these pins is often compared to the raised decoration of pins and brooches from Britain, especially Yorkshire, and has been seen as "a development of East Second B flamboyance" (Simpson and Simpson, 1968, 144). The raised ornament on the imitation coral inlay which ornaments the second/first century B.C. brooch from Danes' Grave 57 in Yorkshire (Stead, 1965, 62-63, Fig. 35; 1979, 69-70, Fig. 26:1) is comparable to the ornament of the Irish pins but not compellingly so. The possibility that direct Continental influence played a part in giving rise to this distinctive type of pin-head decoration is not lightly to be dismissed.

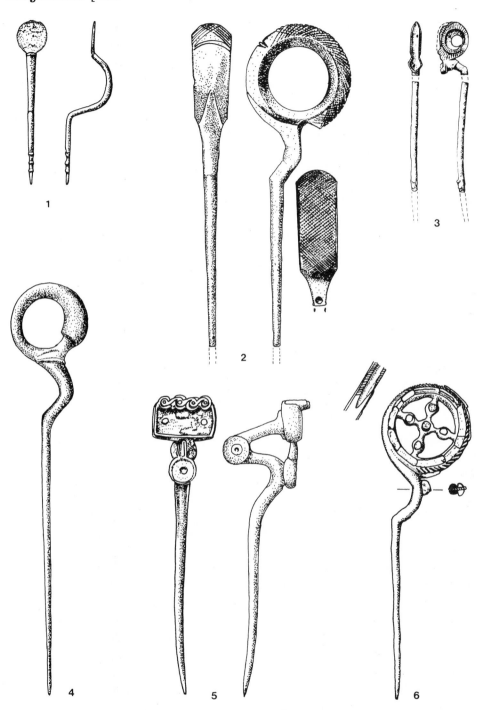

Fig. 90. British ringheaded pins. 1 Meare, Somerset, England. 2 Balla-cagan, Isle of Man. 3 Alnham, Northumberland, England. 4 Sasaig, Skye, Inverness-shire, Scotland. 5 River Thames, Hammersmith, England. 6 Kilham, Yorkshire, England. – Various scales.

There are numerous parallels for the boss decoration on the Continent from Early and Middle La Tène contexts. On bronze torcs such as those from the Marne (Jacobsthal, 1944, Nos 222, 223) and Dammelberg in Hessen, Germany (idem., No. 224), for instance, are to be found many of the motifs which adorn these Irish pins; there is even a hint of the strange boss which occurs on the shoulder of an unlocalised pin in the Ulster Museum, Belfast (Fig. 85:3; Pl. 54), to be recognised on the terminals of the Marne torcs. On the Dammelberg torc (Megaw, 1970, Pl. 148) the interlocking S-scrolls which flank the terminal features could be seen as a flattened version of the curvilinear design which adorns the heads of the Irish pins. On a Middle La Tène fibula from Kosd in Hungary (Jacobsthal, 1944, No. 347) and on a similar example from Chotin, Grave 14, in south-west Slovakia (Ratimorska, 1975, Taf. 11:2), there are ornamental bosses which are close in concept and execution to the raised ornament on the Irish ringheaded pins. Even more striking is a comparison between the raised motifs on the unlocalised pin in the Armagh library (Fig. 85:1) and the virtually identical designs on the hollow bronze bosses on the pair of Middle La Tène rings from Klettham in Upper Bavaria (Jacobsthal, 1944, No. 267). On these German objects the same hemispherical domes as on the Armagh Library pin occur, each further elaborated with a triple arrangement of small bosses joined together by curved lines which, in combination with the bosses, form a triskele pattern. The way in which the major domes on the German bracelet are linked and enclosed by raised, curving lines is also found on the Irish pin-heads. Similarly, the bronze bracelet from the Tarn in the M.A.N., Saint-Germain-en-Laye, France with its raised scrolls encircling prominent domed bosses and its thick fleshy S-scrolls, is comparable to the organisation of the design on these Irish Type 2 pins (Jacobsthal, 1944, No. 275). Their dating could thus be substantially earlier than suggested heretofore.

Pins of Type 3 represent a peculiarly Irish version of the insular ringheaded pin but, as with the other types, hints of contact with foreign traditions of pin-making are evident in some details of their manufacture. Seaby compared the moulded points, particularly the version which he termed the "elongated lobe", with similar features on the ends of Roman bronze surgical instruments (1964, 70). He accordingly dated the Irish pins to the early centuries A.D. Such a late dating was queried by the Simpsons (1968, 144), who pointed to the presence of point moulding on earlier southern English involuted pins, emphasising especially the pin from Meare in Somerset (Fig. 90:1; Dunning, 1934, Fig. 5:3), the moulding of which is closest in form to that on the relevant Irish pins. On English chronology these pins are generally placed in the last two centuries or so B.C. (Harding, 1974, 189).

As already stated the chief distinguishing feature of the type is the concavity on the ringhead which formerly held a decorative stud or inlay. Only on the pair from Lisnacrogher are these studs partly preserved (Fig. 86:3,4; Pl. 55), held in place in each case by a single slender rivet. The expanded heads of the rivets have been hammered to trefoil shape.

Dunning compared the stud form on these Irish pins to similar, though larger, studs on a bronze disc from the Bugthorpe warrior burial in Yorkshire (1934, 286; Stead, 1979, Fig. 20), and on this basis he suggested a first century B.C. date, and a Yorkshire background, for the Irish pins. Such a superficial analogy is, however, hardly a firm basis for wide-reaching conclusions, especially since comparable studs of coral and enamel are known in far earlier European contexts (e.g. Jacobsthal, 1944, No. 348; K.I.G., 1978, No. 45).

Attempts have, however, been made on other grounds to link these Irish pins with north British developments. MacGregor wondered if the ring moulding of a pin from Sasaig, Isle of Skye, Scotland (Fig. 90:4), "could relate to the shaped enamel 'cushions' of Irish pins" (1976, 138). Jobey went so far as to suggest that the Irish Type 3 pin which came from a cremation deposit at Alnham in Northumberland (Fig. 90:3) was directly ancestral to the Irish series (Jobey and Tait, 1966, 29-34). He saw the type as springing ultimately from pins such as that from Danes' Graves, Kilham, in Yorkshire (Fig. 90:6; Stead, 1965, 57, Fig. 32; 1979, Fig. 30:3). Jobey based his belief on an acceptance of Seaby's late date for the Irish group, on the almost identical form of the Alnham and the Irish pins and the difficulty of dating the Alnham pin (assumed to be British) as late as the Roman period, which he believed to be the date of the Irish specimens. The Simpsons, too, regarded the Alnham pin as a "direct and close relative (probably ancestor), of the Irish series" and went on to state that "whatever the duration of this fashion in Ireland, its arrival must be attributed to the first century B.C. at least" (1968, 144). More recently, however, one of the Simpsons (MacGregor, 1976, 139) seems less certain in viewing the Alnham pin as ancestral to the entire Irish group.

When the ten pins of our Type 3 are looked at together it is readily apparent that they form a closely knit group distinct from the other insular ringheaded pins. Nine of the ten come from Ireland and it seems quite unreasonable to regard the Alnham specimen as other than an export to Northumberland from Ireland. Significantly, the burial from which it came represents a type more at home in an Irish than a British context so that it is not beyond the bounds of possibility that it represents the presence of an actual Irish emigrant group in the vicinity (see below p. 331).

In view of the possible Yorkshire connection suggested by the presence in Ireland of two knob-ringed pins it is, of course, conceivable that pins such as that from Kilham in Yorkshire played a part in the development of the Irish Type 3 examples. On this eastern English specimen such features as the inlays on the ringhead, the milled edges to the setting and a stud riveted to the shoulder occur - all of which have parallels on the Irish pins. The openwork design on the ring is also reminiscent of the openwork triskele on one of the Type 3 pins (Fig. 86:1; Pls 53:3; 56:2). Such superficial similarities, however, between selected features of the Irish pins and those on a single English specimen seem of themselves too generalised to demonstrate Yorkshire influence on the Irish group. They certainly do not demonstrate a Yorkshire origin for this Irish pin type.

The Kilham pin is not the only English pin which shares some decorative features with the Irish Type 3 examples. One from the River Thames at Hammersmith (Fig. 90:5; Fox, 1958, Pl. 2,E) has settings for enamel or coral on the head, the arrangement of which is somewhat similar to that on the Irish pins. Again, however, the comparison is not close enough for any direct link between the relevant pins in the two islands to be postulated.

The only other British pin which bears close comparison with those of the Irish group under discussion is that recovered from an embanked settlement site at Ballacagan on the Isle of Man (Fig. 90:2; Bersu, 1977, 60-61, Fig. 19). The closest parallel for this object is the example from Clough, Co. Antrim (Fig. 86:6; Pl. 56:3), and it could, indeed, be argued that the Man pin is of Irish manufacture. Its stratigraphical context at any rate is important for the dating of the Irish pins.

At Ballacagan there were three similar settlement sites, none separated appreciably from the other in time. Ballacagan B appears to have been the earliest but Ballacagan A and C were built not long after B and probably continued in use alongside it. Bersu suggested that the total duration of occupation at the three sites cannot have exceeded three centuries. The pin in question came from the earliest phase of Site A.

Amongst the more important of the dating material from the site are two bronze brooches, both attributed by the excavator to the Phase II occupation layer of Site B. These are a Late La Tène fibula and a brooch of Romano-British derivation. Relying largely on the latter brooch, Bersu took 200 A.D. as a central date for the occupation of the three sites. Radford, however, who edited and posthumously published the excavation report, argues that the stratigraphical position of this brooch is questionable (op. cit., 84, fn. 3) and, in addition, he points to Continental analogies dating to the last century B.C. for the La Tène III brooch and

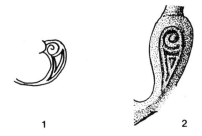

Fig. 91. Details of decoration. 1 Horn, Torrs, Kircudbrightshire, Scotland. 2 Irish Type 4 ringheaded pin, River Shannon. - Various scales.

for glass-work from the site (op. cit., 63, fn. 2; 85, fn. 1). On these and other grounds he is more inclined to take c. 50 B.C. as a central date for the occupation. The two Carbon 14 determinations from Ballacagan (which were not available to Bersu) increase the likelihood of the earlier rather than the later dating. One, from Site B, which belongs to the earliest phase of the three sites, is 2235 ± 45 B.P. (± 285 b.c.). The other, which probably applies to an early stage of Phase A, is 2155 ± 75 B.P. (± 205 b.c.). It is, therefore, possible that the Ballacagan pin may date somewhat before rather than after the birth of Christ.

The Isle of Man find is the nearest we can as yet come to an independently dated pin with Irish Type 3 affinities. The Alnham pin is undatable on its own. The date of the Kilham pin, if it is related to the Irish group at all, is uncertain but belongs somewhere in the last centuries B.C. Only Lisnacrogher, which produced two such pins, offers a possible dating range for the type: the material from this Co. Antrim site, as already noted, probably extends from the third or second century B.C. to the first century A.D. and it seems likely that it is within these parameters that the use of the pin-type in Ireland is to be sought.

Type 4 pins comprise of a small group the most striking characteristic of which (with two exceptions) is the extreme forward curvature of pin. Apart from this feature there is considerable variation amongst them, and individual examples can be seen to share details of form with pins from other Irish groups. Two pins, for instance, one grouped with Type 1 (Pl. 53:2), the other with Type 4 (Fig. 85:10), have very similar hourglass-shaped openings in the ringhead. The bulbous mouldings on the tips of two Type 4 pins (Fig. 85:9,10) may also indicate technical overlap with workshops producing pins of Type 3. The fragmentary, unlocalised pin shown in Fig. 85:7 is the clearest hybrid of all. This specimen possesses on its head a convex setting for some form of inlay exactly as on Type 3 pins and it also has a series of projecting cylindrical elements not unlike those on the Bawnboy, Co. Cavan pin (Fig. 84:4).

The Beaghmore, Co. Galway, pin (Pl. 58) is without parallel in Ireland, its closest counterpart here being an unlocalised specimen in the Armagh Museum.

Prototypes for this group of pins are not readily forthcoming. In Ireland there is a pin from Tullamore, Co. Offaly (Fig. 87:1) which has an exaggerated, forward-curving shank like the Irish Type 4 pins (Wood-Martin, 1904, 13, Fig. 2:1). This example is not, however, a ringheaded pin but has a solid cylindrical head, with transverse perforation. This form of pin-head is closely comparable to a straight-shanked pin from a Late Bronze Age hoard at Lough Gara, Co. Sligo (unpublished; information courtesy of Dr. J. Raftery, former Director, National Museum of Ireland).

There are also north European cast bronze pins which have features in common with some of the Irish specimens. A bronze pin from Denmark (Bronsted, 1940, Vol. III, 23, Fig. 9g) has a curved shank, a sharply angled shoulder and a moulded tip[1]. The significant difference between this example and those of the Irish series, however, is that instead of possessing a ringhead, the pin has a cup-shaped feature at the top which has no parallel on any of the Irish examples. Cup-headed pins with straight shanks, are, of course, known in the Irish Late Bronze Age (Eogan, 1974, 98-101). Bronsted includes the Danish pin in his "older Celtic period" from 400-200 B.C. While overlap between the Irish and Danish pins is conceivable, the analogy is remote and the shared features need reflect no more than a common response to a common mode of wearing the pins.

Scandinavian analogies of Late Bronze Age date for the cruciform arrangements of discs on the Beaghmore pin seem equally obscure, (Bronsted, 1940, 243, Fig. 231d). Comparable ornament also occurs in sub-Roman contexts (e.g. Fox, 1923, Pl. XXII:6). The date of the Beaghmore pin is thus highly speculative.

The S-shape of the heads of the Type 4 pins could hark back to early swan's-neck pins or could even suggest a link with the heads of Scottish crook-headed pins (Dunning, 1934, 283, Fig. 7:1-3). The dating of the Scottish group is vague but it seems now that they can be at least as early as the third century B.C. (Stevenson, 1967, 20) and, with the backdating of the Scottish Iron Age (MacKie, 1969), could even be earlier. The similarity between these Irish pins and the Scottish crook-headed examples may be entirely fortuitous, or may even be based on a common ultimate ancestry rooted in common Hallstatt prototypes. It is however,

1. Comparison suggested in conversation by Richard Warner, Ulster Museum, Belfast.

Fig. 92. Projecting ringheaded pin. Keady
Mountain, Cashel, Co. Derry. - 1/2.

interesting to note the close correspondence between the design on the
eyes of the bird which forms the head of one Type 4 Irish pin (Figs 85:8;
91:2; Pl. 57), and a motif filling one of the incised crescentic patterns
on a horn of the Torrs "chamfrein" (Fig. 91:1; Atkinson and Piggott, 1955,
Pl. LXXII:b; 220, Fig. 4).

Lastly, the projecting-ringheaded pin from Keady Mountain, Cashel,
Co. Derry (Fig. 92), may be briefly referred to. The pin is the only
example in Ireland of this essentially Scottish type. Its precise
chronological position is unclear, however, for in Scotland these pins
appear to have had a long life from perhaps as early as the middle of
the last millennium B.C. to the beginning of the Christian era (MacKie,
1974, 128-129).

The Clonmacnois Hoard

A buffer torc and a ribbon torc, both of gold, are stated to have been
found together around the middle of the last century in a bog near
Clonmacnois, Co. Offaly (Wilde, 1862, 47-9). There are otherwise no
recorded details of find circumstances but there is no reason not to accept
the association as legitimate.

The Clonmacnois buffer torc is a well-known piece often illustrated
and frequently discussed in the literature (e.g. Evans, 1897, 405, Fig. 8,
Pl. 42; Armstrong, 1923, 14-16, Fig. 9; Jacobsthal, 1944, No. 49; Megaw,
1970, No. 174; IK, 1983, No. 26; CIIAA No. 451). It consists of two plain
tubes of hammered sheet-gold which fit into separately-made decorative
expansions at front and back. At the front the pseudo "buffers" take
the form of a hollow, biconical unit, flattened around the centre and

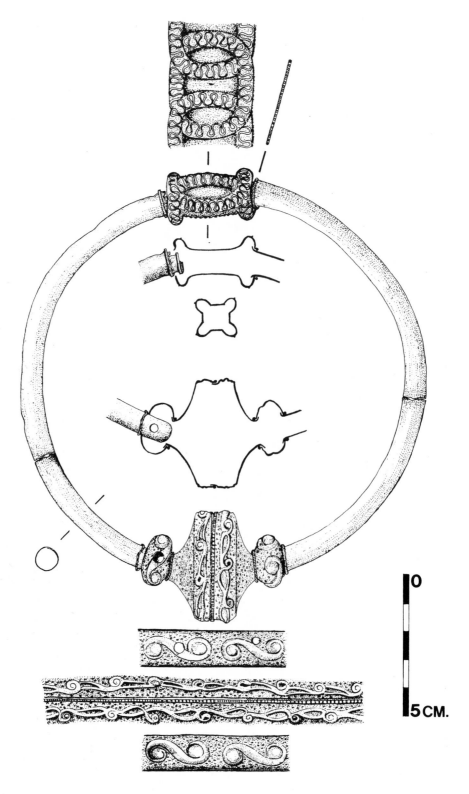

Fig. 93. Gold, fused-buffer torc. Clonmacnois, Co. Offaly. – 3/4.

flanked on either side by a flattened-spherical boss. Each of the bosses is decorated with a pair of raised, spiral-ended S-scrolls. The "buffer" element is divided centrally by a thin line of beading which separates two repoussé bands of loose tendril ornament set against a finely stippled background. At the back of the torc there is a subrectangular box-like feature the edges of which are emphasised by pronounced convex mouldings. These are arranged to form a pair of interlocking, oval loops which are decorated with a continuous meander ornament of applied gold wire.

The torc was closed by inserting one of the side-tubes into one of the hollow bosses at the front where it was secured in place by a transverse pin (now lost).

The Clonmacnois torc takes its place in a well-known class of neck ornament examples of which occur frequently in burials of Early La Tène date on the Continent. The majority are of bronze but exceptional examples of gold are known (e.g. Jacobstal, 1944, Nos 41–56; Keller, 1965, Taf. 12,13; Wyss, 1975). Most of the classic European buffer torcs are penannular, with a space of varying width between the terminals. On some torcs, however, the terminals are joined to form a single unit. These have been described as "fused-buffer" torcs and it is to this group that the Clonmacnois torc has been compared (Megaw, 1970, 114). Fused-buffer torcs in Europe belong in Voigt's Type H (1968, 159–161) and good examples are recorded in Germany from Leimbach, Kr. Bad Selzungen, (Voigt, op. cit., 217, Abb. 7a), Praunheim near Frankfurt, (Jacobsthal, op. cit., No. 210), Darmstadt (Jacobsthal, op. cit., No. 224) and Dammelberg, Kr. Groß Gerau (Megaw, op. cit., No. 148). There are other examples and it seems that the Middle Rhine was an important centre of their manufacture.

The affinities of the Clonmacnois torc with these examples are evident not only in the "fused-buffer" terminals but also in the common presence on the bosses of raised S-scrolls. The absence on the Irish piece of the proliferation of bosses which characterise the German torcs should, however, be noted. The loose, somewhat irregular scrolls on the "buffers" of the Co. Offaly example are also difficult to parallel precisely on the European torcs. Nonetheless, there is a distinctly Waldalgesheim flavour about the ornament, especially in the way in which, on three occasions, tendrils cut straight across other tendrils. It is likely that the source of the Clonmacnois torc is to be sought in the area of the Middle Rhine and there are, indeed, strong grounds for regarding it as an import to Ireland. Megaw, in fact, described the torc as "apart from brooches, probably the only undisputed example of imported La Tène art to be found in the British Isles" (1970, 114). Jope, too, expressed a similar opinion but, conscious of the absence of good parallels in Europe for the "junction-box" on the Clonmacnois specimen, he speculated that this might be a native addition to the imported torc, its form influenced by that of some of the Irish glass beads (1958, 80). This latter suggestion does not seem likely. The "box" on the back of the torc need be no more than an atypical version of the expanded ornamental units present in considerable variety on many European torcs. Indeed, on a "torc ternaire" from grave 4, Villeseneux (Marne), there are decorative expansions which in fact resemble, to an extent, the Clonmacnois "junction-box" (Roualet and Kruta, 1980, Pl. VI:14952). As well as this, the applied meander design on the "box" is otherwise unknown in Ireland but has an impeccable La Tène pedigree back to the Mediterranean (e.g. Jacobstal, 1944, Nos. 120-122; Joffroy, 1962, Pl. p. 107). Finally, it is of interest to note the pattern produced when the interlocking mouldings on the "box" are drawn on a flat plane; the design thus presented resembles strikingly the nodus Herculeus so typical of the Hellenistic world (e.g. Marshall, 1911, Pl. XXVII:1608; Becatti, 1955, Tav. CXX:436; CXXI:438).[1]

The Continental background to the Clonmacnois torc is clear, and the dating range of the relevant comparisons in Europe is well established. These fall consistently into a late phase of the Early La Tène period (i.e. La Tène B2). In absolute terms, therefore, the Irish torc should date to the end of the fourth or the beginning of the third century B.C. It therefore represents the earliest certain evidence of a La Tène presence in the country.

The ribbon torc from the Clonmacnois hoard is not as readily placed in its chronological and cultural context. This object, though belonging to a group which occurs with relative frequency in Ireland, differs from all the other examples in having large, hollow, pear-shaped terminals.

About 60 ribbon torcs of gold are known from the country (Eogan, 1983), but only in four instances are they associated with an object other than another ribbon torc. Apart from two recorded Iron Age associations (Clonmacnois, Co. Offaly (Fig. 94:1), and Somerset, Co. Galway (Fig. 94:2; above p. 155), ribbon torcs are otherwise found with a penannular gold ring of rectangular section and a sheet gold fragment at Largatreany, Co. Donegal (Hartmann, 1970, 29-30), and with an untwisted, flanged bar torc of sub-triangular section at Coolmanagh Upper, Co. Carlow (Manning and Eogan, 1979). A fragment of a gold ribbon torc is said to have come from Lisnacrogher, Co. Antrim (Knowles, Sale Cat., 1924, 48, Lot 707, Pl. 8), but in this instance the genuineness of the find spot

---

1. The comparison has been suggested to me by Dr. Venceslas Kruta.

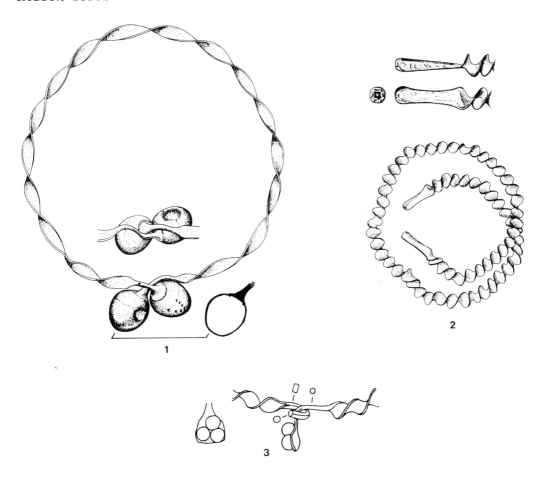

Fig. 94. Gold ribbon torcs. 1 Clonmacnois, Co. Offaly. 2 Somerset, Co. Galway. 3 detail of gold ribbon torc terminal. The Law Farm, Morayshire, Scotland. (3, after Coles, 1975).

is open to question.

The archaeological contexts presented by these four finds appear thus to indicate a wide divergence in date for gold ribbon torcs in Ireland. The bar torc from Coolmanagh is conventionally seen as a type belonging to Eogan's Bishopsland Phase of the Later Bronze Age i.e. between about 1200 B.C. and 1000 B.C. (1964, 171-188), while the Iron Age finds are anything up to a thousand years later than this. The Largatreany association cannot be dated with any confidence (Eogan, 1964, 180; Hartmann, 1970, 29).

Clearly, therefore, the chronological position of the large number of unassociated ribbon torcs is uncertain. Eogan regarded the ribbon torcs in Ireland as an essentially Bishopsland Phase type and considered them as a development of cast bronze torcs of the southern English Middle Bronze Age Ornament Horizon (1964, 336; e.g. Smith, 1959, 147, Fig. 2:4). The absence of any evidence for the manufacture or use of the ribbon torc during the Dowris Phase of the Irish Late Bronze Age was accepted by Eogan as creating something of a problem and he wondered if the Iron Age associations could be explained as evidence for continuity or revival of ribbon torc manufacture.

The matter is further complicated by Hartmann's gold analysis, which shows that the gold content of the Irish ribbon torcs differs from that of gold objects belonging both to the Bishopsland and Dowris Phases of the Irish Later Bronze Age. The ribbon torcs, in fact, belong to his Group PC (platinum-rich gold) and share the same category with all the other Iron Age gold objects in Ireland, apart from the gold strip from Lambay (Hartmann, 1970, 29). While it is possible to disagree with Hartmann's views on the source of the Irish prehistoric gold (see Raftery, J., 1971; Harbison, 1971b; Briggs et al., 1973; Scott, 1976b; Hartmann, 1980), it is difficult to ignore the fact that the ribbon torcs belong to a metal group which differs consistently from that of all the gold objects alleged to be contemporary with them and which, both in Ireland (where datable) and on the Continent, is essentially a La Tène phenomenon.

Outside Ireland, ribbon torcs of gold are uncommon and in general uncertainly dated (Eogan, 1964, 280). Early Roman bronze statuettes of the god Mercury are sometimes shown wearing on their necks what appear to be ribbon torcs (e.g. AuhV, 1900, Taf. 69:2), but the relevance of these to the Irish series is doubtful. Two ribbon torcs from north Italy are, perhaps, of greater significance for the Irish group. The first, of gold, comes from the Celtic cemetery of Montefortino, Ancona (Montelius, 1904, Pl. 155:9). This has simple hooked terminals and seems in every detail to match the Irish torcs. The second was found in Tomb 5 at the Celtic cemetery of Carzaghetto, Mantua (Ferraresi, 1976, Fig. 20:2). This is a ribbon torc of iron but it possesses solid, more or less pear-shaped terminals which bear a striking resemblance to those on the Clonmacnois ribbon torc. Both these cemeteries overlap in time with the period of manufacture of the buffer torc from Clonmacnois. Thus, if the presence of Iron Age gold ribbon torcs in Ireland is to be seen as a revival of torc manufacture after a lapse of more than a millennium, it is conceivable that specimens such as those from Italy inspired the development.

Apart from these few Continental examples, only Scotland has produced ribbon torcs of gold which are closely similar to those in Ireland (Coles, 1959-60, 92). As with the majority of Irish specimens, those from

Scotland, too, are from uninformative contexts. One example, however, displays a unique decorative detail on one of its terminals which may be relevant in the present discussion. The torc comes from the famous Law Farm hoard near Elgin in Morayshire. One of the terminals has been hammered flat, and applied to the surface is a triangular arrangement of three tiny gold balls (Coles, 1975; Fig. 94:3). The only close parallel for this decorative motif is to be found on one of the gold necklaces from the hoard at Broighter, Co. Derry (Fig. 97:4; Pl. 63), an object which, along with the ribbon torcs, belongs in Hartmann's PC gold group.

It can be seen, therefore, that a date in the Middle Bronze Age for the gold ribbon torcs as a group is by no means overwhelmingly established. Future discoveries may yet reveal that the Iron Age was the period of major ribbon torc manufacture in Ireland.

The Broighter hoard

Seven gold objects were found close to the old shore line of Lough Foyle in the townland of Broighter, not far from Limavady, Co. Derry. These consist of the following items: a complete and a fragmentary bar torc of circular section elaborated in each case by the inclusion of a length of thin, twisted gold wire within the torsion grooves of the twisted bar (Fig. 97:1,2); two necklaces of loop-in-loop gold wire chain, one composed of a single strand (Fig. 97:3;Pl. 63), the other made up of three strands (Fig. 97:4; Pl. 63) and each having a complex clasp mechanism; a spectacularly decorated buffer torc with repoussé ornament on the tube, set off by a background of compass-drawn "engine-turned" arcs, with pseudo-granulation on the terminals which are closed by the insertion of a T-shaped tenon (projecting from one terminal face) into a rectangular slot in the opposing terminal face (Fig. 96; Pl. 62); a beaten bowl of hemispherical form with four tiny loops of gold wire equally spaced around the edge (Fig. 95:2); a model ship of beaten gold complete with mast and yardarm, rowers' benches, oars, grappling hook and other implements (Fig. 95:1).

The hoard was found in the year 1896 on the farm of Mr. Joseph L. Gibson of Broighter, Co. Derry. He sold the objects to Mr. Day of Cork and from Mr. Day they were acquired by the British Museum. The find was published one year later (Evans, 1897, 391-408). After some questions about the Broighter find had been asked in the British Parliament, a Royal Commission was appointed to consider the relations between the British and Dublin Museums. The Commission issued its findings in January, 1899, and the whole matter was brought before Mr. Justice Farwell in the High Court in London in 1903. As is well known, after

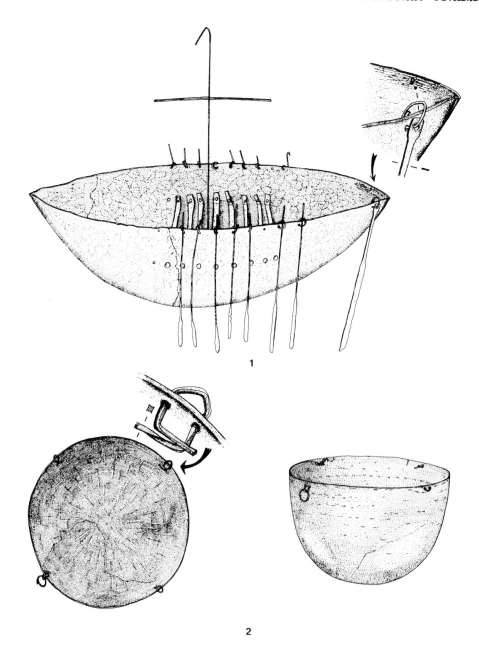

Fig. 95. Objects from hoard, Broighter, Co. Derry. 1 model gold boat.
2 gold bowl. – 1/2.

a lengthy court case the objects were adjudged to be treasure trove and thus the property of the Crown.   Shortly afterwards, at the behest of King Edward VII they were returned to Ireland and given to the Royal Irish Academy (Harbison, 1976, 57-59).   At the time there was no doubt about the genuine nature of the deposit.

Over forty years after the discovery doubts began to be cast on the integrity of the hoard.   Henry (1940, 13, fn.) stated that the "so-called 'Broighter hoard', having been found inside an old umbrella lying in a ditch, is hardly likely to be a deposit of the Iron Age". Mahr (1941, 11,12) stated that the hoard must be "struck off the list almost completely as a discovery illustrating La Tène art in Ireland and he referred to the Broighter hoard as "an exploded myth".   He went on to describe the material as a nineteenth century hoard and dismissed the majority of the objects, with the exception of the collar, as of Oriental, "probably Indian", workmanship.   He hinted that he was not at liberty to divulge the full facts.   Macalister (1949, 239) added some more details regarding the story then circulating.   It was alleged that the gold objects represented loot which had been stolen from the house of a local collector.   Praeger, however, who at the time was the last surviving member of the Government team which investigated the circumstances of the finding, strongly challenged these allegations and pointed out that no such reservations had ever arisen during the lengthy court proceedings (1942, 31-32).   To him it was "all rather mysterious and fantastic".

Lingering doubts have remained almost to the present day.   As recently as 1970 Megaw stated that "the find conditions .... are distressingly uncertain" (167) and he also, in the same publication, referred to "the great torc found under an old umbrella in 1895 at Broighter, Co. Derry" (114).

On the basis of Hartmann's gold analysis it seems now unreasonable to doubt the genuineness of the hoard.   This demonstrated that every item in the hoard is of the same platinum gold which is a characteristic of virtually the entire body of Irish La Tène gold material (Hartmann, 1970, 98-99).   On this analysis alone the material may be regarded as a genuine, prehistoric hoard.

The origin of the strange "umbrella story" has, however, never been explained and its very persistence might be construed as a source of some continued misgivings.   As stated above, Mahr felt he could not divulge the source or the full details of the story and thus he added a further ingredient to the mystery.   The background to the story has not been ascertained, however, and to dispel finally any lingering doubts about Broighter the full account of the "umbrella story" will be given here.

   The source of the writer's information is an affidavit signed by Mr. Joseph H. Hamill, which has been preserved for over twenty years in a safe in the National Museum of Ireland. Thanks are here expressed to the former Director, Dr. Joseph Raftery, for permission to use this document. Mr. Hamill, who was from the Broighter area of Derry, was the originator of the "umbrella story" and he placed on record all he knew of the find circumstances with the proviso that the document was not to be used until after his death and then only in the interests of genuine research.

   Mr. Hamill was a young man of twenty-three at the time of the discovery and he was a close friend of the Gibson family upon whose land the discovery was made. In the course of his affidavit he states "when they (the ornaments) were discovered and carefully collected, there was found in the same spot the remains of an old umbrella. What was left of it was a small portion, about two or three inches long, of that part of the ribs where they were attached to the collar through which a rather thick wooden shaft had passed. No portion of this shaft remained and what was left of the ribs was badly rusted, but there was sufficient to show that it was the remains of a very old umbrella".

   He continues: "I was not present at the finding of the ornaments, Mr. Gibson taking immediate possession of them, but Mrs. Gibson took what was left of the umbrella and wrapping it in paper hid it in a drawer of her bedroom. Afterwards she took me to her room, opened the drawer and handed me the parcel..... It was while I still held the remains of the umbrella in my hand that Mrs. Gibson told me of her early recollections as follows:-

   "She said she remembered having heard years ago that at one time a robbery had taken place in a house called 'Oatlands' less than a mile away. She remembered having been told that two brothers of an earlier generation of the family had been in India and she thought that if it should be proved that the ornaments were of Indian workmanship there might be someone still alive who had heard of a robbery at Oatlands and claim that the ornaments were part of the stolen 'loot' ....

   "The story of this robbery rests on no stronger evidence than the recollections of Mrs. Gibson but there is no doubt whatever that the divided torque bears evidence of a hurried division of spoils and that one of the robbers, perhaps because he was being followed, dropped his portion of the loot into the ditch intending to recover it at some future time...."

   Mr. Hamill concludes: "Somewhere about the year 1930 I had related my knowledge of the finding of the Broighter ornaments to a friend in Dublin, never thinking that he would retail it but he must have done so for subsequently some of the leading antiquarians made use of it .... About this time I related what I knew to Dr. Quane of the Department of Education who, in view of what had already been published, urged me to put in writing what was known to me at first hand. For these reasons it seemed to have become incumbent on me to relate the facts – hence this statement".

From the foregoing account it can be seen that the factual basis for the "umbrella story" is virtually nil. Mr. Hamill, who clearly was the inadvertant originator of the story, was not a witness to the discovery. It can be taken that an umbrella was found near the gold objects but there is nothing in Mr. Hamill's statement to indicate that it was associated with the hoard, much less that the objects were inside it. Similarly, the account of the alleged robbery at "Oatlands" is at best a dim and distant memory on the part of Mrs. Gibson and there is nothing in what she says to connect the alleged robbery with the hoard. The lady only "remembered having heard" and such vagueness is worthless in the present context. The only "evidence" put forward by Mr. Hamill to indicate that the material was loot was the presence in the hoard of an incomplete torc. The break in the torc is, however, almost certainly an ancient one but even if it were recent, such a fracture alone would be a flimsy foundation indeed upon which to base the elaborate story of buried loot.

It is thus clear, once the source of the story is known, that the account of the umbrella and the burglary cannot be shown to have the slightest relevance to the context of the hoard. Even without the Hartmann analysis, the integrity of the Broighter hoard would remain intact. It may truly be said that the "umbrella story" is now an exploded myth!

Affinities and chronology

The magnificent buffer torc is the outstanding piece from the hoard and has, inevitably, occupied the attention of those who have studied the material from Broighter. The object belongs to a small but widely dispersed class of Late La Tène torcs (all of gold) which have been found, in varying contexts, in eastern England, Belgium, France, Germany, Switzerland and northern Italy (Map 18; Clarke, 1954, 41-5; Furger-Gunti, 1982). They are quite distinct from the buffer torcs of Early La Tène Europe. They are characterised by thick, hollow tubes of sheet-gold with large, moulded terminals usually of squat cylindrical or flattened-spherical shape. The tubes are generally plain with the exception of partially decorated specimens from Mailly-le-Camp, Aube in France (Joffroy, 1969; Furger-Gunti, op. cit., 23, Abb. 14) and Frasnes-lez-Buissenal, Hainaut in Belgium (Jacobsthal, 1944, No. 70; Clarke, 1954,

43-4, Pls V, VI; Duval, 1977, 158, Fig. 165; Furger-Gunti, op. cit., 23, Abb. 14). Short decorated cylinders are preserved on the back of two specimens, one from Hoard A, Snettisham (Clarke, op. cit., Pl. I; Fig. 4) and that from Frasnes-lez-Buissenal just referred to. The other of the two torcs from Frasnes and a second from Snettisham Hoard A have twisted or ribbed gold wires soldered to the tube at the back of the torc. Two examples, one from Frasnes, the other from Mailly-le-Camp display between the buffers a ring of gold beading.

In three instances cores are present within the gold tubes and other preserved backing material consists of resin, beeswax and sand; on one of the Snettisham examples traces of a woven material were found wrapped around the iron core at one end (Clarke, op. cit., 38). It may be assumed that the Irish torc, too, was once filled with a backing of some sort.

Furger-Gunti has distinguished two sub-types within this group of torcs on the basis of their closing mechanism (op. cit., 22). The first (the majority) includes those members of the group which opened at the back where there was usually a detachable cylindrical unit or where the simple device of inserting one tube into the other was used. In a sense these could almost be described as "fused-buffer" torcs. The second sub-type (to which Broighter belongs) comprises of torcs which were closed at the front by means of a tenon junction.

There is a considerable measure of uniformity amongst these European torcs and they must surely be the product of a small number of closely related workshops, one at least of which is likely to have been in north Gaul. Some of the Snettisham buffer torcs could, indeed, have been imported from there for three of the torcs from Hoard A have rows of tiny punched circles on the tube, a detail matched on one of the Frasnes torcs (Clarke, op. cit., 37-9, 43; compare Pls II and V). The Irish example is clearly related to this group but not one offers a precise parallel for it and the elaborate decoration on the tubes establishes its native character. It has, however, been suggested that its terminals are from an imported Continental torc which were joined in Ireland to locally-made tubes. Undoubtedly the distinctive tenon-junction on the Irish object has extremely close counterparts amongst the European torcs, especially on the pair from Niederzier/Düren on the lower Rhine in Germany (Joachim, 1979; Furger-Gunti, 1982, 25, Abb. 20; K.I.M., 1980, No. 267). Such fastening mechanism is also found on older torcs of gold in Europe, notably on a group from south-west France with an outlier in Jugoslavia (Megaw, 1970, Nos. 151,2; Mohen, 1979, 35, 37-40, Figs. 5,7). These, however, date to the third century B.C. and have no direct connection with the group of torcs to which the Broighter example belongs. The gold beading (granulation?) between the "buffers" of two of the Late

La Tène torcs (Frasnes and Mailly) calls to mind the pseudo-granulation on the Broighter terminals and could again be taken as indicating foreign manufacture. But the imitation granulation on the Irish object might equally be interpreted as a local attempt at imitating the true granulation which occurs on one of the wire necklaces in the hoard (Fig. 97:4; Pl. 63). Finally, the presence of platinum in the gold of torcs from Mailly and St. Louis/Basel should be noted in this context for platinum also occurs in the composition of the Broighter torc. At the very least, this should indicate a common source for the Irish and the Continental gold - either Middle Rhine, or East Mediterranean (Hartmann, 1970, 50; 1976, 120-123).

The date of these European torcs is clearly established by the informative contexts in which several have been found and the surprising frequency with which examples have been discovered in association with Celtic coinage. In every instance deposition in the last century B.C. is evident and this can be narrowed to the middle or second half of the century in most cases. The possibility that the torcs from Frasnes were made earlier than this has been discussed (Jacobsthal, 1944, 135; Clarke, 1954, 44; Megaw, 1970, 114), but the date of their deposition around the middle of the last century B.C. is indicated by the accompanying coins. The chronological context of the Broighter torc seems thus assured.

The decoration on the torc has been frequently discussed in the context of insular La Tène art and here, too, there is substantial agreement regarding its position within the native artistic development sequence (e.g. Henry, 1954, 17-18; Megaw, 1970, No. 289; Duval, 1977, 200-202; Warner, 1982). Stylistically the object represents an important stage in the evolution of the distinctively Irish variant of the La Tène art style. The elegantly expanding trumpet curves with crisp, pointed-oval bosses foreshadow the characteristically insular trumpet and lentoid-boss design which becomes the dominant decorative motif on metalwork of the early centuries of Christianity. On the Broighter piece they retain elements of their vegetal ancestry. There are good native parallels for the ornament. Especially close comparisons are to be found amongst the designs on the Lough Crew, Co. Meath flakes (below pp. 251-263). One in particular, in its ornamental arrangement, is strikingly similar to the patterning on the torc (Fig. 128:11,12). Other motifs on the torc such as the rows of tiny semicircles, the "engine-turned" background to the raised curves, and some of the elaborate triskele motifs can be precisely matched on the flakes (Fig. 127:1,3-5). "Engine-turning" is also present on the "gaming-piece" from Mentrim Lough, Co. Meath (Fig. 122:1) and, in openwork bronze, on a Somerset-type mount from Cornalaragh, Co. Monaghan (Fig. 140:8; Pl. 99). On stone, too, the ornament on the

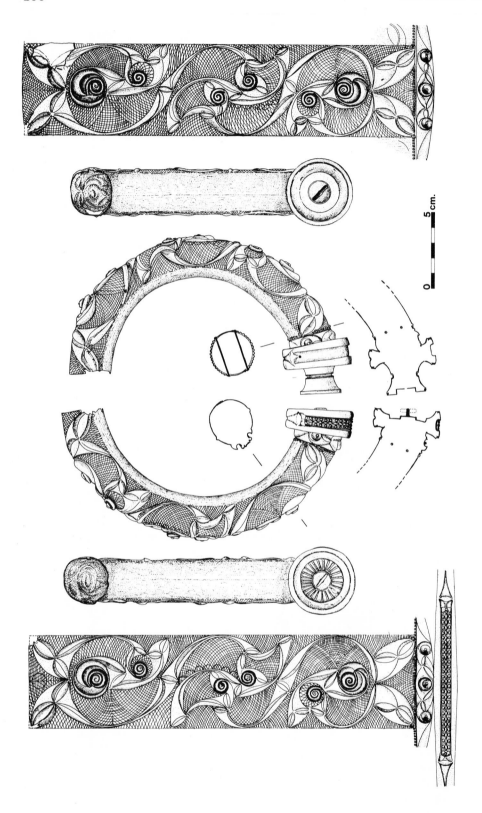

Fig. 96. Gold collar. Broighter, Co. Derry. – 2/5.

5 cm.

0

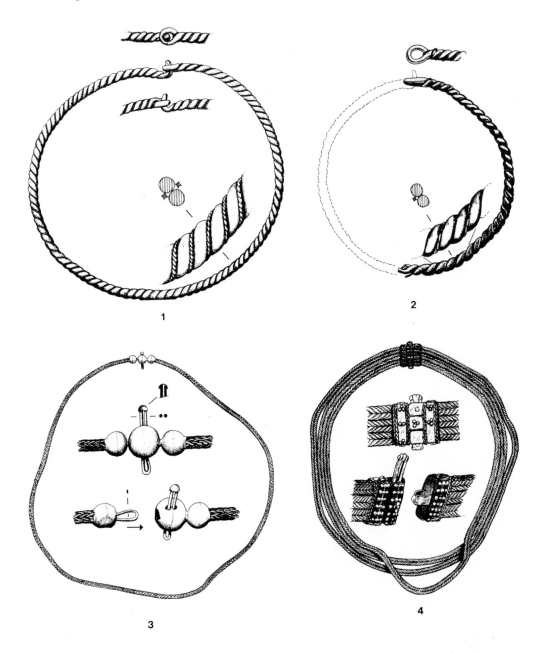

Fig. 97. Gold neck ornaments. Broighter, Co. Derry. - 1/2.

torc can be compared with that on the granite monolith from Turoe, Co. Galway (Fig. 143:2; Pl. 102).

There are also some elements of the decoration on the torc which bear comparison with British metalwork pieces. The decorated cylinder at the back of torc 1 from Hoard A at Snettisham has hammered arcs forming a background to the main decorative units (Clarke, op. cit., Fig. 4) in a manner reminiscent of the way in which the incised arcs highlight the repoussé curves on the Broighter specimen. Another of the objects from Snettisham (a bracelet from Hoard E: Clarke, op. cit., Fig. 12) seems also to share some features with the ornament on the Irish torc and some of the designs on the ends of Snettisham loop-terminal torcs are vaguely comparable to the Broighter designs (Clarke, op. cit., Pls XV, XVI; Fox, 1958, Figs 33,34). In detail, however, the similarities are not close. On the whole the gold objects from Broighter and Snettisham are likely to represent parallel stylistic development.

There can be little doubt that the torc from Broighter is a product of Irish workmanship. Other objects in the hoard are less clearly native and several are certainly imported. The twisted bar torcs of circular section can be paralleled at Snettisham and also Bawsey, in Norfolk, England (Clarke, op. cit., 46-51, Pls VIII-XII). The British examples differ from those in Ireland, however, in having a loop at each extremity rather than the hook-and-loop terminals of the Irish objects. Furthermore, the twisted wire within the torsion grooves on the two Irish torcs is not found on any of the British examples; this can be traced back to Greek objects of the mid-fourth century B.C. at least (Higgins, 1961, Pl. 30B, 129). In Early La Tène contexts twisted bar torcs and bracelets of gold are known, such as one from Toulouse (Jacobsthal, 1944, No. 64), while an annular gold bracelet from Waldalgesheim, Kr. Kreuznach, in Germany, has narrow, ribbed bands in the torsion grooves recalling the inset wires on the Broighter torc (op. cit., No. 54). The hook-and-loop terminals on the Irish bar torcs are readily paralleled on twisted torcs from Early La Tène contexts in the Champagne (Bretz-Mahler, 1971, Pl. 27, 34-39) but none of these examples is really close to the arrangement on the Irish specimens. Perhaps a more relevant parallel for the Broighter bar torcs is a twisted torc of gold with hook-and-loop terminals from the Roman hoard found in 1842 near Newgrange, Co. Meath (Topp, 1956, 53; Carson and O'Kelly, 1977, 54, Pl. III), to which Warner has recently drawn attention (1982, 29).

The two gold-wire necklaces (Fig. 97:3; Pl. 63) are exceptional pieces, which are unparalleled in these islands. Their ultimate background is Mediterranean, though it is difficult to establish the precise area of their probable manufacture. Evans, however, pointed to close parallels from Roman Alexandria in north Africa which date around the birth of Christ (1897, 396-8) and it may be in this area that the objects were made. They are clearly non-native. The chains in both cases are constructed in the loop-in-loop technique, which gives a more flexible type of wire than true plait (Higgins, 1961, 14-16). The technique is found as early as the middle of the third millennium B.C. in Mesopotamia, where it is first encountered at Ur. It spread westwards rapidly and remained popular throughout the whole of the ancient world. The triple-strand necklace from Broighter consists in each case of the simplest form of single-loop chain; the single-strand necklace is more complex consisting of multiple-loops skilfully threaded into one another (CIIAA, Fig. 146). It is probably in the interlocking of Etruscan, Hellenistic and early Roman elements that the inspiration behind the Broighter necklaces is to be found; the immediate background is likely to be Roman.

The clasps of the two wire necklaces from Broighter can be paralleled in Etruscan and Roman contexts, as for example on a pair of seventh century B.C. bracelets from Tarquinii (Higgins, 1961, Pl. 35). An even better comparison is to be found, however, on a third century A.D. Roman openwork bracelet from Tunis (Higgins, 1961, Pl. 60B). Clearly this type of clasp mechanism was long favoured in the Mediterranean world. It was in the Mediterranean, too, that the technique of granulation was brought to its highest standard of perfection, especially amongst the Etruscans and, to a lesser extent, the Romans (Carroll, 1974).

Furger-Gunti felt that the heavy backing materials found within a number of the torcs, in contrast to the thin and fragile sheet-gold of their tubes, indicated a non-utilitarian role for them (op. cit., 22). He argued at length that the function of the torcs, and the reasons for their deposition, were wholly related to cult practises (op. cit., 37-42). The find circumstances of many of the torcs support this hypothesis. Not one has ever come from a grave, as is the normal context of the torcs of Early La Tène Europe. The Late La Tène torcs are commonly found in hoards along with other objects of gold which often include gold coins. Not infrequently the environment in which they are located is marshy or riverine. Two noteworthy examples, from Pommereul in Belgium (Furger-Gunti, op. cit., 22, Abb. 13) and, of course, La Tène in Switzerland (Vouga, 1923, 67-8, Fig. 8, Pl. XXI:21; Clarke, 1954, 44; Furger-Gunti, op. cit., 25, Abb. 16b) were associated with a mass of material, including iron tools and swords in their scabbards. These are best interpreted (*pace* Schwab, 1972), as votive deposits. The position of the Broighter hoard in the flood plain of the River Roe, not far from the seashore corresponds to the sort of environment in which the majority of the European torcs have come to light. Warner has recently discussed the implications of the Broighter findspot and he too has argued in favour of votive deposition. This hypothesis has much to commend it in view of the European evidence and the exceptional nature of the hoard. It is interesting also to note the location of Broighter in an area subject to frequent flooding (Warner, op. cit., 31), for the St. Louis/Basel hoard came from a precisely similar situation; it was, in fact, first brought to light as a result of severe flooding of the Rhine in 1883 (Furger-Gunti, op. cit., 5).

But the find circumstances do not in every instance suggest ritual deposition. Clarke, for example, regarded the five Snettisham hoards together "as a smith's or founder's hoard and not a series of votive deposits or share-out of loot" (op. cit., 70), for fragmentary objects, scrap and other raw materials predominated. The two Niederzier/Düren torcs were found with 46 coins buried in the side of a rubbish pit within a Late La Tène settlement (Joachim, 1979, 56), hardly a compellingly votive context; the excavator does not, however, rule out this possibility (op. cit., 57).

The Broighter hoard is thus a unique and important assemblage. The buffer torc, decorated in Ireland, shows the country to have been in close contact with Continental traditions of gold-working and the object, along with its mode of burial, may be an indicator of common religious customs and beliefs in Ireland and Celtic Europe. The wire necklaces were clearly imported from the Mediterranean and the bar torcs may reflect cultural links with eastern England. Whereas the buffer torc is undoubtedly a product of the last century B.C., it is possible that the hoard was placed in the ground after the turn of the millennium.

Miscellaneous neck ornaments

A number of necklets of bronze is known from Ireland. From one of the Lambay, Co. Dublin, inhumations comes a beaded torc of north British type (Fig. 98:1; Map 16). The object has long been regarded as an import from Brigantia (most recent summary: Rynne, 1976) and its date, around the middle of the first Christian century, is hardly in question (for the type: MacGregor, 1976, 97-99). A penannular bronze loop with simply moulded ends from Lisnacrogher, Co. Antrim (Fig. 98:2; Wakeman, 1890-1, 544 and Pl. III:2), may also be a neck ornament, though its restricted internal dimensions (14.6 cm by 7.9 cm) do not rule out the possibility that it could have been worn on the upper arm. The object has no parallels in Ireland but the similarity between its moulded terminals and the moulding on Type 3 ringheaded pins (two of which came from Lisnacrogher, Fig. 86:3,4) should be noted. In view of the suggested

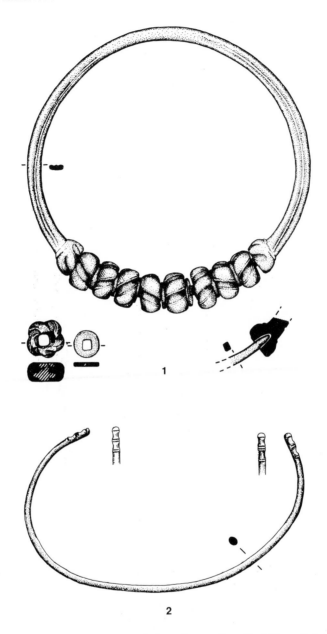

Fig. 98. Bronze neck ornaments. 1 Lambay, Co. Dublin. 2 Lisnacrogher, Co. Antrim. - 1/2.

early Continental elements at Lisnacrogher (above pp. 99-107) it is, perhaps, of interest to compare the terminals on the Irish object with the similarly moulded ends of bracelets of the European "Dux" horizon (e.g. Kruta, 1979, 101, Fig. 16a).

Two fragmentary bar torcs of cast bronze from Annesborough, Co. Armagh, were included by MacGregor in her list of Iron Age torcs (1976, 111). While admitting that these objects could be contemporary with the first century A.D. Roman fibula allegedly found with them (Eogan, 1964, 274, 332, Fig. 4) it is likely that the bronze palstave from the "hoard" gives a more correct indication of the date of the torcs (Eogan, 1964, 273; see Hennig, 1980, 115, Abb. 12:2 for close Bronze Age comparison).

Reference may finally be made to the alleged representation of a buffer torc on the neck of a stone head from Beltany, Co. Donegal (Fig. 153; Rynne, 1972, 87, Fig. 18). The features on the neck are, however, so worn as to make the identification uncertain.

Bracelets of bronze

The number of bracelets of bronze from Iron Age Ireland is small but includes several important examples. The bronze penannular bracelet with bulbous terminals from the Kilmurry, Co. Kerry, hoard is a Hallstatt C import, possibly from Alsace (Fig. 2:3; Eogan, 1964, 320). Five "nut-moulded" bracelets of Hallstatt D type are preserved (Fig. 2:1,2,4,5) and a sixth (one of a pair), is now missing (Armstrong, 1911b, 58-60). All the localised examples come from Co. Antrim.

Two bronze bracelets were found at Lisnacrogher. The first (Fig. 99:3) can be compared with a specimen from Lambay (Fig. 99:4). The probable first century date for the Lambay bracelet may be a clue to the dating of the Co. Antrim piece. The other example from Lisnacrogher (Fig. 99:2) is less certainly a bracelet. It is now incomplete and the remaining portion consists of two coils of bronze wire, the outer surfaces of which bear incised decoration. It has no close parallels.

Two hollow bronze rings, one plain, the other adorned along its outer surface with incised linear ornament, were found with other bronzes in a hoard at Kishawanny, Co. Kildare (Pl. 18). These objects may be bracelets (cf. Fox, 1946, 21, 24-25, 69, Pl. IX:86) but the possibility that they could have served another purpose, conceivably as the bronze casing of iron horsebit rings, cannot be discounted.

From Newry, Co. Down, comes the only Irish example of the essentially eastern Scottish "massive armlet" (Fig. 99:1a,b; Map 17). These objects have been subjected to detailed study on more than one occasion, most recently and comprehensively by Simpson (1968, 233-254) and summarised by her (now MacGregor, 1976, 106-110). She concludes by regarding them as "products of a renaissance of decorative skills in the late first and second centuries A.D.". The chronological position of the Irish piece

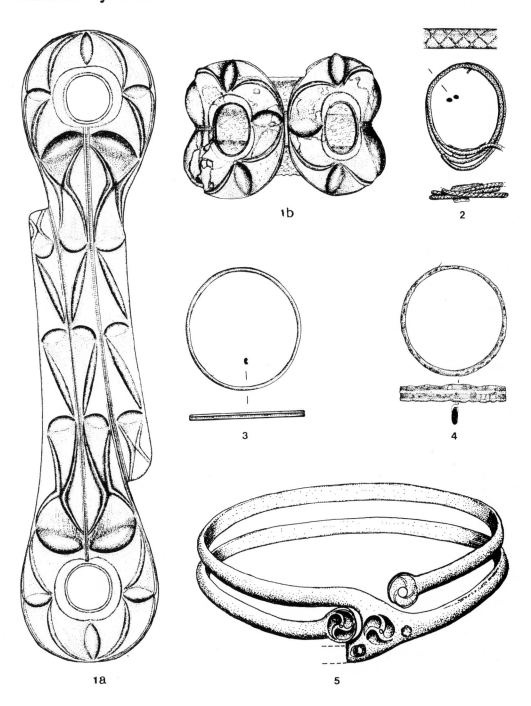

Fig. 99. Bronze bracelets. 1a,b Newry, Co. Down. 2,3 Lisnacrogher,
Co. Antrim. 4 Lambay, Co. Dublin. 5 Ballymahon, Co. Meath.
– 5 approx. 3/4, otherwise 1/2.

may be regarded as secure and it takes its place with the Antrim terret, the Lambay beaded torc and other material as a clearly recognisable import to Ireland from northern Britain at the beginning of our era (below pp. 328-330).

The Ballymahon coiled armlet (Fig. 99:5) is tentatively included in this discussion because of the uncertainty of its date. Rynne (1964) suggested that it belonged to the fifth or sixth century A.D. but this date is based on nothing more than a few not very convincing stylistic parallels for the triskele ornament on the object. Parallels of presumably earlier date, such as the triskeles on the stop-studs of an unlocalised Irish horsebit (Fig. 17:1) could equally be postulated as relevant comparisons, as could those on the knob-ends of the Attymon and Drumanone pendants (Fig. 35:1,3; Pl. 16). Rynne's contention that chronological significance may be attached to the presence of a centrally-perforated triskele is unjustified as the design on the undoubtedly Iron Age mount from Ballycastle, Co. Antrim (Fig. 140:6; Pl. 97:2) demonstrates. Rings of presumed Iron Age date from Scotland also bear comparable triskele designs (e.g. MacGregor, 1976, Nos 40,258,259) and the same design is present on a wooden plaque from Lochlee crannog also in Scotland (ibid., No. 337). There are many more examples.

The Ballymahon bracelet is, however, a unique piece. It is conceivable that its coiled form was influenced by the coiled snake bracelets found in north Britain during the early centuries A.D., but in the last analysis it must be accepted that, as long as dating rests on a consideration of the triskele ornament which adorns it, so long shall its date be open for discussion.

Bracelets of glass and jet

A number of bracelets of glass and jet, belonging in broad terms to the Iron Age, is known from Ireland. The date of the two glass specimens from the Loughey, Co. Down, burial deposit has already been commented upon above (p. 151). The Freestone Hill, Co. Kilkenny, fragment (Raftery, B., 1969, 51, 83, Fig. 30) presumably dates to the third or fourth century A.D. on the basis of associated Roman material. The Feerwore, Co. Galway, fragment may be a few centuries earlier than this but is at present hardly susceptible to close dating (Raftery, J., 1944, 33, Fig. 4:23). The Dunadry, Co. Antrim, fragment of clear glass, found in association with a jet bracelet fragment in a burial mound, is undatable (Macalister, 1928, 203; Raftery, B., 1981, 181-3).

Apart from the jet example from Dunadry (CIIAA No. 466), the only other relevant bracelet of this substance is the complete specimen from

Lambay, Co. Dublin (CIIAA No. 467). This piece, bent slightly off a horizontal plane, may have once adorned an ankle rather than a wrist. Its presumed contemporaneity with the dated metalwork from the site places it firmly in a first century A.D. context (Rynne, 1976, 240).

Spiral rings

The number of spiral rings known from Ireland is small and the dating of individual specimens is not always clear. There are, however, several instances where a date within the Iron Age is probable. The ring from the Loughey, Co. Down, burial (Jope and Wilson, 1957a) is obviously Iron Age in date and that from Lisnacrogher, Co. Antrim (CIIAA No. 469), may well be also. The Feerwore, Co. Galway, ring (Raftery, J., 1944, 33, Figs 4, 26) was also associated with Iron Age material; the ring from Cairn H, Lough Crew, Co. Meath, cannot be considered apart from the decorated flakes and the melon bead from the tomb and must surely be contemporary with them (Herity, 1974, Fig. 139:37). The spiral finger/toe ring from Site 4 at the Curragh, Co. Kildare (Ó Ríordáin, 1950, 258, Fig. 8,4:3), may be a further Iron Age ring, though its relationship to the burial on the site is not certain, nor, indeed, has the date of the burial itself been established. The two ribbed, spiral rings of silver from Newgrange, Co. Meath, are more elaborate than the bronze examples and are probably Roman (Carson and O'Kelly, 1977, 51, Pl. VIIIa). A closely similar ring comes from the broch of Dun Mor Vaul on Tiree off the west coast of Scotland (MacKie, 1974, 132, Fig. 17:327). Spiral rings are present amongst the material from the unpublished excavations at Ballingarry Down, Co. Limerick (a ringfort), and Dooey, Co. Donegal (sandhill occupation: Ó Ríordáin and Rynne, 1961, 58-64). In neither instance is dating clear though at the latter site, at least, bronzes of sub-Roman appearance, as well as a large body of material of the Early Historic period, are certainly present. Lastly, attention may be drawn to the stray rings in the National Museum from Feltrim Hill, Co. Dublin, Deredis Upper, Co. Cavan, and Dalkey Island, Co. Dublin, none of which is, however, datable. The possibility of a late dating for some, at least, of the spiral rings is indicated by the presence of one example at Garranes, Co. Cork, a ringfort dated to the Early Historic period (Ó Ríordáin, 1942, 100, 97, Fig. 4:176), and the presence of spiral loops of bronze wire on pennanular brooches of the Early Historic centuries should also be noted (e.g. Henry, 1965, Pl. 24).

Thus it can be seen that the evidence for dating these rings as a group is not overwhelming but certain tentative deductions can be made. The Loughey specimen dates to the beginning of the Christian era (above

p. 151) and a comparable date for the Lough Crew specimen is likely.
The ring from Feerwore could date to just before or just after the birth
of Christ, and if the ring from Lisnacrogher is contemporary with the
dated Iron Age material from that site it can be placed somewhere in
the period between the third century B.C. and the first century or so
A.D.   On the basis of their study of the Loughey burial, Jope and Wilson
considered southern England as the source of the spiral rings (1957a,
79-82) but the concentration of spiral rings in Scotland should not be
forgotten (MacKie, 1970).   The type is, however, widespread in Europe
and has no recognisable chronological limits.   Devoid of firm context
the rings are valueless as an indicator of date (Clarke, 1971, 25-28).

Annular rings

A few plain, circular, cast bronze rings are also known from Ireland.
That from one of the Lambay inhumations was found encircling a middle
finger joint (Macalister, 1929, 234, No. 26, Pl. XXII:13; Rynne, 1976,
240).

Beads of glass

Glass beads are recorded from Ireland at least as early as the Late
Bronze Age (as shown by recent excavations at Rathgall, Co. Wicklow;
Raftery, B., 1976b) and it is clear that they were an important means
of self-adornment throughout the Iron Age and Early Historic periods.
In the latter era, at least, there can be no doubt that the beads were
made in native workshops and a great variety of bead types was produced.
There is no reason not to believe that beads were also being made here
during the pagan Iron Age.

There are many problems involved in trying to isolate from the huge
mass of glass beads which exist in our museums those specimens which
belong to the Early Iron Age.   Not only is the very volume of the material
itself an obstacle, compounded by the high percentage of unlocalised
and unstratified examples, but also there is the added problem posed
by the apparent continuity of Iron Age types well into historic centuries.
Thus, if beads from allegedly Early Historic contexts can be precisely
paralleled by beads from undoubtedly Iron Age burials, do we take the
former as representing early beads which somehow found their way into
a late level, do we take them as demonstrating the unchanging techniques
of bead manufacture over many centuries, should we see them as family
heirlooms or should we perhaps doubt the original dating assigned to
the sites?   There is no easy answer to these questions.

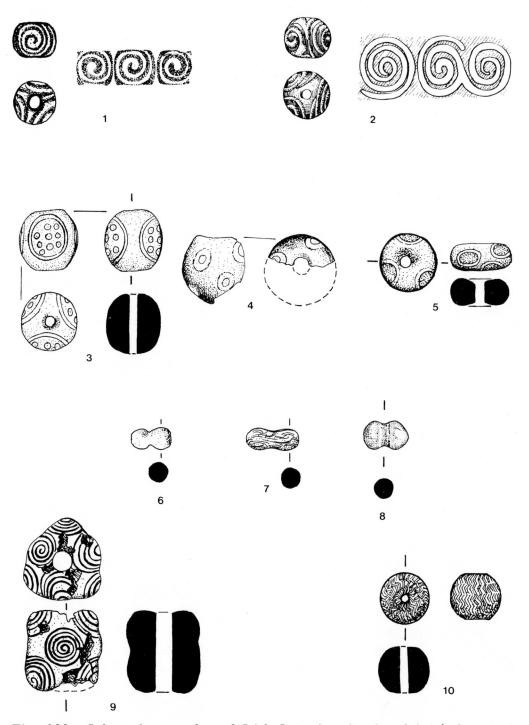

Fig. 100. Selected examples of Irish Iron Age beads. 1,3,4,6 Grannagh, Co. Galway. 2 Loughey, Co. Down. 5,7,9,10 Kiltierney, Co. Fermanagh. 8 Carrowjames, Co. Mayo. – 6,8 bone, otherwise glass. – 1/1.

Clearly a specialist study of the Irish glass material is urgently needed. A start has been made by Guido (1978) but for Ireland there is much to do. Scientific analysis of the Irish beads on a large scale is a prerequisite. Until this has been carried out it is possible to make only the most generalised of observations. The first serious attempt at such an analysis has recently taken place (Warner and Meighan, 1981).

Comment on the Irish material is here largely confined to those examples which come from reasonably reliable contexts but where a bead type is sufficiently distinctive, stray specimens may also be considered.

Notwithstanding the fairly limited number of beads in Ireland which may reasonably be regarded as of Iron Age date there is no small amount of variety amongst them. The best contexts are burials (Raftery, B., 1981) but a number of occupation sites have also yielded relevant glass material. Of the latter, however, Cairn H, Lough Crew, Co. Meath, and the Rath of the Synods, Tara, Co. Meath, are as yet unpublished so that little can be said of the precise stratigraphical positions of beads which they yielded. Recently excavated hilltop sites of Iron Age date at Dún Ailinne, Co. Kildare, and Emain Macha, Co. Armagh, have also produced glass material but these, too, await publication.

Perhaps the most interesting collection of Irish beads has come from a ring-barrow at Grannagh, Co. Galway. No fewer than ten glass beads have been recovered from the monument, some from cremation deposits, some unstratified within the body of the mound. Four bone beads have also come from Grannagh as well as some safety-pin fibula fragments and a number of other artifacts (for recent discussion of the Grannagh material, see Hawkes, 1982, 59-62).

Included amongst the glass objects from Grannagh are two essentially colourless beads with marvered-in spiral decoration covering almost their entire surface (Fig. 100:1). The most significant parallels in Ireland for these are the eight comparable specimens from the cremation burial at Loughey, Co. Down (Fig. 100:2; Jope and Wilson, 1957a), but a number of other examples of the type are recorded in the country from sandhill sites in Donegal, from a ringfort at Garryduff, Co. Cork, and from a crannog at Lagore, Co. Meath (Guido, 1978, 188).

Outside Ireland comparable beads are concentrated in the south-western portion of Britain centred on the Meare lake settlement and the possibility that the latter site was a centre for the manufacture of these beads has prompted Guido to name the group "Meare spiral" beads (1978, 79-81). A few outliers of the type are also recorded from Scotland. Tentative dating for such beads in Britain lies between c. 250 B.C. and 50 A.D. Within Ireland, the best fixed point remains the Loughey burial, where the beads were associated with a number of important bronzes, notably a Nauheim-derivative brooch, now to be dated around the beginning of the Christian era, or slightly before (above p. 151). A southern English origin for the person buried at Loughey seems reasonably probable and, indeed, the distribution of these beads on either side of the Irish Sea could perhaps be interpreted as indicating movement of some sort northward along that important routeway.

The longevity of "Meare spiral" beads as a type in Ireland is, however, uncertain, for some examples come from excavated sites which, on conventional grounds, are dated well into the historic period. At Lagore, Co. Meath, for instance, two examples were found though neither was stratified. The excavator could only compare them to Iron Age beads from Meare and Maiden Castle in Dorset. He felt, however, that they "would seem to be a survival in Ireland" (Hencken, 1950, 145). Guido on the other hand regarded such beads as "treasured heirlooms perhaps accidentally found and kept" (1978, 80), and she referred to the Garryduff, Co. Cork, ringfort find as "probably an earlier stray" (1978, 188). It can be seen that these examples clearly illustrate the difficulties already adverted to with regard to the recognition of those beads which in Ireland belong to the Iron Age and those which do not.

While the Loughey "spirals" date either just before or just after the birth of Christ, it may be that at Grannagh the latter of the two possibilities is preferable. At that site one of the "spirals" was directly associated in a cremation deposit not only with some bone beads and a glass dumb-bell toggle (see below) but also with a tiny segmented bead of translucent blue glass which seems most appropriately compared to early Roman specimens (Guido, 1978, 91-92, Fig. 37:1). A putative Roman context for burial activity at the Grannagh monument is further enhanced by Macalister's early discovery there of two fragmentary beads of bluish-green glass which, according to Guido, may well be made of re-used Roman bottle glass (ibid., 69, 167).

Grannagh also produced an interesting blue glass bead ornamented with inlaid nests of eyes (Fig. 100:3); this, oddly, has its closest parallel in the fourth-century B.C. grave from Reinheim in south-west Germany (Keller, 1965, 49 and Taf. 26:1,2). It hardly seems likely that the Irish specimen is as early as the Reinheim bead though this cannot be entirely ruled out. The object could be a late survival. Closer to home, the beads of "Garrow Tor" type as isolated by Guido (ibid., 61-62), may also be compared to the Irish bead and indeed Guido herself noted the similarities between these beads and the Reinheim example and saw the latter as representing the probable prototypes for this group. Two specimens of this type of bead (apart from Grannagh) are listed by her for Ireland but she is cautious on dating, for these may have been revived here in Early Historic times.

The other "eyed" bead from Grannagh (Fig. 100:4) has also some general affinities with several of Guido's classes, notably her South Harting and Findon types (ibid., 49-51) but in neither case are the parallels precise. Neither of these two "eyed" beads came from a closed deposit at Grannagh.

The presence of a glass dumb-bell bead from Grannagh (Fig. 100:6) invites comparison with the Kiltierney burial monument, where secondary cremation deposits in an earlier mound apparently yielded such a bead (Fig. 100:7), along with three other glass beads (Fig. 100:5,9,10) and a bronze safety-pin fibula (above p. 151). Recent inhumation burials at Knowth, Co. Meath, have also produced, among other grave-goods, a dumb-bell bead of colourless glass. Dumb-bell beads seem essentially an Irish form but they are known from Britain (e.g. Gelling, 1958, 95, Fig. 4:5,6). The occurrence of three specimens from Iron Age burials in Ireland indicates for the first time an early dating for the type in the country and it is likely that the glass dumb-bell beads from Cairn H, Lough Crew (Herity, 1974, 282, Fig. 139:33-5), are also of Iron Age date. The occurrence of glass dumb-bell beads at Lagore and other sites said to belong to the Early Historic period (Hencken, 1950, 141, Fig. 67:1471) indicates the possibility that the type could have continued late in this country (but note the reservations expressed above regarding such apparent survivals). However, Grannagh, Kiltierney and probably Lough Crew show that by the first century A.D. at least, and possibly even a century or so earlier, dumb-bell beads were already being made in Ireland. A pagan, Iron Age context for such beads is also shown by a bone version from cremation 18, Tumulus 8, at Carrowjames, Co. Mayo (Fig. 100:8; Raftery, J., 1940-1, 70-1).

A date either just before or just after the birth of Christ for the dumb-bell beads is supported by the other material from Kiltierney. The fine, trumpet-ornamented brooch has already been considered (above, p. 151), and a date in the centuries spanning the birth of Christ has been suggested for it on formal and stylistic grounds. In addition, the large, spiral-decorated bead from Kiltierney (Fig. 100:9) is a classic example of Guido's Class 6 (Oldbury type) beads. These are an ultimately Continental type with a southern English concentration and a lesser scatter in north Wales and southern Scotland (ibid., 53-57). Dating evidence for the type points consistently to the last two centuries B.C. and the first Christian century. Guido does not, however, discount the possibility of a late revival of such beads in Ireland. Six other specimens of this bead group are listed by her, all from eastern Ulster.

The "eyed" bead from Kiltierney (Fig. 100:5) may be a variant of

Fig. 101. Late La Tène glass ringbeads from Ireland. 1 Denhamstown, Co. Meath. 2 Cloughwater, Co. Antrim. 3 Co. Antrim? 4 Co. Antrim? 5 Hawk Hill, Co. Kildare. – 1/1.

Guido's South Harting type (ibid., 49-50) which according to her belong to the Early Romano-British period, but there are differences in detail, particularly in size, between the Irish example and the British beads.

The fourth Kiltierney bead, that with horizontal bands of herring-bone ornament (Fig. 100:10), has almost exact parallels in a number of beads from the Carrowjames tumulus (Raftery, J., 1940a, Pl. I:8). As with the dumb-bell beads, herring-bone beads are also recorded from sites of the Early Historic period, such as Lagore, Co. Meath (Hencken, 1950, 139, Fig. 67:984). The dating of individual specimens is thus again problematical but it is interesting to note Beck's comments on the Lagore herring-bone bead (in Hencken, ibid., 139). He stated that the Lagore bead "is so like a bead from Meare Lake Village that I think these two may be identical in manufacture and that, either the bead .... is an old bead, or else that beads like them have continued to be made for a thousand years or more". At any rate, the Carrowjames and Kiltierney finds show that these beads begin in the pagan Iron Age and it may be that appropriate parallels for them are to be found in beads such as the Roman specimen illustrated by Guido from South Shields (ibid., 101, Fig. 38:10).

The remaining Irish beads of likely Iron Age date call for little comment here. Parallels for the tiny horned bead from Loughey are not readily forthcoming (Guido, ibid., 74-75, Fig. 23:2). The small opaque, yellow beads from Loughey were included by Guido in her Class 8 and similar beads from Oranbeg are comparable to those from the same Co. Down burial. According to Guido such beads overlap in culture and in time with the "Meare spirals" (ibid., 73-76). They are an insular type and in Britain they occur in two principal areas, south-west England and eastern, south-eastern and western Scotland. The small blue beads which came from Loughey, Oranbeg, the Knowth inhumation and Pollacorragune, Co. Galway (Riley, 1936), require specialist study before their significance can be assessed.

In view of the problems earlier referred to concerning a study of the Irish glass material, it is difficult to know how much emphasis should be placed on unstratified and unassociated glass beads. A number of differing types are listed by Guido but only two specific forms may be referred to here. The single Irish example of her "Hanging Langford" type (Class 5), from Newcastle, Co. Down (ibid., 51-53), is of great potential interest if a north-west French or Breton origin for it should be demonstrated by future research. The large ringbeads with whirl or ray design (Fig. 101; Guido's Class 7, ibid., 57-59; Haevernick, 1960, Group 23), of which nine specimens are listed by Guido for Ireland, are a well-known Late La Tène Continental type which were imported to these islands and may have been imitated here (Raftery, B., 1972a, 14-18).

Fig. 102. Bone and stone beads. 1 Grannagh, Co. Galway. 2,3 Knowth,
Co. Meath. 4 Lisnacrogher, Co. Antrim. - 1,3 bone. 4 stone.
1-3:1/1. 4:1/2.

Beads of bone and stone

As well as glass beads a number of burials has also produced beads
of bone. The simple cylindrical or globular specimens such as those
from Carrowbeg North, Co. Galway (Willmot, 1939), or Oranbeg, Co.
Galway are on their own hardly susceptible to dating, for the type seems
timeless. The more pear-shaped beads, however, with a cylindrical or,
more characteristically, with a V-perforation piercing the narrower end
(Fig. 102:1-3), may well prove to be a recognisable Iron Age form here
for such have now come from Grannagh and Knowth (Eogan, 1968, 369,
Fig. 37), the former certainly, the latter probably, of Iron Age date.
The beads from a possible grave at Newgrange (Flanagan, 1960, 61-2)
probably also belong to this group. The bone dumb-bell bead from
Carrowjames has already been noted above.

A stone bead from Lisnacrogher (Fig. 102:4) has oblique ribbing around
its outer surface; this calls to mind the designs on Roman melon beads
and also the central boss of the bronze triangular plaque from the first
century burial at Lambay, Co. Dublin (Fig. 139:2; Rynne, 1976, 235-236,
Pl. XXXIII:I).

Bronze "Locket"

The bronze locket-like object from Carrowbeg North, Co. Galway
(Fig. 103:2; Pl. 64), was found in the left shoulder area of an extended
female skeleton (Willmot, 1939; Raftery, B., 1982, 187, Fig. 40). Close
to one of her feet an anklet of twelve bone beads was found. The burial
was one of four (the other three devoid of gravegoods) which had been
placed as secondary interments in the ditch fill of a Bronze Age burial
mound.

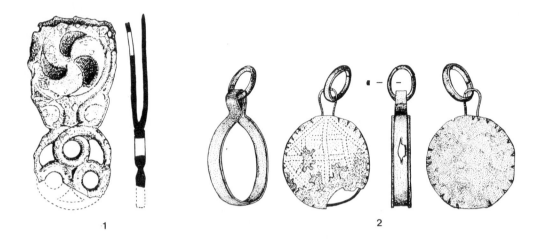

Fig. 103. Items of personal ornament. 1 bronze strap-tag, Rathgall, Co. Wicklow. 2 bronze "locket", Carrowbeg North, Co. Galway. - 1/1.

Neither in form nor in ornament can the "locket" be precisely paralleled. Superficial similarities with Roman seal-boxes must be fortuitous for the Carrowbeg bronze was never intended to open. Nonetheless the angular designs which sometimes occur on the seal-boxes or on other small Roman bronzes of the early centuries A.D. (e.g. Thompson, 1975, 190, 193, Fig. 26:13) may have some bearing on the dating of the Irish object. The design on a silver disc-chape from a Roman cemetery at Cologne in Germany also resembles that on the Carrowbeg specimen (AuhV, 1900, IV, Taf. 57:1b).

Better parallels are to be found, however, in two cremation burials (one at least of a woman), Nos 1216 and 1252, at Wederath-Belginum, near Trier in south-western Germany (Haffner, 1977, 180-202; 1978, 67-71, Taf. 310:4f., 79, Taf. 321:14). Here, small, circular, hollow objects of iron with loops for suspension, as on the Carrowbeg bronze, were found accompanied in one grave by Middle/Late La Tène ring-beads, in the other by an iron shaft-hole axehead. Each one is described as an "Amulettkapsel" and such a function is likely for the Irish piece. It could once have contained some organic substance, now perished, which bestowed upon it properties of a protective or magico-ritual nature.

The Wederath-Belginum burials date to the last centuries B.C. The possibility of similar dating for the Carrowbeg interments cannot be dismissed so that they may, in fact, be considerably earlier than recently suggested by the writer (1981, 197).

The presence of some textile fragments adhering to the back of the Carrowbeg specimen (Pl. 64) adds to its interest for this is the only piece of textile from Ireland for which an Iron Age date may be argued.

Strap-tag

The decorated bronze strap-tag found at Rathgall, Co. Wicklow (Fig. 103:1; Pl. 65) has been fully discussed by the present writer (1970, 200-211). The object, with its loop-end and its openwork ornament clearly reflects provincial Roman influence and a date in the late first or early second century A.D. was argued for it. Strap-tags of this type are a Continental Roman feature and the object probably implies contact with the European mainland. It is of wholly insular (probably Irish) manufacture, however, and is an indication of likely Roman cultural influences here in the early centuries A.D.

TOILET EQUIPMENT

Mirrors

Two handled Iron Age mirrors are known from Ireland (Ballymoney, Co. Antrim and Lambay, Co. Dublin), and an imported Roman disc mirror of bronze was found in a burial at Stoneyford, Co. Kilkenny (Raftery, B., 1981, Fig. 41:1). A bronze handle from Inishkea North, Co. Mayo has been regarded as possibly from a mirror but it is likely to be the handle of a patera (Henry, 1952, 169-171, Pl. XXVIII). An unlocalised object of enamelled bronze could possibly be the handle portion of a mirror (CIIAA No. 818; Pl. 67). The object consists of a perforated sub-circular disc 5.1 cm in maximum external width, from one edge of which a narrow moulded socket projects.

The most interesting mirror is that from Ballybogey Bog, Ballymoney, Co. Antrim (Fig. 104:1; Pl. 66; Jope, 1954b). This is represented by a heavy, double-looped handle with cast ornithomorphic modelling. Only a small portion of the original iron disc remains. It is not certain to which of Fox's categories the Irish example belongs (1958, 84ff.), but perhaps the closest in form is that from Ingleton in Yorkshire, which has a pair of loops joined by a straight ribbed section. On this mirror, the place of the Ballymoney bird heads is taken by bovine masks. The Ingleton piece is included by Fox in his Group 1 mirrors with bar handles and he is inclined, though, as he admits himself, on limited evidence, to see the type as fundamentally north British. MacGregor (1976, 140-141) also stresses the northerly aspect of these objects though an isolated example is found as far south as Devon. Comparable forms are also present, engraved on the presumably later Pictish slabs.

MacGregor compares the ribbing on the Ballymoney handle with ribbing on a late Yorkshire horsebit from Rise and goes so far as to wonder

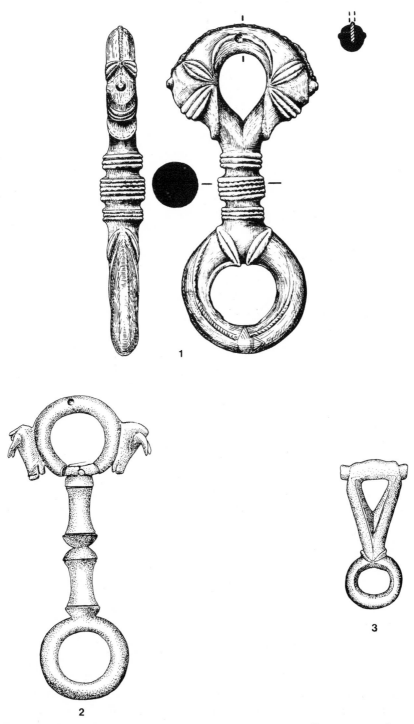

Fig. 104. Mirror handles. 1 Ballybogey Bog, Ballymoney, Co. Antrim. 2 Ingleton, Yorkshire, England. 3 Bac Mhic Connain, North Uist, Scotland. 1:3/4. 2,3:1/2.

whether this might suggest Yorkshire manufacture for the Irish object. The comparison, however, seems hardly close enough to substantiate such a hypothesis. Her comparison between the "split-lip detail" on the ring-terminal of the Ballymoney piece and the ridge of bone which separates the grip from the ring-terminal of a supposed mirror handle from Bac Mhic Connain, North Uist (Fig. 104:3), is more appropriate. Such a detail is, however, also present on the earlier iron mirror handle from Arras (Stead, 1979, 81-83, Fig. 32).

Jope, on the other hand, saw the Ballymoney object as an import from southern Britain (1954b. 94). He compared, for instance, the birds on the Irish mirror handle with "bird-head hints" on the Old Warden, Bedfordshire, mirror plaque and also with moulding on the Desborough, Northamptonshire, mirror handle. Whereas the representations on the Desborough handle are to some extent comparable with the Ballymoney bird heads, the Old Warden ornament has, it seems, little in common with the Irish piece and in neither case is there clearly detectable ornithomorphic representation. The modelling on the handle of the Antrim bronze is also compared by Jope with that on the handle of a mirror from Stamford Hill, Plymouth, but again the parallel is hardly close. Ingleton in Yorkshire seems far more relevant (Fig. 104:2) and perhaps it is in northern rather than southern Britain that the immediate background of the Irish mirror should be sought, even though ultimate origins for the type may lie further to the south in that island. It should be noted, however, that the bird's heads on the Irish mirror have good parallels on metalwork of undoubtedly Irish manufacture (e.g. Fig. 11:1) so that the possibility that it was cast on Irish soil cannot be discounted.

The Lambay, Co. Dublin, mirror is corroded and fragmentary and can be considered only in the context of the burial deposit as a whole. The material from the island clearly points to north Britain and can hardly be other than an exotic assemblage of the mid-first century A.D. (Rynne, 1976).

Combs

Fourteen fragmentary bone combs are preserved from Lough Crew, Co. Meath, Passage Grave H (see below p. 251; Fig. 105; Pl. 68) and a possible fifteenth is represented by a tiny fragment from the same site. An unstratified comb from Lagore, Co. Meath (Hencken, 1950, 189, 190, Fig. 102A), may also be contemporary with the Lough Crew group and two comparable specimens from uncertainly dated contexts have been recovered from the recent excavations at Knowth, Co. Meath (information courtesy excavator, Professor George Eogan). Though sometimes referred

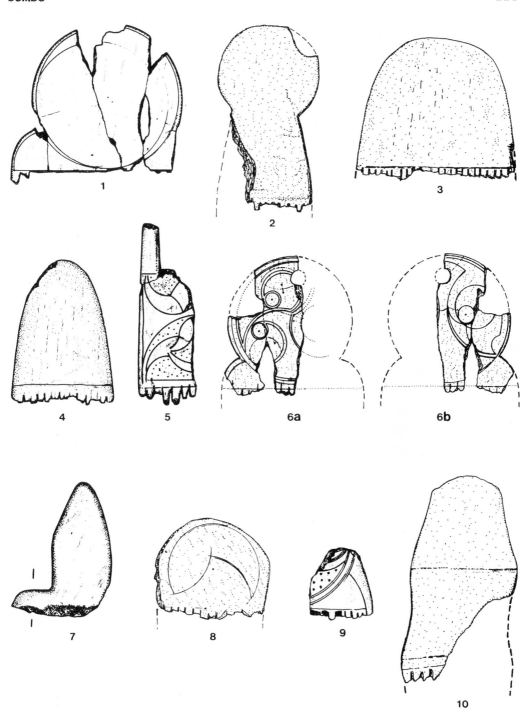

Fig. 105. Bone combs. Lough Crew, Co. Meath. – 1/1.

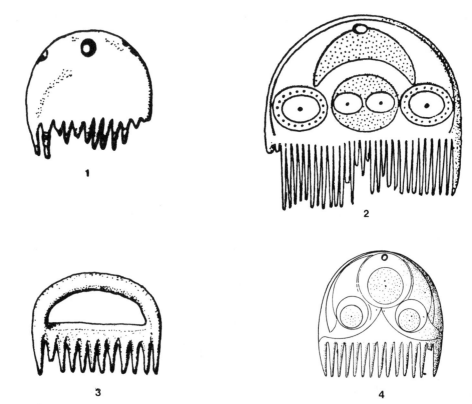

Fig. 106. British bone combs. 1 Close ny Collagh, Isle of Man. 2 Ghegan Rock, Seacliff, East Lothian, Scotland. 3 Bowermadden, Caithness, Scotland. 4 Langbank, Renfrewshire, Scotland. - 1/1. (1 after Gelling, 1958. 2,4 after MacGregor, 1976. 3 after Anderson, 1883).

to as weaving combs, the small size of these combs and their slender form seem more in keeping with use as toilet implements.

That the combs from Lough Crew belong to the same cultural and chronological context as the flakes from that site is beyond question so that what is written regarding the dating and affinities of the flakes (below p. 258) applies equally to the combs. But additional evidence, independent of a stylistic analysis of the flakes, is arrived at by a study of the combs themselves and a consideration of related pieces outside the country.

Closest parallels are to be found in Scotland. From a crannog at Langbank in Renfrewshire (Fig. 106:4) and a midden site at Ghegan Rock, Seacliff, East Lothian (Fig. 106:2; MacGregor, 1976, Nos 274, 275), come two combs similar in form to the Irish specimens and each one bears incised, compass-drawn ornament on the handle. The Langbank comb, in form and decoration, is particularly close to several from Lough Crew.

It could, indeed, be an Irish piece: compare, for instance, its ornament with that on the Petrie Crown (Fig. 133) or on the Monasterevin-type discs (Figs 136, 137). MacGregor (ibid., 143) drew attention to another undecorated comb of similar type from a promontory fort at Close ny Chollagh, Man (Fig. 106:1).

Dating for these British combs seems to centre on the first century A.D. Occupation at the Isle of Man fort, according to the excavator, ceased c. 75-80 A.D. (Gelling, 1958, 97), and at the two other sites relevantly dated Roman and sub-Roman material was recovered.

Another Scottish comb of possible significance for the Lough Crew series is a tiny example with openwork handle from a broch at Bowermadden in Caithness (Fig. 106:3; Anderson, 1883, 233, Fig. 205). It seems that one of the fragmentary combs from Lough Crew (Fig. 105:5) also had an openwork handle and when complete its form may have resembled that of the Bowermadden piece. Material from the broch included what appears to be an example of Guido's Meare-spiral glass bead (Anderson, op. cit., Fig. 204) and an ibex-headed pin (ibid., Fig. 206), both objects not out of place in a first century B.C./first century A.D. context. It must be admitted, however, that neither can be shown to have been directly associated with the comb.

Combs of the type under consideration are widely known in Europe, especially in northern areas, and there is considerable support from the European evidence for the insular dating (e.g. Breidel, 1930, 259, 368, Abb. 465; Eggers, 1964, 170-171, Taf. 12:11 and 19:3; Kytlicova, 1970, 305, Obr. 8:A1; Stiglitz, 1975, 76, Abb. 100; Adler, 1976, 20, Abb. 2). Thomas, in her major study of these combs (1960), isolates a group identical in form to those from Lough Crew - her Type A1 - and demonstrates that their dating centres on Eggers' phase B2 of the Roman Imperial Period (i.e. roughly between 50 and 150 A.D.). The type continues somewhat later, e.g. Pollwitten (Eggers, op. cit.), which belongs to Eggers' phase C1 (roughly 150-200 A.D.).

Tweezers

The only other toilet implement of insular Iron Age, as opposed to Roman, type in Ireland (a sizeable selection of Roman toilet implements is known from the country) is the bronze tweezers from Loughey, near Donaghadee, Co. Down (Jope and Wilson, 1957a), a burial already referred to on more than one occasion above (p. 151).

DOMESTIC EQUIPMENT

Cups and bowls

Eight bronze bowls and the cast-bronze handle of a ninth, which are possibly or probably of Iron Age date, have been found in Ireland (Figs 107, 108). Two wooden bowls with handles also survive (Fig. 109). Of the bronze vessels, two - from Lisnacrogher, Co. Antrim (CIIAA No. 562), and from Athlone, Co. Westmeath (CIIAA No. 570) - must be regarded as of doubtfully Iron Age date; they may well belong to the end rather than the beginning of the first millennium A.D.

Bronze bowls of this type belong to an insular group, many of which exhibit evidence for the use of the lathe in their manufacture. It seems that in a number of cases these objects were initially cast, after which they were "lathe-cleaned" or "spin-finished" by pressing the bowl, while turning, into a prepared wooden mould (Megaw, 1970, 160; Tylecote, 1962, 149-152). Not all the Irish examples have been subjected to detailed technical examination but the Westmeath and Keshcarrigan examples exhibit chuck marks in central positions on their bases, while on several others faint striations, which may derive from the spinning process, are detectable. Hammer marks are also present on some bowls and in several cases (e.g. Cookstown, Co. Tyrone: Fig. 108:4) it seems that the vessel was fashioned entirely by hammering.

These bowls bear little decoration. Apart from the finely-cast, bird's-head handles of two examples (Somerset, Co. Galway, and Keshcarrigan, Co. Leitrim: Fig. 107:1,2), decoration consists otherwise of the reserved zig-zag band around the rim of the Keshcarrigan vessel, oblique hatching on the rim of one from the River Bann (Fig. 108; Pl. 70) and the crudely-incised triquetra on the inner and outer surfaces of the base of the Lisnacrogher bowl. As stated above, the latter specimen

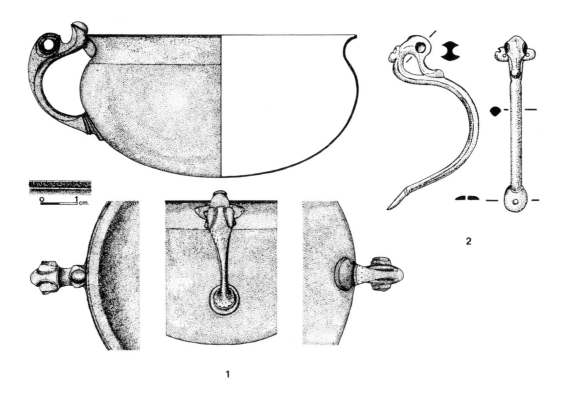

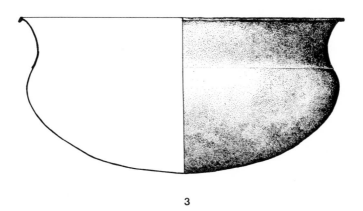

Fig. 107. Bronze bowls. 1 Keshcarrigan, Co. Leitrim. 2 Somerset, Co. Galway. 3 Co. Westmeath. – 1,3:1/2. 2:3/4.

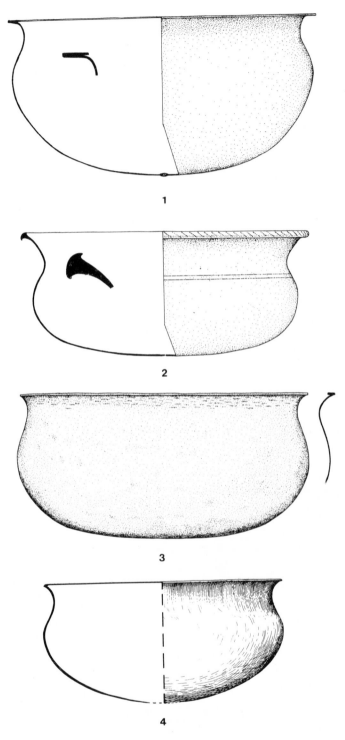

Fig. 108. Bronze bowls. 1-3 River Bann. 4 Cookstown, Co. Tyrone. - 1/2.

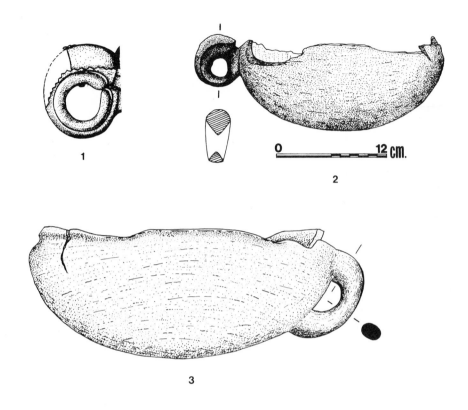

Fig. 109. Wooden bowls. 2 Co. Armagh. 3 no prov. 1 detail of Type 3
ringheaded pin, Lisnacrogher, Co. Antrim. – 1:c.2/1. 2:1/4. 3:1/2.

may, however, be post-Iron Age. The disposition of the hammer marks
on the base of one of the River Bann bowls (Fig. 108:3; CIIAA No. 565)
also appears to represent a simple attempt at ornamentation. The carved
wooden handle of the Armagh bowl (Fig. 109:2) may perhaps be construed
as a stylised bird's head, but more relevant is the similarity between
its shape and that of the rings of Type 3 ringheaded pins (Fig. 109:1).
This is the only clue as to its date.

The Keshcarrigan bowl found, not in the Shannon as so often stated,
but in a tributary of that river between Lough Scur and Lough Marrave,
is the best known and most elaborate of the Irish series (Fig. 107:1; Pl. 69;
Jope, 1954b; Megaw, 1970, No. 273; Duval, 1977, 205, Fig. 413). Discussion
of the origins and chronology of the group has, inevitably, revolved around

this very fine specimen. A southern or south-western British background is generally argued for it and it is normally considered to date just before or just after the birth of Christ. The bowl is almost universally seen as a direct import into Ireland. However, while features of the Irish bowl have close and obvious parallels amongst vessels of the British group, it remains possible to question this assertion.

The presence of lathe-turning on some of the Irish vessels has been repeatedly emphasised as a major factor in demonstrating an alleged British origin for them. The reserved zig-zag ornament on the rim of the Keshcarrigan bowl has also been stressed, for this is closely paralleled on the rim of a bowl from Rose Ash, Devon, in the south of England (Fox, 1961, 190-192) and on an outlying British export at Łeg Piekarski in Poland (Megaw, 1963, 27-33; Jazdzewski and Rycel, 1981, 30-48), where the wavy line is doubled. There are also two bands of zig-zag ornament under the rim of a bowl from Glastonbury, Somerset, in England (Bulleid and Gray, 1911, 179-181), which is, however, otherwise quite different from the bowls under discussion. On vessels from Youlton in Cornwall (Fox, A., 1961, 192 and Pl. XXXIII) and Birdlip in Gloucestershire (Fox, op. cit., 194-195, Pl. XXXIV), a hyphenated instead of a wavy line adorns the rim. Dotted decoration is present on the Youlton and Łeg Piekarski examples.

The handle of the Keshcarrigan bowl has also been compared to the handle of a bronze bowl from Colchester, Essex, in England (Fig. 110; Pl. 71). The frequent implicit assumption is that Colchester provides the prototype for Keshcarrigan. Undoubtedly, there is a morphological similarity between the two handles, especially between their expanded extremities, but the stylised English version is but a pale shadow of the lively Keshcarrigan bird. Indeed both Megaw and Lady Fox have suggested that the Colchester specimen should be regarded as later than that from Keshcarrigan (Fox, A., 1961, 195). A very generalised comparison might also be made between the snout-ended escutcheon of the Rose Ash bowl and the Keshcarrigan bird, but the similarity is somewhat remote.

If the substantially complete southern English bowls are regarded as a group, it becomes evident that, in profile, the Irish bowls in fact differ generally from their English counterparts. The shallow, flat-bottomed examples such as Rose Ash, Łeg Piekarski, Welwyn Garden City (Stead, 1967, 23-25) or Felmersham (Watson, 1949, 42-45; Kennet, 1970, 86-89) are wholly distinct from the deeper, more globular Irish versions. Somewhat closer are the profiles of bowls from Birdlip, Youlton or Bulbury (Cunliffe, 1972, 298-299), but again they are squatter than the Irish bowls, have a stronger tendency towards a flat bottom, and their necks are more pronouncedly vertical than on any Irish specimen.

for example, strongly recalls the pattern on the Stamford Hill mirror in some of its details (Fig. 112:3; Fox, 1958, 95, Fig. 60). This mirror, according to Fox, is no earlier than the mid-first century. The pointed "ears" on the Irish piece are also paralleled on insular metalwork of the early centuries A.D. (Jope, 1955, 42-44). The use of triangles as a border for curvilinear ornament is also known on late metalwork in Britain such as on a harness mount from a hoard of the first century A.D. at Polden Hill, Somerset (Fox, 1958, Pl. 72:c).

Perhaps the closest stylistic analogy for the ornament on the escutcheon of the Carrickfergus tankard is to be found on the escutcheon of a hammered bronze bowl from Snowdon, Caernarvonshire, in Wales (Figs 110:5; 112:2; Savory, 1976, 62, 108, Fig. 38a). On this object not only does the pseudo-face design closely resemble the design on the Irish escutcheon (though here it is of inlaid glass), but the actual shape of the Snowdon escutcheon, with its curved edge and its pair of projecting "ears", is clearly recognisable in the Carrickfergus rendering. The Welsh bowl belongs to that group of insular bowls discussed above and may be reasonably dated to the early first century A.D.

It is appropriate that one of the closest stylistic parallels for the tankard ornament should come from Wales, for in terms of form and details of manufacture the same country provides by far the best comparison for the Irish vessel. The tankard in question is, of course the famous Trawsfynydd specimen (Fox, 1958, 109, Pls 64, 5). This shares with the Carrickfergus piece the elegant, concave-sided form which in other surviving British examples seems less pronounced. Stave-built and bronze-bound like the Irish tankard, it also shares with the latter the raised concentric bands on its lathe-turned base. The base, too, is centrally perforated as is that of the Carrickfergus tankard, but the Welsh specimen still retains the bronze stud which plugs this perforation; such a stud must once have existed on the Carrickfergus vessel. A double circle of wavy metal strips hammered into the ends of the staves around the basal circumference of the Trawsfynydd object once existed in exactly the same form on the Carrickfergus tankard.

On the basis of its ornamented handle a date within the first century A.D. has been suggested for the Trawsfynydd tankard (Corcoran, 1952, 88-93) and, on formal similarities alone, it seems the Irish specimen cannot be far removed from it in time. The decorative analogies for the Carrickfergus escutcheon are entirely in keeping with such a dating and it is likely that the Irish piece was imported from western Britain, possibly from the area of north-west Wales, some time in that century.

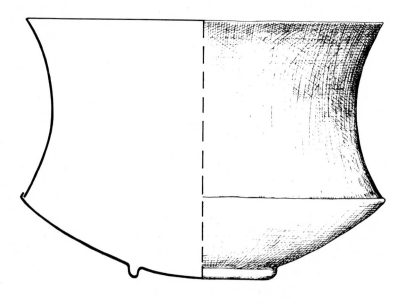

Fig. 113. Bronze tazza. Edenderry, Co. Offaly. - 3/4.

Tazza

The sheet-bronze tazza allegedly from Edenderry, Co. Offaly (Fig. 113), is thus far unique in Ireland. Though no precise parallels are to be found in bronze, the form is fairly well reproduced in pottery from southern and western British contexts of the last century B.C. and the early first century A.D. These vessels are associated in the main with Belgic intrusions in those areas (Fox, 1958, 63) and relevant comparisons occur at Aylsford, Kent (ibid., Pl. 26A), Essex (ibid., Pl. 30b) and Barnwell, Cambridgeshire (ibid., Pl. 45). The Irish vessel, if it is a genuine, ancient find, can hardly be other than an import from Belgic Britain dating sometime around the birth of Christ.

Cauldrons

The number of cauldrons in Ireland which may be regarded as of Iron Age date is small compared with the impressive array of such vessels which were produced here during the preceding Late Bronze Age. There are seven extant specimens which may with reasonable probability be accepted as belonging to the Iron Age and a small number of doubtful and uncertain examples also exists.   Two principal forms occur: those with a more or less globular body and those which are made up of a roughly hemispherical base joined to a roughly cylindrical neck.   These last are known technically as "projecting-bellied cauldrons".

Globular cauldrons

Three examples are included here and all differ from one another not only in size and form but also in the material of which they are composed.   Only their general globular shape links them and they may well be widely separated from one another in time.

The fragmentary wooden cauldron from Altartate Glebe, Co. Monaghan, carved from a single piece of poplar (Fig. 114:1), could be amongst the earliest of the Irish Iron Age cauldrons (Mahr, 1934, 11-29).   Its form is similar to that of some of the Atlantic B Bronze Age cauldrons but there are notable differences, especially in rim and neck profile.   The ribbed, cylindrical handle attachment also bears comparison with those on the Atlantic cauldrons but a significant difference lies in the fact that the handle on the Altartate vessel is attached to the body whereas on the Atlantic cauldrons it is, without exception, joined to the rim of the bronze container.

The handle attachment on the Altartate cauldron can be even more closely paralleled on Greek pottery cauldrons of the eighth and seventh centuries B.C., not only in form but also in its positioning on the vessel, and the general profile of such containers is not unlike that of the Co. Monaghan specimen.   A good example of this type from Rhodes is illustrated by Leeds (1930, Pl. X:26).   It is thus conceivable that influence ultimately from the Mediterranean world may be seen in the morphology of the wooden vessel from Altartate, but it is certainly a native piece and its likely Iron Age context is indicated by the simple incised ornament which encircles the rim.

It is not, however, possible to date the Altartate cauldron with any degree of precision.   Hawkes and Smith referred to it as an Irish adaptation of Hallstatt D cauldron forms but went on to state that "its ornament, derived from the La Tène style, must place it late before the Christian era" (1957, 198).   The form is, indeed, similar to that of some Hallstatt D cauldrons (e.g. Reinecke, 1911, Taf. 56:1034; 329, Abb. 3b; Hawkes and Smith, op. cit., Fig. 11; Harding, 1974, Fig. 36; Jacobi, 1974, Abb. 34 above) and the similarity of form continues with

Continental vessels of Early La Tène date (Jacobi, op. cit., Abb. 34). The handle attachments of these Iron Age cauldrons are, however, quite different from those on the Irish example. It is interesting, nonetheless, that Jacobi could write (op. cit., 148, n. 650): "Nach der Form mit einbeigendem Rand, der mit einem Muster in der Art des 'laufenden Hundes' verzierten Schulter sowie der Scharniergriffe würde er gut zu den festländischen Stücken der Frühlatènezeit passen". He went on, however, to state: "Hawkes hat aber gewiß recht, wenn er diesen Kessel spät datiert", but offered no reason for this assertion.

Altartate clearly embodies early elements but its absolute chronology remains vague. In this context a decorated potsherd from a hillfort on Blewburton Hill, Berkshire in England, may be relevant (Fig. 114:2). The piece (Harding, 1972, 95-96, Pl. 58:G) comes from a vessel which formerly had around its rim incised ornament strongly reminiscent of the design on the Monaghan cauldron. In discussing this sherd, Harding compared the ornament with the compass-drawn pattern on a scabbard from Minster Ditch, Oxford and he concluded that it could be regarded as a piece transitional between his Early and Middle La Tène phases in Britain, implying thereby a period of experimentation in pottery decoration. He thus suggested for it a date in the first half of the fourth century B.C. Such a dating would not be inappropriate for the Altartate cauldron.

Insular parallels for the vessel are virtually non-existent, though Mahr (1934, 20, Fig. 3) drew attention to another single-piece wooden vessel in the National Museum. It also has cylindrical lugs. It was found at Clogh, Co. Fermanagh, and could be contemporary with the Altartate piece. Another specimen from Gortagowan bog, Co. Tyrone (Mahr, 1934, 20), could equally belong to the same period. Such undecorated containers are, however, at present undatable. In Scotland, the bronze cauldron from Kyleakin, Skye, Invernesshire, is not unlike the Altartate example in form (MacGregor, 1976, No. 306) but its date, too, is uncertain.

Like Altartate, the sheet-iron cauldron from Drumlane, Co. Cavan (Fig. 4:3), can be compared with Continental Hallstatt D and Early La Tène cauldrons but the method of manufacture is quite different and it is possible that the concept of riveting iron sheets together reflects influence from Late Bronze Age cauldron traditions. As has been suggested frequently (e.g. Scott, 1974, 16-17: above p. 9) the object may well be an early transitional piece between bronze-using and iron-using periods. Mahr compared it with the bronze cauldron from Kyleakin in Skye already referred to but, because several kegs of bog butter were found near it, he was inclined to view the Scottish piece and the

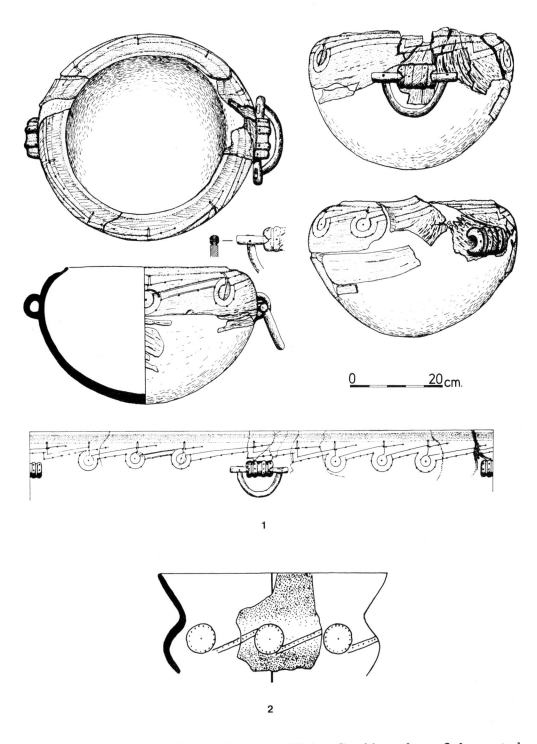

Fig. 114. Wooden cauldron, Altartate Glebe, Co. Monaghan. 2 decorated potsherd, Blewburton Hill, Berkshire, England. – (after Harding, 1974).

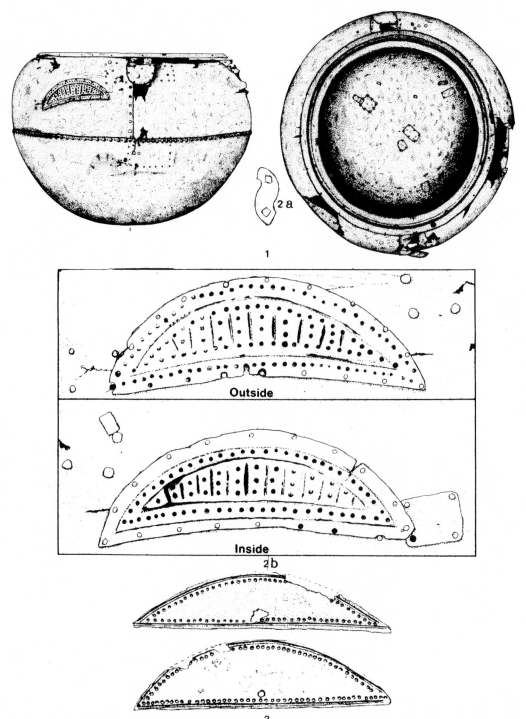

Fig. 115. Bronze cauldron, Ballyedmond, Co. Galway, (1) and details
of its decorative patches (2a,b). 3 bronze bucket escutcheons, Birdlip,
Gloucester, England. – 1:c. 1/10. 2–3:1/2. (3 after Green, 1949).

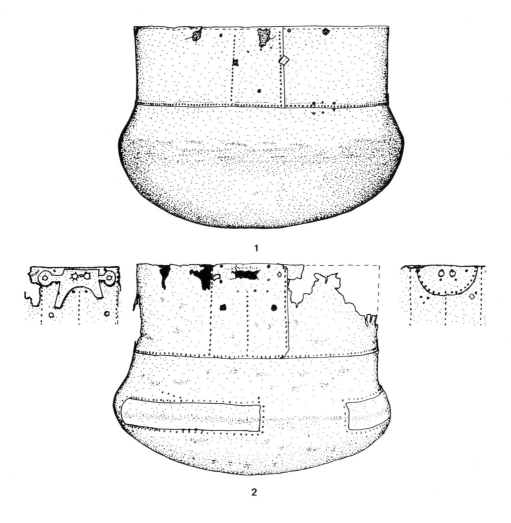

Fig. 116. Bronze projecting-bellied cauldrons. 1 Ballymoney, Co. Antrim.
2 no prov. - approx. 1/10.

Ireland.

In Britain such cauldrons are referred to as "Santon type" and six examples are known there (MacGregor, 1976, 151, Map 21). They are found in two areas of that island, four in the south-east and two in the north. Of the latter, one from Carlingwark Loch in the south-west of Scotland, is especially close to the Irish examples (Pl. 75:2) not only in its form, but also in the presence on it of D-shaped and "paper-clip" patches. This Scottish cauldron was found on the bed of a lake, filled with metal objects of both Roman and native manufacture for which

a date in the late first or early second century A.D. could be advanced
(Piggott, 1952-3b, 1-50).   A similar cauldron from Santon, Suffolk, in
southern England was also filled with metal objects, in this instance
of Belgic type, "usually attributed to the Claudian period" (MacGregor,
1976, 151).

The chronological range within which these Irish cauldrons are likely
to have been in use is thus clear.   It is tempting, in view of the close
analogy between Carlingwark on the eastern side of the North Channel
and Ballymoney on the western side of the Channel, to postulate a direct
link between the Irish projecting-bellied cauldrons and those in Britain,
especially the north British group.   Indeed, if the late dating of
Ballyedmond and Kincardine Moss is correct, then these cauldrons would
overlap in time with the projecting-bellied specimens and would thus
further emphasise an Irish/south-west Scottish connection about the
beginning of the Christian era.   It might even be argued that the Irish
cauldrons could be imports from the neighbouring island.

Certainly, evidence for direct links between Ireland and Britain in
the centuries spanning the birth of Christ is considerable (see below
P. 328) and Ireland not only received imports, but also undoubtedly absorbed
influences from Britain, especially from the north.   But it is equally
evident that Ireland exported to Britain, so that, lacking a reliable relative
chronology for the cauldrons in the two islands, it is unwise as yet to
argue chronological priority for one or other of the insular groups.
Moreover, it should be noted that the Irish projecting-bellied cauldrons
can be as closely paralleled on the Continent as in Britain. For example,
the fine vessel found near a Gallo-Roman villa at Sainte Sixte (Loire)
in France (Rauchon and Périchon, op. cit.) resembles very closely the
cauldrons from Ireland, so that direct Continental influence on them
cannot be ruled out.

Weaving Appliances

The so-called weaving comb is, without doubt, one of the commonest
artifacts of the British Iron Age, so much so, in fact, that Hodson was
moved to include it as one of the type fossils of his Woodbury Culture
(1964, 103).   It remains to be demonstrated that these appliances were,
in fact, used as weaving combs (Hodder and Hedges, 1977, 17-19). The
term is, however, retained here as it is widely used in the literature.

In Ireland these objects are rare.   While it is possible that some of
the Lough Crew combs (Fig. 105:2,10) were for weaving (Henshall, 1950,
Fig. 5; Megaw, 1970, 25; Wheeler, 1943, 298), this seems unlikely, for
they appear to have been slender objects unlike any of the robust specimens

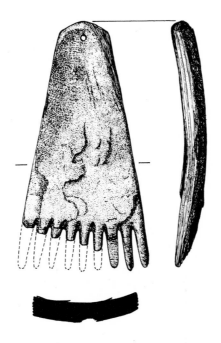

Fig. 117. Weaver's comb of horn, Glassamucky Brakes, Co. Dublin. - 1/2.

from Britain and it is likely that they were for personal use. Two undoubted examples of the weaving comb class are, however, known from this country, one from a bog at Glassamucky Brakes in south Co. Dublin (Fig. 117), the other from the recent excavations at Navan Fort, Co. Armagh. The Co. Dublin find was an isolated discovery. The Navan comb seems to have come from an unstratified position and as material from the site extends from the Late Bronze Age to the beginning of the Christian era at least, the exact context of this object cannot be indicated in advance of the excavation report.

On the Continent, comparable implements are occasionally recorded from Early La Tène contexts (e.g. Marquis and Brunaux, 1975, 14, 16, Fig. 4; Cadoux, 1977, 311, Fig. 17). In Britain such combs were in use from Iron Age A times onwards (as defined by Hawkes), e.g. Maiden Castle, Dorset (Wheeler, 1943, 298), and in Scotland they can, apparently, be as late as the fifth century A.D. (Henshall, 1950, 146). They are especially common during the period termed by Hawkes as Iron Age B. In Scotland, their appearance has been interpreted, along with that of spiral finger/toe rings, bone dice and certain types of querns and other evidence, as reflecting the presence there of refugees from southern England (e.g. MacKie, 1970 and references), a view not, however, universally accepted (e.g. Clarke, 1970, 218-220).

The Irish weaving combs may best be compared with those in Britain but equally with examples both in the north and the south of that country. Two from the Maiden Castle hillfort in Dorset, for instance, coming, it is stated, from first century A.D. contexts (Wheeler, 1943, 301-303, Nos 13, 20) resemble the Glassamucky Brakes specimen. A recent study of the insular weaving combs suggests, however, that the Irish example is most closely related to a form concentrated on the Orkney Islands, off the north coast of Scotland (Hodder and Hodges, 1977, 16).

None of the parallels is close enough to provide, on its own, firm indications of date for the Irish combs and it is not possible to decide if they are imports or of native fabrication. The objects are, however, important for they appear to represent a humbler, more mundane aspect of domestic economy in sharp contrast to the martial or aristocratic nature of the bulk of the decorated metalwork.

The only other evidence for weaving from Iron Age Ireland (apart from the traces of textile found adhering to the surface of a bronze locket in a burial at Carrowbeg North, Co. Galway: above p. 206; Pl. 64) is the small collection of presumed spindle whorls from the third/fourth century hillfort at Freestone Hill, Co. Kilkenny (Raftery, B., 1969, 83-84, Fig. 13) and a possible wooden spindle allegedly from Lisnacrogher, Co. Antrim (NMI 1928:329). The provenance of this last object need not necessarily be accurate, however, and neither its function nor its date can be firmly established.

Tools and Implements

Tools and implements of recognisably Iron Age date are poorly represented in Ireland. Because of the essentially unchanging form of so many of the simple domestic artifacts of iron it is clear that the chronological position of individual specimens can be established only if recovered from a datable context. Thus, for example, an unassociated, tanged, single-edged knife of iron is undatable.

As well as the basic absence of diagnostically Iron Age features, a factor which should also be borne in mind when considering domestic implements of iron is that the chances of their being retained by casual finders, much less sent to a museum, must be regarded as remote. Would, for instance, the fragmentary and corroded iron "pendant" from Kilbeg, Co. Westmeath (CIIAA No. 232), have reached the National Museum had it not been found in association with a bronze object and other more clearly recognisable artifacts? The imbalance in the archaeological record between decorative bronzes and domestic implements should

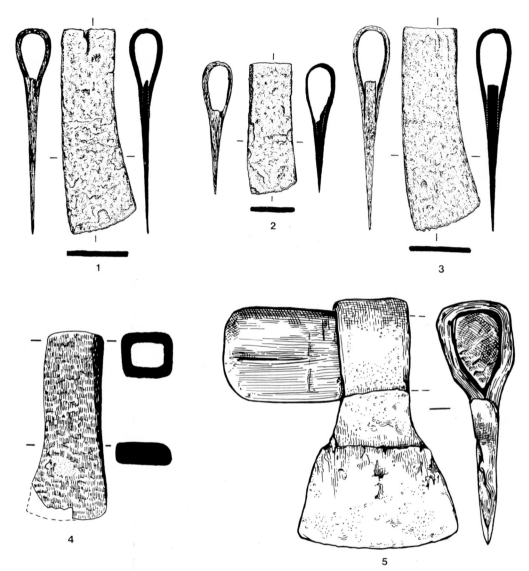

Fig. 118. Iron axeheads. 1-3 Kilbeg, Co. Westmeath. 4 Feerwore, Co.
Galway. 5 Rathtinaun, Co. Sligo. - 1-3:1/4. 4-5:1/2.
(4 after Raftery, J., 1944).

thus not be overstressed.

Axeheads form the only moderately sizeable group of iron domestic implements from the country relevant to the present discussion (Fig. 118). Three types exist: looped, socketed specimens, a single unlooped, socketed example and several of shafthole form. Inevitably, dating is, in most instances, only tentatively suggested.

There are two looped, socketed axeheads from Ireland, one from

Toome, Co. Antrim, the other from Lough Mourne, Co. Down (Fig. 4:1,2; Scott, 1974).   In technique of manufacture they are quite distinct from the single unlooped specimen (see below) and, as has already been suggested (above, p. 9), they may represent an early phase of iron-working in the country, where influences from Late Bronze Age industries are present. Manning and Saunders, in considering the fourteen similar axeheads from Britain (1972, 277-279), refer to the possibility of such a transitional role for them but point out the scarcity of dating evidence for the insular examples.   While allowing for the possible early dating of these axeheads, they suggest that this type may well have been in use "throughout the whole of the pre-Roman Iron Age and not until the Roman period was it completely superseded by the shaft-hole axe ...." (1972, 281).

The sole Irish unlooped, socketed axehead (Fig. 118:4) was discovered in the course of excavations at the ringfort of Feerwore, Co. Galway (Raftery, J., 1944, Fig. 4:38; Scott, 1974, 12-13), a site which also produced an iron safety-pin fibula (above, p. 151).   The axehead may be intrusive. Similar axeheads are found in Middle and Late La Tène contexts in Europe (Jacobi, 1977, 21-23; Manning and Saunders, 1972, 277-279), but the type is not common in Britain.   The Feerwore axehead may reasonably be seen as dating to the late second or early first century B.C. and it may well indicate some sort of movement at this time along the western seaways to Ireland direct from the Continent.

The shafthole axeheads form an interesting but somewhat disparate group of artifacts nowhere clearly datable in Ireland.   Three of varying size were found associated with a pair of horse "pendants" at Kilbeg, Co. Westmeath (Fig. 118:1-3; Scott, 1980, 195, Fig. 6).   One is a stray find from Castlereban North, Co. Kildare (Rynne, 1958, 149-150), and one came from an occupation level at a crannog at Rathtinaun, Lough Gara, Co. Sligo (Fig. 118:5; CIIAA No. 583).

The Kilbeg axeheads and the Castlereban specimen are all made of two sheets of iron, one forming the blade, the other folded over and forged to the blade to provide the loop.   This method of manufacture is, it seems, unrecorded outside the country.   The only hint at dating is in the Kilbeg association and here, of course, precision is impossible because the "pendants" themselves are not susceptible to close dating. However, in discussing the chronology of the "pendants" (above, pp. 47-56) tentative suggestions of dating just before and more especially in the centuries shortly after the birth of Christ were mooted.

The Lough Gara axehead was made in a manner somewhat similar to that of the Kilbeg and Castlereban specimens, but in this instance three sheets of iron were used.   The axehead was associated with bronzes of Late Bronze Age type as well as a swan's-neck pin (Fig. 5:3) and some other iron objects. This level has already been adverted to above (pp. 9-13), as it seems to demonstrate the overlap of two metalworking traditions. On conventional archaeological grounds the axehead, on the basis of the associations, should date to the middle of the last millennium B.C. or just before it. This dating is in conflict with the second/first century b.c. carbon 14 determinations which the level yielded (see above p. 11). The accuracy of these dates has, however, been questioned (e.g. Alcock, 1972, 105).

A shafthole axehead of different type came from Lisnacrogher, Co. Antrim (Wakeman, 1891, Pl. II:1). The object is forged as a unit with a cylindrical eye and a flat, hammer-shaped head. Ultimately the type is Roman but almost exact parallels come from Lagore, Co. Meath (Hencken, 1950, 106, Fig. 40a), Lough Faughan, Co. Down (Collins, 1955, 61, Fig. 11), Cahercommaun, Co. Clare (Hencken, 1938, 51) and elsewhere, so that the Lisnacrogher specimen may be post-Iron Age in date. The evidence from the three sites referred to should not, however, be regarded as an infallible index of late date for this axehead type in Ireland, as there are increasing grounds for dating their initial occupation somewhat earlier than has hitherto been generally accepted (Raftery, B., 1972, 51-53).

Apart from the axeheads there are few remaining iron tools which may with any confidence be ascribed to the Iron Age. A socketed adze from Newgrange, Co. Meath, is probably sub-Roman (Carson and O'Kelly, 1977, 52). From Feerwore, Co. Galway, come an iron knife and chisel (Raftery, J., 1944, 34, Fig. 4), and a shafthole adze was found at Lisnacrogher. The adze, like the axehead from the same site, has good Roman parallels as, for instance, at Carlingwark in Scotland (Piggott, 1952-3b, 36, Fig. 9:C50), but such a basic type could continue later. The same chronological uncertainty applies to the sickle and the lost billhook both allegedly from Lisnacrogher (Wakeman, 1891, Pl. II:3). An iron shears from Carbury Hill, Co. Kildare (Willmot, 1938, 133, Fig. 3), and a lost example from Seskin, Co. Kilkenny (Macalister, 1928, 203), were probably for personal use. Both came from burial monuments and it is likely that their date falls within the Iron Age but where within that imprecisely determined period it is, as yet, impossible to say.

The remaining domestic implements probably belong to the early centuries of the Christian era. The bronze hook and the Roman bell from Kishawanny, Co. Kildare (Pl. 18), have already been referred to (above, p. 54). Freestone Hill, Co. Kilkenny, one of the very rare settlement sites of broadly Iron Age date to be excavated in Ireland (Raftery, B., 1969), produced a range of household items scarcely represented elsewhere. These included iron needles, spindle whorls,

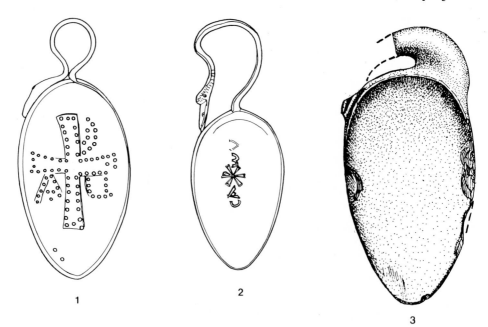

Fig. 119. Loop-handled spoons. 1, Canoscio, Prov. Perugia, Italy. 2 Ibener Hof, Kr. Alzey, Germany. 3 Carbury Hill, Co. Kildare. 1,2 silver (after Milojčić, 1968). 3 jet. - 1,2 various scales. 3:1/1.

whetstones and other objects, the date of which is indicated by the third/fourth century Roman imports.

A final object of great potential interest is the finely made jet spoon from Carbury Hill, Co. Kildare (Fig. 119:3; Pl. 76; Willmot, 1938, 135, Fig. 3). This implement, from a burial monument – though not specifically associated with a burial – appears to have its best parallels in some of the late Roman loop-handled spoons of silver, in particular those of the swan's-neck, handled group (Fig. 119:1,2; Laur-Belart, 1963, 4-5, Abb. 21; Strong, 1966, 205, Fig. 40e; Milojčić, 1968; Böhme, 1970, 185-186, Abb. 11). These belong to the fourth and early fifth centuries A.D. and may, in some cases, have been associated with the Roman rite of communion (Milojčić, op. cit.), but hardly exclusively so. The Irish object could thus just as easily have been used in the home.

Metalworking

No single mould fragment for the manufacture of an Iron Age object has as yet been found in Ireland, nor has a crucible of the period or any metalworking implement ever come to light. Unfinished bronzes are, of course, known; these give us some direct insight into the casting process but the absence in Ireland of a bronzeworking centre such as Gussage All Saints in Britain (Wainwright and Spratling, 1973; Spratling, 1979;

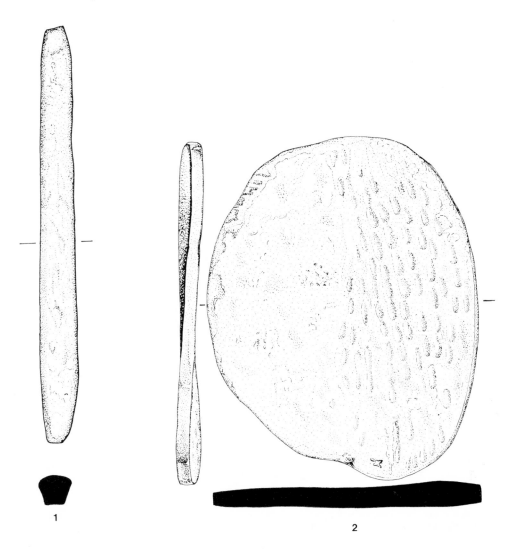

Fig. 120. Bronze ingot (1) and cake (2). Somerset, Co. Galway. -3/4.

Foster, 1980) constitutes a major gap in our knowledge of Iron Age metalworking in this country.

The only information we have regarding the techniques of metalworking in Ireland, apart from the objects themselves, is provided by a few lumps of enamel/glass and a few cakes and ingots of bronze. The enamel fragments, reportedly from the Hill of Tara, Co. Meath, and Kilmessan, not far distant in the same county, have most recently been considered by Hughes (1972). The possibility of a date spanning the birth of Christ is considered and the likelihood, on the basis of high lead oxide content, of a Mediterranean origin for them is put forward.

The presence of an ingot and a cake of bronze from the Somerset, Co. Galway, hoard (Raftery, J., 1960, 2-5; above, p. 154) indicate that this was a metalworker's assemblage. The cake has extensive hammer-marks on it and it may have been intended to raise a bowl from it. A similar cake comes from the River Bann at Toome, Co. Antrim, and outside the country the closest parallel for the type is found at Ringstead, Norfolk in England (Clarke, 1951, 223, Pl. XIXb). The first century B.C. assemblage from Gussage All Saints included an ingot (or billet) of bronze closely similar to that from Somerset (Spratling, op. cit., 130, Fig. 98:1)

Beehive Querns

The principal evidence for agriculture in Iron Age Ireland comes from the extensive number of beehive querns which are now recorded from the country. Up to relatively recently their existence in Ireland was scarcely acknowledged, and it is only in the last decade or so, due to the work of S. Caulfield, that the importance of these objects has been realised.

In his extensive study of the beehive quern in Ireland (1977), Caulfield numbered 215 specimens from the country and several more examples have since come to light. The upper stone in each instance is "unpierced", that is, the socket, into which the detachable wooden handle fitted, does not perforate the stone. All were iron-mounted and in every case the central perforation is funnel-shaped. Based on the form and position of the handle-hole, Caulfield has isolated three types – B1, B2 and B3. B1 querns are taken as the earliest group and these are concentrated mainly in central Ulster, the upper Shannon and the west of the country. B2 stones are virtually absent in the west of Ireland, displaying in their distribution a more easterly bias. B3 are more widely dispersed. Beehive querns are unknown in the southern half of Ireland. Their distribution in the northern half of the country overlaps superficially with that of the La Tène metalwork but in detail, metalwork and querns are, to a large extent, mutually exclusive (*pace* Caulfield, op. cit., 127-8).

None of the Irish beehive querns comes from a datable context. Their chronological position is thus imprecisely fixed, and within the country only the decoration which adorns a few examples gives a clue to their dating, a clue which is, however, in most instances only of the most generalised kind. The strange curves and almost "Gothic" arches on a specimen from Glaslough, Co. Monaghan, are undatable (Griffiths,

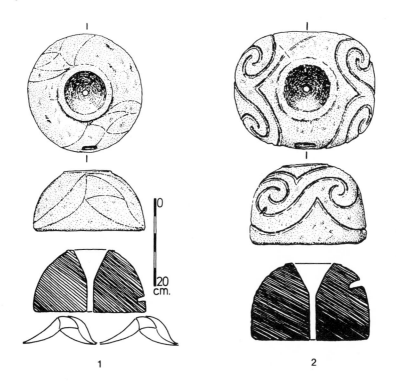

Fig. 121. Beehive quernstones. 1 Clonmacnois, Co. Offaly.
.2 Ticooly-O'Kelly, Co. Galway.

1951, Pl. 7:11). The S-spirals on a quern from Ticooly-O'Kelly, Co. Galway (Fig. 121:2; Pl. 78; Caulfield, op. cit., 122, Fig. 28B), are also difficult to date closely but the disposition of the ornament recalls such metalwork renderings as the decorated spearbutt from Lisnacrogher (above p. 125; Fig. 60:2; Pl. 34:1) or the S-scrolls on the circular plaque from Lambay (Fig. 139:1; Pl. 96). The comparisons are not, however, compelling enough to form a convincing basis for dating. The relief S-scroll with circular boss-ending on a quern from Clones, Co. Monaghan, (Barron, 1976, Pl. 6) has, perhaps, somewhat more in common with the two metalwork analogies cited above and there seems to be in the decoration of these objects a hint of overlap in details of their ornament with the northern British "Boss Style" (Leeds, 1933, 110). The worn S-scrolls on another north of Ireland quern (Raftery, J., 1951, 202, Fig. 255) are even less susceptible to close dating. Only the quern from Clonmacnois, Co. Offaly, bears ornament for which a slightly narrower dating range may be suggested (Fig. 121:1; Caulfield, op. cit., 123, Fig. 21A, 28A). Comparable decorative treatment is present on a number of native artifacts (Fig. 127:6-8), of which the most notable are the bone flakes from Lough Crew, Co. Meath and the bronze "spoons" (see below). Dating for these objects in the first century A.D. or slightly earlier is suggested.

Outside Ireland the custom of decorating quernstones is rare. Only in north-west Wales are comparable ornamented stones to be found (Griffiths, 1951). Although the Welsh querns differ in form from those in Ireland (Caulfield, op. cit., 123), it may be that some sort of interaction between the two insular groups was responsible for the common custom of embellishing quernstones. It cannot, however, be stated which area had chronological priority.

Evidence for the dating of the Irish querns both on internal and external grounds is thus meagre and Caulfield is suitably cautious on this topic (op. cit., 125). He suggests, however, that the beehive quern was introduced to Ireland probably in the final centuries B.C. or first A.D. (op. cit., 127).

There can be little doubt that the beehive quern in Ireland represents a radical change in the technique of grinding corn and clearly this must have been introduced from outside. Caulfield looks to the northeast-English/south-Scottish area as the source of the Irish beehive querns. He interprets their presence in Ireland as indicative of an extensive folk movement from Britain and considers this alleged folk movement as being also responsible for the introduction of La Tène metalworking traditions to the country.

The arguments for such a migration to Ireland are not conclusive (see below, pp. 330-331). The absence of B1 querns in east Ulster is striking, especially if the querns are, as Caulfield implies, to be equated with the decorated scabbards (op. cit., 127). The absence of beehive querns from settlement sites of native aspect seems also a less important argument than Caulfield suggests (op. cit., 126), since our knowledge of relevant Irish settlement types, either native or exotic, which could be regarded as certainly contemporary with the beehive quern tradition in the country is negligible.

It remains to be proven that the beehive quern in Ireland represents the appearance here of alien intruders. Writing in a Scottish context MacKie considered the significance of the spread of the beehive quern in that country. He wrote ".... they illustrate well how a new artifact could spread by example without any evidence of population movements. There can be little doubt that this clear and obvious improvement in a technique fundamental to a peasant economy - that of grinding corn - could have spread quite rapidly among communities otherwise notoriously conservative" (1970, 52). Such a model could apply equally to Ireland.

Gaming Pieces

The term "gaming piece" is often used in archaeological literature to describe objects of doubtful function. In the case of some of the objects briefly considered below, an element of uncertainty as to their original purpose also exists but it seems likely, on balance, that the items included here once served in some sort of gaming activities, either as dice, as pieces for a board game or as counters.

Dice

Dice of the so-called parallelopiped shape form a small but important group of antiquities in late prehistoric and early historic Ireland. Some sixteen examples of the type have been listed (Dornan, 1975), all but one of bone. The exception, from Ballinderry crannog No. 2, Co. Offaly, is of wood.

Although twelve of the sixteen known dice have come from excavations, the exact dating range of these objects has not as yet been established precisely and, although several at least are of undoubtedly Iron Age date, the possibility that others were in use well into the first millennium A.D. cannot be ruled out. At Carraig Aille 1, Co. Limerick, for instance (Ó Ríordáin, 1949, 99, Fig. 13), the dice could well date to post-500 A.D., while the examples from both Lagore crannog (Hencken, 1950, Fig. 106:999, 1000) and Ballinderry crannog No. 2, Co. Offaly (Hencken, 1942, 54, 61, Fig. 22:17,45; Fig. 26:W.147), may be equally late.

Three sites have, however, produced dice of the shorter type which in each case might be assigned to the Iron Age with somewhat more confidence. The three dice in the inhumation burial at Knowth (Eogan, 1974a, 76, Fig. 31, Nos 150-152) must be regarded as coming from a pagan interment and the occurrence in other burials at the Knowth inhumation cemetery of V-perforated bone beads (see above, p. 205) and conical stone objects (below p. 250; Raftery, B., 1969, 79-82, Fig. 29) may prove to be of significance in the dating of the Knowth inhumations. The unfinished bone dice from the Newgrange excavation (Fig. 122:5,8), though not clearly stratified, were found in an area which produced exclusively Roman and sub-Roman material (Carson and O'Kelly, C., 1977, 51, Pl. VIIa). Finally, the dice from Navan Fort, whatever about its precise stratigraphical position, undoubtedly belongs to the Iron Age phase of occupation on the site (information courtesy the late D.M. Waterman, Archaeological Survey of Northern Ireland), and it is unlikely to be later than the beginning of the Christian era. Outside Ireland, the closest parallels for the Irish objects are to be found in the Atlantic Province of Scotland.   Continental examples are also known, generally dating to the Late La Tène and early Roman periods (e.g. Eichhorn, 1927, Fig. p. 180; Meduna, 1961, Taf. 10:1; Fouet, 1968, 90, Fig. 17:224; Motykova, 1974, 504, Figs 3,6; Py, 1978, 294, Fig. 139:4; Collis, 1980, 42, Fig. 2:14-16).

In Scotland the dice come in the main from brochs and wheelhouses but their dating is hardly more securely established than is the case for their Irish counterparts.   Twenty-one Scottish examples are known and the dating evidence for them is summarised by Clarke (1970). He concluded that their appearance in northern Britain "cannot be dated, on present evidence, earlier than the second century A.D." This was, however, criticised by MacKie (1970, 68), who pointed out that the crucial earliest examples, the Clickhimin dice, can be dated at least as early as the beginning of the Christian era and possibly even just before the birth of Christ.   Apart from this, however, wherever a hint of dating evidence is present, including Coygan Camp in Carmarthenshire (Wainwright, 1967, 183-4, Fig. 48:8), or Maiden Castle, Dorset (Wheeler, 1943, 310, Fig. 106:5,6), the weight of probability suggests for these objects a date in the first two or three centuries A.D.

Rectangular Plaques

Within Ireland there are two decorated bone plaques - one from Mentrim Lough crannog, Co. Meath (Fig. 122:1), the other from Cush, Co. Limerick (Fig. 122:2; Pl. 79).   Portion of a third undecorated specimen from Lough Crew, Co. Meath (Fig. 122:3) may be an unfinished example of the type.   The object which was found at Cush is thin in section and rectangular in shape and bears on each face ornament which is close in concept and execution to that on one of the Lough Crew, Co. Meath, slips (Fig. 127:9,11,14,15; see below, p. 258).   The narrow edges along two sides of the Cush plaque also have a series of small, dot-in-circle motifs.   The Co. Limerick object came from a cremation burial under a tumulus of "bowl-barrow" type near a series of ringforts (Ó Ríordáin, 1940, 137-138 and 154-156, Fig. 38).   There were no other grave goods. Mentrim Lough is a surface find without archaeological context.   It is a carefully fashioned rectangular plaque decorated with a series of sub-peltate motifs on one flat surface and a strange wavy, almost horse-like creature on the other.   This design is highlighted by a background formed of an extremely fine mesh of closely-spaced, compass-drawn arcs.   On each of the long edges a row of small, dot-in-circle motifs occurs as on the Cush specimen. The object, which may no doubt also be regarded as a "gaming piece" is, like the Cush piece, difficult to date

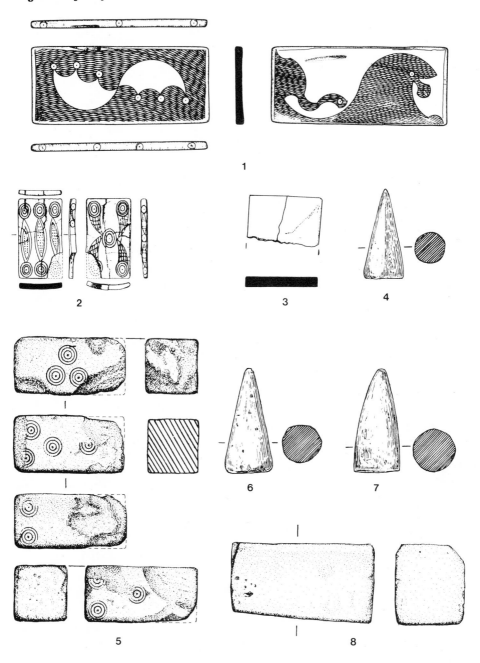

Fig. 122. "Gaming pieces". 1 Mentrim Lough, Co. Meath. 2 Cush, Co. Limerick. 3 Lough Crew, Co. Meath. 4 Freestone Hill, Co. Kilkenny. 5,8 Newgrange, Co. Meath. 6 Rath of the Synods, Tara, Co. Meath. 7 Dunbell Big, Co. Kilkenny. 1-3,5,8 bone; 4,6,7 stone. - 3/4.

on its own. The "mouth" of the creature which adorns one face, and its curving, semi-abstract body are both, perhaps, reminiscent of some of the horses on Gaulish coins, such as a first century B.C. example from the Seine (Megaw, 1970, Pl. IV:c), but the analogy is somewhat obscure. More relevant decorative parallels for the ornament on the Mentrim Lough piece might be sought on pottery from the south-west English lake settlements (e.g. Meare: Bulleid and Gray, I, 1948, 37, Fig. 7).

Of greater relevance from the point of view of local dating is the similarity in form between the Mentrim Lough and Cush plaques and the common relationship which both share with the ornament on the Lough Crew flakes. The fine mesh of compass-drawn arcs on the Mentrim Lough object ("engine-turning") has earlier been referred to in a consideration of the ornament on the gold collar from Broighter, Co. Derry, where comparable "engine-turning" forms a background to the raised decoration (above, p. 187). In the same context it was pointed out that such ornamentation was also present on a bronze mount from Cornalaragh, Co. Monaghan, as well as on the Lough Crew flakes. Dating just before or just after the birth of Christ for these comparanda seems likely.

Miscellaneous

The only other objects from Iron Age Ireland which might be regarded as "gaming pieces" are a few small, polished stone cones (Fig. 122:4,6-7), some pegged bone objects from a burial at Knowth, Co. Meath, and some rounded, water-rolled pebbles from the same Knowth burial (Eogan, 1974a, 76-80, Figs 31-32). One of the cremations at Grannagh, Co. Galway, produced a small rounded object of bone or chalk which might also have served as a counter (CIIAA No. 618).

The stone cones have been considered elsewhere by the writer (1969, 79-82). Where contexts are present the indications appear to be of a date in the early centuries of our era. They could, of course, have continued in use into later times. The pegged objects and the pebbles from Knowth are likely also to date to the first half of the first Christian millennium.

THE LOUGH CREW FLAKES

In the years between 1863 and 1943 sporadic investigation at the Passage Grave cemetery of Lough Crew, Co. Meath, has revealed evidence of a substantial Iron Age presence there, concentrated principally in that tomb designated Cairn H by the original explorer of the site, Eugene Conwell (1873). Only the latest phase of the investigations at Lough Crew were on a scientific basis - the 1943 excavations of J. Raftery - so that many of the stratigraphical details of the site are lost to us. It is clear, however, that the tomb was the scene of some specialised and intensive activity for a time during the Iron Age, the precise nature of which is uncertain.

The site is remarkable for the large amount of worked bone flakes which came from it (Figs 123-126; Pls 80, 81; Crawford, 1925), but it also produced a collection of glass, bone and amber beads, bronze and iron rings, bone combs, bone pins and an iron object described as the leg of a compass (CIIAA No. 296; Conwell, 1873, 51-58; Herity, 1974, 235-237). Not all of these items are preserved but it seems reasonable to assume that all derive from the same archaeological horizon.

As well as Cairn H, it is possible that some Iron Age material was also found in another of the tombs. A label, written in what appears to be E.C. Rotherham's hand, accompanies a box of 21 flakes in the National Museum and ascribes them to Cairn L. A bone pin, possibly contemporary with the flakes, is stated to have come from Cairn R2 (Crawford, 1925, 23, 27, Fig. 93; Herity, 1974, 242, Fig. 142:57).

Conwell, in enumerating the finds from Cairn H, lists a total of 4884 fragmentary bone flakes as coming from this site. These included 13 combs (7 of which were ornamented with "rows of fine, parallel, transverse lines"). He also referred to 14 fragments perforated near one end.

Not all the flakes appear to have survived. The present writer has counted or traced records of some 4350 fragments in the National Museum, which included 14 (or possibly 15) incomplete combs, 11 perforated flakes, 138 decorated fragments, portion of a small, carefully-worked, rectangular plaque (Fig. 122:3) and two bone pins. Drawings of 22 further decorated fragments occur in Crawford, 1925.

The sizes of the flakes vary to such an extent that it is impossible to estimate with any degree of precision the number of complete flakes which once existed. One way of establishing a rough estimate of the original quantity is by counting the number of end pieces and halving the total. Another possible method is by weighing all the fragments, determining the weight of an average complete flake and dividing this into the total weight. Obviously, both methods are crude in the extreme and provide at best a mere inkling of the minimum original total. In each case, for what it is worth, the number arrived at was between 500 and 600.

The fragments, which seem all to be composed of the bones of cattle, are highly polished on all surfaces and carefully worked to shape. Some exhibit considerable evidence of weathering. In outline they may be oval or ovoid, sometimes with parallel sides, convex sides or having one edge straight, the other edge convex. A small number have one edge convex, the other concave. The ends are most usually pointed or rounded. The points have at times been polished almost to needle sharpness and there are instances where the thinness of the pointed end is so pronounced and the surface so highly polished that the feel and the appearance of the object approaches that of ivory. There are some flakes which have blunter, flattened ends, sometimes cut transversely, sometimes obliquely to the long axis of the object and there are several instances of notched or forked extremities. There is one flake the end of which has been cut to a gently curving "beaked" form (Fig. 123:8). In the small number of substantially complete specimens there are some examples which have both ends rounded and others which have one rounded end and which taper to a point at the other end.

It is difficult to estimate the average size of the flakes because of their extremely fragmentary state. The longest piece (which is incomplete) is 13.4 cm and there are several more or less complete examples the lengths of which range between 12 cm and 13 cm. The average length may have varied between 9 cm and 10 cm. The minimum size is represented by an almost complete specimen 5.2 cm in length, (Fig. 123:11), but this seems to be exceptional. The greatest width of individual flakes ranges on average between 2 cm and 2.5 cm but widths in excess of 3 cm occur. The narrowest specimen has a maximum width

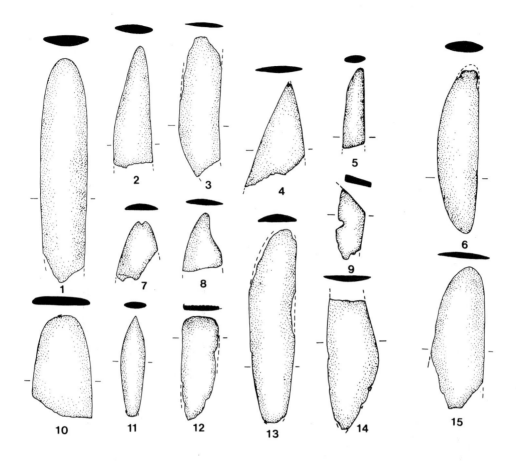

Fig. 123. Undecorated bone flakes, selection of forms. Lough Crew, Co. Meath. - 1/2.

of 1.25 cm.

In section the flakes are usually either pointed-oval or D-shaped. Flattened-oval, plano-convex and somewhat more irregularly-shaped sections are also present. In thickness the flakes also vary considerably. The greatest thickness is from 6 mm to 7.5 mm, while at the other extreme there are flakes which have been polished almost to the thinness of paper. Thicknesses of 3 mm to 4 mm appear to be the most usual.

Only a tiny fraction of the total number of fragments bears decoration. Overwhelmingly this consists of compass-drawn motifs, sometimes deeply and crisply incised, sometimes lightly scratched. Occasional attempts at free-hand curves have been made - usually with unimpressive results. The straight line is sparingly used, being confined for the most part to framing curvilinear compositions and defining the edges of flakes. The nature and quality of the designs varies greatly. On the one hand, there

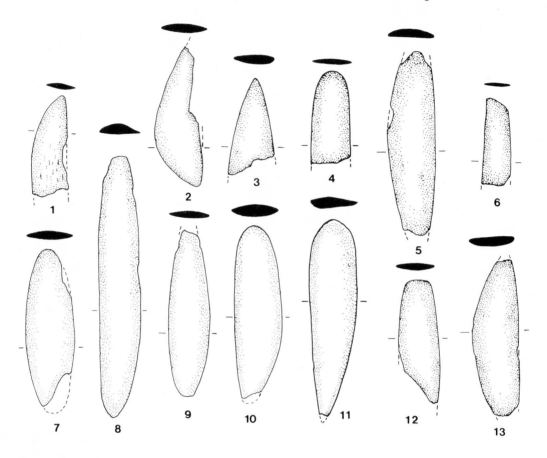

Fig. 124. Undecorated bone flakes, selection of forms. Lough Crew,
Co. Meath. – 1/2.

are carefully composed and expertly executed patterns; on the other
there are haphazard doodles, aimlessly-drawn arcs or nests of poorly-
produced, overlapping circles. Another type of design comprises carefully
drawn but unfinished patterns. Occasionally the ornament extends along
the length of a flake but more often a pattern or even a single motif
may occur on a flake confined to one part of the surface only, leaving
the rest plain. There appears no obvious reasoning behind the positioning
of the design on individual flakes.

As well as the compass-drawn arcs which compose the main motifs,
minor decorative elements are also used, such as stippling, bands of dots,
hyphenated lines, hatching and cross-hatching. Areas of cross-hatched,
compass-drawn arcs are also used on several occasions. In ten instances,
ornament occurs on both surfaces of the flake.

The inept attempt at producing curvilinear ornament without use

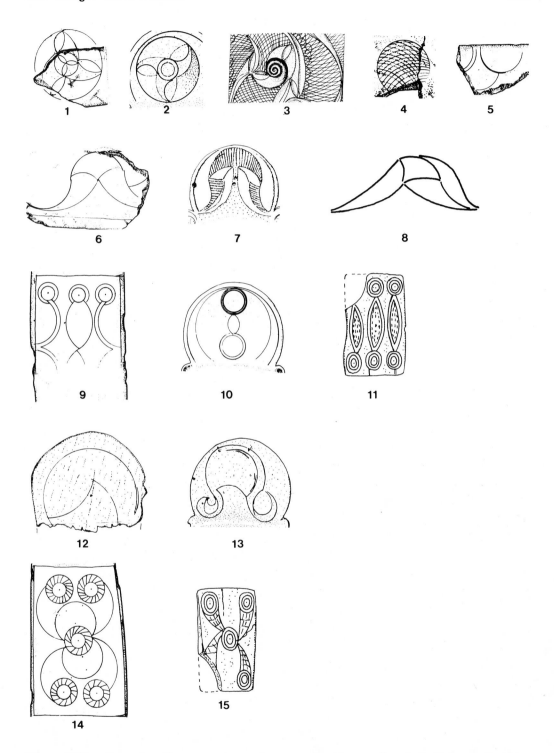

Fig. 127. Lough Crew art and a selection of stylistic analogies. 1,4-6,9,12,14 bone flakes, Lough Crew, Co. Meath. 2,7,10,13 bronze "spoons". 3 gold collar, Broighter, Co. Derry. 8 quernstone, Clonmacnois, Co. Offaly. 4,15 "gaming piece", Cush, Co. Limerick. - Various scales.

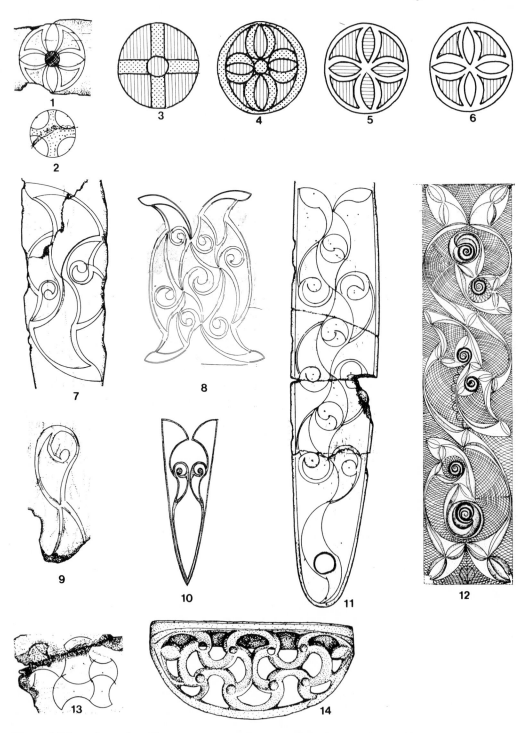

Fig. 128. Lough Crew art and a selection of stylistic analogies.
1-2,7,9,11,13 bone flakes, Lough Crew, Co. Meath. 3-4 enamelled studs,
Pitkelloney, Perthshire, Scotland. 5 enamelled inlay, Rise, Holderness,
Yorkshire, England. 6 enamelled inlay, Seven Sisters, Glamorganshire,
Wales. 8 stone, Derrykeighan, Co. Antrim. 10 ornament on Irish tubular
spearbutt. 12 gold collar, Broighter, Co. Derry. 14 scabbard mount,
Lambay, Co. Dublin. - Various scales.

is not, however, entirely hopeless. The Broighter collar probably dates to the last century B.C. (above p. 187) and the Somerset-type mounts may well date within the first century of the Christian era. Beehive querns, though by no means securely dated in individual cases, are likely to have been in use in the centuries spanning the birth of Christ (above pp. 245-246).

The meagre body of associated material from Lough Crew is of little assistance in further pinpointing the date of the flakes. A bronze spiral finger/toe ring and three glass dumb-bell beads from the site (Herity, 1974, 282, Fig. 139:33-35, 37) do little more than add to the possibility of a dating range for the Lough Crew material within the centuries on either side of the birth of Christ.

Though the flakes are of local manufacture, it is clear that the Lough Crew artificers and their native contemporaries were in close touch with artistic developments outside the country. In Britain, especially in northern and western areas, many decorative parallels for the art on the Lough Crew flakes are to be found. Some of the motifs at Lough Crew are, indeed, otherwise absent in Ireland but are well represented in Scotland. One interesting flake from Lough Crew, for instance, is adorned along its length by a continuous series of broken-backed curves (Fig. 129:1; Though the motif was only partly understood by the Irish craftsman, it is likely that renderings such as that on a beaded torc from Lochar Moss in Scotland (Fig. 129:2; MacGregor, 1976, No. 204), or that on a scabbard from Mortonhall in the same country (op. cit., No. 150), could have provided the inspiration for the Irish version of the design. The date of these two Scottish objects within the first century A.D. is hardly in dispute.

The broken-backed curve is also a recurring theme on the broadly contemporary "massisve" armlets of north Britain (e.g. MacGregor, 1976, Nos 236-239). In discussing these armlets MacGregor saw a direct cousinly relationship between their art and that on the Lough Crew flakes (Simpson, 1968, 250-251). The latter, she wrote, "provide engraved analogies not only for the slender trumpet, but also the sinuous saltire, the paired and opposed trumpet-domes of Castle Newe, the broken-backed S-unit and even the more elaborate of the diaphragms of the Pitkelloney armlets". To these last may be added (Fig. 128:1-6) the enamelled studs which occur on a horsebit from Holderness in Yorkshire, England (MacGregor, 1976, No. 10), and on a terret from Seven Sisters, Glamorganshire, Wales (Davis and Spratling, 1976, 131, Fig. 7:20). MacGregor invoked a common source for the ornament on the two insular groups back as far as Broighter/Snettisham, and the close relationship between the art of the Irish and north British groups at the beginning of the Christian era is

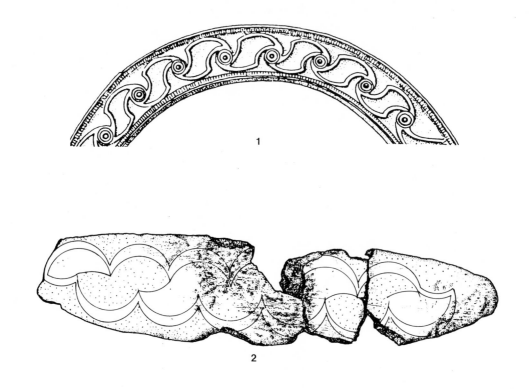

Fig. 129. 1 Beaded torc, decorative detail, Lochar Moss, Dumfriesshire, Scotland. 2 bone flake, Lough Crew, Co. Meath. - 1:3/4. 2:1/1. (1 after MacGregor, 1976).

taken by her as reflecting "a common decorative atmosphere". The pattern-book of the Lough Crew craftsmen clearly borrowed much that was directly Scottish.

The design on the flake fragment here illustrated as Fig. 128:13 is also of note in the context of possible stylistic overlaps with British workshop traditions. The pattern on this piece is undoubtedly a confused version of that so finely cast in openwork bronze on one of the scabbard mounts from the Lambay, Co. Dublin, cemetery (Fig. 128:14). A first century date for the Lambay material is well established (Rynne, 1976) and, significantly perhaps, it is in north Britain that the source of much of the material at the site is sought.

The decorative parallels noted above date consistently to the beginning of the Christian era and the preponderantly north British bias in their distribution is noteworthy. It should also be borne in mind that a similar picture emerged when the bone combs from Lough Crew were independently considered above (pp. 212-213). For these, too, parallels in Scotland (and the Isle of Man) were noted and dating evidence, where present, pointed to manufacture in the first century or so after Christ.

There can be little doubt that these stylistic overlaps indicate cultural interaction between groups on either side of the north Irish Sea. Equally, it seems that the datable British parallels imply a date slightly after, rather than slightly before, the birth of Christ for the Lough Crew school of craftsmanship.

As well as the northern parts of Britain, however, it is possible that the Lough Crew craftsmen also shared areas of artistic inspiration with the potters and woodworkers of south-west England. At the marsh settlements of both Meare and Glastonbury in Somerset (Bulleid and Gray, 1911; 1917; 1948), the same experimentation with compass designs gave rise to patterns there which can be closely paralleled amongst the Lough Crew and related pieces. The lotus-like forms, the continuous, broken-backed scroll, the comma curve, the background dotting, the concentric, overlapping arcs, the circles asymmetrically placed within one another, and the spindly, knob-ended triskele are all common to the Irish and the Somerset stylistic repertoires. Absent at Lough Crew, however, is any trace of the straight-line ornamentation so frequent at Meare and Glastonbury and it should not be forgotten that no Iron Age pottery, decorated or otherwise, has ever been found in Ireland.

The possibility of contacts between the Lough Crew school of craftsmen and the Somerset potters is worth pursuing, however, because of the likelihood of Breton influence on the development of the south-west English pottery style (Peacock, 1969, 52-54; Avery, 1973). The Irish decorated stones are stylistically linked with the Lough Crew flakes (see below, p. 295) and if the latter could be taken to indicate contact with an area where Breton influences are manifestly evident then the argument put forward below for a Breton ingredient in the genesis of the custom of raising carved stones in Ireland is enhanced (below p. 299).

BRONZE "SPOONS"

Six of the objects referred to as either "spoons" or "castanets" are recorded from Ireland. Outside that country a further seventeen are known, all but a single pair (from France; Dechelette, 1927, 783, Fig. 552) coming from various parts of Britain (Way, 1869; Craw, 1923-4; MacGregor, 1976, 145-146). The function of these objects is unknown.

The "spoons" are all of cast bronze (Figs 130-131; Pls 82, 83). On nine occasions they have been found in pairs. In each case one unit of the pair has a circular hole set close to one edge of the larger dished portion of the object (the "bowl"), and on the other unit, also on the "bowl" portion, an incised cross, either simple or emerging from a small, central incised circle, occurs. Decoration may occur on one or both faces of the "handle" portion and it may be engraved or cast.

Two broad groups of insular "spoons" may be recognised according to their shape. The first group comprises examples with a circular "handle" portion. Where the "bowl" and the "handle" meet there is on each side a tiny petal or tear-shaped feature which projects characteristically from the "angle" of junction. At times this ornamental device becomes so enlarged as almost to swallow the circular "handle" itself, such as on the Penbryn, Cardigan (Fox, 1958, Pl. 70a), and River Thames (Jope and Wilson, 1957a, Pl. VIII) specimens. "Spoons" of this group have a pear-shaped, markedly concave "bowl". The second type of "spoon" is that in which the "handle" is roughly D-shaped and for the most part only slightly narrrower than the greatest width of the "bowl" portion. The "bowls" of Type 2 "spoons" tend to be shallower than in the case of Type 1 specimens and they are on the whole more elongated than is the case on the latter group.

Five of the six "spoons" from Ireland belong to Type 2. Outside Ireland

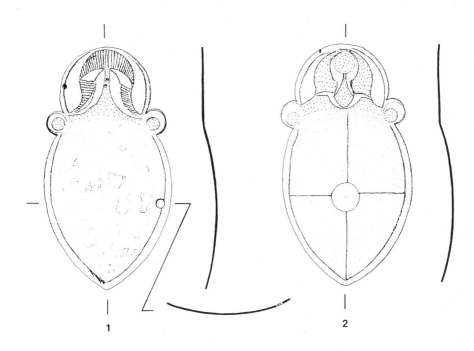

Fig. 130. Bronze "spoons". No prov. - 1/2.

the only Type 2 "spoons" known are the two found together in a grave at Berwick in Scotland (Craw, 1925). Thus an interesting distinction emerges between the "spoons" of southern Britain on the one hand and those of Scotland and Ireland on the other.

The sixth example from Ireland (Fig. 131:3) is closer to those from southern England and could be an import from there. It has raised, concentric circles on its "handle" similar to the ornament on specimens from London, Deal and Bath in the south of England (Craw, 1925, Fig. 4); it is quite unlike the other Irish "spoons". Jope included these Irish objects in his list of material in Ireland "of earlier 1st century A.D. southern British origin" (Jope and Wilson, 1957a, 85-88), though he did concede that "a case could just be made out for considering these an Irish variant" (ibid., 87). As stated above, only one of the "spoons" from Ireland has southern British connotations and the other five probably constitute a local version of the type.

These five Irish "spoons" (which include two pairs) bear engraved decoration on their "handles". It is in several instances compass-drawn but in two cases it is produced by the free-hand rocked-tracer technique

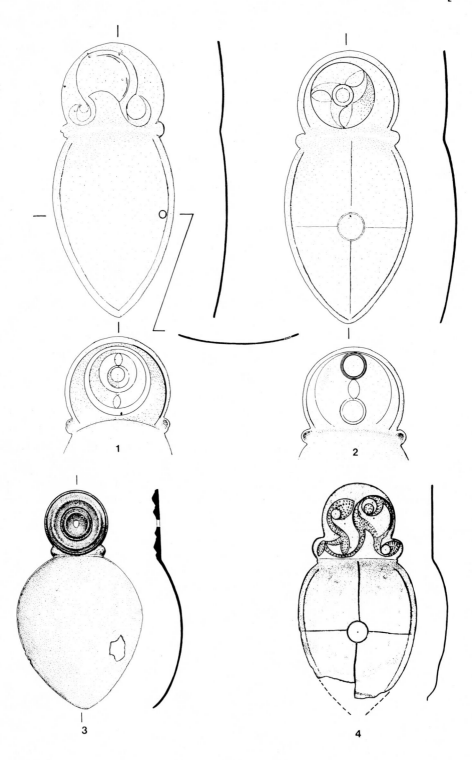

Fig. 131. Bronze "spoons". No prov. – 1/2.

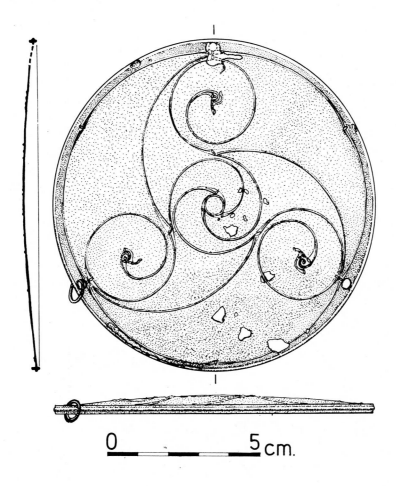

Fig. 134. Bronze disc, Loughan Island, River Bann, Co. Derry.

(Fig. 134; Pl 88; Raftery, J., 1940b, c; Jope and Wilson, 1957b). It is circular, gently convex to the front and about 10 cm in diameter. A tiny loop of thin bronze wire was threaded through a circular hole at three points equally spaced around its circumference. One of the loops survives. Presumably the object was suspended in some way by these, in a manner which calls to mind the pan of a scales. But such a humble function is surely belied by the exceptional craftsmanship of the object; its purpose remains enigmatic.

All three pieces are decorated and it is the technique of their ornamentation which establishes them as outstanding masterpieces of Irish Iron Age metalworking. O'Kelly subjected the Cork and Petrie specimens to detailed and rigorous scientific examination (1961) and concluded that the ornament on them could only have been produced by the meticulous and painstaking method of finely cutting down the background bronze leaving the curving lines in low relief. He pointed out that had the design been cast in the flat the bending of the sheet to the required form would have stretched and damaged the ornament. Equally, if the horns had been initially cast in the round they would have been cast as complete cones thus obviating the necessity for riveting-on a sealing strip. Even if, for some reason, this was in fact done the drilling of rivetholes could not have avoided causing some damage to the ornament immediately adjacent to them. In spite of the most detailed examination, no such damage was detectable.

O'Kelly's arguments carry conviction and his conclusions are supported by Jope who accepted that the original description of the Bann Disc as cast was incorrect (in O'Kelly, op. cit., 12). He wrote that its ornament "was in fact formed by tooling down from the convex surface of a cast, saucer-shaped disc initially at least about 1 mm thick".

The skill and virtuosity which is implied by such a technique and the flawlessness with which the compass-drawn curves were produced is breathtaking. Hodges has demonstrated the geometrical precision of the layout of the Bann Disc design (in Jope and Wilson, 1957b, Fig. 2). Pencil-thin trumpet curves flow across the bronze surfaces forming designs of deceptive complexity for, as different areas of the composition are allowed to take prominence in the eye of the beholder, so differing patterns appear. The decoration of these objects is enhanced by a rare element of restraint, for extensive areas of the surface of each piece are left plain.

All units of the design in each case are composed of elegant, sinuous trumpet-and-lentoid curves; indeed, on the "Petrie Crown" there is an almost obsessive quality about the use of lentoid-bosses. On this object, as on the Bann Disc there are bird's-head endings to several of the curves. On the Bann object each of the birds is a semi-abstract creation composed of a series of trumpet-and-lentoid units. On the "crown" there are three separate versions of the bird's head (Fig. 111:4-6) varying from fine, crested representations on the horn to those on one of the discs which resemble the Bann Disc birds in the way in which they are made up of a series of tiny, trumpet curves. Birds are absent on the Cork horns but this object has, in decorative details, much in common with the other two specimens.

Affinities and chronology

The chronology of these three objects is uncertain and it has been

suggested that their date could be as late as the fifth or sixth century
A.D. (e.g. Henry, 1954, 26).   A date early in the first Christian millennium
seems more likely.   The bird's-head representations on the Bann and
"Petrie" pieces have good parallels on the bowl handles from Keshcarrigan
and Somerset (Figs 107:1,2; 111:7, 8) those on one of the discs of the
"crown" being especially close to the birds on the handles.   Outside Ireland
the crested "birds" on some of the north British dragonesque brooches
resemble those on the "Petrie Crown" horn (Fig. 135:2-4; Feachem, 1951,
32-44; MacGregor, 1976, 127-9, Fig. 6).   The crested bird-silhouettes
on a bronze ball from Walston, Lanarkshire in Scotland are also similar
to the same "Petrie Crown" birds (Fig. 135:5; Pl. 89; MacGregor, op.
cit., No. 350).   The comparanda date to the early centuries A.D.   Their
ultimate ancestry no doubt lies in such early renderings as the birds of
the Early La Tène *Vogelkopffibeln* (e.g. Jacobsthal, 1944, Pls 154-5)
and the crested bird's-head of the Cernon-sur-Coole (Marne), scabbard
(Fig. 56:2; above pp. 103ff.).

Close comparisons for the Irish birds are to be found in the north
of Britain and it is thus interesting that Scotland also supplies a bronze
object with decoration executed by the technique of background tooling
as on the three Irish bronzes.   The relevant object is a bronze collar
from Stichill, Roxburghshire (MacGregor, op. cit., No. 210) the nape
portion of which is tooled in the manner of the Irish pieces (MacGregor
op. cit., 101). As well as this, details of the decoration are closely matched
on the Irish bronzes particularly on the Cork horns.   Megaw, too, compared
the art on the collar with that on the three Irish objects here under
discussion, and stated that "one might consider an Irish link far from
out of the question" (1971, 150).   The Stichill collar, on stylistic grounds,
is assigned to the first or second century A.D. and the probable association
with it of one (or two) "massive" armlets supports this dating.

Another object, again from north Britain, of possible relevance to
the dating of these Irish bronzes is the bone comb from Langbank,
Renfrewshire in Scotland earlier referred to (above p. 212; Fig. 106:4;
MacGregor, 1976, No. 275; Lenerz de Wilde, 1982, 104, Figs 21, 22, 24).
The organisation of the engraved design on this specimen is sufficiently
close to that on one of the discs of the "Petrie Crown" and, indeed, also
to the ornament on the Monasterevin-type discs (see below) to suggest
chronological overlap.   The postulated first century A.D. dating for
the comb is again in keeping with the date of the other comparisons
here put forward for the bronzes in question.

There is one final decorative detail which seems important in the
present context.   On one of the discs of the "Petrie Crown" there is
a small cross-in-circle motif (Fig. 135:1).   This design has only one parallel

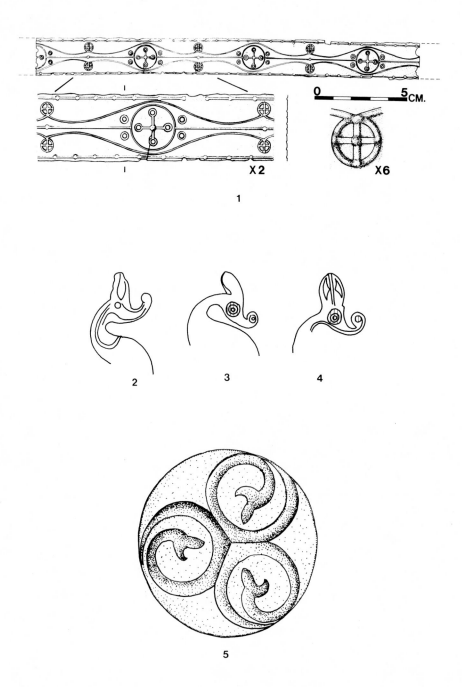

Fig. 135. 1 gold strip, Lambay, Co. Dublin. 2-4 north British dragonesque brooches, details. 5 Walston, Lanarkshire, bronze sphere. - Various scales. (2-5 after MacGregor, 1976).

in the entire repertoire of Irish Iron Age art, on the gold strip from Lambay Island, Co. Dublin (Fig. 135:1). This object was found on the island more than a century ago, allegedly with an iron sword, but the find circumstances are vague (Wilde, 1862, 39; Rynne, 1976, 231-2). If, as seems likely, the strip comes from the Iron Age cemetery found there more recently (Macalister, 1929; Rynne, op. cit.), then a date in the first century is established for it, a date which should, in consequence, also apply to the "Petrie Crown".

DISCS, MOUNTS AND OTHER BRONZES

Monasterevin-type discs

There are seven discs of this type from Ireland, four complete and three fragmentary (Figs 136, 137; Pls 90-95). The only provenanced examples are a pair found together at Monasterevin, Co. Kildare (Fig. 136), and this discovery has given its name to the group. Each consists of a circular sheet of bronze, the diameter of which varies from about 24 cm to approximately 30 cm. They are usually slightly dished, and their concave surface is decorated by bold, curvilinear, repoussé scrolls. The edges have been folded over for strengthening. The patterns on the discs resemble each other closely, but in no two cases are the designs identical. It is likely, however, that all emanate from the same craft-working centre. Their function is unknown.

A feature common to all the discs is a plain, eccentrically-placed, circular area defined in every case by a raised ring of rounded section. The surface within the ring is either flat, gently concave, or hammered to a deep, bowl-shaped hollow. In one case (Fig. 136:1; Pl. 90:2), there is a carefully executed, oval opening through the centre of the sunken, circular area.

The hollow space seems to be the pivotal feature of the decoration. In six of the seven discs, a pair of semi-circular arcs encloses the circle (one from Monasterevin - Fig. 136:1 - has only a single arc) and in each case a snail-shell coil occurs at each extremity of the outer curves. This coil is joined to the end of the inner curve by a short, curved line almost giving the impression of eyebrows. In fact, Megaw compared the design to "a grotesque face with large staring eyes ...." (1970, 158). At the

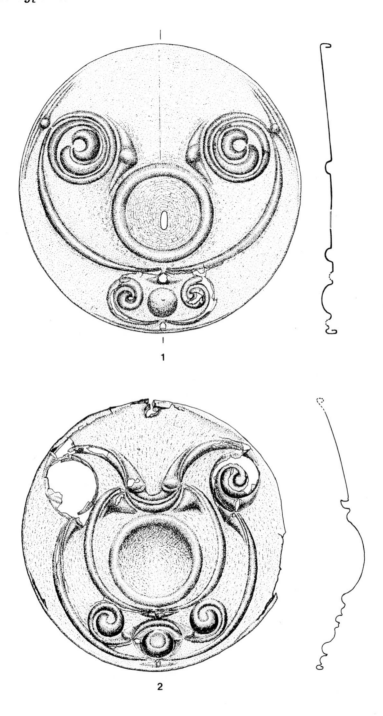

Fig. 136. Bronze, repoussé, Monasterevin-type discs.
1,2 Monasterevin, Co. Kildare. Scale 1/4.

opposite end to the "eyebrows", near the edge of the disc, a triple motif occurs. This comprises a central domed boss (which may have a circular concavity in it) flanked on each side by a snail-shell spiral. This triple motif is absent only on the specimen in the British Museum (CIIAA No. 792; Megaw, 1970, No. 269), where a simple trumpet junction occurs in its place. Trumpet junctions with raised lentoid bosses are common, but their quality varies from crisply executed, sharp-edged units, to barely recognisable, rounded bumps. Tool marks are evident on all examples, culminating in the extreme case of the B.M. piece, where the background to the raised design is emphasised by carefully organised panels of short linear tool marks, set at varying angles to one another to form a pleasing, and undoubtedly intentional, pattern (Pl. 95).

There is general consistency in the nature of the design on these discs, but the quality of their craftsmanship is not uniform. In the first place, the cross-section of the raised curves varies. It can be rounded, or of sharply "keeled" form, with one surface convex, the other concave. In the case of those with "keeled" section, there may be a sharp spine forming a narrow ridge along the apex of the curve. In several instances both variants occur on the same object and, indeed, in the case of one (Fig. 137; Pl. 92) there is a third type of raised curve present, consisting of a spiral, the upper surface of which is flat and which has sharp edges and concave sides. This type of curve does not occur on any of the other discs. This disc is particularly interesting for there seem to be indications of more than a single hand at work on it and several features occur, which are not found on the other examples. The raised curves of this specimen are, for the most part, of rounded profile. The triple boss and snail-shell spiral element, on the other hand, has "keeled" curves. The two "eye-brows" and one of the accompanying spirals are also of rounded profile, but the other spiral (the flat-topped, concave-sided version alluded to above) is completely out of proportion and balance in relation to its counterpart on the opposite side of the disc. Most striking of all, however, is the perfectly executed minor motif set within the sunken space formed by this spiral (Pls 92, 93). This design consists of a thin, tendril-like curve with lobed extremity. The latter is filled with a tiny concentric-circle design, and from this extends a series of trumpet curves with minute, crisp, lentoid bosses to produce a generally ornithomorphic effect. Elsewhere on this disc, lentoid-bosses, comprising rounded bumps which give every appearance of a degenerate or careless hand, are discernible. The contrast in the two styles on this piece is striking and the conclusion is that two craftsmen of widely differing skill were, for some reason, involved in its manufacture and decoration.

The disc shown as Pl. 90:4 (CIIAA No. 790) and that in the British

Fig. 139. Bronze discs, Lambay, Co. Dublin. - 1/2.

and a strong north English element in the Lambay material is likely. Roman influence, so clearly demonstrated in the burial assemblage by the presence of five distinctive brooches (Rynne, op. cit., 240-241; Raftery, B., 1981, Fig. 41:3-7), is stylistically represented on the circular disc by the beaded rim and the rosette stud. Lloyd-Morgan draws attention to sub-Roman parallels from the Lower Rhine region for the art on the circular Lambay disc, while both she and Rynne compared the triskele on the Irish object to one on a lozenge-shaped plaque from a hoard at Moel Hiraddug in north Wales. Attention was also drawn by them to the presence, in the same hoard, of a triangular plaque closely comparable with that from Lambay. Fragment of a third such plaque came from Godmanchester, a Roman farm site in Cambridgeshire (Lloyd-Morgan, op. cit., 221).

Somerset-type mounts

Ten bronze mounts may be grouped together and referred to as "Somerset-type" because half the known number come from the Somerset, Co. Galway hoard (Raftery, J., 1960; 1961, 93, Fig. 24).

The objects are circular and normally take the form of a shallow cylinder with one end closed (Fig. 140; Pls 97-99). The closed end is usually adorned with cast, openwork or repoussé patterns, but is occasionally plain. Two of the ten mounts differ somewhat from this general form. One (from Somerset, Fig. 140:5; Pl. 97:1) is made entirely of openwork bronze and retains at its centre a large enamel inset (see Henry, 1965, 71, Fig. 6:C). Another mount (from Ballycastle, Co. Antrim), is clearly a skeuomorphic version of this (Fig. 140:6; Pl. 97:2).

Apart from assuming that these objects were originally intended as decorative mounts, it is not possible to ascertain their precise function. In two instances (Somerset and Athlone), two similar mounts were inserted into one another and used as containers, but this was obviously not their original purpose; there is no correspondence between the rivetholes on opposed surfaces of the joined mounts in either case. Where rivets remain in situ they project inwards to such a limited extent that it is difficult to envisage the nature of the material to which they were attached.

The type is unknown in Iron Age contexts outside the country. A Scottish Late Bronze Age hoard, from Horsehope in Peebleshire, has produced a pair of superficially similar bronze mounts, which Piggott interpreted as having been cart fittings (1952-3a, 175-186, Fig. 1:4), and a Continental Hallstatt background for them was postulated. The clear chronological disparity between the Scottish and the Irish objects seems, however, to preclude any direct relationship between the two groups

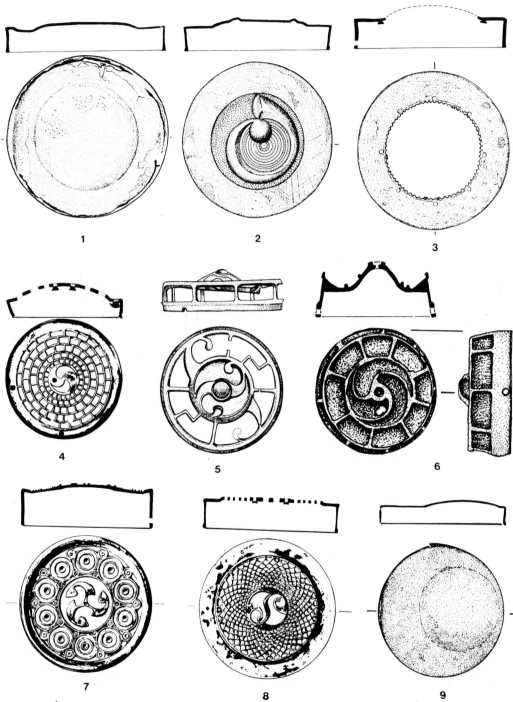

Fig. 140. Bronze Somerset-type mounts. 1-5 Somerset, Co. Galway.
6 Ballycastle, Co. Antrim. 7 Navan Fort, Co. Armagh. 8 Cornalaragh,
Co. Monaghan. 9 River Shannon, near Athlone, Co. Westmeath. - 1-3,
7-9, 1/2; 4-6, 1/1.

and equally, there can be no question that the Irish bronzes, with their small, marginally-projecting rivets, were ever used as cart fittings.

Within Ireland, only at Somerset are mounts of the type under discussion found in significant association. Material from this hoard has elsewhere been discussed (above p. 154) and there are compelling reasons for placing the date of its deposition within the first century A.D. or, at the very earliest, in the latter part of the last century B.C. Such a dating range finds support in a consideration of the stylistic analogies of the ornament which adorns the Somerset-type mounts. Occasionally, however, an echo of earlier traditions is detectable. The openwork "engine-turning" on the Cornalaragh mount, for instance, can be closely compared with the openwork on the Early La Tène disc from Cuperly in France (Jacobsthal, 1944, No. 185), but chronologically more appropriate parallels for this decorative feature have already been referred to (above p. 187).

The stiff, rather jagged triskele on the Navan Fort mount (the arms of which are, in effect, three angular versions of the thick-lobed spiral motif, arranged to form a triskele pattern), call to mind such insular versions of the design as that on the lozenge-shaped bronze plaque from Moel Hiraddug (Fox, 1958, Pl. 45b). Comparison might also be made with a similar, angular triskele on a sub-Roman disc brooch in the University Museum, Newcastle-upon-Tyne (MacGregor, 1976, Fig. 5:7).

The raised trumpet with lentoid boss on one of the mounts from Somerset (Fig. 140:2; Pl. 98), brings discussion back to the Navan-type brooches with their proliferating trumpet patterns, and to the whole range of related insular bronzes of the early centuries A.D., bronzes which have sometimes an almost obsessive fixation with the trumpet-and-lentoid idea. The stippling on the same Somerset mount may also be paralleled on the large Navan brooch, and, in somewhat coarser form, is to be found on the neck of the Kescarrigan bird.

The central openwork design of fan-shaped, spiral-ended trumpets on the Cornalaragh mount (Fig. 140:8; Pl. 99:2), return us to the British mirrors, where precise parallels are to be found on the mid-first century A.D. "Gibbs" mirror, incised and filled with hatching (Fox, 1958, 85, 148). The pattern can also be seen in numerous examples of British craftsmanship of the early Christian era, such as on a hame from Suffolk (Fox, 1958, Fig. 75) and, of course, in a multiplicity of variations on the mirrors, both as positive motifs and as voids. Similarly, the design can be closely compared with that on the front of one of the spoons from Penbryn, Cardiganshire (Fox, 1958, Pl. 70a). The central design on the smallest of the Somerset mounts (Fig. 140:4), derives from the same chronological context; it may best be compared, perhaps, to the pattern on the Balmaclellan mirror (Fox, 1958, 99, Fig. 65) or to an enamelled mount from Santon, Norfolk (Megaw, 1970, Pl. VIIIa). The pattern on the other small Somerset mount (Fig. 140:5; Pl. 97:1) shares exactly the same artistic milieu with the last-mentioned specimen, and the enamel-filled voids left by the central S-shaped design provide a pair of fan-shaped trumpets, precisely similar to those on the Cornalaragh mount. The central motif on this object has already been compared to the designs on the ends of the Lough Gur "chariot" mounts (above, p. 61; Fig. 41).

Miscellaneous mounts

Four centrally-perforated, circular, bronze mounts of phalera-type (Fig. 141:1-4) and two damaged foil mounts of uncertain original shape (Fig. 141:5,6) came from the Lisnacrogher, Co. Antrim site. The spindly, repoussé, boss-ended triskele on one of the circular mounts (Fig. 141:3) recalls, perhaps, the cast ornament on one of the spearbutts from the same site (above, p. 125; Fig. 60:2) and in concept and execution, it seems also to share something with the design on the repoussé disc from Killeevan, Co. Monaghan (Fig. 26:2). The Killeevan analogy may be particularly relevant, as the closest parallels for the whirligigs on the two damaged foil mounts from Lisnacrogher are also to be found on the same Co. Monaghan object (Fig. 27:2). The Killeevan piece could well be a horse-phalera and might thus shed light on the function of the smaller Lisnacrogher mounts. Its probable date in the first century A.D. or so (above, pp. 42-44), may be appropriate for the Co. Antrim objects.

A final mount briefly to be noted here is a sub-oval loop of cast bronze from the upper surface of which a pair of stylised birds (Fig. 141:7) projects. Around its sides there are two parallel bands of reserved zig-zags which had formerly been set in a field of red enamel. It has been suggested (Jope and Wilson, 1957a, 87), that the object could have served as the hilt-mount of a sword but the writer does not find this suggestion convincing.

Dating is not easy. The birds have a strangely archaic appearance and have good parallels of Hallstatt, even of Urnfield date (e.g. Wells, 1981, Fig. 32a; cf. also Fig. 3:1 above). But such early dating seems unlikely for the Irish mount. In the double zig-zag may be a better clue to its chronological position for, in an insular context, this design, as already suggested, seems to belong just before and shortly after the birth of Christ (see Megaw, 1963, 28-30).

Rings of uncertain function

The most interesting of the rings is that in the Ulster Museum, which

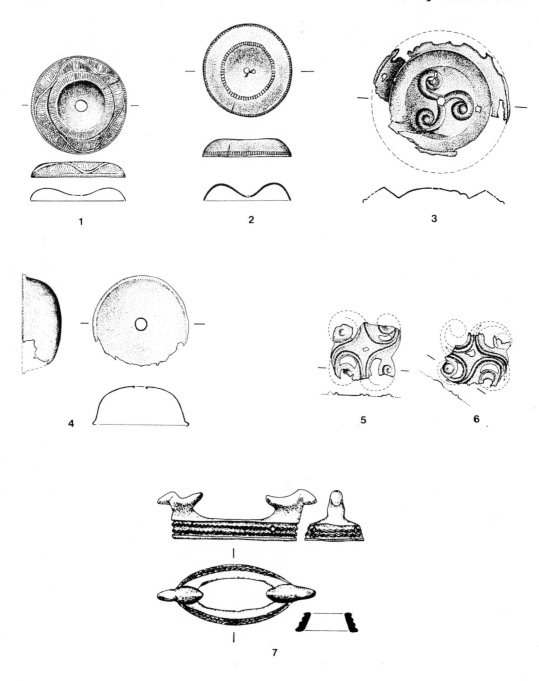

Fig. 141. Miscellaneous bronze mounts, Lisnacrogher, Co. Antrim.
1–6:1/2. 7:3/4

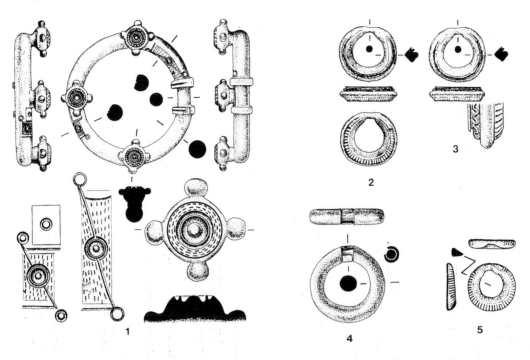

Fig. 142. Miscellaneous bronze rings. 1 possibly north of Ireland. 2-5 Lisnacrogher, Co. Antrim. - 1:c.2/5. 2-5:1/2.

probably comes from northern Ireland (Fig. 142:1; Pl. 100). The object, recessed at one point on its circumference, might be a harness loop or may be part of a belt. Three hemispherical bosses, from each one of which projects a cruciform arrangement of lesser bosses, adorn one face of the ring, and a series of strange designs, combining rectilinear, linear and circular motifs, are engraved on the same face. Hyphenated stippling occurs on the upper surface of each of the main bosses, and also within several of the engraved rectangles on the ring.

The object is unparalleled in Ireland. The cruciform bosses on it can, however, be matched on a mount from Portstewart, Co. Derry. (Fig. 38:1, above p. 59) while the peculiar combinations of circles and straight lines on it are found, in closely similar form, on the unique spearhead from Boho, Co. Fermanagh (Fig. 58:1; above p. 108). In neither case is dating little more than a guess, however, but the possibility of manufacture sometime within the early centuries A.D. has been tentatively put forward.

Outside Ireland the only rings which bear any resemblance to the object in question are belt rings of the local Late La Tène period, found

on the island of Gotland off the south-east coast of Sweden.   Though
differing in important formal details from the Irish specimen, these rings
possess two, and sometimes three, bosses projecting prominently from
one face, in precisely the same manner as on the north of Ireland ring
(Nylen, 1955, 452-7, Fig. 286).   It could be that the similarities are merely
coincidental.   In the foregoing pages, however, occasional hints of possible
influence from the north of Europe on Irish metalworking traditions have
from time to time been noted, and it may be that future research will
add substance to what remains, for the moment, no more than an
interesting possibility.

Other bronze rings, smaller and less elaborate than that just described,
are also known from Ireland.   One plain example from Lisnacrogher
is of uncertain date (Fig. 142:4).   Others are more probably Iron Age.
An interesting group is represented by five examples from north-east
Ireland (three from Lisnacrogher, two from the River Bann), all decorated
and all possessing, at one point on their circumference, a recess for the
likely attachment of a leather strap (Fig. 142:2,3,5).   In three cases,
the cross-section is sub-trapezoidal or D-shaped and one face bears simple,
radially-ribbed ornament (Fig. 142:5).   The other two examples, both
from Lisnacrogher, have cross-sections of sub-lozenge shape.   A band
of ornament adorns each face (cast, reserved zig-zag on one face, simple
hatching on the other), separated by a plain, convex rib around the outer
circumference of the ring (Fig. 142:2,3).

Rings of this group may well have been attached to leather belts
(note the ring-pairs from cremation deposits at Carbury Hill, Co. Kildare
- Willmot, 1938, 136, Fig. 4 - and Carrowjames, Co. Mayo - Raftery, J.,
1940a, 31, Pl. I:9, 11), but their precise function can only be demonstrated
if such objects are found in situ in an inhumation burial.   The type seems
essentially native with the reserved zig-zag ornament in particular,
recalling insular versions of the design for which a date around, or shortly
after, the birth of Christ can be argued.   The possibility of an earlier,
Continental background for these rings should, however, be borne in
mind (e.g. Pajot and Vernhet, in Guilaine, 1976, 696, Fig. 5:20; Chossenot
et al., 1981, Fig. 11 d-f).

DECORATED STONES

Five standing stones, bearing abstract curvilinear decoration, and at least one undecorated stone of Iron Age date are known from Ireland. Though these stones are generally treated of as a group, they differ from each other in size, in form and in details of ornamentation; there is, in fact, no reason for regarding them as a single chronological grouping.

The best known and most frequently discussed of the Irish monoliths is that from Turoe, Co. Galway (Fig. 143:2; Pl. 102). Its original position was close to a ringfort in the townland of Turoe, Co. Galway (Knox, 1915-16; Raftery, J., 1944), and it was initially brought to public attention in 1902 (Reddington, 1902, 118). The first person to discuss its significance, however, was Coffey (1902-04, 26ff.) and since then it has always figured prominently in discussions of the Irish Iron Age. A detailed stylistic analysis, with a summary of the earlier views on the stone, was published by Duignan (1976), and important new conclusions were reached by him regarding the place of the stone in the native artistic development. The latest statement on the stone is by Waddell (1982).

The ornament on the Turoe stone is produced by chiselling away the background, leaving the curvilinear designs in low relief. The horizontal band of step or meandroid ornament which defines the base of the main decorated area is rather inexpertly executed by the less laborious technique of incising the design into the stone. The curvilinear ornament on the stone as Duignan demonstrated, is carefully organised into four distinct panels - D-shaped on the broader faces of the stone and sub-triangular on the narrower sides (Fig. 143:2).

The stone now standing at Castlestrange, Co. Roscommon (its original position is unknown), is smaller and squatter than that at Turoe (maximum height c. 90) and the ornament on it, unlike the curvilinear ornament

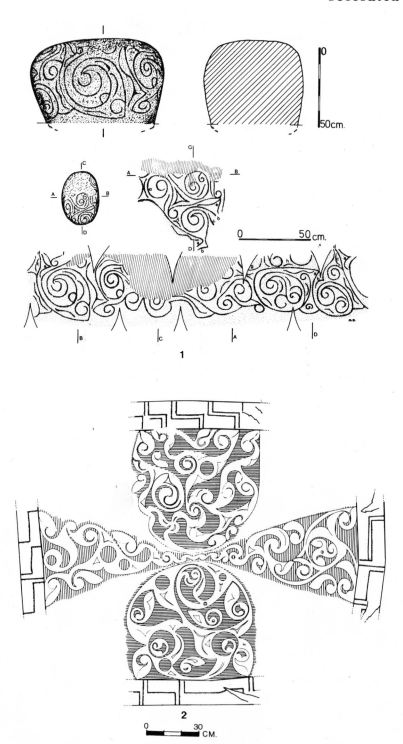

Fig. 143. Decorated stones. 1 Castlestrange, Co. Roscommon. 2 Turoe,
Co. Galway. (2 after Duignan, 1976, with 'step' pattern added).

on the Galway stela, is pecked into its surface (Fig. 143:1; Pl. 103; Coffey, 1902-4, 262-263, Pl.XXI).   The design which it bears comprises of a continuous series of thin, freehand curves, flowing tendril-like over the surface of the stone without any clearly discernible order. Spirals, spiral-ended triskeles, peltate patterns, disjointed curves and wavy lines are the principal motifs present.   Duignan regarded its art as "inferior to Turoe's"; indeed, he went so far as to describe it as a "degenerate piece of work" (op. cit., 215).   Undoubtedly it does not exhibit the same excellence of craftsmanship as the Galway specimen, but it should not be forgotten that poor craftsmanship and lateness in date need not necessarily be synonymous.

Only portions of the third stone, that from Killycluggin Co. Cavan, survive (Fig. 144; Pls 104, 105; Macalister, 1922; Ó Ríordáin, 1952; Raftery, B., 1978).   If it can be assumed (as seems reasonable) that the domed fragment which lay downslope from the shattered stump is, in fact, the upper part of the original stone (Pl. 105), then it may be surmised that the object, when complete, resembled the Turoe stone in shape.

The decoration on the principal surviving fragment (the basal portion), has been deeply and crisply carved into the surface of the monolith. Tight, hair-spring spirals dominate, joined by spindly, curving lines. As on Turoe, the ornament appears to have been divided into panels, here separated from one another by vertical lines.   Remains of two such vertical lines are visible and it is likely that this stone also had a fourfold arrangement of the ornament. Traces of similar, curvilinear ornament survive on the domed piece, but the main decoration on it consists of a series of deep, parallel lines, now considerably weathered, extending across the rounded surface of the stone.

The most recently discovered of the carved stones is that which was found built into the gable wall of a church at Derrykeighan, Co. Antrim (Fig. 145; Pl. 106; Waterman, 1975).   The stone is rectangular in shape and section, and at the time of writing only one decorated face is exposed. When removed from the wall it is likely that further ornament will come to light[1].   The decoration now visible consists of a carefully organised, geometrically-balanced, compass-drawn pattern, incised expertly into the surface of the stone.

The final stone, that from Mullaghmast, Co. Kildare, differs substantially from those briefly noted above and will be separately considered below (Fig. 147; Coffey, 1902-4, 263-6, Pl. XXII).   It is probably a far later piece than the other four examples.

---

1. Since the above was written the stone has been removed from the church wall revealing a second decorated face.

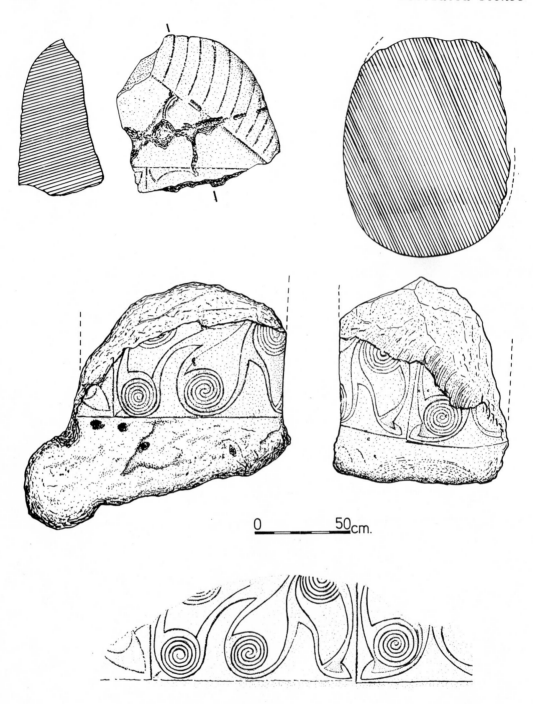

Fig. 144. Decorated stone, Killycluggin, Co. Cavan.

5cm.

Fig. 145. Decorated stone, Derrykeighan, Co. Antrim.
(after Waterman, 1975).

Affinities and chronology

Discussion of these Irish stones has been dominated by consideration
of the fine granite monolith at Turoe. As Duignan pointed out (1976),
most commentators regarded it as evidence of direct contact via the
western seaways between Ireland and the Breton peninsula, where a large
series of comparable stones exists. Some went so far as to regard it
as indicating the presence in Ireland of a Breton carver, sometime in
the third century B.C.

In his detailed study of the art on the stone, however, Duignan
compared the various elements of the design with insular patterns in
bronze and concluded that the ornament on it "shows us a mixture of
insular styles and represents an advanced stage of insular La Tène art"
(op. cit., 210). There can now be little doubt as to the correctness of
this view. Most of the decorative analogies for the stone's decoration

to which Duignan drew attention, however, come from Britain and implicit
in Duignan's arguments seemed to be the contention that the art of the
Turoe stone has a wholly British background.   Undoubtedly the stone
shares much in common with British Iron Age decoration, especially
with so-called "mirror-art" but the stone fits well into the native family
of La Tène art and it is in this context, along with the other stones, that
it is best considered.

The Turoe stone shares with Killycluggin not merely an assumed
similarity of shape but also a subdivision of the ornament into clearly
defined panels.   The two stones also share details of ornamentation
even though contrasting sculptural techniques are used. For instance,
the manner in which the corner of each surviving angular panel of ornament
on the Killycluggin stone is filled with a pointed, convex-sided "ear"
provides, in combination with a spiral, what is, in effect, a version of
the "domed trumpet" or "lobed spiral" motif filling each basal corner
of the four panels of ornament on the Turoe stone.   The tight, hair-
spring spirals are, of course, absent in this form on the Turoe stone.
Such two-dimensional spirals are otherwise known in Ireland only on
the decorated scabbards but these share little else with the Co. Cavan
stone.   Perhaps we should look rather to the engraved decoration on
some of the Lough Crew flakes for better comparisons.   Here, though
the true spiral is absent, the manner in which concentric-circle motifs
are occasionally linked by double, curved lines (e.g. Fig. 126:18-21) calls
to mind the treatment of the curves on the Killycluggin stone.

Reference to the Lough Crew flakes brings discussion to the
Derrykeighan stone, the ornament of which is so close to that on several
of the flakes as to compel the view that a common school of craftsmen
was involved both in the carving of the stone and of the flakes
(Fig. 128:7,8).   Here, indeed, it is possible to imagine that the artist
at Derrykeighan had a Lough Crew flake as a pattern before him as he
worked.

The stylistic analogies of the flakes have been considered above (p. 258)
and a case has been put forward for dating them no later than the first
century A.D.   That the flakes were generically related to the Broighter
collar (Fig. 128:11,12) was also evident and so it is not surprising to note
that the collar, too, shares decorative features with the stones.   At
Broighter, as well as at Derrykeighan and Killycluggin, the decoration
is set in rectangular fields and the corners of these panels on the collar
are filled with the same pointed "ears" as on the other stones.   The
affinities between Broighter and Killycluggin are especially close in this
respect and, indeed, the two-dimensional spirals on this stone can be
compared with the three-dimensional spirals on the collar.   Broighter

Fig. 146. Comparative triskele designs. 1 Scabbard No 49, La Tène, Switzerland (after De Navarro, 1972,). 2 Castlestrange stone. Various scales.

and Turoe are also linked, especially by their domed trumpets, their peltate patterns and their similarly shaped voids.

The Castlestrange stone, however, stands apart as a work apparently less organised and less disciplined than is the case with the other examples. It is not easy to relate the ornament on it with that on other native pieces and the coherence of the design is difficult to assess, especially in view of the extensive weathering on the surface of the stone.

In occasional details, there may be overlap with the decoration on other Irish objects. For instance, some elements of the design on the Loughnashade disc seem to be echoed on the stone and the asymmetrical triskeles on one of the Lough Crew flakes (Fig. 126:9) are also, to an extent, matched on the Castlestrange monolith. But on the whole, its ornament appears distinct from the mainstream of native art. Stylistic comparisons, far closer in detail than anything in Ireland are, however, to be found on some of the scabbards from the Swiss site of La Tène. On these scabbards the spindly, spiral-ended triskele was a common motif and those on the Castlestrange stone are strikingly paralleled there. In particular, the triskele with central triangle, occurring near the top of the Co. Roscommon stone, has an astoundingly close parallel on scabbard No. 49 from La Tène (Fig. 146; De Navarro, 1972, 385, Pl. LXXVIII:2; CXLIX:1a).

The stone from Co. Roscommon is thus a tantalising piece. Some details on it may be early and it is not impossible that it is this piece, with its squat shape and its atypical ornament, which may stand near the head of the Irish series.

The final Irish stone, that from Mullaghmast, Co. Kildare (Fig. 147), is, perhaps, the most difficult of all to place in its exact context. The stone is somewhat irregular in shape but there is a definite tendency

towards rectangular section, which seems to be partly a natural feature
and partly due to deliberate working.   The disposition of the ornament,
however, emphasises its essentially quadripartite nature, and the design
varies in content and technique from one face to the next. One surface
bears a pattern of incised, interlocking compass-drawn curves while
another has a pair of thick-lobed spirals in false relief, enclosed within
a more or less pointed-oval frame.   Below this, there are some unclear
patterns which resemble the "muzzles" as defined by MacGregor (1976,
I, XVIII) and under these there is a band of pseudo-step design, again
in false relief, the lines of which run obliquely to provide the appearance
of a zig-zag.   On the flat, sloping top of the stone there is a regular,
open-limbed triskele, enclosed within a circle, and from this a number
of trumpet curves with flattened, lentoid bosses extend.

Several different styles appear to be represented on the Mullaghmast
stone.   The band of zig-zag design is dimly reminiscent of the framing
band along the base of Turoe, but the analogy is not close.   The panel
of interlocking curves, the thick-lobed spirals, the triskele and the trumpet
curves on the other hand give every impression of deriving inspiration
from metal prototypes, and close comparisons for these motifs can be
found on bronzes which are conventionally dated to the Early Historic
Period.   The thick-lobed spirals can be closely paralleled, for instance,
on latchets, especially the unlocalised specimen, Reg. No. W. 492, in
the National Museum (Henry, 1965, Pl. 13).   Similar designs may also
be noted on a carved bone "trial piece" from Dooey sandhills, Co. Donegal
(Ó Ríordáin and Rynne, 1961, 63, Fig. 8).

Outside the country, parallels for some of the motifs on the
Mullaghmast stone are to be found in surprisingly early contexts.   Amongst
the art of the Somerset potters in south-west England are to be found
versions of the Mullaghmast zig-zag and X designs (e.g. Bulleid and Gray,
1948, Pl. IX: P165, P163), and a false relief variant of the latter is present
on one face of the four-sided Kermaria stela (Duval, 1977, Fig. 289;
Waddell, 1982, Fig. 1:II).   The early dating of these foreign comparisons
seems to rule out the possibility of any direct overlap between them
and the Co. Kildare example.   It could be, however, that the presence
of such designs on an Irish stone represents archaic survival of long-
established traditions.   Such ornamental details could, indeed, be a clue
to the direction from which the tradition of stone carving travelled to
Ireland.

The unresolved question remains, however, as to whether the
Mullaghmast stone is a late (fourth or fifth century A.D.?) survival of
the decorated stone group or whether it contains in its ornamental details
evidence for the early beginnings of some of the standard motifs of the

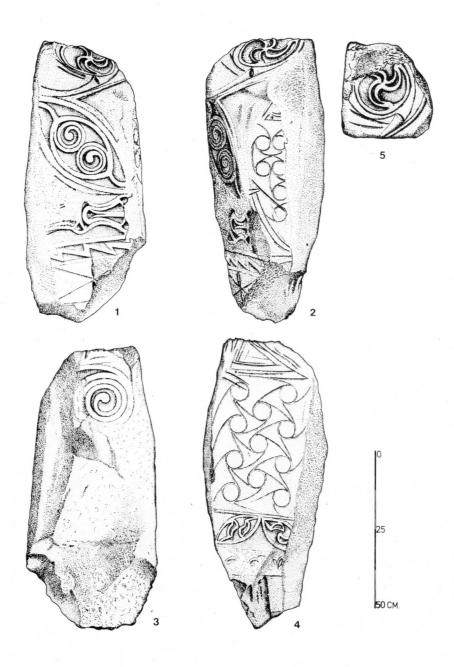

Fig. 147. Decorated stone, Mullaghmast, Co. Kildare.

Early Historic Period in Ireland.   Or should we, perhaps, view the decorative latchets and penannular brooches as themselves commencing several centuries earlier than is normally accepted?

On balance, it seems that the Mullaghmast stone is likely to be the latest of the Irish group and a date for it somewhere towards the middle of the first Christian millennium is the most probable.

The Breton Connection

The art on the Irish stones is clearly the product of local craftsmen whose work is dominated by insular traditions of ornamentation.   This and the suggested late dating for them within the native artistic development have given rise to a tendency among some commentators to reject the concept of an ultimately Breton background for the custom of erecting ornamented stones in Ireland (for recent discussion, see Waddell, 1982). Duignan, for instance, in his published discourse delivered in 1972 to the Oxford Colloquy on Celtic Art (1976) made no reference to the possibility of a French connection for the Irish stones and, by implication, appeared to dismiss such a possibility.

It is interesting, however, that in the discussion which followed Duignan's paper on the Turoe stone (reproduced verbatim in Duignan, 1976, 214-217), Brittany was repeatedly referred to as a likely source of inspiration for the tradition of raising carved stones in Ireland.   As Schwappach rightly pointed out, there are two elements germane to the discussion: firstly, that the curvilinear art on the Turoe stone is insular and, secondly, that the custom of adorning the stone, the quadripartite basis for the ornament on it and the meandroid band around its base, are all Continental features (op. cit., 214).   As regards the second element Schwappach stated firmly: "With Brittany alone (the Armorican north-west of Gaul), where besides stones that are tall there are many essentially hemispherical, can we certainly connect it: through its shape and its basal band ...."   No serious disagreement with this view was expressed and, indeed, Duignan himself conceded "one must of course relate the Brittany stones to the Irish in idea" (op. cit., 215).

It is indeed difficult to dismiss the possibility that inspiration of some sort emanating from the Breton peninsula contributed to the tradition of erecting and carving stones in Ireland.   Large numbers of stones of varied form exist in Brittany but, as Schwappach pointed out, two dominant types occur - tall stones of cylindrical, truncated-conical or rectangular-sectioned type and low, squat stones of hemispherical profile (Giot, 1959; 1960, 179-184; Giot et al., 1979, 261-274). Of the hundreds of stones known in Brittany only a handful now bear decoration.   The decoration is, however, always engraved in very low relief and Giot refers to the liklihood that in many cases decoration might have been obliterated by weathering (1979, 270). It is also possible, even likely, that painted decoration occurred on many of the French stones.

Virtually all the forms present in Ireland can be matched in Brittany and the parallelism is at times strikingly close. Compare, for instance, the hemispherical stones in the Vannes and Penmarc'h museums, at Audierne, at Carnac or the massive specimen at Ploudaniel, with the round-topped Irish stones (Pls 107,108). The squat outline of Castlestrange is typically Breton. The undecorated stone at Tara in Co. Meath - the Lia Fáil - would also excite little undue comment if it were to be transplanted to Brittany (Pl. 109; Macalister, 1931, 29-31 and Pl.). It is possible, too, though hardly provable, that some of the other undecorated pillarstones in Ireland, which are generally regarded as of Christian date because of the crosses inscribed on them, could represent pagan Iron Age monoliths with secondary Christian symbols added. The cylindrical granite pillar at Kilnasaggart, Co. Armagh, for example, some 2.10 m tall and with rounded top would, like the Lia Fáil, be completely at home in an Iron Age Breton context, were it not for the inscription and the proliferation of crosses upon it (Henry, 1965, 119-120 and Pl. 49). One of the undecorated stones at the Early Christian site of Killadeas in Co. Fermanagh could also be of pre-Christian date (Evans, 1966, 115).

The carefully quadripartite arrangement of the ornament on the Turoe stone is likely to indicate that the layout of the decoration was influenced by stones of rectangular section (see comments on this aspect of the problem by Schwappach and Duval, in Duignan, 1976, 215-216). Inevitably the famous, ornamented, four-sided stone from Kermaria comes to mind here but many other, undecorated four-sided stones are also known on the Breton peninsula (e.g. Beg-an-Toul, Plouguerneau; Giot et al., 1979, Fig. p. 262, no. 4). The ornament on the Kermaria stone has, however, little in common with that on any of the Irish specimens apart from the horizontal band of meandroid ornament on it which is frequently compared with that on the Turoe stone. But even this is not precisely the same as that on the Galway example. Some of the other Breton stones, notably one from Treguennec, Finistère (Giot et al., 1979, 271) also possess meandroid bands. The S-spirals on the stone at Trégastel, Côtes du Nord, are perhaps, distantly reminiscent of the spirals on the Killycluggin fragment (Duval, 1977, 262, Fig. 33; Giot et al., op. cit., 271), and it is interesting to ponder on the possibility that the strange parallel grooves present on the smaller of the fragments from Killycluggin (Fig. 144) may be, in some way, related to the vertical grooving not infrequently present on Breton stones (e.g. Goulien and Roz-an-Treman, both in

Finistère; Giot et al., op. cit., Fig. p. 262, nos. 7,8).   On the whole, however, it has to be accepted that such decoration as survives on the Breton stones (with the exception of the meandroid bands) is unlike that on any of the Irish examples.

The precise chronological range of the Breton stones is uncertain, as only those few with decoration or those coming from cemetery contexts can be dated.   They are probably distantly related to the Rhenish group and ultimately, no doubt, to the Etruscan cippi (Jacobsthal, 1944, 8-9); a date for the earliest of the French stones (including Kermaria), in the late fifth or early fourth century B.C. is likely.   There are no firmly dated stones later than the Early La Tène period but there are grounds for believing that the type continued in use into the Late La Tène or even the Gallo-Roman periods (Giot et al., 1979, 273).

If, therefore, a late survival for the custom of raising carved monoliths in Brittany can be demonstrated, then the apparent chronological difficulties involved in relating the Irish stones to those in Brittany are diminished. But if such a relationship can be sustained it is evident from all that has been written above that it was only the idea of the decorated stone which was introduced to Ireland or, more correctly perhaps, only the religious beliefs with which the stones were presumably associated. The art on them, with the possible exception of a few individual motifs, is essentially insular.   Thus again the decorated stones seem to illustrate the recurring conundrum of the Irish Iron Age - a foreign concept rendered in an entirely native form.

The mechanism by which the relevant innovations could have been introduced into the country is unknown.   In Brittany, the concentration of the lower, domed stones in the area of the Veneti tribe (Giot, 1960, Figs 59 and 67) might give rise to the suggestion that it was through the agency of this sea-faring group that the idea was transported to Ireland. The presence in Ireland of promontory forts similar to those in the Venetic region could also be seen as deriving from the same Breton influences.

Unfortunately, the objections to such an hypothesis are at present daunting.   Dating evidence for the Irish promontory forts is virtually non-existent and there is, at any rate, no distributional overlap between them and the carved stones.   In southern and south-western Britain, where a Venetic presence is manifestly recognisable (e.g. Schwappach, 1975, 88-90, Abb. 2; Cunliffe, 1982) no carved stones exist.   No pottery, coins or other Breton material have ever come to light in Ireland.

For the moment the matter of possible Breton background for the Irish stones remains no more than an unproven hypothesis.   It cannot, however, be dismissed as "untenable" (Waddell, 1978, 126). The suggestion that the Irish stones are "scattered lithic survivors of a more widespread timber form" (Waddell, 1982, 26) is also no more than an interesting hypothesis.

Other aniconic carving

Apart from the monoliths just discussed, and a handful of ornamented beehive querns (above pp. 244-245), the only other decorative carving of possible Iron Age date from Ireland is that which occurs on the chamber wall of a Portal Dolmen at Rathkenny, Co. Meath (Raftery, J., 1937-40, 258-261). The designs present on this monument include an apparent triskele motif enclosed within a circle (Pl. 110) and an odd figure-of-eight-shaped pattern described as a "Pictish mirror-case".

The so-called "Pictish" analogy for the latter motif is somewhat obscure and Rynne is doubtless correct in regarding the Rathkenny "mirror" as no more than a slightly aberrant version of the more normal circle and "cupmark" designs, generally regarded as of pre-Iron Age date, which are also present elsewhere on the stone (1972, 94 Ref. 1). The triskele is, however, less easily dismissed. J. Raftery compared it with the repoussé triskele on the Lambay disc (above p. 282; Fig. 139:1; Pl. 96:1) and also with a rock-sculptured triskele at Ilkley, Yorkshire, in England (Leeds, 1933, Fig. 24c). The comparisons may well be valid, but because of the worn condition of the stone caution is necessary. If, however, an Iron Age dating should prove acceptable for the Rathkenny triskele, then an interesting avenue of speculation is opened as to the reasons why such a design should appear on a tomb of conventionally Neolithic type.

HUMAN AND ANIMAL REPRESENTATIONS

Animal representations

⌈Only seven or eight animal representations which may be regarded as of probable or possible Iron Age date are known from Ireland (Fig. 148; Pl. 111). These include two small, cast bronze pigs, a hollow bronze mask of stylised bovine form, a small bronze ring with two projecting animal heads, a zoomorphic, pelta-shaped mount, a stag-form scratched on a bone flake and the strange animal faces on an unlocalised horsebit⌋ (Figs 11:2; 23; Pl. 3). Some of the other horsebits such as that from Ballymoney, Co. Antrim (Fig. 24:16), are distinctly zoomorphic in the treatment of their curvilinear ornament and one or two of the safety-pin fibulae appear to have their foot portion cast in serpentine form (e.g. Fig. 80:3; Pl. 48:2).

⌈Few of these animals are closely dated. The pigs (Fig. 148:2,3; Pl. 111:1) may be compared with the widespread pan-Celtic family of model, cast-bronze pigs.⌋ The evidence for tinning on one of the Irish specimens might suggest a sub-Roman dating, for both Tylecote (1962, 156) and Forbes (1950, 259) regarded this as a Roman technique invented in Gaul (but see Savory, 1971, 68 and refs.). The dotting on the snout of one of the pigs and the hinted trumpet design on one of the eyes of the other would not conflict with such a dating. Indeed, the worn pattern on the latter pig's eye calls vaguely to mind the obviously far more elaborate ornament surrounding the eyes of the Deskford carnyx boar (Fig. 138:1; Piggott, 1959; MacGregor, 1976, No. 188). Foster, too, (1977, 23) drew attention to a certain similarity of treatment between the same

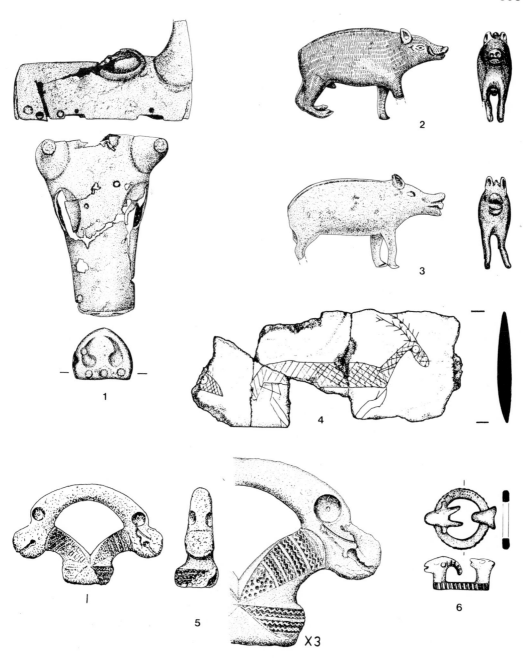

Fig. 148. Animal representations. 4 Lough Crew, Co. Meath.
Otherwise no prov. 4:1/1. 5:c.4/5. otherwise 1/2.

Irish pig and a cast bronze version of the animal on a cult wagon from
Merida in Spain (Megaw, 1970, No. 37), the date of which may be second
or first century B.C. A comparable specimen is also recorded from
Czechoslavakia (Filip, 1956, 313, Obr. 91:1). On the whole, however,
none of the foreign parallels for the Irish pigs is entirely convincing and,
in fact, the possibility of a date for them considerably later than generally
accepted is not to be entirely dismissed. A sixteenth century German
sander of cast bronze, in the form of a pig, illustrated in the auction
catalogue of the Hirsch Collection (Sothebys, 1978, Vol. 2, 141, No. 319),
bears more than a passing resemblance to the more elablorate of the
Irish specimens. It could be, therefore, that these pigs should be removed
entirely from the list of Irish Iron Age material.

The bovine head (Fig. 148:1) differs substantially in concept and design
from the two model pigs just discussed, and it obviously served a different
function. It is a highly stylised, hollow casting and is in fact a mask
rather than a model in the round. It was originally mounted on some
object. It could have been an escutcheon for a bucket or might have
been mounted on top of a pole for use, perhaps, in a procession.

Cast-bronze representations of the bull/cow form are known in Celtic
Europe (Klindt-Jensen, 1950, 110-119; Déchelette, 1927, Figs 568:6;
570:2) and are not infrequent in Britain where MacGregor has counted
no fewer than thirty-nine examples (1976, 153-155). As Hawkes pointed
out, bovine (ox) representations are rare in Celtic Europe before the
late La Tène period but continue into Roman times (Hawkes, 1951, 192).
According to MacGregor "no known member of the British series can
much predate the early first century A.D. and long popularity is confirmed
by the fourth century finds from Wilcote, Oxfordshire, and Mountsorrel,
Leicestershire."

Within this chronological range the exact position of the Irish example
is unknown because, as in the case of the pigs, no specimen outside the
country is quite like it. The casting from Burrow in Lancashire
(MacGregor, 1976, No. 313) is superficially comparable in form with
the Irish object in that it has flat edges, is open at the back, has inward-
curving horns the ends of which are flattened rather than knobbed. But
even this north English piece, which was found with pottery of the 2nd
to 4th century A.D., differs in detail from the Irish representation, for
it has ears, rounded eyes, circular nostrils and a mouth. Moreover, like
the majority of the British bovine representations, it is considerably
smaller than that from Ireland. Jope (1954b, 95) compared the Irish
object to the carnyx head from Deskford, but the analogy is not close.
He regarded it, along with the two cast pigs considered above, as being
comparable with the "more naturalistic styles which were gaining ground

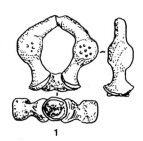

Fig. 149. Bronze loops. 1 Wilford Down, Devizes, Wiltshire, England. 2 Maiden Castle, Dorset, England. - 1/1. (1 after Goddard 1907-8; 2 after Wheeler, 1943).

in the Belgic workshops of Britain".

The unlocalised, cast-bronze ring with projecting animal heads (Fig. 148:6) is probably an Iron Age piece, but it too is an object not easy to parallel precisely. A drinking horn from Keilstrup in Jutland is adorned with a series of animal and bird forms which include a ram/goat with backward-sweeping horns, treated in a manner not unlike that on the Irish ring. The Danish piece is dated to the period between 150 A.D. and 300 A.D. (Eggers et al., 1964, 49, Abb. 100b and Pl. p. 50; Klindt-Jensen, 1950, 156, Fig. 101). An even closer parallel, however, is a bronze ring from southern Germany, which, like the Irish example, has cast animal representations projecting from one surface. This comes from Garchinger Heide, Ldkr. München, and is said to be from a burial deposit (Dannheimer, 1975, 59-68). The ring is somewhat larger than that of the Irish specimen (its maximum diameter is 4.3 cm) and there are three figures projecting from it. One is a bird with spread wings, a second is possibly a snake and the third appears to be a goat's or ram's head. The last is strongly reminiscent of the goat/ram on the Irish ring.

In all liklihood the German and the Irish rings served the same purpose but what this might have been is unknown. Equally uncertain is the date of the German example; varying dates from Early La Tène times to the Imperial Roman period have been proposed. If the Danish example cited earlier has any dating relevance in this matter, it might be suggested that the later rather than the earlier dating is the more likely for the German object, and it might further be postulated that such is also possible for the Irish ring.

A date in the first century A.D. for the unlocalised, bronze, pelta-shaped mount (Fig. 148:5; Pl. 101) with its strange animal heads can be suggested with slightly more confidence than in the case of the objects just discussed. At Maiden Castle, Dorset a similar though somewhat

smaller mount, referred to as a "terret-like loop", was found stratified
in a Romano-Belgic level and was assigned by the excavator to between
25 and 50 A.D. (Wheeler, 1943, 275, Fig. 90:7).   The ends of the upper
curve of the loop of the Maiden Castle object (Fig. 149:2) are moulded
in apparent simulation of a bird's head.   Another mount in the Devizes
Museum, "probably from Wilford Down", to which Jope drew attention,
is also comparable with the Irish object in question, though it too is a
trifle smaller than the Irish piece (Fig. 149:1).   Here also, bird-head
representations, more realistic than on the Maiden Castle piece, are
recognisable at the ends of the upper loop.   Dotted decoration appears,
from the unclear illustration, also to be present on this object (Goddard,
1907-8, 406, Fig. 35).

The date provided by the context of the Maiden Castle parallel is
the most likely for the Irish object.   It is thus interesting to encounter
again the reserved zig-zag motif and the dotted ornament which
increasingly appear as important elements in the artistic repertoire of
the immediately pre- and post-Christian period in Ireland.

The animal heads on this Irish mount have no exact comparison. The
nearest analogy to them is perhaps to be found on the pseudo-faces which
are recognisable on the ends of the side-links of the Ballymoney, Co.
Antrim, Type D horsebit (Fig. 24:16).

Human Representations

Apart from a fairly extensive series of stone heads, the human form
is poorly represented in the repertoire of surviving Irish Iron Age material.
The anthropoid hilt of the Ballyshannon sword (Fig. 43:1; Pls 23, 112:2)
is presumably of Gaulish fabrication, and the strange little cast bronze
head, now in the Hunt Collection (Fig. 150:2) is also likely to be an import
to Ireland though whether, in this instance, ancient or modern, is open
to question.   On native metalwork, only one object, an unlocalised horsebit
bears recognisably anthropomorphic decoration (Figs 11:1; 150:2; Pl. 1;
Raftery, B., 1974).   The fine carving of a human figure from Ralaghan,
Co. Cavan (Fig. 150:1; Pl. 112:1; Mahr, 1930; Megaw, 1970, No. 280)
serves to remind us of what once must have existed in wood.   By itself
it cannot be closely dated, for parallels ranging from the Late Bronze
Age to the beginning of our era can be quoted (see Megaw, 1970, 164).
Some of the Gallo-Roman carvings from the source of the Seine are,
however, especially close in details of form and treatment to the carving
of the Ralaghan figure (e.g. Deyts, 1970, Figs 8,13,20).

The stone heads are scattered throughout the country in museums,
in private collections and in the field.   Rynne, who summarised the main

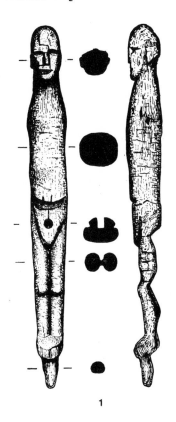

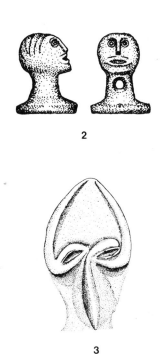

Fig. 150. Human representations. 1 wooden carving, Ralaghan, Co. Cavan. 2 bronze, no prov. 3 horsebit decoration, no prov. 1:1/12. 2,3:1/1.

features of Irish stone heads (1972), divided them into seven main groups (apart from a few isolated specimens), six of which are in Ulster, the seventh far to the south of the country in Kilkenny. None can be closely dated, and it is not certain that all the heads included by him are of demonstrably Iron Age manufacture. Some may be considerably later than this (e.g. Rynne, 1972, Pls X:3; XI:3) and, indeed, Hickey has demonstrated the timelessness of the tradition of stone-head carving in Ireland (1976, esp. 95ff). There can, of course, be no doubt that examples such as the three-faced specimen from Corleck, Co. Cavan (Pl. 113:1), the "Tandaragee" idol, the Boa Island carvings, the Cavan Town head (Pl. 113:2) and that from Beltany, Co. Donegal (Fig. 151) belong to the pagan Iron Age.

The cult of the human head is a pan-Celtic phenomenon (Lambrechts, 1954; Ross, 1967), and heads represented in stone are found right across the Celtic area of Europe. A common treatment of the human form

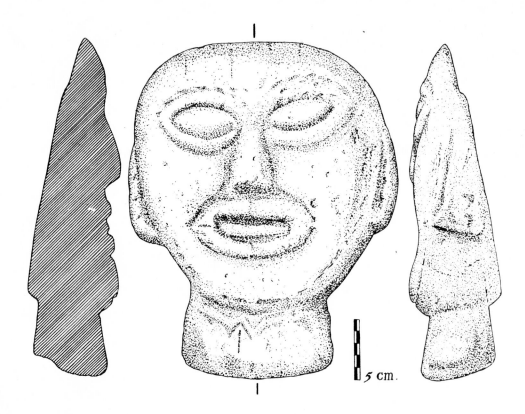

Fig. 151. Stone head, Beltany, Co. Donegal. (after Rynne, 1972).

is evident and details such as the apparent torc around the neck of the Beltany idol (Fig. 151), and the "whistle-hole" mouth-depressions present on Corleck and other Irish heads (Rynne, 1966) stress the unity of the religious beliefs which gave rise to the tradition of head carving. The Irish heads belong in this widespread tradition and it is virtually impossible to determine with any confidence which area outside the country influenced the native development.

Rynne favoured Britain as the source of the Irish head tradition and wrote that ".... it is unlikely that any of the Irish carvings antedate Romano-British influence ...." (1972, 79). Nonetheless Continental analogies for many of the features of the Irish carvings are recognisable. The faces on the Corleck head are closely similar to those, arranged in groups of three, on the Entremont pillar (Duval, 1977, Fig. 135); the stance of the Tanderagee idol is reminiscent of that of the Holzgerlingen stone (Megaw, 1970, No. 14). Rynne himself compared details of the Cathedral Hill, Armagh bears to carvings from Limoges and Euffigneix in France (op. cit., 85) and he also referred to Rhenish features on the Boa Island busts. [In Iberia too, numerous heads of stone directly comparable with the Irish ones are known.] Examples from castros such as Santa Iria, Castro de Cortes, Armea of Baran (Civite, 1965, 10-18) would give rise to no unusual comment if discovered in Ireland.

The precise chronological and cultural affinities of the Irish stone heads thus clearly remain to be established.

SUMMARY AND CONCLUSIONS

Find Circumstances

A large proportion of Irish La Tène objects is made up of old finds, that is, finds made before the days of scientific archaeological recording. All too often they are unprovenanced and, even when the place of discovery is noted, only rarely is any information regarding find circumstances supplied. A bare handful of significantly associated groups of objects has come to light and of these only that from Somerset, Co. Galway, is of real assistance in determining the chronology and assessing the inter-relationships of the native La Tène industries. Table 1 illustrates the extent of the problem. The three main sources of archaeological material are bogs, rivers and lakes. Some objects have been dug up in fields and a small number come from sandhill deposits. The paucity of relevant settlement and burial evidence from the country is reflected in the limited number of artifacts listed in Table 1 from such contexts.

There is little to be deduced from such meagre information. Concentrations of objects from specific spots on rivers (Banagher or Carrick on the Shannon, Toome on the Bann) could indicate the existence at these places of ancient crossing points. The question remains, however, as to whether such riverine discoveries represent accidental loss or deliberate deposition. The relatively high proportion of weapons and decorated scabbards from rivers and lakes should be noted in this context and it is not impossible that some, at least, came to their final resting places in the course of ritual activity. Such an interpretation might be deemed appropriate for the deposition of the four horns at Loughnashade, Co. Armagh. A similar explanation might also apply to the Broighter hoard and, perhaps, the Cork horns.

	Total Number	Localised	Bog	River	Lake / Lakeshore	Sandhills	'Field'	Occupation Site	Burial	Other
HORSEBITS	141	59	8	5	4		2	2		1
'PENDANTS'	95	42	4	2	1		3			4
CART FITTINGS	4	4	1	2						
SWORDS	22	21	5	5	1			1	1	1
SCABBARDS & CHAPES	11	11	4	4				1		
SPEARHEADS	5	5	3	1	1					
SPEARBUTTS, TYPES 1 & 2	39	28	20	1	1					1
SPEARBUTTS, TYPES 3 & 4	30	19	14				1			1
SPEARMOUNTS	4	4	4							
SHIELDS	2	2	1					1		
HORNS	5	4	4							
SAFETY-PIN FIBULAE	25	20	1		1	2		6	5	
RINGHEADED PINS	38	24	3	4		2		1	1	
NAVAN-TYPE BROOCHES	5	4				1	1	2		
NECK ORNAMENTS	11	11	2	1			6		1	
ARM ORNAMENTS	14	14	2	1				3	7	
TOILET IMPLEMENTS	18	18	1					15	2	
BOWLS, CAULDRONS, ETC.	21	18	7	4			2			1
BEEHIVE QUERNS	215	178	25	3						
TOOLS & IMPLEMENTS	23	23	4	1	1		1	8	3	3
MISC. BRONZES	46	30	10	3		1		5	1	

Table 1. Principal categories of Irish La Tène material: find circumstances

Uncertainty exists also regarding the significance of the dry-land discoveries. Obviously, little can be said about isolated finds but when two or more items are associated it must be deemed likely that they were deliberately buried. Whether this was for reasons of expediency or otherwise remains a matter for speculation. In the case of the bronzesmith's hoard from Somerset, Co. Galway, however, expediency and not ritual is the probable explanation.

The one major complex of La Tène material from Ireland – Lisnacrogher, Co. Antrim – remains an enigma. Discovered during turf-cutting activities in the latter half of the nineteenth century, the site was totally obliterated without any archaeological supervision (Wakeman, 1883-4; 1889; 1891; Wood-Martin, 1886, 173; Munro, 1890, 379; 386; Knowles, 1897, 114-5; CIIAA, pp. 287-288). We do not know what Lisnacrogher was. It is often referred to as a crannog but, even if such a structure existed at the site, it cannot be shown to have been contemporary with the La Tène metalwork. The possibility that the Iron Age material from Lisnacrogher represents a votive deposit, perhaps extending over a number of generations, remains strong. Other interpretations such as those put forward for La Tène and Cornaux in Switzerland should, however, also be borne in mind (Schwab, 1972).

Distribution

The relevance of the gross distribution map of La Tène finds from Ireland must be judged, not only in the light of the deficiencies outlined above, but also against the likely chronological range of the material. The spots on the map may represent the industrial and artistic output of anything up to half a millennium. It is thus possible that future discoveries will alter somewhat the distributional pattern as at present known to us, but it is submitted that any such change will not be dramatic.

Specific regional concentrations of La Tène material in the country emerge from the distribution map (Map 27) and it is evident that in certain areas of Ireland La Tène influences were either negligible or entirely absent. In some cases, the absence of La Tène objects may be explicable in terms of an inhospitable environment as, for example, the rugged mountain areas of Donegal in the north-west of the country, or the barren and stony region of west Galway. But in other areas the scarcity of La Tène objects must be seen as having cultural significance. In the south of the country, for instance, i.e. in Munster and south Leinster, only small scattered pockets of La Tène objects occur. Clearly, the south of Ireland was not depopulated in the centuries around the birth of Christ and some form of non-La Tène culture, contemporary with the manufacture

does there appear to be a geographical overlap between querns and other La Tène material.

The main areas of La Tène influence in the country are, thus, the Lower Bann Valley, south-central Ulster and a Central Plain region extending across the country from Meath to Galway. Isolated discoveries are recorded from Down and small pockets of material have been recovered from the south of Ireland. Little can be said of these single finds. The small, local concentration of La Tène artifacts from the north Limerick lowlands is, however, worth noting.

The objects from this small area form an interesting group, including bronze "chariot mounts" (Fig. 38:3; Pl. 19), a fibula of late La Tène flattened-bow form (Fig. 79:6) and a sword (Pl. 22:1), all from Lough Gur, and a bone plaque from a burial not far away at Cush (Fig. 122:2; Pl. 79). The cheek-ring of a horsebit was found at Kilmallock, just south of Lough Gur. This group may represent a body of related material, perhaps indicating the presence in the area of a contemporary settlement. It is also possible that the scatter of artifacts may mark the line of an ancient route extending due south along the River Maigue, across the Blackwater at Mallow and thence to Cork harbour (see Warner, 1976, 277, Fig. 3). Such a possibility is, perhaps, enhanced by the presence of a small number of La Tène objects from the immediate vicinity of Cork harbour.

Stylistic considerations

It is clear from the foregoing section that differing regional emphases in the manufacture of certain artifact types give rise to the recognition of several regions within the Irish La Tène province, and it is equally clear that types common to, and probably made in, one area found their way into other areas, thereby demonstrating contact and interaction between one region and another. But since artifacts of one type are practically never found in association with artifacts of another type, the cultural and chronological relationships between the different objects within a region, and between the objects of one region and those of another, are difficult to establish.

Thus, lacking physical association, the only possibility of determining links between different artifact types is by examining the ornament which adorns them, thereby attempting to recognise stylistic groups for which some tentative dating may be postulated.

In the Irish La Tène material a number of distinct styles or schools of craftsmanship can be recognised. Perhaps the most obvious and the most geographically defined is that which may be called the Irish Scabbard

Style, represented by two-dimensional scabbard engraving and confined to the Bann Valley area. Leaving aside the possibility of an early date for the Altertate cauldron, it is probable that these scabbards represent the earliest native Irish renderings of the pan-European La Tène art style. A date in the third or second century B.C. for the earliest of them is likely. Nothing directly comparable is known outside Antrim though the tight hair-spring spirals on the Killycluggin stone may derive from the Antrim Scabbard Style. Lisnacrogher-type chapes from Galway and north Tipperary, too, may suggest that the style was more widespread than the paucity of finds allows us to suppose.

It is difficult to know what material in the country may be taken as contemporary with the scabbards. Some of the ringheaded pins could belong to the same horizon and the presence of two Type 3 pins at Lisnacrogher should be noted. Some of the earliest Irish horsebits may also be contemporary with the scabbards but, as already stressed, no independent dating for either horsebits or ringheaded pins exists. The absence of horsebits from Lisnacrogher may well be important. The Loughnashade horn disc may be related to this style too, but this problematical piece is difficult to categorize stylistically. It could be later. It is clear, however, that Antrim remained a centre of metalworking into the early centuries A.D. The Derrykeighan stone, probably some centuries later in date than the scabbards, may provide us with a focus of artistic production in the north of the same county. Lisnacrogher itself must, however, have remained important, for material, in all probability contemporary with Derrykeighan and the later schools of craftsmanship, has come from that site.

The Derrykeighan stone signifies a new and far more widespread phase of artistic production in the country, which spread to every area of the La Tène province in Ireland. From about the latter half of the last century B.C. or so, and extending into the first and possibly the second century A.D., a distinctive native art style emerges, within which, irrespective of the techniques employed or the medium upon which the art occurs, a wide measure of homogeneity may be recognised. The impression is of a deep sense of conservatism amongst the artificers of the time, who displayed in their works a considerable reluctance to deviate from the constraints of artistic convention. Where variety occurs, it is based on a number of set themes which, in the last analysis, draw on an established and recurring grammar of ornament.

When dealing with this second phase of native La Tène art, two sites stand out, because each has produced an important body of material and because each may legitimately be regarded as a local focus of fine metalworking. The two sites are Lough Crew in Co. Meath and Somerset in Co. Galway.

Both Lough Crew and Somerset are representative of regional schools of artistic production, but, while differences of artistic emphasis between them can be readily recognised, it is clearly evident that both drew on common wells of inspiration; there can be little doubt that the two schools are broadly contemporary. It may thus be appropriate to term the ornamental output of these two schools the Lough Crew-Somerset Style.

The art of the Lough Crew school is two-dimensional, and lays emphasis on combinations of compass-drawn curves. The broken-backed curve is a recurring theme; dotting and "engine-turning" are also used. The trumpet-and-lentoid motif is rare, occurring occasionally at Lough Crew itself, but not always, it seems, in fully understood form (Figs. 125:2,3; 127:1). Unmistakable works of this school, apart from the Lough Crew flakes themselves are the Cush, Co. Limerick, and Mentrim Lough, Co. Meath "gaming pieces" (Fig. 122:1,2; Pl. 79), the Derrykeighan, Co. Antrim, stone (Fig. 145; Pl. 106) and the beehive quern from Clonmacnois, Co. Offaly (Fig. 121:1). The wide geographical range of the Lough Crew school is at once apparent from these examples. The bronze "spoons", too (Figs. 130-1; Pls 82-3), all unfortunately without provenance, belong firmly in this two-dimensional, compass-drawn artistic milieu, though on these objects the occasional lines, hand-drawn in rocked-graver technique, could hark back to earlier traditions. The Modeenagh fibula with its compass-drawn circles (Fig. 80:2) may also display influence from this school of craftsmanship and some of the later decorated horsebits, too, share decorative details with the art on the flakes (Figs 23:13; 152:3-5).

The Broighter collar obviously shares much with the Lough Crew flakes in terms of artistic design, especially in the "engine-turning" and the use of the broken-backed curve, but there are differences, for the raised curves and the snail-shell spirals of Broighter, even allowing for the two-dimensional nature of the Lough Crew art, are hardly hinted at on works of the latter group. The relief trumpet curves on the collar are related rather to the trumpet-and-lentoid boss designs which are found on material from Somerset and related pieces - the Navan-type brooches, the Somerset "box" (both of which also include dotted decoration - Figs 82:2; 140:2; Pls 50; 98:2), the Kiltierney fibula (Fig. 80:8) possibly even the Ballinderry sword-hilt guard (Fig. 43:12). The Clogher, Co. Tyrone, fibula may perhaps also be included here (Fig. 79:8; Pl. 45). The formal, somewhat stereotyped nature of the trumpet designs on these objects, however, with the exception of the Clogher fibula, contrasts with the more sinuous, vegetal treatment of the design on the collar and it may be that the Broighter specimen stands near the head of the development which gave rise to the Lough Crew-Somerset style.

But the collar is critical in considering the complex inter-relationships between material of the Lough Crew and Somerset groups. Along with Derrykeighan, the collar brings discussion to Turoe and the other carved stones; the trumpet patterns on the object lead to Somerset and beyond, the "engine-turning" recalls Cornalaragh and thence the Somerset-type mounts. With these last may be included, in all probability, the Lough Gur mounts (see Fig. 38:3). The raised, snail-shell spirals on the Broighter collar may relate to cast spiral renderings on Type 2 ringheaded pins (Fig. 85:1-6), and the repoussé-spiral variants on the Monasterevin-type discs (see below) could also, ultimately, owe something to a common artistic inspiration.

The special importance of the Somerset hoard lies in the varied nature of the objects found there in closed association - a situation all but unique in the Irish Iron Age. Because of this find the extent of the Somerset school may be widened considerably. The bird's-head handle from the hoard (Fig. 107:2) automatically allows the Keshcarrigan bowl (Fig. 107:1; Pl. 69) and maybe also the other related bronze bowls (Fig. 108; Pl. 70) to be included in the group. With Keshcarrigan, an additional motif, the reserved zig-zag, appears. This is found elsewhere on a variety of unassociated bronzes - a tubular spearbutt from the River Bann (Fig. 63:5; Pl. 35:2), rings and mounts from Lisnacrogher (Figs 59; 141:7; 142:2,3; Pl. 32) and on an unlocalised mount (Fig. 148:5; Pl. 101) where, in common with one of the above-mentioned Lisnacrogher bronzes, the zig-zags are doubled. This same unlocalised mount also bears dotted decoration, a feature already encountered on other objects of the Lough Crew-Somerset Style.

Related to this is what might be described provisionally as the "Petrie Crown" style. The "Petrie Crown" is the pièce de resistance of a small, interconnected group of ornate bronzes which includes the Cork Horns, the Bann disc, and the Monasterevin-type discs (Figs 132-4; 136-7). Though differing from one another in scale and, at times, in technique of ornament, these objects have sufficient in common to suggest that they may emanate from a single workshop tradition. They undoubtedly overlap in time with material of the Lough Crew-Somerset schools and once again appear to have shared to a large extent with the latter group a common decorative repertoire. The trumpet-and-lentoid is there, the bird's head, the raised spiral on the discs; but their treatment differs from that on the objects of the Lough Crew-Somerset Style. The delicate nature of the trumpet curves and the minuteness of the lentoids on both the horned objects and the Bann disc have no parallel on Lough Crew-Somerset material nor, indeed, has the technique of background tooling.

Eastern Gaul may have been a key area for these early Irish developments and it is through this region that ornamental details of ultimately Danubian origin could have been transmitted to Ireland.

The best parallel for the two-link horsebit from the River Bann also comes from eastern Gaul; it may be from a destroyed, Early La Tène burial, but its context is uncertain. The extent to which the main Irish three-link horsebit series derives directly from Gaulish prototypes remains, however, unresolved, and details of their form may reflect contact with British metalworking traditions.

A west Gaulish source for the anthropoid sword-hilt from Ballyshannon, Co. Donegal is hardly in doubt and this piece suggests the continued use of the Atlantic seaways into the first century B.C. Some of the iron objects from Feerwore, Co. Galway could have come to Ireland, about the same time by the same route. The Broighter collar, also a Late La Tène specimen, belongs to a widespread European family of torcs which may have developed in north Gaul (Map 18). The decoration on the Irish example is native but Continental manufacture for the terminals has been suggested. Close parallels for them occur, notably on the Lower Rhine. Other material from the hoard points to the Roman Mediterranean and it is interesting that such a source for the enamel blocks from Tara has also been sought. The grooved blade of the Ballinderry sword could indicate influence from European traditions of sword manufacture at the beginning of our era and there are a few glass beads in the country which may be of European derivation. Some decorative details, such as the raised ornament on Type 2 ringheaded pins, could have a European, Middle La Tène background, and some elements of Irish leaf-bow fibulae might also emanate from the Continent. Here, however, the absence of firm chronology is acutely felt and uncertainty persists.

The problem of the carved stones has been discussed at length above, and these demonstrate well the difficulties of interpretation which the Irish material poses. North-west France may have supplied the idea, but there is nothing else in the Irish archaeological record to indicate contact with that area of Europe. There is no evidence to support the notion of a substantial folk movement from the Continent to Ireland.

The external antecedents of the Irish stone heads are even more difficult to determine than is the case with the aniconic carvings and there are, for the moment, few grounds for preferrring one group of foreign heads over another as supplying the prototypes of the Irish examples.

Britain

Contacts between Ireland and Britain are increasingly evident as the Iron Age progresses. Stylistic overlaps, common forms, common techniques of manufacture, and imports from one island to the other combine to indicate close and continuing links across the Irish Sea. In many areas of art and technology the distinctions between the two islands blur. Ireland's British connections were not confined to any one region but extended to widely dispersed areas of that island.

Contacts with Scotland, particularly the south-west and the Western Isles were especially close. The Torrs horns, for instance, in details of their engraved ornament, may well reflect influence from Ulster scabbard engraving traditions. Two Ayrshire finds - a scabbard from Bargany and a sword from Stevenston Sands - could also indicate an Irish presence in the same south-west area of Scotland shortly before the birth of Christ. The form of the crude, leaf-bow fibula from Lochlee crannog, also in Ayrshire, might have been inspired by an Irish prototype and the same could be true of the decorated bone comb from Langbank in Renfrewshire; the latter could, in fact, be an Irish piece. Both technically and geographically, the closest parallel for the thick-bellied Ballymoney cauldron is to be found at Carlingwark in Kircudbrightshire and somewhat to the north of this, in Stirlingshire, a globular cauldron from Kincardine Moss provides the only close comparison for the cauldron from Ballyedmond, Co. Galway. A notable concentration of beehive quernstones of Caulfield's B2 group is found in south-west Scotland and these could represent influence there from Ireland (1977, 119). Finally, in view of proposed Irish-Scottish links, the presence of a local concentration of "Meare spiral" beads in the Luce Sands area of Wigtownshire should be noted.

Maritime contacts between Ireland and the Scottish islands also undoubtedly existed throughout the Iron Age. An Irish-made ringheaded pin of Type 2 found its way to the Isle of Coll and another ringheaded pin from Sasaig on the Isle of Skye betrays Irish influence, and may even be of Irish manufacture. Knobbed spearbutts and the moulds for making them have come from brochs and duns on the islands of Bute, Tiree and Mainland Orkney. The butts are virtually indistinguishable from those found in Ireland and, though coming from purely local settlement types, must surely indicate movement of some sort, between Ireland and the western Atlantic fringe of Scotland (Raftery, B., 1982). Good parallels for the Irish organic-hilted swords (referred to above as Class 2) can also be found on the Scottish islands and the Glassamucky Brakes, Co. Dublin weaving comb belongs, it seems, to a sub-type of the weaving comb group otherwise confined to the Orkneys. The projecting ringheaded pin from Keady Mountain, Co. Derry may also reflect contact between Ireland and the western Scottish islands (Clarke, 1971) and the Irish parallelopiped dice may indicate similar contacts.

In the case of the butts, the dice and the swords our evidence is insufficient to establish which area contains the earliest examples so we cannot say which area, Ireland or western Scotland, had cultural priority. Nor do we know the precise means by which such selective influences moved from one area to another. It is perhaps worth remembering, however, that ample documentation exists for the early historic period to show that long journeys by sea took place between Ireland and western Scottish islands. The casual way, for instance, in which sixth century annalists refer to military expeditions from Ireland to the Hebrides and even to the Orkneys (MacNiocaill, 1972, 76, 78) suggests that such trips were unexceptional. There is no reason to doubt that similar journeys would have been equally common a few centuries earlier in the pagan Iron Age. Such seafaring movement, not necessarily always of a military nature, could provide us with a means by which the selective transfer of cultural traits from one area to another could have taken place. It may be that the curious concentration of multivallate promontory forts in the Orkney and Shetland islands fits, in some obscure way, into such a pattern of movement from the Atlantic coast of Europe, northwards along the Irish sea and thence, via Ireland, to the Scottish Isles (Lamb, 1980).

A single import of ultimately east Scottish manufacture is the "massive" armlet from Newry, Co. Down, which reached Ireland probably around the end of the first century A.D. At Crichie, Inverurrie, in the heart of the "massive" armlet distribution, a doorknob spearbutt was found which is identical in every way with the classic versions of the type from Ireland. The Crichie specimen could have come from Ireland, or could reflect contact with Ireland. It should be remembered, however, that, apart from their known manufacture in western Scotland, similar butts were being made at Traprain Law in the east Scottish lowlands so that the extent to which such butts in east Scotland indicate a direct Irish involvement is uncertain.

It is also possible that overlap of some sort with Irish metalworking traditions is indicated by the two bronze "spoons" found in a burial at Burnmouth in Berwickshire. These are likely to be of local manufacture, but their form provides perhaps the closest parallel for that of the main Irish variant of the type, which includes five of the six known examples.

Common decorative details in Ireland and Scotland emphasise further the close ties between the two areas in the centuries spanning the birth of Christ. The arrangement of the ornament on the Langbank comb is paralleled on the Monasterevin-type discs and on the "Petrie Crown" and the Stichill collar bears tooled ornament close in treatment and technique to that on the "crown" and related pieces. The "Petrie" birds have good comparanda in Scotland and the keeled, repoussé spirals of the Monasterevin-type discs are precisely matched on the Norries Law, Fife, plaque and the Deskford, Banffshire, carnyx-head. The petal-loop terminals of two Irish horse "pendants" provide clear evidence of Scottish inspiration and the developed "Swash-N" design on one of the Irish "spoons" may reflect further influence from that country. Most important of all, however, are the Lough Crew flakes which include in their decorative repertoire a number of motifs otherwise found only in Scotland.

Northern and eastern areas of England, especially Yorkshire, have been regarded by many commentators as critical regions in a consideration of Irish La Tène beginnings and, as noted above, folk-movement from eastern England has been invoked on more than one occasion, to account for the La Tène presence in Ireland.

Evidence for cultural interaction between Ireland and the northern and eastern areas of England undoubtedly exists. The earliest Irish horsebits bear some resemblance to their east English counterparts and an argument may plausibly be made for relating the two insular groups. The knob-ringed, ringheaded pins from Ireland could well be imports from Yorkshire but might also be regarded as sharing with Yorkshire a common southern British origin. Beehive querns of Caulfield's Type B1 have been taken as deriving from eastern or north-eastern English forms (Map 23), and eastern England may also provide the immediate background for the Ballymoney, Co. Antrim, mirror handle (Map 19). It is possible, too, that influence from north-English/south Scottish bowl forms is detectable in the Irish bowls, though the latter are not here regarded as necessarily of British manufacture (Map 20).

Two undoubted imports to Ireland from north-east England, roughly contemporary with the Newry armlet referred to above, are the Antrim platform-terret and the Lambay beaded torc. Moving in the opposite direction, the Type 3 ringheaded pin from a cremation burial at Alnham, Northumberland can only be regarded as of Irish manufacture.

A historical interpretation for these Irish/east English links is difficult. Evidence for contact between the two regions, is sporadic and selective and spread over several centuries. It hardly seems sufficient to support the concept of a large-scale population migration to Ireland, one which, moreover, could be held responsible for the introduction of the earliest La Tène to the country. Only at Lambay can we recognise the unequivocal presence of foreigners, in this instance, perhaps, a small band of north English fugitives (Brigantians?), settling for a time, in the first century A.D., on an isolated, eastern Irish island.

Caulfield argued, however, that the near identity in form between the beehive querns in Ireland and those in eastern England, allied to the absence from Ireland of all British regional variations of the type, could only be interpreted as indicating a population spread from England which, in his view, was responsible for the introduction of the beehive quern (and the La Tène tradition) to Ireland. Another interpretation is, however, possible, an interpretation largely hypothetical but one which, it is submitted, seems more in keeping with the available archaeological evidence than is the simple invasion theory. Could it be that Irishmen, travelling to east England, encountered the beehive quern and there learned how to make and use it before eventually returning home with the knowledge? To a people accustomed for centuries to the cumbersome saddle quern the rotary quern must have seemed near miraculous and the idea, once introduced to Ireland, would have spread rapidly. Such a reflux movement from eastern England could have brought, along with the idea of the rotary quern, such other eastern English elements as are detectable in the Irish material while at the same time explaining the absence from the country of so much that is typical of the Yorkshire Iron Age. Above all, the absence from Ireland of the square-ditched barrow, the standard burial rite of the eastern English Iron Age (Stead, 1979, 7-39), is thus explicable, for the absence of this burial form from Ireland is one of the strongest arguments against the idea of a large scale La Tène incursion from that region to Ireland.

The proposed concept of returning emigrants, as an explanation for the existence in Ireland of some eastern English features and the absence of others, can only be regarded as a speculative attempt to explain a given set of archaeological data. There is, however, one interesting piece of evidence which might enhance this speculation.

The Irish Type 3 ringheaded pin from Alnham in north-eastern England came from a simple cremation burial-pit in a low, circular cairn. Both the burial monument, and the rite of cremation, are anomalous in the region and the excavators were unable to quote any adequate comparative sites in Britain (Tait and Jobey, 1966, 32). In Ireland such a burial monument would not be out of place and in Ireland, too, contrasting with eastern England, cremation was the normal rite observed in contemporary burials (see Raftery, B., 1981). Is it thus possible that the Alnham burial with its Irish pin is, in fact, the last resting place of an Irishman? Could it even be that somewhere in the area a migrant Irish group had established itself?

Contact between Ireland and north-west Wales sometime before the birth of Christ is demonstrated by the presence in the hoard at Llyn Cerrig Bach, Anglesey, of three objects of probable Irish origin: a horsebit, a horn fragment and a sword. It is also possible, as Savory has suggested (1964, 468ff.), that at about the same time the Ulster armourers responsible for the Irish Scabbard Style shared inspiration with the important contemporary schools of north Welsh metalworking. Continued links between the two areas after the birth of Christ are suggested by the recently reported discovery in north-west Wales of two Irish Type D horsebits. The first came from the River Conway, Denbighshire (Pryor, 1980, 19, No. 160), the other, allegedly, from Dollgellau, Montgomeryshire (CIIAA No. 136). Obviously, we can never know if these two objects represent genuine ancient loss. There is, however, nothing inherently improbable in the possibility of Irish objects finding their way to Wales in the early centuries A.D. It may, indeed, be significant that both alleged find spots are in river valleys, Dollgellau, in particular, straddling what was probably an important routeway across Wales from the coast towards the southern English lowlands.

Movement in the opposite direction from Wales to Ireland is suggested by two Irish objects, both of which could have come from Wales. These are the Carrickfergus tankard and the triangular bronze plaque from the Lambay, Co. Dublin, cemetery. The latter, indeed, may indicate the route by which eastern English migrants made their way to Ireland. The localised concentration of decorated beehive querns in northern and north-western Wales should also be noted. Decorated quernstones of beehive type are otherwise recorded only from Ireland. While the Irish and Welsh querns differ from one another in important details, it may be that the custom of decorating the stones reflects interaction between the two areas.

Cultural overlaps between Ireland and southern areas of England can be recognised from the last centuries B.C. but often these are of a generalised and diffuse nature, difficult to interpret in practical terms. Shared details of technique and decoration between Witham-Wandsworth and Irish Scabbard Style bronzes are perhaps best seen as representing parallel metalworking traditions, each enriched by mutual workshop contacts. Similarly, the Broighter-Snettisham inter-relationships could be a result of common inspiration from the European mainland. One object, however, which may be regarded as of unequivocally south-east English manufacture is the linch-pin from Dunmore, Co. Galway noted above. This piece belongs to Ward-Perkins' Type II, a Belgic form (1939, 187, Map 10). The specimen is now in the Royal Museum of Ontario, Canada, having come there from a private collection so that, inevitably, an element of uncertainty exists as to the genuiness of the find spot.

Around the beginning of our era, however, there is evidence that the Irish bronzesmiths were absorbing stylistic and technological ideas from the English south, especially from the south-west. The latter area probably played a part in the development of the Irish ringheaded pin and some of the Irish examples could be imports from there. The background to the Irish flattened-bow fibula has also been sought in the same region. The two closest comparisons for an unlocalised Irish mount (Fig. 148:5; Pl. 101) come from Somerset and Dorset, and Somerset may be the source of the Irish "Meare-spiral" beads. The Somerset potters, too, could have supplied one source of inspiration for the artists of the Lough Crew bone flakes. The few horsebits of English type from Ireland are all of south-west English forms. The D-shaped mounts, reused as patches on the Ballyedmond cauldron, have their closest parallels on a bucket from Birdlip, Gloucester again in the English south-west.

Southern England also supplies good comparisons for such Irish bronzes as the bowls, the projecting-bellied cauldrons and the Ballymoney mirror handle, but here, northern rather than southern areas of Britain may be of more immediate relevance. Such objects as the Edenderry tazza, the Nauheim-derivative and Colchester-type fibulae and one of the six Irish "spoons" (Fig. 127:3), are likely imports from the south of England.

A few Irish objects found their way to southern England. These include a Type E horsebit from Devon, a doorknob spearbutt from Wiltshire and, perhaps, a fibula from Somerset (Hawkes, 1982, 57, Fig. 6:4).

In view of the evidence for movement between Ireland and Britain in the centuries spanning the birth of Christ, it is scarcely surprising that objects should be encountered on the Isle of Man which exhibit influence from Irish craft traditions. Some may even be of Irish origin. The most obvious of these is the Type 3 ringheaded pin from the embanked settlement at Ballacagan, which is surely of Irish manufacture. The same site has produced beehive querns of Caulfield's Irish B 2 type, here probably of Irish derivation (1977, 119). A small fort, Close ny Collagh (Gelling, 1958), has also produced material with a distinctly Irish flavour including a bone comb and a glass dumb-bell bead.

Conclusions

It is evident from the foregoing that Ireland throughout her La Tène Iron Age had extensive contacts with the outside world, both with the west European mainland and with the neighbouring island of Britain. These contacts manifest themselves in the archaeological record as selective and piecemeal and in the case of Britain the links are with widely scattered parts of the island.   It is impossible, no matter what archaeological criteria are used, to interpret the evidence as indicating that the Irish La Tène tradition was introduced from a single area in a single wave at a single time.   As Hawkes has recently written "…. no fully-formed La Tène can be seen as sweeping over Britain throughout, in a manner to show that this was the culture that made the island Celtic. Still less can this be declared of La Tène in Ireland …." (1976, 2). Clearly, the surviving archaeological remains represent the fragmentary end product of a long and complicated sequence of events and the realities of history must have been infinitely more complex than the simple invasion model would allow.   Change and innovation must have been initiated and introduced by a multiplicity of means, slowly and gradually and often in a way which would scarcely impinge on the archaeological record. Trade and exchange must have taken place between the two countries as often as not in perishable as well as imperishable goods. Small-scale migrations crossing the sea in both directions must have been a recurring feature of the late prehistoric period, bringing people who sought land or plunder or, perhaps, as at Anglesey, to visit a holy shrine.   People travelled and returned.   Thriving craft centres undoubtedly existed in both islands where skilled metalworkers, heirs to the mastery of the Bronze Age artificers, were ready and eager to adapt and transform introduced ideas of technique and ornament.

Burials such as those at Lambay (Rynne, 1976) and "Loughey" (Jope and Wilson, 1957a) undoubtedly represent in each instance an alien assemblage and here at least we can speak of the presence in the country of foreigners from Britain firmly reflected in the archaeological record. But such exotic burial groups are otherwise rare in Ireland and the numbers represented by them are small.   Apart from a few burials in the country of Roman type dating to the early centuries A.D., the bulk of recognisable Iron Age interments from Ireland, few though they be, emphasise continuity from the past rather than exotic innovation (Raftery, B., 1981).

However inadequate our knowledge of Iron Age burial customs in Ireland is, firm information regarding the settlement types of the period in the country is virtually non-existent.   There is doubt as regards the precise nature of the settlement associated with the La Tène metalwork at Feerwore, Co. Galway (Raftery, J., 1944).   We do not know if Lisnacrogher was a settlement or a place of votive deposition (Wakeman, 1883-4; 1889; 1890-1). Lough Crew, whatever activities took place there in Iron Age times (Crawford, 1925), can hardly have been typical of contemporary settlement forms. The relationship of the fibula to the fort of Dun Aengus on the Aran Islands is unknown (Harbison, 1971, 205). We have no knowledge of the context of the fibula from Lough Gur, Co.

Limerick (Ó Ríordáin, 1954, 340).

Otherwise, the only occupation sites firmly related to the La Tène metalwork horizon in Ireland are the great hilltop enclosures of Emain Macha (Selkirk and Waterman, 1970) and Dún Ailinne (Wailes, 1976) which, with their internal ditches and their obviously royal connotations, must have been exceptional centres in Ireland during the Iron Age. Thus the normal domestic habitations of those people responsible for the production of La Tène material in the country continue to elude us.

But Emain Macha and Dún Ailinne teach us important lessons. There is nothing at either site which requires explanation in terms of intrusive populations; in fact, the contrary is evident, for the internally-ditched enclosure is a long-established native phenomenon (Wailes, 1982, 21), and at Emain Macha, at least, the excavation evidence seems to point to long and continuous occupation from the Later Bronze Age through to the last centuries B.C. (Selkirk and Waterman, op. cit.).

The appearance of hillforts in the country cannot, in the present state of our knowledge, be linked to the introduction of La Tène traditions to Ireland (Raftery, B., 1976, 352-3), much less to the introduction of "the Celts". Promontory forts (both coastal and inland), and related structures, may prove ultimately to be more significant in this regard but without extensive excavation this remains to be established.

We are left then with a situation which is problematical and confusing. The La Tène art style, technology and artifact types clearly represent a foreign, introduced tradition in the country. They appear fully developed but, from the very beginning, in a wholly Irish manifestation. The number of imported items is insignificant and, with the exception of a few late burials, we lack any intrusive assemblage of artifacts. There are no foreign burials in the country contemporary with the earliest metalwork and no proven exotic settlement types. Most of the metal types diagnostic of the La Tène culture outside the country are either poorly represented in Ireland, or are entirely absent. The total absence of recognisable La Tène pottery from the country is striking.

Cú Chulainn, striding heroically across the pages of our epic literature, is often seen as the living embodiment of La Tène Ireland, as the flesh and blood bestowing life on an Irish La Tène skeleton. The reality is that the skeleton is a ghost of deceptive substance, dissipating when subjected to close scrutiny. The Irish La Tène material gives us tantalising glimpses into a Celtic, Iron Age society but, more often than not, the evidence can be said to "speak in riddles, for the most part hinting at things and leaving a great deal to be understood".

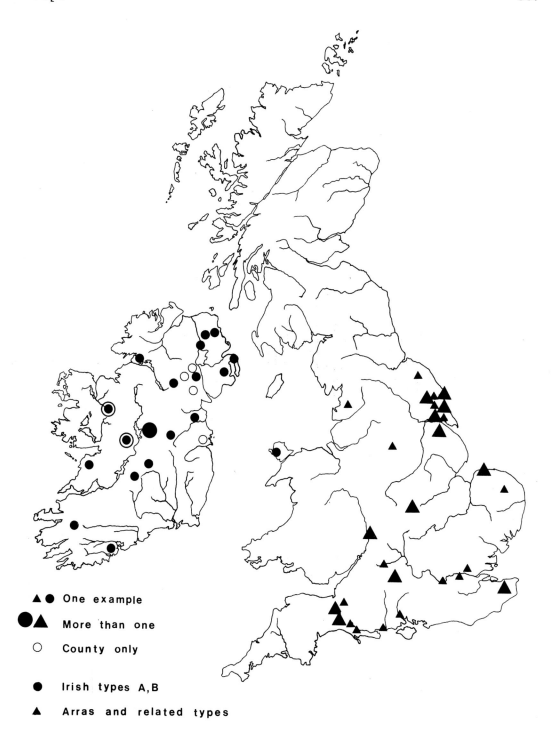

Map 1. Early three-link horsebits. Symbol within circle = harness hoard.
(After Haworth, 1971, MacGregor, 1976, with additions).

▲ ● One example

● ▲ More than one

○ County only

● Irish types A, B

▲ Arras and related types

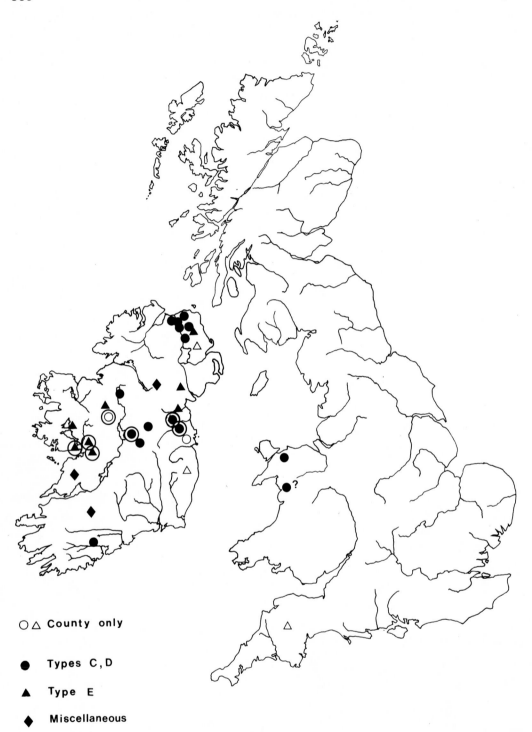

○△ **County only**

● **Types C, D**

▲ **Type E**

◆ **Miscellaneous**

Map 2. Later three-link horsebits. Symbol within circle = harness hoard.
(After Haworth, 1971, with additions).

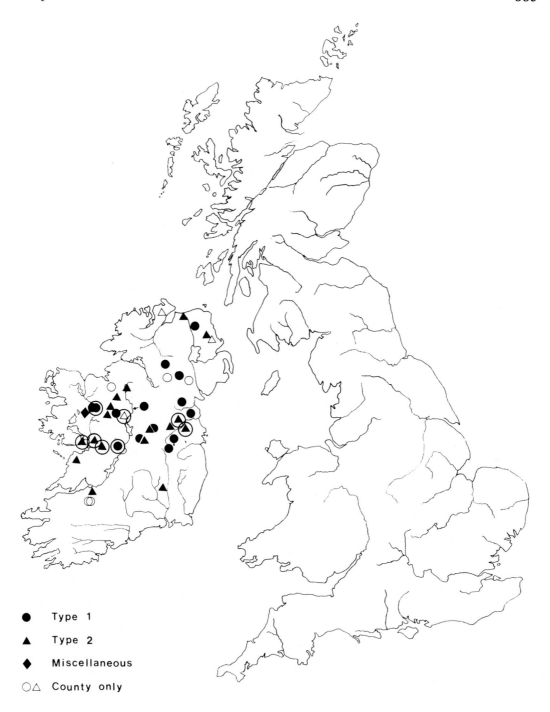

Map 3. Horse "pendants". Symbol within circle = harness hoard. (After Haworth, 1971, with additions).

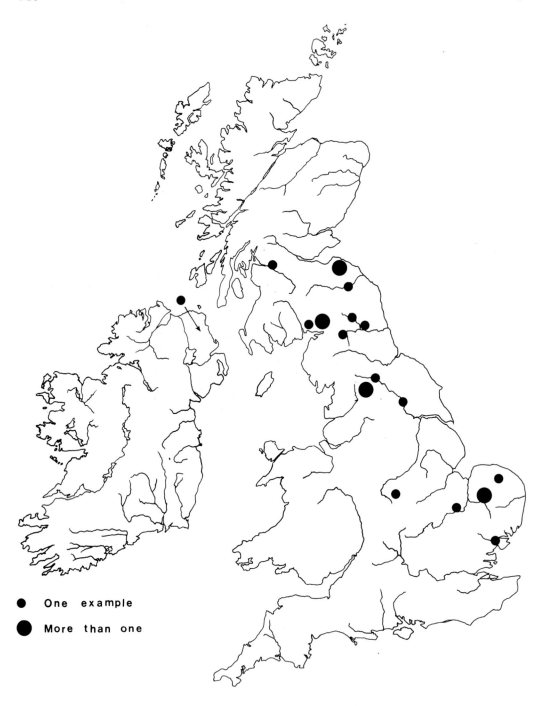

Map 4. Platform terrets. (After MacGregor, 1976).

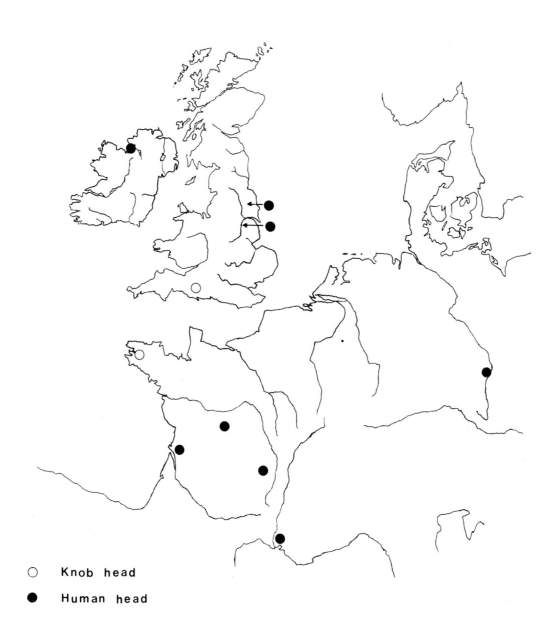

Map 5. Anthropoid-hilted swords. (After Clarke and Hawkes, 1955).

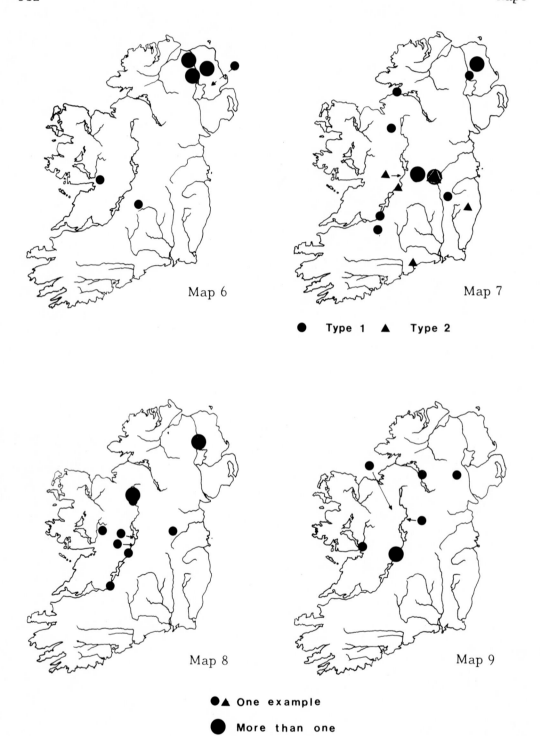

Maps 6-9.   6 Scabbards.   7 Swords of La Tène type.   8 tubular spearbutts.
9 Conical spearbutts.

Map 18. Late La Tène gold torcs of 'Broighter' type.
(After Furger-Gunti, 1982).

Map 19. Mirror-handles, bar form. (After MacGregor, 1976).

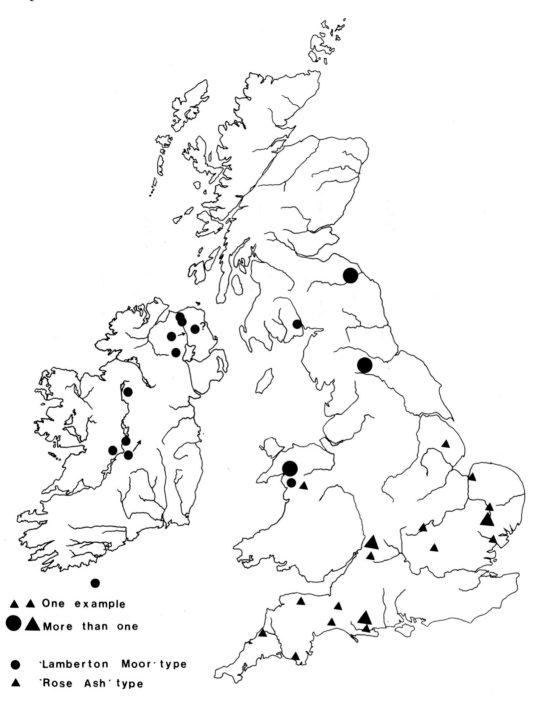

Map 20. Bronze bowls. (After MacGregor, 1976, with additions).

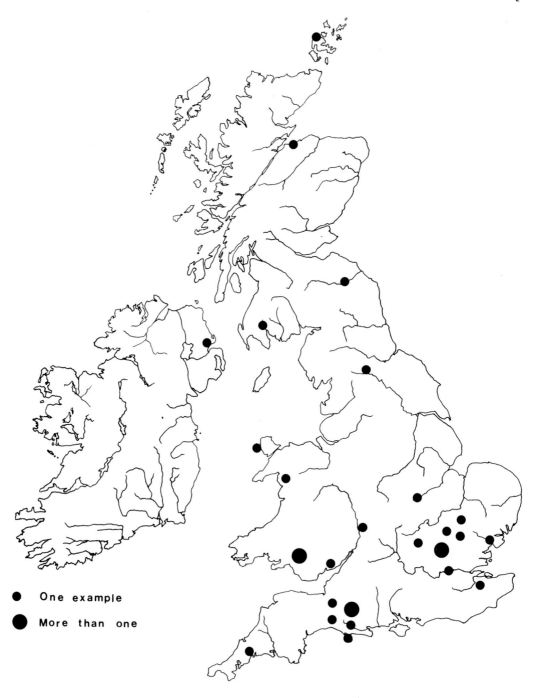

Map 21. Tankards. (After MacGregor, 1976, with addition).

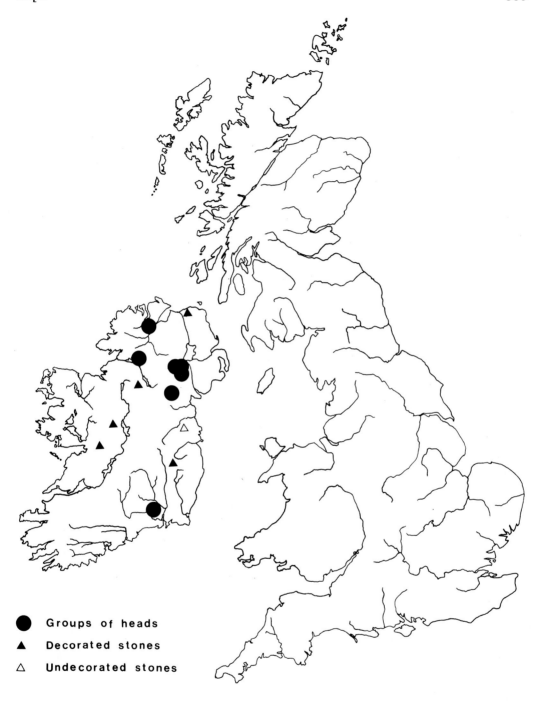

Map 26. Stone carvings in Ireland. (After Rynne, 1972, with additions).

Map 27. General distribution map of La Tène metalwork and related material in Ireland. Querns and stone heads omitted. Arrows indicate county or river provenance only. Important sites numbered as follows: 1 Dunadry, Co. Antrim. 2 "Loughey", Co. Down. 3 Lambay, Co. Dublin. 4 Kiltierney, Co. Fermanagh. 5 Carrowbeg North, Co. Galway. 6 Grannagh, Co. Galway. 7 Oranbeg, Co. Galway. 8 Pollacorragune, Co. Galway. 9 Carbury Hill, Co. Kildare. 10 Cush, Co. Limerick. 11 Carrowjames, Co. Mayo. 12/13 Knowth, Co. Meath. 14 Longstone, Cullen, Co. Tipperary. 15 Lisnacrogher, Co. Antrim. 16 Navan Fort, Co. Armagh. 17 Broighter, Co. Derry. 18 Feerwore, Co. Galway. 19 Somerset, Co. Galway. 20 Dún Ailinne, Co. Kildare. 21 Kisawanny, Co. Kildare. 22 Freestone Hill, Co. Kilkenny. 23 Hill of Tara, Co. Meath. 24 Lough Crew, Co. Meath. 25 Killeevan, Co. Monaghan. 26 Newgrange, Co. Meath. 27 Ballinderry, Co. Westmeath. 28 Clonmacnois, Co. Offaly. 29 Edenderry, Co. Offaly. 30 Kilbeg, Co. Westmeath. 31 Rathgall, Co. Wicklow.

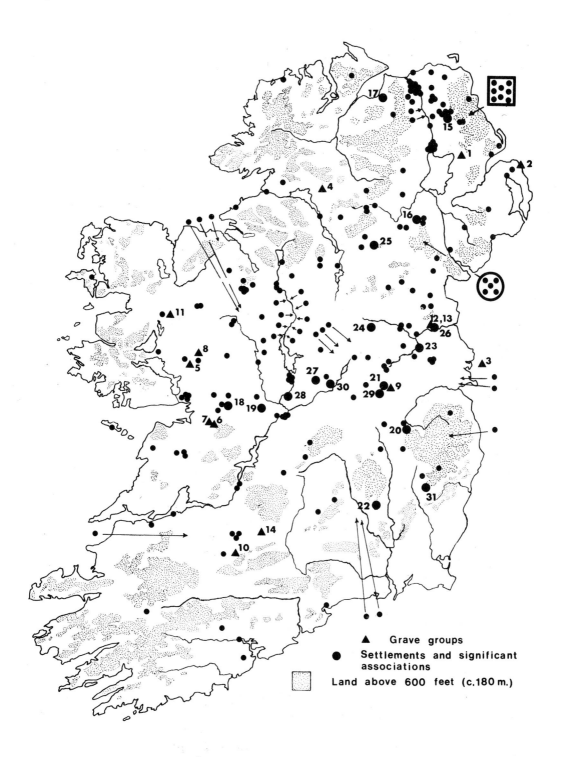

Grave groups

Settlements and significant associations

Land above 600 feet (c.180 m.)

BIBLIOGRAPHY

Adler, H., 1976. "Zur Datierung einiger Beinkämme aus der römischen Kaiserzeit in Bernhardsthal", **Fundberichte aus Österreich** 15, 19-30.

Alcock, L., 1963. **Celtic Archaeology and Art**, 3-46.
1971. **Arthur's Britain**, London.
1972a "The Irish Sea Zone in the Pre-Roman Iron Age" in **The Iron Age in the Irish Sea Province** (ed. C. Thomas), Council for British Archaeology, Research Report No. 9, 99-112.
1972b. '**By South Cadbury is that Camelot ....' Excavations at Cadbury Castle, 1966-70**, London.

Anderson, J., 1883. **The Pagan Iron Age in Scotland**, Edinburgh.

Anon., 1893-4. "Donations to the Museum", **Proc. Soc. Antiq. Scotland** 28, 237.

Armstrong, E.C.R., 1911a. "Note on the Block of Red Enamel from Tara", **J. Roy. Soc. Antiq. Ireland** 41, 61-2.
1911b "A bronze bracelet of Hallstatt type said to have been found near the town of Antrim", **J. Roy. Soc. Antiq. Ireland** 41, 58-60.
1923. "The La Tène Period in Ireland", **J. Roy. Soc. Antiq. Ireland** 53, 1-33.
1924. "The Early Iron Age or Hallstatt Period in Ireland", **J. Roy. Soc. Antiq. Ireland** 54, 1-14; 109-127.

A.S.D. 1966. **An Archaeological Survey of County Down**, Belfast.

Atkinson, D., 1942. **Report on the Excavations at Wroxeter, 1923-27.**

Atkinson, R.J.C. and Piggott, S., 1955. "The Torrs Chamfrein", **Arch.** 96, 197-235.

AuhV **Die Alterthümer unserer heidnischen Vorzeit**, Mainz, 1858-1911 (5 vols.)

Avery, M., 1973. "British La Tène Decorated Pottery: an Outline", **Études Celtiques** (Actes du quatrième congrès international d'études celtiques, Rennes 18-25 juillet 1971) 13, 522-551.

Ball, V. (and Stokes, M.), 1893. "On a block of red glass said to have been found at Tara Hill", **Trans Roy. Irish Acad.** 30, 277-281.

Barber, L. and Megaw, J.V.S., 1963. "A decorated Iron Age Bridle-bit in the London Museum: its place in Art and Archaeology", **Proc. Prehist. Soc.** 29, 206-213.

Baring C., 1907. "Contributions to the Natural History of Lambay, County Dublin: Historical Notes", **Irish Naturalist** 16, 17-19.

Barron, T.J. 1976. "Some Beehive Quernstones from counties Cavan and Monaghan", **Clogher Record** 9, 95-107.

Bateson, J.D., 1973. "Roman Material from Ireland: a Re-consideration", **Proc. Roy. Irish Acad.** 73C, 21-97.

Becatti, G., 1955. **Oreficerie Antiche dalle Minoiche alle Barbariche,** Rome.

Behn, R., 1954. **Musikleben im Altertum und Frühen Mittelalter,** Berlin.

Bersu, G., 1977. **Three Iron Age Round Houses in the Isle of Man** (The Manx Museum and National Trust).

Bienkowski, P.R., 1908. **Die Darstellung der Gallier in der hellenistischen Kunst,** Vienna.

Bigger, F.J., 1903. Note in **Ulster J. Arch.** 9, 138-9.

Böhme, H.W., 1970. "Löffelbeigabe in spätrömischen gräbern nördlich der Alpen", **Jahrbuch. Röm–Germ. Zentralmuseums Mainz** 17, 172-200.

Bonnamour, L. et Bulard, A., 1976. "Une epée celtique à fourreau décoré découverte a Montbellet (Sâone-et-Loire)", **Gallia** 34, 279-284.

Boon, G.C., 1974. "A 'Worton'-type Bronze Sword-Hilt at Caerleon", **Proc. Prehist. Soc.** 40, 205-6.

Brailsford, J., 1953. **Later Prehistoric Antiquities of the British Isles,** London.
1958. "Early Iron Age 'C' in Wessex", **Proc. Prehist. Soc.** 24, 101-119.
1975. **Early Celtic Masterpieces from Britain in the British Museum,** London.

Breidel, H., 1930. **Die germanischen Kulturen in Böhmen und ihre Träger,** I, Kassel.

Bremer, W., 1928. **Ireland's Place in Prehistoric and Early Historic Europe.** (A translation of an essay by the late Walther Bremer, published in his memory under the auspices of the Royal Irish Academy and the Royal Society of Antiquaries of Ireland).

Bretz-Mahler, D., 1971. **La Civilisation de La Tène I en Champagne,** Paris.

Briggs, S., Brennan, J. and Freeburn, G., 1973. "Irish Prehistoric Gold-Working: some Geological and Metallurgical Considerations", **Bulletin of the Historical Metallurgy Group** 7, No. 2, 18-26.

Brisson, A., 1935. "Lance ajourée (Villevenard)", **Bull. Soc. Arch. Champenoise** 29, 79-80, Fig. p. 80.

Bronsted, J., 1940. **Danmarks Oldtid,** Copenhagen.

Browne, A., 1802. "An Account of some Ancient Trumpets dug up in a Bog near Armagh", **Trans. Roy. Irish Acad.** 8, 11-12.

Bulard, A., 1979. "Fourreaux ornés d'animaux fantastiques affrontés découverts en France", **Études Celtiques** 16, 27-52.

1980. "Sur deux poignards de la fin de l'époque de la Tène", **Études Celtiques** 17, 33-49.

Bulleid, A. and Gray, H. St. G., 1911, 1917. **The Glastonbury Lake Village.** Vols I and II.

1948. **The Meare Lake Village,** Vol. I.

Burgess, C., 1974. "The Bronze Age" in **British Prehistory: A New Outline** (ed. C. Renfrew), London, 165-232.

Burley, E., 1955-6. "A Catalogue and Survey of the Metalwork from Traprain Law", **Proc. Soc. Antiq. Scotland** 89, 118-221.

Bushe-Fox, J.P., 1949. **Fourth Report on the Excavations of the Roman Fort at Richborough, Kent.**

Byrne, F.J., 1973. **Irish Kings and High Kings,** London.

Cadoux, J.-L., 1977. "Circonscription de Picardie", **Gallia** 35, 295-320.

Callander, J., 1926-7. "An Early Iron Age Hoard from Crichie, Aberdeen", **Proc. Soc. Antiq. Scotland** 61, 243-6.

Carroll, D.L. 1974. "A Classification for Granulation in Ancient Metalwork", **American J. Arch.** 78, 33-39.

Carson, R.A.G. and O'Kelly, C., 1977. "A Catalogue of the Roman Coins from Newgrange, Co. Meath, and Notes on the Coins and Related Finds", **Proc. Roy. Irish Acad.** 77C, 35-55.

Caulfield, S., 1977. "The Beehive Quern in Ireland", **J. Roy. Soc. Antiq. Ireland** 107, 104-139.

Challis, A.J. and Harding, D.W., 1975. "Later Prehistory from the Trent to the Tyne", **Brit. Arch. Reports** 20 (ii).

Champion, T., 1971. "The End of the Irish Bronze Age", **North Munster Antiquarian Journal** 14, 17-24.

Chivite, J.T., 1965. **Cuadernos de Arte Gallego, 3: Escultura Celto-Romana,** Ediciones Castrelos, Vigo.

CIIAA. See Raftery, B., 1983.

Chossenot, D., Neiss, R. et Sauget, J.M., 1981. "Fouille de sauvetage d'une nécropole de la Tène I à Vrigny (Marne)" in **L'Age du Fer en France Septentrionale,** Reims, 131-150.

Clarke, D.V., 1970. "Bone Dice and the Scottish Iron Age", **Proc. Prehist. Soc.** 36, 214-232.

1971. "Small finds in the Atlantic Province: Problems of Approach", **Scottish Arch. Forum** 3, 22-54.

Clarke, E.D., 1821. "An Account of some Antiquities found at Fulbourn in Cambridgeshire", **Arch.** 19, 56-61.

Clarke, R.R., 1939. "The Iron Age in Norfolk and Suffolk", **Arch. J.** 96, 1-113.

1951 "A Hoard of Metalwork of the Early Iron Age from Ringstead, Norfolk", **Proc. Prehist. Soc.** 17, 214-225.

1954. "The Early Iron Age Treasure from Snettisham, Norfolk", **Proc. Prehist. Soc.** 20, 27-86.

Clarke, R.R. and Hawkes, C.F.C., 1955. "An Iron Anthropoid Sword from Shouldham, Norfolk, with Related Continental and British Weapons", **Proc. Prehist. Soc.** 21, 198-227.

Coffey, G., 1902-4. "Some Monuments of the La Tène Period recently discovered in Ireland", **Proc. Roy. Irish Acad.** 24C, 257-266.

Coles, J., 1959-60. "Scottish Late Bronze Age Metalwork: Typology, Distribution and Chronology", **Proc. Soc. Antiq. Scotland** 93, 16-134.

1968. "The 1857 Law Farm Hoard", **Ant. J.** 48, 162-174.

1975. "The 1857 Law Farm Hoard: an addition", **Ant. J.** 60, 128.

Collingwood, R.G., 1930. "Roman-Celtic Art in Northumbria", **Arch.** 80 37-58.

Collingwood-Bruce, J., 1880. **A descriptive catalogue of Antiquities, chiefly British, at Alnwick Castle,** Newcastle-upon-Tyne.

Collins, A.E.P., 1955. "Excavations in Lough Faughan Crannog, County Down", **Ulster J. Arch.** 18, 45-80.

1977. "A Sand-dune site at the White Rocks, Co. Antrim", **Ulster J. Arch.** 40, 21-6.

Collis, J., 1980. "Aulnat and Urbanisation in France: a second interim report", **Arch. J.** 137, 40-49.

Conwell, E.A., 1873. **Discovery of the Tomb of Ollamh Fodhla,** Dublin.

Corcoran, J.X.W.P., 1952. "Tankards and Tankard Handles of the British Iron Age", **Proc. Prehist. Soc.** 18, 85-102.

Costello, T.B., 1919-20. "Find of Bronze Pin with La Tène Ornament", **J. Galway Arch. Hist. Soc.** 11, 76.

Craw, J.H., 1923-4. "On Two Bronze Spoons from an Early Iron Age Grave near Burnmouth, Berwickshire", **Proc. Soc. Antiq. Scotland** 58, 143-160.

Crawford, H.S., 1914. "Note on the Bone Implements from Lough Crew", **J. Roy. Soc. Antiq. Ireland** 44, 161-3.

1922. "A Bronze Pin found near Sligo", **J. Roy. Soc. Antiq. Ireland** 52, 178-9.

1925. "The Engraved Bone Objects found at Lough Crew, Co. Meath, in 1865", **J. Roy. Soc. Antiq. Ireland** 55, 15-29.

Cunliffe, B., 1972. "The Late Iron Age Metalwork from Bulbury, Dorset", **Ant. J.** 52, 293-308.

1974. **Iron Age Communities in Britain,** London.

1982. "Britain, the Veneti and Beyond", **Oxford J. Arch.** 1:1, 39-68.

Curle, J., 1911. **A Roman Frontier Post and its People: The Fort of Newstead,** Glasgow.

Dannheimer, H., 1975. "Zu zwei älteren keltischen Fundstücken aus der Münchener Schotterebene", **Arch. Korrespondenzblatt** 5, 59-68

Davis, J.L. and Spratling, M.G., 1976. "The Seven Sisters hoard: a centenary study", in **Welsh Antiquity** (ed. Boon, G.E. and Lewis, J.M.),

Cardiff, 121-137.

Déchelette, J., 1927. **Manuel d'Archéologie Préhistorique Celtique et Gallo-Romaine**, IV.

Degen, R., 1977. "Mont Vully - ein keltisches Oppidum?", **Helvetia Archaeologica** 32, 114-145.

Dehn, W., 1949. "Jahresbericht des Rheinischen Landesmuseums Trier für 1941 bis 1944", **Trierer Zeitschrift** 18, 269-334.
    1966. "Die Doppelvogelkopffibel aus dem Val-de-Travers", **Helvetia Antiqua, Festschrift Emil Vogt**, Zurich, 137-146.

De Navarro, J.M., 1952. "The Celts in Britain and their Art", in **The Heritage of Early Britain** (ed. D. Charlesworth), London, 56-82.
    1972. **The Finds from the Site of La Tène, Vol. I, Scabbards and the Swords found in them**, Oxford.

Deyts, S., 1970. "A propos d'une statue en bois des sources de la Seine", **Rev. Arch. de l'Est et du Centre-Est** 21, 437-460.

Dickinson, C.W. and Waterman, D.M., 1960. "Excavations at Castle Skreen, Co. Down", **Ulster J. Arch.** 23, 63-77.

Dixon, P., 1976. **Barbarian Europe**, Oxford.

Dornan, B., 1975. **Gaming in Pre- and Protohistoric Ireland** (unpublished M.A. Thesis).

Duignan, M.V., 1976. "The Turoe Stone: its Place in insular La Tène Art", in **Celtic Art in Ancient Europe: Five Protohistoric Centuries** (eds P.-M. Duval and C.F.C. Hawkes), London, 201-218.

Dunning, G.C., 1934. "The Swan's-neck and Ring-headed Pins of the Early Iron Age in Britain", **Arch J.** 91, 269-295.

Duval, P.-M., 1975. "La décoration des fourreaux d'epée laténiens en Europe du Centre-Est et en Europe Occidentale", in **Székesféhervár, 1975**, 9-14.
    1977. **Les Celtes**, Paris.

Duval, P.-M. and Kruta, V., (eds), 1979. **Les mouvements celtiques du Ve au Ier siècle avant notre ère** (Actes du XXVIIIe colloque organisé à l'occasion du IXe Congrès International des Sciènces Préhistoriques et Protohistoriques, Nice, le 19 Septembre 1976), Paris.
    1982. **L'art celtique de la période d'expansion (IVe et IIIe siècles avant notre ère)**, Geneva.

Eggers, H.-J., 1951. "Der Römische Import im Freien Germanien", **Atlas der Urgeschichte** I.
    1964. "Das kaiserzeitliche Gräberfeld von Pollwitten, Kr. Mohrungen, Ostpreussen", **Jahrbuch. Röm-Germ. Zentralmuseums Mainz** 11, 154-175.

Eggers, J.A., Will, E., Joffroy, R. and Holmqvist, W., 1964. **Kelten und Germanen in Heidnischer Zeit**, Baden Baden.

Eichhorn, G., 1927. **Der Urnenfriedhof bei Grossromstedt**, Mannus-Bibliothek No. 41, Leipzig.

Eogan, G., 1964. "The Later Bronze Age in Ireland in the light of recent research", **Proc. Prehist. Soc.** 30, 268-351.

Jackson, S., 1973. **Celtic and other stone heads,** Bradford.

Jacobi, G., 1974. **Werkzeug und Gerät aus dem Oppidum von Manching** (Die Ausgrabungen in Manching, Band 5: Römisch-Germanische Kommission des Deutschen Archäologischen Instituts zu Frankfurt am Main), Wiesbaden.

1977. **Die Metallfunde vom Dünsberg,** Wiesbaden.

Jacobsthal, P., 1934. "Keltische Bronzebeschläge in Berlin", **Prähistorische Zeitschrift** 25, 62-104.

1938. "Iberian Statuette from Sligo", **J. Roy. Soc. Antiq. Ireland** 68, 49-54.

1939. "The Witham Sword", **The Burlington Magazine for Connoisseurs** 75, No. 1536, 29-30.

1944. **Early Celtic Art,** Oxford.

Jazdzewski, K. and Rycel, G., 1981. "Habent sua fata tumuli!" **Z Otchlani Wiekow** 47, 1-2, 30-48.

Jenny, W.A. von, 1935. **Keltische Metallarbeiten aus Heidnischer und Christlicher Zeit,** Berlin.

Joachim, H.-E., 1979. **Das Rheinische Landesmuseum, Bonn,** (Sonderheft, Januar 1979, Ausgrabungen im Rheinland '78), Bonn.

Jobey, G. and Tait, J., 1966. "Excavations on Palisaded Settlements and Cairnfields at Alnham, Northumberland", **Arch. Aeliana** 44, 5-48.

Jockenhövel, A., 1974. "Fleischhaken von den Britischen Inseln", **Arch Korrespondenzblatt** 4:4, 329-338.

Joffroy, R., 1957. "Les sépultures à char du premier age du fer en France", **Rev. Arch. de l'Est et du Centre-est** 8, 7-73.

1962. **Le Trésor de Vix,** Paris.

1969. "Le Torque de Mailly-le-Camp", **Monuments et Memoires** 56, 45-59.

Joffroy, R. et Bretz-Mahler, D., 1959. "Les tombes à char de La Tène dans l'est de la France", **Gallia** 17, 5-35.

Johns, C., 1971. "Spur-shaped Bronzes of the Irish Early Iron Age", in **Sieveking (ed.) 1971,** 57-61.

Jope, E.M., 1950. "Two Iron Age Horse Bridle-Bits from the North of Ireland", **Ulster J. Arch.** 13, 57-60.

1951. "A Bronze Butt or Ferrule from the River Bann", **City of Belfast Museum and Art Gallery Bulletin** I, 4, 57-65.

1954a. "An Iron Age decorated sword-scabbard from the River Bann at Toome", **Ulster J. Arch.** 17, 81-91.

1954b. "The Keshcarrigan Bowl and a Bronze Mirror Handle from Ballymoney", **Ulster J. Arch.** 17, 92-6.

1955. "Chariotry and Paired-Draught in Ireland during the Early Iron Age: the Evidence of some Horse-Bridle-Bits", **Ulster J. Arch.** 18, 37-44.

1958. "The Beginnings of the La Tène Ornamental Style in the British Isles" in **Problems of the Iron Age in Southern Britain,** (ed. S.S. Frere), 69-83.

1960. "The Beads from the First Century A.D. Burial at 'Loughey' near Donaghadee: Supplementary Note", **Ulster J. Arch.** 23, 40.

1961. "Daggers of the Early Iron Age in Britain", **Proc. Prehist. Soc.** 27, 307-343.

1961-2. "Iron Age Brooches in Ireland: a Summary", **Ulster J. Arch.** 24-5, 25-38.

1971. "The Witham Shield" in **Sieveking (ed.), 1971**, 61-69.

1974. "Iron Age Sword and Dagger Chapes: Technology, Taxonomy and Prehistory", **Irish Arch. Research Forum** 1:1, 1-8.

1975. "The Style of the Broighter Collar and its Significance", **Irish Arch Research Forum** II;2, 24.

Jope, E.M. and Wilson, B.C.S., 1957a. "A Burial Group of the First Century A.D. from 'Loughey' near Donaghadee", **Ulster J. Arch.** 20, 73-94.

1957b. "The Decorated Cast Bronze Disc from the River Bann, near Coleraine", **Ulster J. Arch.** 20, 95-102.

Keller, J., 1965. **Das Keltische Fürstengrab von Reinheim**, Mainz.

Kelly, E.P., 1974. "Aughinish stone forts", in **Excavations 1974**, (ed. T. Delaney), Belfast.

Kemble, J.M., 1863. **Horae Ferales, or Studies in the Archaeology of the Northern Nations** (with A.W. Franks and R.G. Latham).

Kennet, D.H., 1970. "The Felmersham Fish-head Spout: a Suggested Reconstruction", **Ant. J.** 50, 86-89.

K.I.G., 1978. **Die Kelten in Gallien**, Austellungskatalog, Museum für Völkerkunde, Wien.

Kilbride-Jones, H.E., 1934-5. "An Aberdeenshire Iron Age Miscellany", **Proc. Soc. Antiq. Scotland** 69, 445-454."

K.I.M., 1980. **Die Kelten in Mitteleuropa**, (ed. L. Pauli), Salzburger Landes-ausstellung .... im Keltenmuseum, Hallein, Salzburg.

Klindt-Jensen, O., 1950. **Foreign Influences in Denmark's Early Iron Age**, Copenhagen.

Knowles, W.J., 1897. "Portion of a Harp and other objects found in the Crannoge of Carncoagh, Co. Antrim", **J. Roy. Soc. Antiq. Ireland** 27, 114-5.

1904. "Crannogs or Artificial Islands in the Counties of Antrim and Derry", **Ulster J. Arch.** 10, 49-56.

1924. **Catalogue of the Well-known and Representative Collection of Pre-historic Antiquities etc., Chiefly from Ireland, formed by W.J. Knowles, Esq. M.R.I.A. of Flixton Place, Ballymena.**

Knox, H.T., 1915-16. "The Turoe Stone and the Rath of Feerwore, Co. Galway", **J. Galway Arch. Hist. Soc.** 9, 190-193.

Kolnik, T., 1971. "Übersicht und Stand der Erforschung der römischen Kaiserzeit und Völkerwanderungszeit". **Slovenská Archeológia** 19, 499-558.

Kraft, J., 1980. "Margetshöchheim, Lkr. Würzburg", **Ausgrabungen und Funde in Unterfranken, 1979** (Sonderdruck aus: Frankenland, Zeitschrift für Fränkische Landeskunde und Kulturpflege, NF 32, 1980), 136-139.

Krämer, W., 1949. "Zur Zeitstellung der hölzernen Schilde des Hirsch-sprungfundes", **Prähistorische Zeitschrift** 34-5, 354-360.
1961. "Fremder Frauenschmuck aus Manching", **Germania** 39, 305-322.

Kromer, K., 1959. **Das Gräberfeld von Hallstatt**, Firenze.

Kruta, V., 1971 **Le Trésor de Duchov**, Usti nad Labem.
1975a. **L'Art celtique en Bohême**, Paris.
1975b. "Les deux fibules Laténiennes de Conflans (Marne)", **Études Celtiques** 14, 377-389.
1977. **Les Celtes**, Paris.
1979. "Duchov-Münsingen: nature et diffusion d'une phase laténienne", in **Duval and Kruta (eds), 1979**, 81-115.

Kytlicova, D., 1970. "Das römerzeitliche Gräberfeld in Luzec nad Vltavou (Kr. Melnik)", **Pamatky Arch.** 61, 291-377.

Lamb, R.G., 1980. "Iron Age Promontory Forts in the Northern Isles", **Brit. Arch. Reports** 79.

Lambrechts, P., 1954. "L'Exaltation de la Tête dans la Pensée et dans l'Art des Celtes", **Dissertationes Archaeologicae Gandenses II**, Bruges.

Laur-Belart, R., 1963. **Der spätrömische Silberschatz von Kaiseraugst/ Aargau**, Basle.

Leeds, E.T., 1930. "A Bronze Cauldron from the River Cherwell, Oxford-shire, with notes on cauldrons and other bronze vessels of allied types", **Arch.** 80, 1-36.
1933. **Celtic Ornament in the British Isles down to A.D. 700**, Oxford.

Lenerz de Wilde, M., 1982. "Le 'Style de Cheshire Cat' un phénomène caracteristique de l'art celtique", in **Duval et Kruta (eds), 1982**, 101-114.

Lindenschmit, L., 1900. See **AuhV**.

Licka, M., 1968. "Latensky Kostrovy Hrob z Nymburka-Zalabi", **Arch rozhledy** 20, 353-6.

Livens, R.G., 1976. "A Don Terret from Anglesey, with a discussion of the type", in **Welsh Antiquity** (ed Boon, G.C. and Lewis, J.M.), 142-162.

Lloyd-Morgan, G., 1976. "A note on some Celtic discs from Ireland and the province of Lower Germany", **Proc. Roy. Irish Acad.** 76C, (Colloquium on Hiberno-Roman Relations and Material Remains), 217-222.

Lowery, P.R., Savage, R.D.A. and Wilkins, R.L., 1971. "Scriber, Graver, Scorper, Tracer: notes on Experiments in Bronzeworking Technique", **Proc. Prehist. Soc.** 37, 167-182.

Lynch, F., 1970. **Prehistoric Anglesey**, Llangefri.

Macalister, R.A.S., 1916-7. "A Report on some Excavations recently conducted in Co. Galway", **Proc. Roy. Irish Acad.** 33C, 505-510.
1922. "On a Stone with La Tène Decoration recently discovered in Co. Cavan", **J. Roy. Soc. Antiq. Ireland** 52, 113-6.
1928. **The Archaeology of Ireland**, London.

1929. "On some Antiquities Discovered upon Lambay Island", **Proc. Roy. Irish Acad.** 38C, 240-6.

1931. **Tara: a Pagan Sanctuary of Ancient Ireland**, London.

1935. **Ancient Ireland**, Dublin.

1949. **The Archaeology of Ireland**, London, (2nd Edition).

Macdonald, G., 1934. **The Roman Wall in Scotland**.

MacGregor, M., 1962. "The Early Iron Age Metalwork Hoard from Stanwick, North Riding, Yorkshire", **Proc. Prehist. Soc.** 28, 17-57.

1976. **Early Celtic Art in North Britain**, Leicester.

MacKie, E.W., 1969. "Radio-Carbon Dates and the Scottish Iron Age", **Ant.** 42, 15-26.

1970. "English Migrants and Scottish Brochs", **Glasgow Archaeol. J.** 2, 39-71.

1974. **Dun Mor Vaul, an Iron Age Broch on Tiree**.

MacNiocaill, G., 1972. **Ireland before the Vikings**, Dublin.

Mahr, A., 1930. "A Wooden Idol from Ireland", **Ant.** 4, 487.

1934. "A Wooden Cauldron from Altertate, Co. Monaghan", **Proc. Roy. Irish Acad.** 42C, 11-29.

1937. "New Aspects and Problems in Irish Prehistory", **Proc. Prehist. Soc.** 3, 262-436.

1941. **Celtic Art in Ancient Ireland**, Dublin.

Mann, L. McL., 1925. "Note on the Results of the Exploration of the Fort at Dunagoil", **Trans. Bute Nat. Hist. Soc.** 9, 56-60.

Manning, W. and Saunders, C., 1972. "Socketed axe from Maids Moreton, Buckinghamshire, with a note on the type", **Ant. J.** 52, 276-292.

Manning, C. and Eogan, G., 1979. "A Find of Gold Torcs from Coolmanagh, Co. Carlow", **J: Roy. Soc. Antiq. Ireland** 109, 20-27.

Mariën, M.-E., 1961. **La Période de la Tène en Belgique: la Groupe de la Haine**, Monographies d'Archéologie Nationale 2, Brussels.

Marquis, P. et Brunaux, J.-L., 1975. "Une fosse de La Tène Ia à Verberie (Oise)". **Revue Arch. de l'Oise 6**, 11-17.

Marshall, F.H., 1911. **Catalogue of the Jewellery, Greek, Etruscan and Roman, in the Departments of Antiquities, British Museum**, London.

Maryon, H., 1938. "The Technical Methods of the Irish Smiths in the Bronze and Early Iron Ages", **Proc. Roy. Irish Acad.** 44C, 181-228.

May, J., 1976. **Prehistoric Lincolnshire**, Lincoln.

McEvoy, E., 1854-5. "Note", in **J. Roy. Soc. Antiq. Ireland** 3, 131.

Meduna, J., 1961. **Stare Hradisko: Katalog der Funde im Museum der Stadt Boskovice**, Fontes Archeologia Moravicae II, Brno.

Megaw, J.V.S., 1963. "A British Bronze Bowl of the Belgic Iron Age from Poland", **Ant. J.** 43, 27-37.

1968a. "Une épée de la Tène I, avec fourreau décoré", **Rev. Arch. de l'Est et du Centre-Est** 19, 129-144.

1968b. "Problems and non-problems in Palaeo-organology: a Musical Miscellany", in **Studies in Ancient Europe: Essays presented to Stuart Piggott** (ed. J.M. Coles and D.D.A. Simpson), 333-358.

1970. **Art of the European Iron Age**, Bath.

1971. "A Group of Later Iron Age Collars or Neckrings from Western Britain", in **Sieveking (ed.), 1971,** 145-156.

1973. "The decorated sword-scabbards of iron from Cernon-sur-Coole (Marne) and Drna, Rimavska Sobota (Slovakia)", **Hamburger Beiträge zur Archäologie** III: 2, 119-137.

1975. "The orientalising theme in early celtic art: East or West?", in **Székesfehérvár 1975,** 15-34.

Milojčić, V., 1968. "Zu den spätkaiserzeitlichen und Merowingischen Silberlöffeln", **Ber. Röm-Germ. Kommission** 49, 111-148.

Mohen, J.-P., 1979. "La présence celtique dans le Sud-Ouest de l'Europe: indices archéologiques", in **Duval and Kruta (eds), 1979,** 29-48.

Montelius, O., 1904. **La civilisation primitive en Italie,** Stockholm.

Moosleitner, F., Pauli, L. and Penninger, E., 1974. **Der Dürrnberg bei Hallein,** Vol. II, Munich.

Mordant, C. et D., 1970. **Le site protohistorique des Gours-aux-Lions à Marolles-sur-Seine (Seine-et-Marne),** Mémoires de la Société Préhistorique Française, 8.

Mortillet, G. and A., 1881. **Musée Préhistorique,** Paris.

Motykova, K., 1974. "Ein römerzeitliches Siedlungsobjekt mit Belegen für Spielwürfelerzeugung bei Hostice in Böhmen", **Arch. rozhledy** 26, 504-519.

Müller-Beck, H.J. and Ettlinger, E., 1962-3. "Die Besiedlung der Engehalbinsel in Bern auf Grund des Kentnisstandes vom Februar des Jahres 1962", **Bericht Röm-Germ. Kommission** 43-4, 107-153.

Munro, R., 1882. **Ancient Scottish Lake Dwellings or Crannogs,** Edinburgh.

1890. **The Lake Dwellings of Europe,** London.

Murray, T.R., 1901. "Catalogue of the Collection of Irish Antiquities, formed by the late Thomas R. Murray, Esq. J.P.", **Sixteenth Annual Report of the Antiquarian Committee, University of Cambridge, Museum of Archaeology and Ethnology,** Cambridge.

Norreys, D.J., 1876-8. Note, in **J. Roy. Soc. Antiq. Ireland** 14, 277-279.

Nothdurfter, J., 1979. **Die Eisenfunde von Sanzeno im Nonsberg,** Römisch-Germanische Forschungen 38.

Nylen, E., 1955. **Die Jüngere Vorrömische Eisenzeit Gotlands,** Uppsala.

O'Connor, A. and Clarke, D.V., (eds), 1983. **From the Stone Age to the 'Forty-Five,** Studies Presented to R.B.K. Stevenson, Edinburgh.

Ó Corráin, D. (ed). 1981. **Irish Antiquity: Essays and Studies presented to Professor M.J. O'Kelly,** Cork.

O'Donovan, J., 1839. **Letters containing information relative to the Antiquities of the County of Galway. Collected during the progress of the Ordnance Survey in 1839** (Typescript ed., Vol. III, 1928).

O'Kelly, M.J., 1961. "The Cork Horns, the Petrie Crown and the Bann Disc", **J. Cork Hist. Arch. Soc.** 66, 1-12.

Oldeberg, A., 1947. "A Contribution to the History of the Scandinavian Bronze Lur in the Bronze and Iron Ages", **Act. Arch.** 18, 1-116.

Oldenstein, J., 1976. "Zur Ausrüstung römischer Auxiliareinheiten", **Ber. Röm–Germ. Komm.** 57, 49–284.

O'Rahilly, T.F., 1946. **Early Irish History and Mythology**, Dublin.

ÓRíordáin, A.B.A., Prendergast, E.M. and Rynne, E., 1962. "National Museum of Ireland: Archaeological Acquisitions in the Year 1960", **J. Roy. Soc. Antiq. Ireland** 92, 139–173.

ÓRíordáin, A.B.A. and Rynne, E., 1961. "A Settlement in the Sandhills at Dooey, Co. Donegal", **J. Roy. Soc. Antiq. Ireland** 91, 58–64.

ÓRíordáin, S.P., 1940. "Excavations at Cush, Co. Limerick", **Proc. Roy. Irish Acad.** 45C, 83–181.

1942. "The Excavation of a large Earthen Ringfort at Garranes, Co. Cork", **Proc. Roy. Irish Acad.** 47C, 77–150.

1946. "Prehistory in Ireland, 1937–1946", **Proc. Prehist. Soc.** 12, 142–171.

1949. "Lough Gur Excavations: Carraig Aille and the Spectacles", **Proc. Roy. Irish Acad.** 52C, 39–111.

1950. "Excavations on some Earthworks on the Curragh, Co. Kildare", **Proc. Roy. Irish Acad.** 53C, 249–277.

1952. "Fragment of the Killycluggin Stone", **J. Roy. Soc. Antiq. Ireland** 82, 68.

1954. "Lough Gur Excavations: Neolithic and Bronze Age Houses at Knockadoon", **Proc. Roy. Irish Acad.** 56C, 297–459.

1960. **Tara: The Monuments on the Hill**, 3rd edn., Drogheda.

Osterhaus, U., 1969. "Zu verzierten Frühlatènewaffen", **Marburger Beiträge zur Archäologie der Kelten, Festschrift für Wolfgang Dehn** (ed. O.-H. Frey), Fundberichte aus Hessen, Beiheft 1, 134–144.

O'Toole, E. and Mitchell, G.F., 1939. "A Group of Grooved Standing Stones in North Carlow", **J. Roy. Soc. Antiq. Ireland** 69, 99–111.

Özgan, R., 1981. "Bemerkungen zum großen Gallieranathem", **Archäologischer Anzeiger** 3, 489–510

Pajot, B. and Vernhet, A., 1976. "Les Civilizations de l'Age du Fer dans les Causses", in **La Préhistoire Française**, Tome II (ed. J. Guilaine), 687–698.

Peacock, D.P.S., 1969. "A Contribution to the Study of Glastonbury Ware from South-Western Britain", **Ant. J.** 49, 41–61.

Penninger, E., 1972. **Der Dürrnberg bei Hallein**, Vol. I, Munich.

Petres, E.F., 1979. "Some Remarks on anthropoid and pseudoanthropoid-hilted daggers in Hungary", in **Duval and Kruta (eds), 1979**, 171–178.

Petrie, G., 1833-4. Note in **Dublin Penny Journal** 2, 29–30.

Piggott, S., 1949. "An Iron Age Yoke from Northern Ireland", **Proc. Prehist. Soc.** 15, 192–193.

1950. "Swords and Scabbards of the British Early Iron Age", **Proc. Prehist. Soc** 16, 1–28.

1952-3a. "A Late Bronze Age Hoard from Peebleshire", **Proc. Soc. Antiq. Scotland** 87, 175–186.

1952-3b. "Three Metalwork Hoards of the Roman Period", **Proc. Soc. Antiq. Scotland** 87, 1-50.

1958. "Excavations at Braidwood Fort, Midlothian and Craig's Quarry, Dirleton, East Lothian", **Proc. Soc. Antiq. Scotland** 91, 61-77.

1959. "The Carnyx in Early Iron Age Britain", **Ant. J.** 39, 19-32.

1967. "A Scheme for the Scottish Iron Age", in **The Iron Age in Northern Britain** (ed. A.L.F. Rivet), Edinburgh, 1-16.

1969. "Early Iron Age Horn-caps and Yokes", **Ant. J.** 49, 378-381.

Powell, T.G.E., 1958. **The Celts**, London.

1966. **Prehistoric Art**, London.

Praeger, R.L., 1942. "The Broighter Gold Ornaments", **J. Roy. Soc. Antiq. Ireland** 72, 29-32.

Pryor, F., 1980. **A Catalogue of British and Irish Prehistoric Bronzes in the Royal Ontario Museum**, Toronto.

Py, M., 1978. **L'Oppidum des Castels à Nages-Gard** (XXXVe Supplément à Gallia), Paris.

Radford, C.A.P. Ralegh, 1977. See **Bersu, 1977.**

Raftery, B., 1969. "Freestone Hill: an Iron Age Hillfort and Bronze Age Cairn", **Proc. Roy. Irish Acad.** 68C, 1-108.

1970. "A Decorated Strap-end from Rathgall, Co. Wicklow", **J. Roy. Soc. Antiq. Ireland** 100, 200-211.

1972a. "Some Late La Tène Glass Beads from Ireland", **J. Roy. Soc. Antiq. Ireland** 102, 14-18.

1972b. "Irish Hillforts", in **The Iron Age in the Irish Sea Province** (ed. C. Thomas) C.B.A. Research Reports No. 9, 37-58.

1974. "A Decorated Iron Age Horse-bit Fragment from Ireland", **Proc. Roy. Irish Acad.** 74C, 1-10.

1976a. "Dowris, Hallstatt and La Tène in Ireland: Problems of the Transition from Bronze to Iron", in **Acculturation and Continuity in Atlantic Europe** (Papers presented at the IV Atlantic Colloquium, Ghent, 1975, ed. S.J. De Laet), 189-197.

1976b. "Rathgall and Irish Hillfort Problems", in **Hillforts: Later Prehistoric Earthworks in Britain and Ireland** (ed. D.W. Harding), London, 339-357.

1977. "A much-repaired Horse-bit pair from Iron Age Ireland", **Marburger Studien zu Vor- und Frühgeschichte**, Band 1, Festschrift zum 50 jährigen Bestehen des Vorgeschichtlichen Seminars Marburg, (ed. O.-H. Frey), 299-308.

1978. "Excavations at Killycluggin, Co. Cavan", **Ulster J. Arch.** 41, 49-54.

1980. "Iron Age Cauldrons in Ireland", **Arch. Atlantica** 3, 57-80.

1981. "Iron Age Burials in Ireland" in **Ó Corráin (ed.), 1981**, 173-204.

1982. "Knobbed Spearbutts of the Irish Iron Age" in **Scott (ed.), 1982**, 75-92.

1983. **A Catalogue of Irish Iron Age Antiquities,** Marburg.

Raftery, J., 1937. Abstract, pp. 409-411, in **Mahr, A., 1937.**

1937-40. "Early Iron Age Decoration on the Dolmen at Rathkenny, Co. Meath", **Co. Louth Arch J.** 9, 258-261.

1938-9. "The Tumulus Cemetery of Carrowjames, Co. Mayo, Part I", **J. Galway Hist. Arch. Soc.** 18, 157-167.

1939. "An Early Iron Age Sword from Lough Gur, Co. Limerick", **J. Roy. Soc. Antiq. Ireland** 69, 170-172.

1940a. "The Tumulus Cemetery of Carrowjames, Co. Mayo, Part II, Carrowjames II", **J. Galway Hist. Arch. Soc.** 19, 16-88.

1940b. "A Bronze Disc from the River Bann, Northern Ireland", **Ant. J.** 20, 281-282; also in **Ulster J. Arch.** 3, 1940, 27-30.

1944. "The Turoe Stone and the Rath of Feerwore", **J. Roy. Soc. Antiq. Ireland** 74, 23-52.

1951. **Prehistoric Ireland,** London.

1953. "Lough Crew, Co. Meath – Ein Megalithgrab der La Tène Zeit", in **Congrès International des Sciènces Préhistoriques et Protohistoriques, Actes de la IIIe Session** (ed. E. Vogt), Zurich.

1960. "A Hoard of the Early Iron Age", **J. Roy. Soc. Antiq. Ireland** 90, 2-5.

1961. "National Museum of Ireland: Archaeological Acquisitions in the Year 1959", **J. Roy. Soc. Antiq. Ireland** 91, 43-108.

1966. "National Museum of Ireland: Archaeological Acquisitions in the Year 1963", **J. Roy. Soc. Antiq. Ireland** 96, 7-27.

1970. "National Museum of Ireland: Archaeological Acquisitions in the Year 1967", **J. Roy. Soc. Antiq. Ireland** 100, 145-166.

1971. "Irish Prehistoric Gold Objects: New Light on the Source of the Metal", **J. Roy. Soc. Antiq. Ireland** 101, 101-105.

1972. "Iron Age and Irish Sea: Problems for Research", in **The Iron Age in the Irish Sea Province** (ed. C. Thomas), Council for British Archaeology, Research Report No. 9, 1-10.

1973. "National Museum of Ireland: Archaeological Acquisitions in the Year 1970", **J. Roy. Soc. Antiq. Ireland** 103, 177-213.

Raftery, J., Prendergast, E.M. and Waddell, J., 1968. "National Museum of Ireland: Archaeological Acquisitions in the Year 1965", **J. Roy. Soc. Antiq. Ireland** 98, 93-159.

Raftery, J. and Ryan, M., 1971. "National Museum of Ireland: Archaeological Acquisitions in the Year 1967". **J. Roy. Soc. Antiq. Ireland** 101, 184-244.

1972. "National Museum of Ireland: Archaeological Acquisitions in the Year 1969", **J. Roy. Soc. Antiq. Ireland** 102, 181-223.

Raistrick, A., 1939. "Iron Age Settlements in West Yorkshire, **Yorkshire Arch J.** 34, 115-150.

Ralston, I.B.M., 1979. "The Iron Age (c. 600 B.C. - A.D. 200): Northern Britain", in **Introduction to British Prehistory,** J.V.S. Megaw and D.D.A. Simpson, London, 446-501.

Ratimorská, P., 1975. "Das Keltische Gräberfeld in Chotin (Sudwestslowakei)", in **Székesfehérvár 1975**, 85-96.

Rauchon, C. et Perichon, R., 1979. "Une restauration du Musée du Fer de Nancy". **Rev. Arch. du Centre de la France** 18, 25-27.

Read, C.H., 1915. "On a Bronze Object of the Late Celtic Period recently added to the British Museum", **Arch.** 66, 349-352.

Reddington, M., 1902. "Stone at Turoe", **J. Galway Arch. Hist. Soc.** 2, 118.

Rees, S.E., 1979. "Agricultural Implements in Prehistoric and Roman Britain", **Brit. Arch. Reports** 69.

Reinecke, P., 1911. See **AuhV.**

Riley, F.T., 1936. "Excavation in the Townland of Pollacorragune, Tuam, Co. Galway", **J. Galway Arch. Hist. Soc.** 17, 44-64.

Rilliot, M., 1975. "Épée de La Tène I, à Moroux (Territoire de Belfort)", **Rev. Arch. de l'Est et du Centre-Est** 26, 443-444.

Ritchie, J.N.G., 1969. "Shields in North Britain in the Iron Age", **Scottish Arch. Forum**, 31-40.

Romilly Allen J., 1904. **Celtic Art in Pagan and Christian Times (The Antiquary's Books).**

Rosenberg, G., 1937-43. "Hjortspringfundet", **Nordiske Fortidsminder** 3, 9-111.

Roska, M., 1944. "Les Gaulois en Transylvanie", **Közlemények Kolozsvár** 4, 53-80.

Ross, A., 1967. **Pagan Celtic Britain**, London.

Rotherham, E.C., 1895. "On the Excavation of a Cairn on Slieve-na-Caillighe, Lough Crew", **J. Roy. Soc. Antiq. Ireland** 25, 311-316.
1896. "An Ornamented Bone Flake from Slieve-na-Caillighe", **J. Roy. Soc. Antiq. Ireland** 26, 257-258.

Roualet, P., Rapin, A., Fluzin, P., 1982. "Sépultures du Crayon, à Écury-le-Repos Marne", **Mém. Soc. Ag. Comm. Sciènces et Arts (Marne)** 97, 25-44.

Roualet, P. et Kruta, V., 1980. "Le cimetière gaulois de la Barbière à Villeseneux (Marne)", **Mém. Soc. Ag. Comm. Sciènces et Arts Marne** 95, 27-58.

Rynne, E., 1958. "Iron Axehead of La Tène date", **J. Roy. Soc. Antiq. Ireland** 88, 149-150.
1960a. "La Tène Sword from near Lough Gara", **J. Roy. Soc. Antiq. Ireland** 90, 12-13.
1960b. "A Bronze Cauldron from Ballyedmond, Co. Galway", **J. Galway Arch. Hist. Soc.** 29, 1-2.
1961. "The Introduction of La Tène into Ireland", **Bericht über den V. Internationalen Kongress für Vor- und Frühgeschichte, Hamburg 1958**, 705-709.
1964. "The Coiled Bronze Armlet from Ballymahon, Co. Meath", **J. Roy. Soc. Antiq. Ireland** 94, 69-72.
1966. "Some Irish Affinities with the Msecke Zehrovice Stone Head", **Sbornik Narodniho Muzea v Praze** 20, 151-154.

1972. "Celtic Stone Idols in Ireland", in **The Iron Age in the Irish Sea Province** (ed. C. Thomas), Council for British Archaeology, Research Report No. 9, 79-98.

1976. "The La Tène and Roman Finds from Lambay, Co. Dublin: a re-assessment", **Proc. Roy. Irish Acad.** 76C, Colloquium on Hiberno-Roman Relations and Material Remains 231-244.

1979. "An Early Celtic Spanish-North Munster Connection", **North Munster Ant. J.** 21, 7-10.

1982. "A Classification of Pre-Viking Irish swords" in **Scott (ed.) 1982,** 93-97.

1983. "Some Early Iron Age Sword-Hilts from Ireland and Scotland", in **O'Connor and Clarke (eds) 1983,** 188-196.

Rynne, E. and Raftery, J., 1963. "National Museum of Ireland: Archaeological Acquisitions for the Year 1961", **J. Roy. Soc. Antiq. Ireland** 93, 115-133.

Savory, H.N., 1964. "A New Hoard of La Tène Metalwork from Merionethshire", **Bull. Board Celtic Studies** 20, 449-475.

1971. **Excavations at Dinorben, 1965-9,** Cardiff.

1973. "La Tène Wales", **Études Celtiques** (Actes du quatrième congrès international d'études celtiques, Rennes, 18-25 juillet 1971) 13, 687-709.

1976. **National Museum of Wales: Guide Catalogue of the Early Iron Age Collections,** Cardiff.

Schaaf, U., 1973. "Frühlatènezeitliche Grabfunde mit Helmen vom Typ Berru", **Jahrbuch. Röm.-Germ. Zentralmuseum, Mainz** 20, 81-106.

Scherer, J. et Mordant, C., 1972. "La Nécropole de la Tène de Gravon (S. et M.)" **Rev. Arch. de l'Est et du Centre-Est** 23, 357-384.

Schlette, F., 1980. **Kelten zwischen Alesia und Pergamon,** Leipzig.

Schwab, H., 1972. "Entdeckung einer keltischen Brücke an der Zihl und ihre Bedeutung für La Tène", **Arch. Korrespondenzblatt** 2, 289-294.

Schwantes, G., 1911. **Die ältesten Urnenfriedhöfe bei Uelzen und Luneburg,** Hamburg.

Schwappach, F., 1969. Stempelverzierte Keramik von Armorica", **Marburger Beiträge zur Archäologie der Kelten, Festschrift für Wolfgang Dehn** (ed. O.-H. Frey), Fundberichte aus Hessen, Beiheft 1, 213-287.

1971. "Stempel des Waldalgesheimstils an einer Vase aus Sopron-Bécsidomb (West-Ungarn)" **Hamburger Beiträge zur Archäologie** 1, 131-172.

1975. "Die Bretagne vor Caesar", **Uni-Forschung, Wissenschaftsberichte aus der Universität Hamburg** VIII, 86-113.

Scott, B.G., 1976a. "Some Notes on the Transition from Bronze to Iron in Ireland", **Irish Arch. Research Forum** I:1, 9-24.

1976b. "The occurrence of Platinum as a trace element in Irish gold: comments on Hartmann's gold analyses", **Irish Arch. Research**

Forum 3:2, 21-24.

1980. "The introductions of non-ferrous and ferrous metal technologies to Ireland: Motives and Mechanisms", in **The Origins of Metallurgy in Atlantic Europe: Proceedings of the Fifth Atlantic Colloquium** (ed. M. Ryan), Dublin, 189-204.

Scott, B.G. (ed.) 1982. **Studies on Early Ireland: Essays in Honour of M.V. Duignan**, Belfast.

Seaby, W.A., 1964. "A Ring-headed Bronze Pin from Ulster", **Ulster J. Arch.** 27, 67-72.

Sieveking, G. de G., (ed.) 1971. **Prehistoric and Roman Studies** (Commemorating the Opening of the Department of Prehistoric and Romano-British Antiquities), London.

Selkirk, A. and Waterman, D.M., 1970. "Navan Fort", **Current Arch.** No. 22, September 1970, 304-308.

Simpson, M., 1968. "Massive Armlets in the North British Iron Age", in **Studies in Ancient Europe: Essays presented to Stuart Piggott** (ed. J.M. Coles and D.D.A. Simpson), 233-254.

Simpson, D.D.A. and Simpson, M., 1968. "Decorative Ring-headed pins in Scotland", **Trans. Dumfriesshire and Galloway Nat. Hist. Ant. Soc.** 45, 141-147.

SLZ 1961. **Schweizerisches Landesmuseum in Zürich, Jahresberichte 1959 und 1960.**

Smith, R., 1913. "The Evolution of the Hand-pin in Great Britain and Ireland", **Opuscula Archaeologia Oscari Montelio dicata**, 281-289.

1925. **British Museum: a Guide to the Antiquities of the Early Iron Age in the Department of British and Medieval Antiquities** (Second Edition), London.

Smith, M.A., 1956. "The Limitations of Inference in Archaeology". **Arch. Newsletter**, 6:1, 3-7.

1959. "Some Somerset Hoards and their Place in the Bronze Age of Southern Britain", **Proc. Prehist. Soc.** 25, 144-187.

Spratling, M.G., 1970a. "The Smiths of South Cadbury", **Current Arch.** 188-191.

1970b. "Excavations at South Cadbury Castle, 1969: Bronze Shield Mount", **Ant. J.** 50, 21-22.

1970c. "Bronze Shield Fragments and Metal Workers' Tools from the 1969 Excavations", **Department of Archaeology, University College Cardiff, Wales, South Cadbury Information Sheets,** unnumbered.

1979. "The debris of metalworking" in **Wainwright, G., 1979**, 125-149.

Stead, I.M., 1965. **The La Tène Cultures of Eastern Yorkshire**, York.

1967. "A Late La Tène III Burial at Welwyn Garden City", **Arch.** 101, 1-62.

1979. **The Arras Culture**, York.

1982. "The Cerrig-y-Drudion 'Hanging Bowl'", **Ant. J.** 52, 221-234.

1983. "La Tène Swords and Scabbards in Champagne", **Germania**

61, 487-510.

Stevenson, R.B.K., 1955. "Pins and the Chronology of the Brochs", **Proc. Prehist. Soc.** 21, 282-294.

1967. "Metalwork and some other Objects in Scotland and their Cultural Affinities", in **The Iron Age in Northern Britain** (ed. A.L.F. Rivet), Edinburgh, 17-44.

Stiglitz, H., 1975. **Der römische Limes in Österreich, Heft XXVI: das römische Donaukastell Zwentendorf in Niederösterreich**, Vienna.

Stimming, R., 1912. "Waffen der römischen Kaiserzeit aus der Mark Brandenburg", **Mannus** 4, 309-315.

Stokes, M., 1882. "On Two Bronze Fragments of an Unknown Object Portions of the Petrie Collection in the Museum of the Royal Irish Academy, Dublin", **Arch.** 47, 1-8.

Strong, D.E., 1966. **Greek and Roman Gold and Silver Plate**, London.

Stuart, J., 1819. **Historical Memoirs of the City of Armagh.**

Szabó, M., 1976. "A 'Magyar Kardstílus' Kialakulása", **Alba Regia** 15, 25-37.

1977. "The origins of the Hungarian sword style", **Ant** 51, 211-220.

1982. "Remarques sur la classification des fourreaux d'épée dits hongrois" in **Duval and Kruta (eds), 1982,** 175-190.

Székesféhervár, 1975. **The Celts in Central Europe**, Papers of the II Pannonia Conference (ed. J. Fitz), Székesféhervár.

Tanner, A., 1980. **Das Latènegräberfeld von Trun-Darvella**, Schriften des Seminars für Urgeschichte der Universität Bern.

Tempest, H.G., 1949. "Bone Objects from an Irish Burial Cairn", **Man, Royal Anthropological Institute of Gt. Britain and Ireland** 64, 13-16.

Thomas, C., 1961. "The Animal Art of the Scottish Iron Age and its Origins", **Arch J.** 118, 14-64.

Thomas, S., 1960. "Studien zu den germanischen Kämmen der römischen Kaiserzeit", **Arbeits- und Forschungsberichte zu sächsischen Bodendenkmalpflege** 8, 54-215.

1968. "Zu den Fibeln vom Mittellatèneschema und den Fibeln mit umgeschlagenem fuß der frühen Kaiserzeit" in **Provinciala, Festschrift für Rudolf Laur-Belart** (eds E. Schmid, L. Berger, P Bürgin), Basle, 464-469.

Thompson, F.H., 1975. "The Excavation of the Roman Amphitheatre at Chester", **Arch.** 105, 127-239.

Tierney, J.J., 1960. "The Celtic Ethnography of Poseidonius", **Proc. Roy. Irish Acad.** 60C, 189-275.

Todorovic, J., 1968. **Kelti u Jugoistocnoj Evropi**, Belgrade.

1973-4. "Une tombe double de guerriers scordisques à Ritopek", **Starinar** 24/25, 79-83.

Topp, C., 1956. "The Gold Ornaments Reputedly Found near the Entrance to Newgrange in 1842", **Ann. Report of Inst. Arch. London** 12, 53-62.

Torbrügge, W. und Uenze, H.P., 1968. **Bilder zur Vorgeschichte Bayerns,**

PLATES

1

2

Pl. 1. Decorative details on unlocalised Type B horsebit.

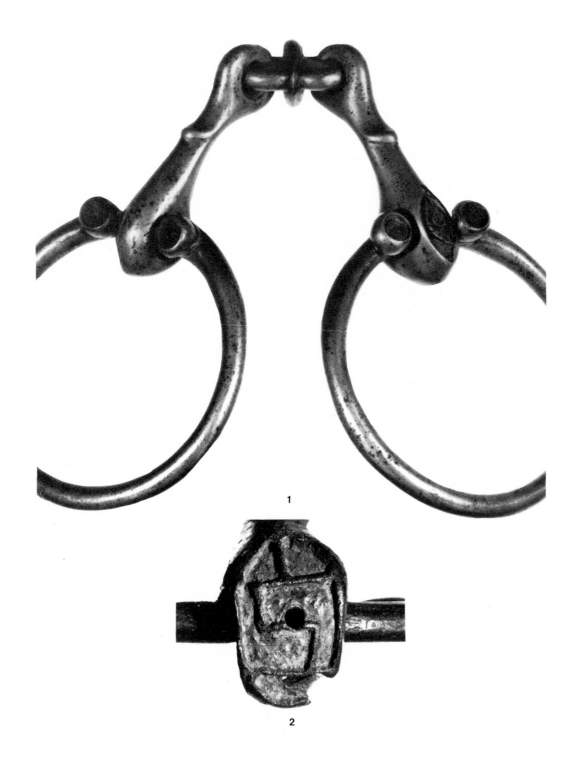

Pl. 2. Type B horsebits with champlevé ornament. 1 Lough Beg,
Co. Antrim. 2 no prov.

Pl. 3. Type B horsebit. Decorative details of stop-studs and link-end.
No prov.

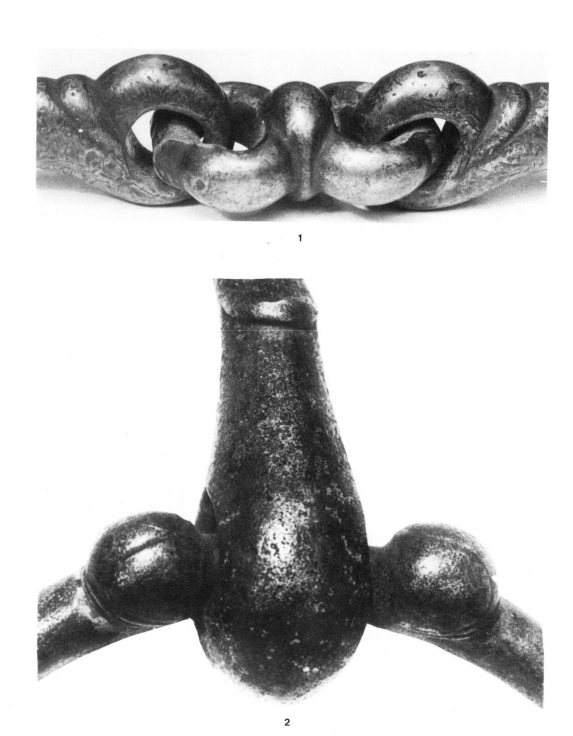

Pl. 4. Type B horsebit details. 1 no prov. 2 Abbeyshrule,
Co. Longford.

Pl. 5. Type B horsebit detail. No prov.

Pl. 6. Type B horsebits. Details of central-links. No prov.

Pl. 7. Type D horsebit. Champlevé ornament on side-link. No prov.

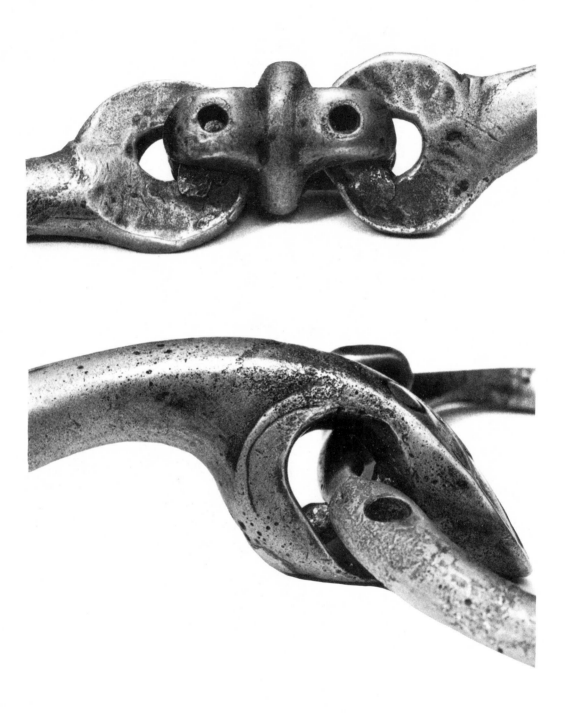

Pl. 8. Type D horsebit. Streamstown, Co. Westmeath. Details of repairs.

Pl. 9. Type D horsebit. Detail of decorated side-link. No prov.

Pl. 10. Type D horsebit. Detail of decorated side-link. No prov.

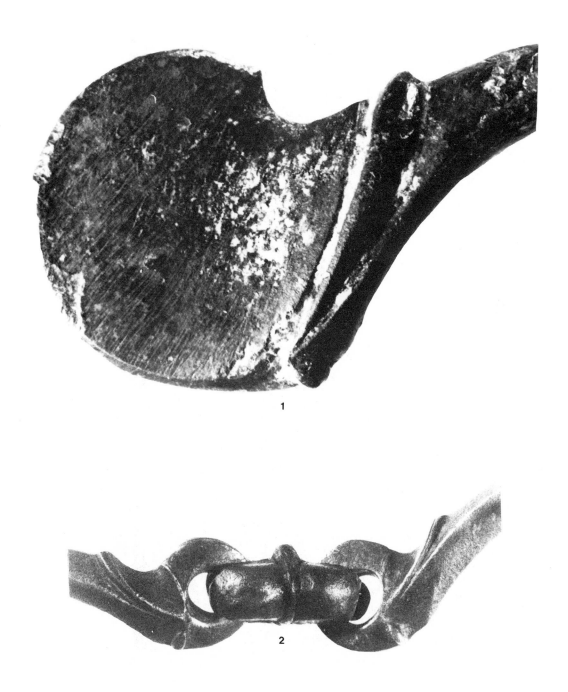

1

2

Pl. 11. Type E horsebits. Details of link-ends. No prov.

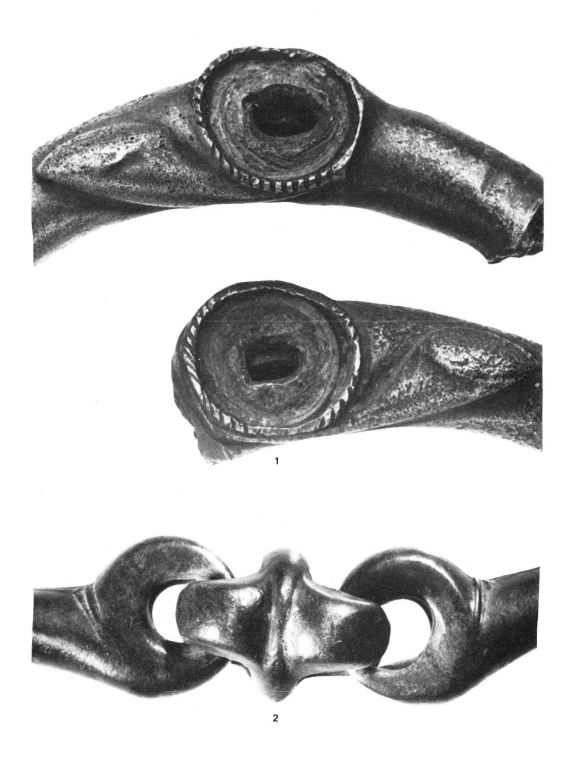

Pl. 12. 1 fragmentary bridle-ring, details of decorative stop-studs.
2 Type D horsebit, detail. No prov.

Pl. 13. Killeevan, Anlore, Co. Monaghan. Horsebit and repoussé bronze disc.

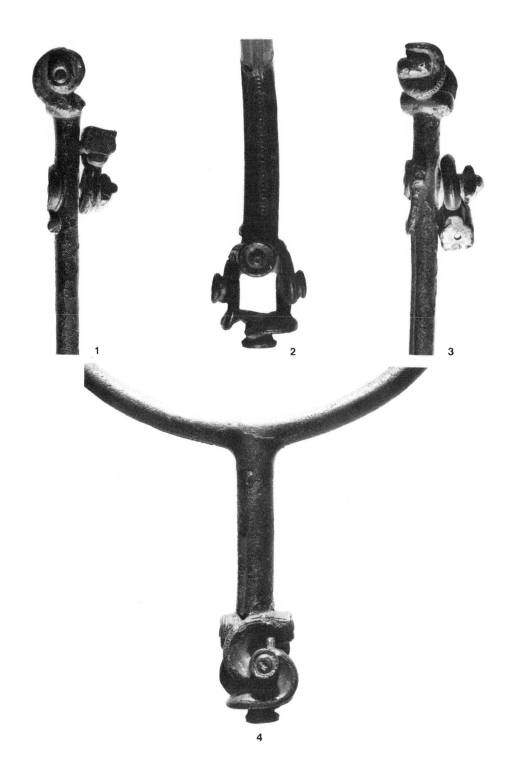

Pl. 14. Decorative details of stem- and prong-terminals of horse "pendant".

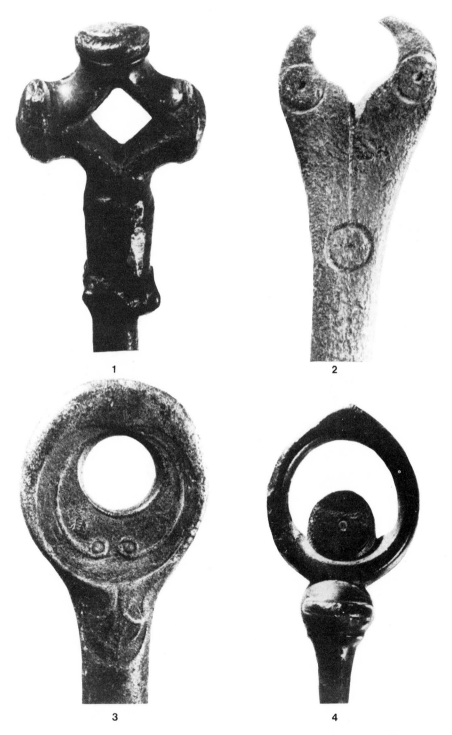

Pl. 15. Decorative details of prong-terminals of bronze horse "pendants".
All no prov.

1   2

Pl. 16. Decorative details of stem- and prong-terminals, Type 2a "pendant".
Attymon, Co. Galway.

Pl. 17. "Pendant" prong-terminals. 1 Tara-Skreen, Co. Meath (Type 2a).
2 no prov. (Type 1d).

Pl. 18. Penannular rings, hook and hand-bell. Kishawanny, Co. Kildare.

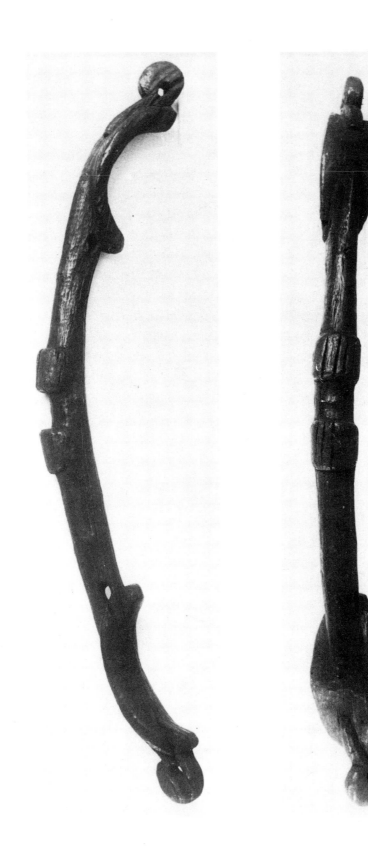

Pl. 19. Wooden horse yoke. Co. Antrim.

Pl. 20. Bronze yoke (?) mounts. Lough Gur, Co. Limerick.

1

2

3

Pl. 25. Bronze scabbard-mounts, Lambay, Co. Dublin.

Pl. 26. Decorated bronze scabbard-plate. Lisnacrogher, Co. Antrim.

Pl. 27. Chape and scabbard-end. Lisnacrogher No. 3, Co. Antrim. Bronze.

Pl. 28. Decorated bronze scabbard-detail. Lisnacrogher No. 3, Co. Antrim.

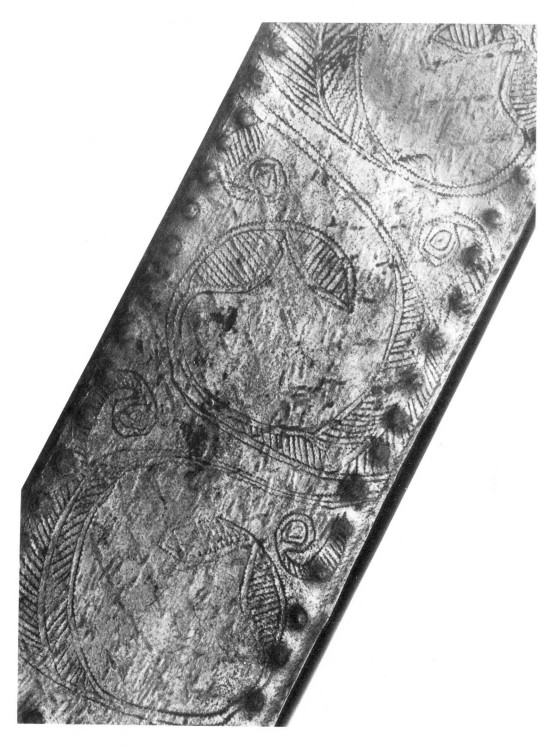

Pl. 29. Decorated bronze scabbard-detail. River Bann, Toome,
Co. Antrim.

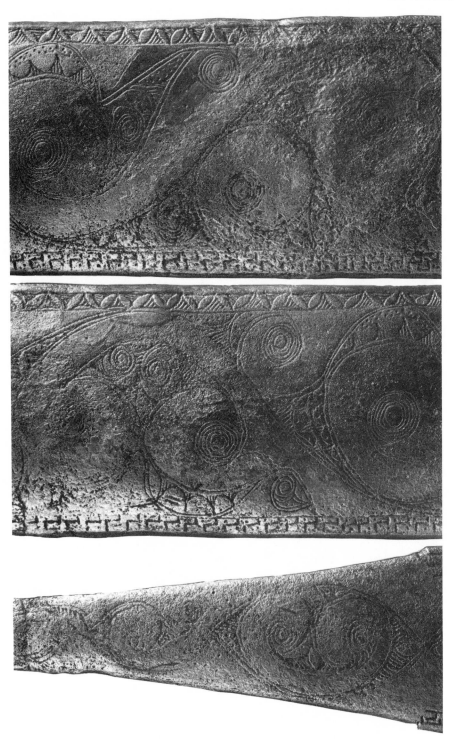

Pl. 30. Decorated bronze scabbard-details. River Bann, Co. Derry.
(photos of copy made in British Museum).

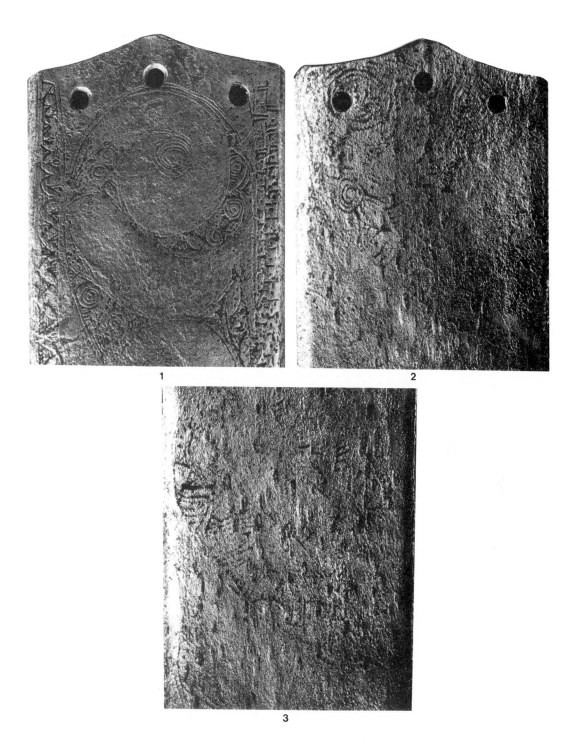

1

2

3

Pl. 31. Decorated bronze scabbard-details. River Bann, Co. Derry. 1 front.
2-3 back, showing traces of ornament and hammer marks. (Photos of
copy made in British Museum).

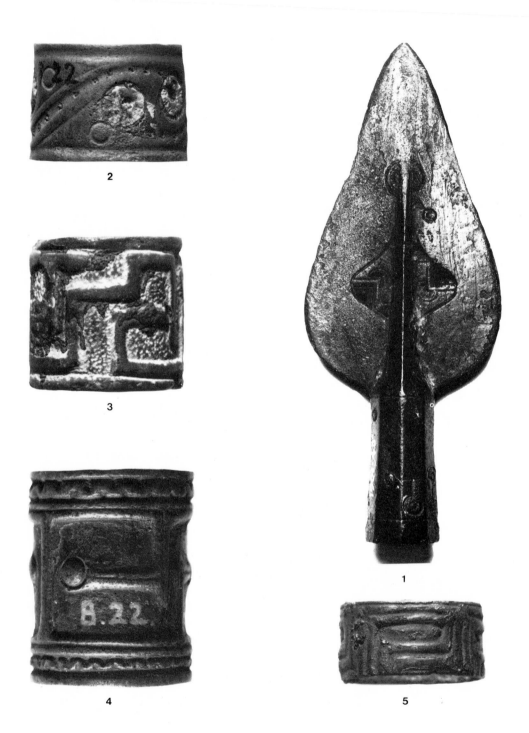

Pl. 32. 1 bronze spearhead, Boho, Co. Fermanagh. 2-5, bronze ferrules, Lisnacrogher, Co. Antrim.

Pl. 33. Knobbed bronze spearbutts. 1 Coleraine, Co. Derry (Type 1b).
2 no prov. (Type 2).

Pl. 34. 1, 3 Spearbutts (Type 1a), Lisnacrogher, Co. Antrim.
2 Detail of tubular bronze spearbutt. No prov.

Pl. 35. Tubular bronze spearbutts. 1 (Type 3b), Clondalee, Co. Meath.
2 (Type 3c), River Bann, Toome, Co. Antrim.

Pl. 36. Type 4 spearbutt. Ballybrit, Co. Galway.

Pl. 37. Silver plaque. Bewcastle, Cumberland, England. The god Cocidius
is shown holding a knob-ended spear in his right hand.
(After Richmond, 1958, Pl. 7).

Pl. 38. Scottish spearbutt and spearbutt moulds. 1 Harray, Orkney.
2, 4 Dunagoil, Buteshire. 3, 5 Traprain Law, East Lothian.
2, 4 replicas.

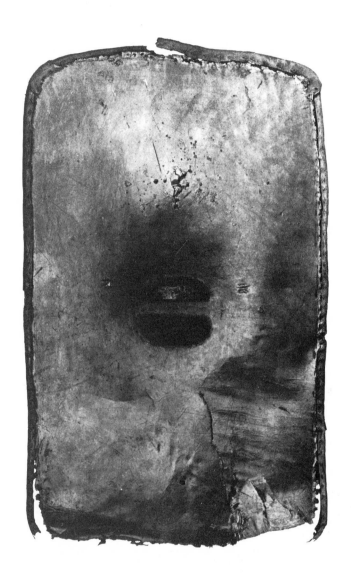

Pl. 39. Leather-covered wooden shield. Clonoura, Co. Tipperary. Back.

Pl. 40. Shield representations in stone, north of Britain. 1 Maryport, Cumberland, England. 2 Roman distance slab, Bridgeness, West Lothian, Scotland. (1 Photo Anne Ross, courtesy National Museum of Ireland. 2 after Richmond, 1958, Pl. 6).

1

2

Pl. 41. Bronze horn. Ardbrin, Co. Down. 1 General view. 2 Detail of
internal, riveted sealing-strip.

Pl. 42. Bronze horn. Loughnashade, Co. Armagh. 1 Detail of bell, showing internal, riveted sealing-strip. 2 Detail of exterior, showing repair patches. 3 Repoussé disc. 4 General view.

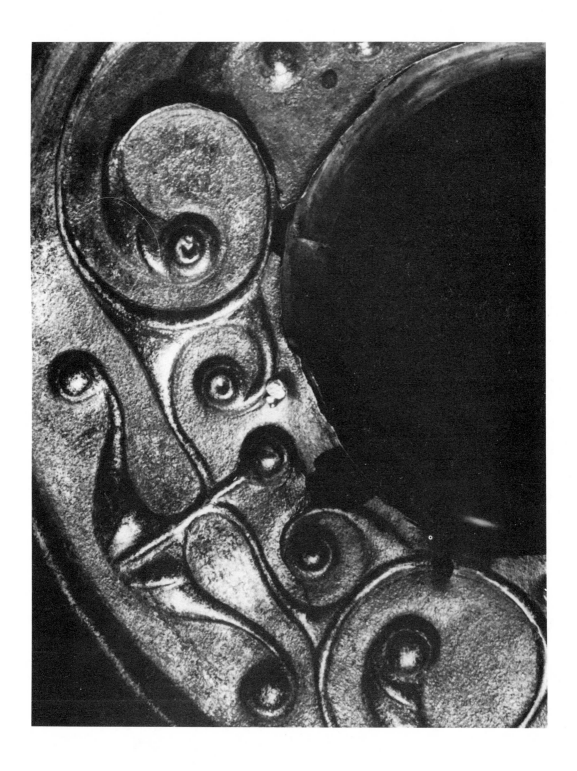

Pl. 43. Loughnashade, Co. Armagh, repoussé disc.
Detail of decoration.

Pl. 44. Bronze horn fragment, detail. No prov.

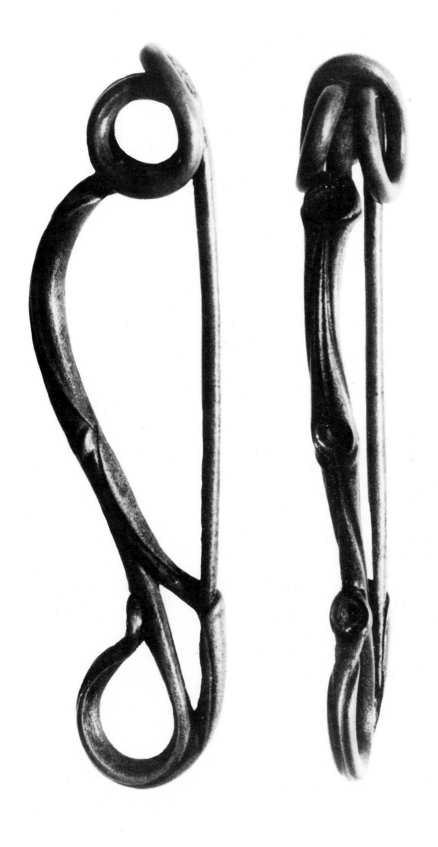

Pl. 45. Bronze fibula. Clogher, Co. Tyrone.

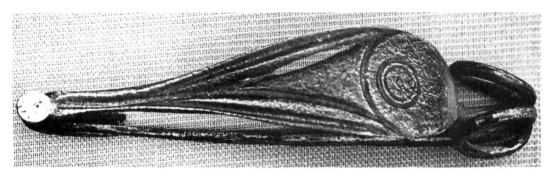

2

1

Pl. 46. Bronze fibulae. 1 Bondville, Co. Armagh. 2 Modeenagh, Co. Fermanagh. 3 no. prov.

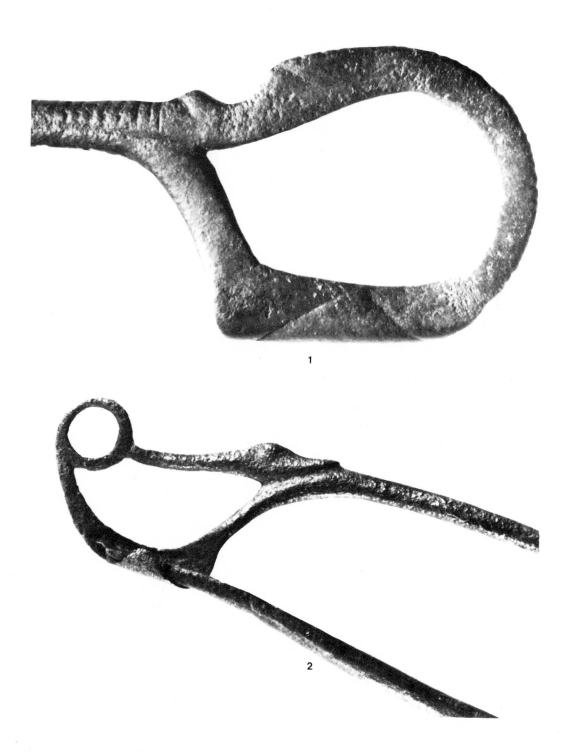

Pl. 47. Bronze fibulae. Details showing bird's-head modelling. 1 Dun Aengus, Aran, Co. Galway. 2 Lecarrow, Co. Sligo.

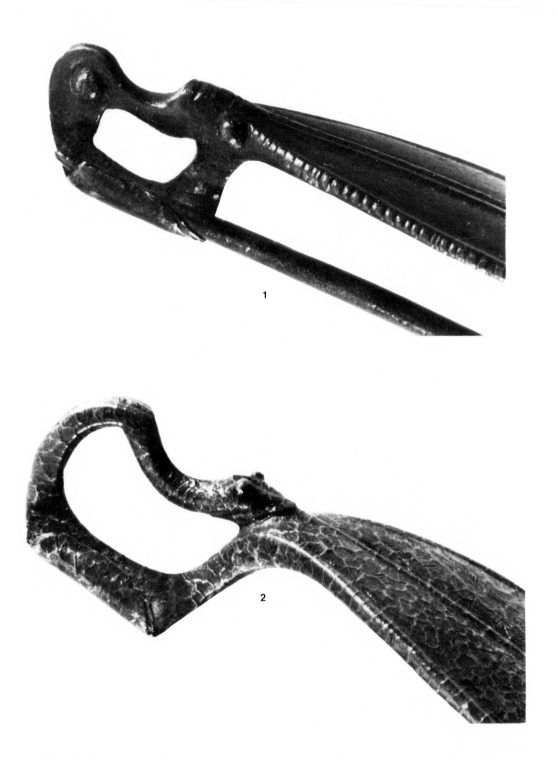

Pl. 48. Bronze fibulae. Details showing bird's-head and snake's-head modelling. Both no prov.

Pl. 49. Navan-type brooch, front and side views.
Navan Fort, Co. Armagh.

Pl. 50. Detail of Navan-type brooch, showing fine stippling,
Navan Fort, Co. Armagh.

Pl. 51. Navan-type brooches. 1 Somerset, Co. Galway. 2 Dunfanaghy, Co. Donegal. – Various scales.

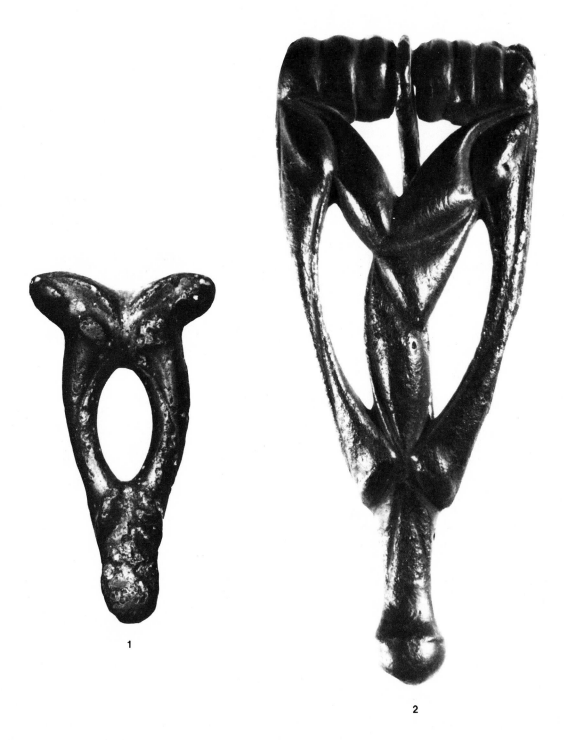

Pl. 52. Navan-type brooches. 1 Navan Fort, Co. Armagh.
2 no prov. – Various scales.

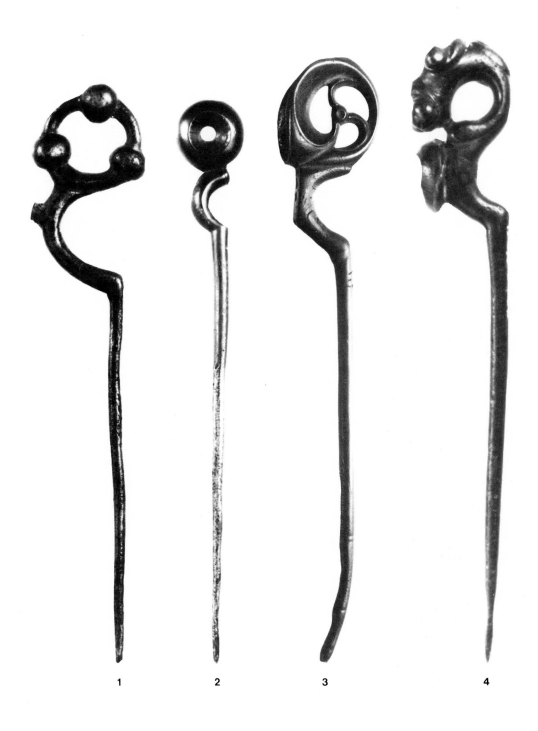

Pl. 53. Irish ringheaded pins. 1–2 type 1. 3 Type 3. 4 Type 2,
Co. Sligo. – Various scales.

Pl. 54. Irish Type 2 ringheaded pin, general view and detail. No prov.

1a   1b

2

Pl. 55. Irish Type 3 ringheaded pins. Lisnacrogher, Co. Antrim.

Pl. 56. Irish ringheaded pins, details. 1 Grange, Co. Sligo. 2 no prov.
3 Clough, Co. Antrim. – Various scales.

Pl. 57. Irish Type 4 ringheaded pin, details. River Shannon.

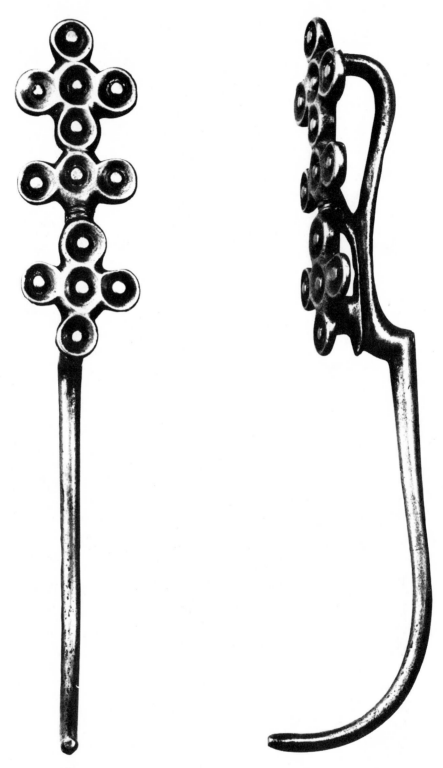

Pl. 58. Irish Type 4 ringheaded pin, front and side views.
Beaghmore, Co. Galway.

Pl. 59. Gold buffer torc. Clonmacnois, Co. Offaly.

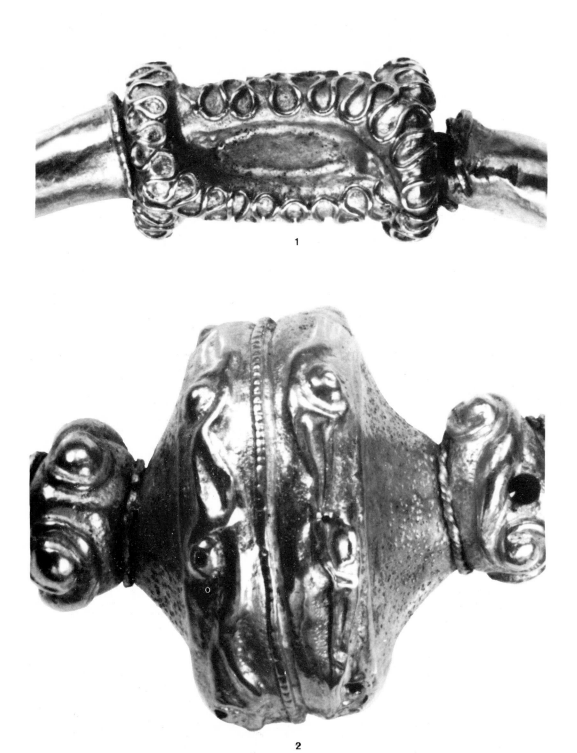

1

2

Pl. 60. Gold buffer-torc, Clonmacnois, Co. Offaly. Details.

Pl. 65. Bronze strap-tag. Rathgall, Co. Wicklow.

Pl. 66. Bronze mirror handle, Ballybogey Bog, Ballymoney, Co. Antrim.

Pl. 67. Enamelled bronze object. No prov.

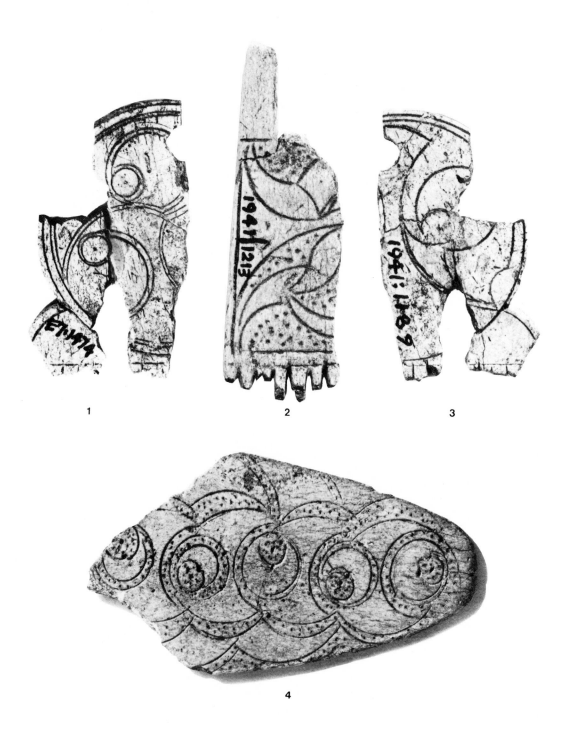

Pl. 68. 1–3 decorated bone comb fragments. 4 decorated flake.
Lough Crew, Co. Meath.

1

2   3

Pl. 69. Bronze bowl, general view and details of bird's-head handle.
Keshcarrigan, Co. Leitrim.

Pl. 70. Bronze bowls. River Bann.

Pl. 71. Bronze bowl, general view and detail of pseudo bird's-head handle.
Colchester, Essex, England.

Pl. 72. Bronze-bound wooden tankard. Carrickfergus, Co. Antrim.

Pl. 73. Decorated bronze tankard escutcheon. Carrickfergus, Co. Antrim.

1

2

Pl. 74. Globular bronze cauldrons. 1 Kincardine Moss, Stirlingshire, Scotland. 2 detail of Ballyedmond, Co. Galway, cauldron, showing decorative patch.

Pl. 75. Bronze projecting-bellied cauldrons. 1 Ballymoney, Co. Antrim.
2 Carlingwark Loch, Kirkcudbrightshire, Scotland. ·

Pl. 76. Jet spoon. Carbury Hill, Co. Kildare.

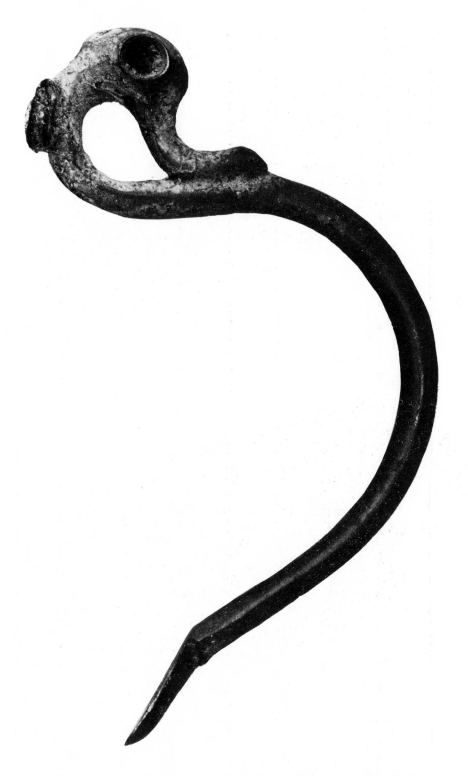

Pl. 77. Bronze, bird's-head handle. Somerset, Co. Galway.

Pl. 78. Beehive quernstone. Ticooly-O'Kelly, Co. Galway.

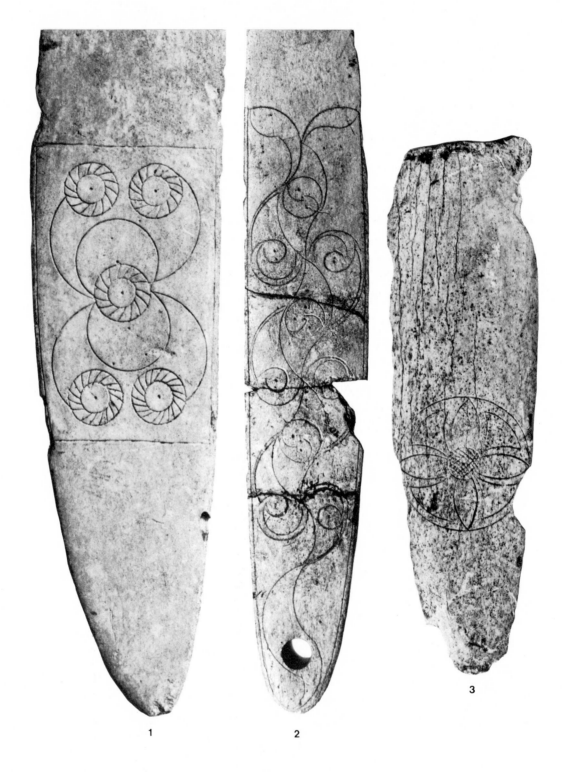

1 2 3

Pl. 80. Decorated bone flakes. Lough Crew, Co. Meath.

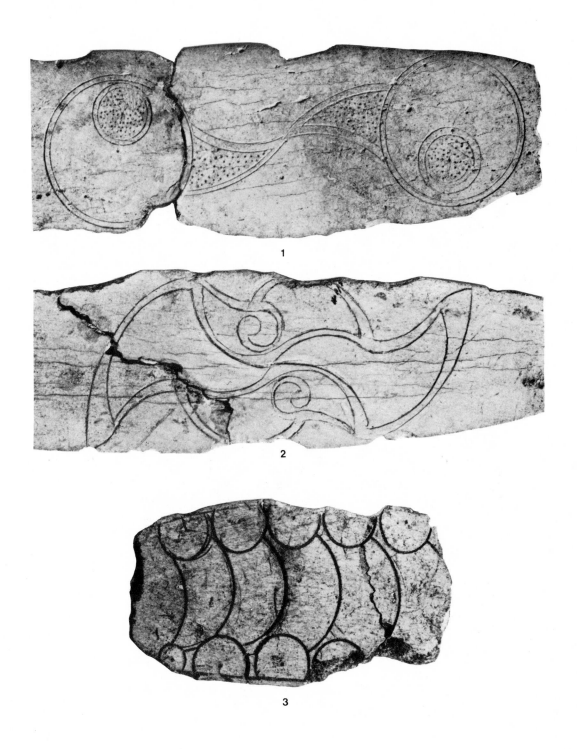

1

2

3

Pl. 81. Decorated bone flakes. Lough Crew, Co. Meath.

Pl. 82. Irish bronze "spoon", detail. No prov.

Pl. 83. Irish bronze "spoons", details. No prov.

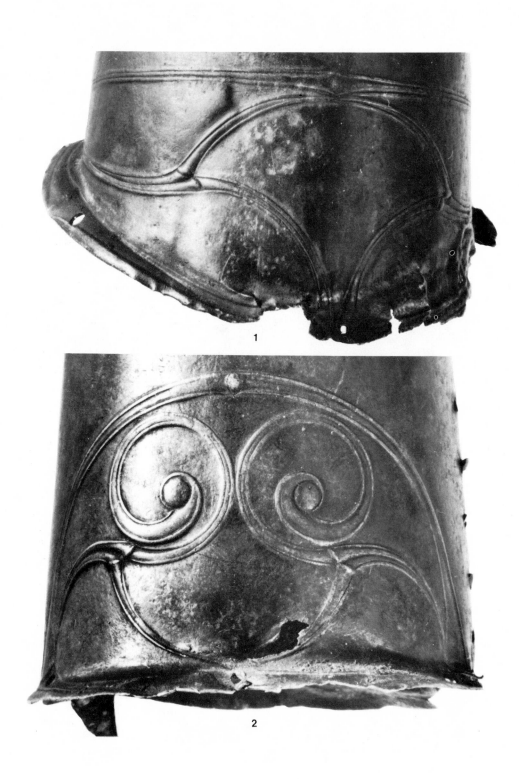

Pl. 84. Cork Horns. Details of decoration.

Pl. 85. The "Petrie Crown".

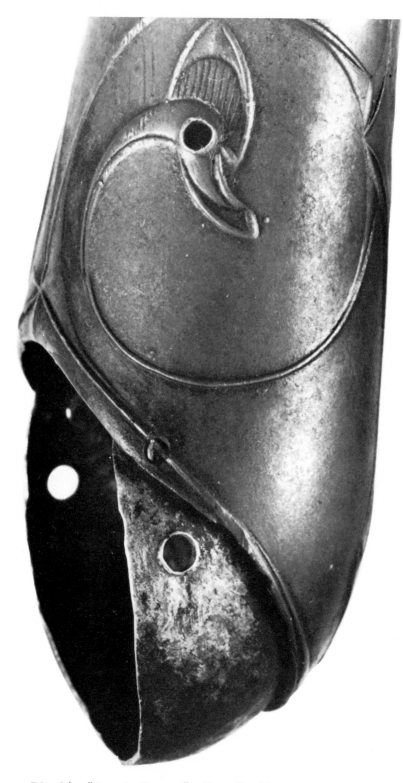

Pl. 86. "Petrie Crown". Detail of horn.

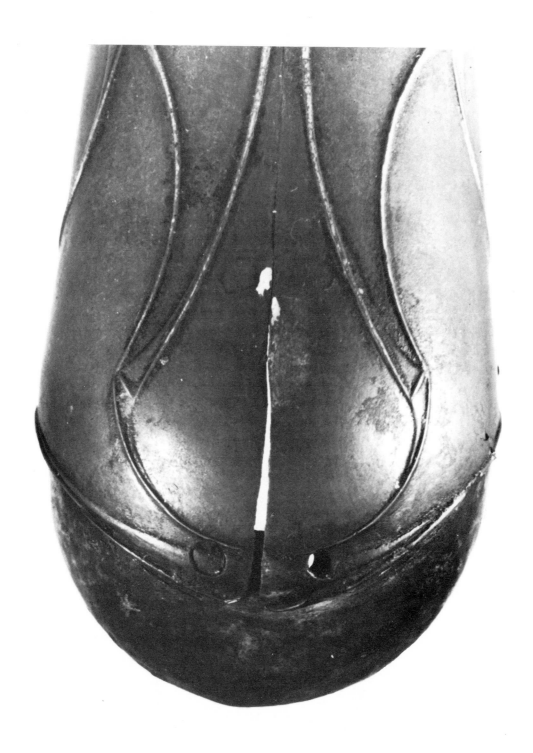

Pl. 87. "Petrie Crown". Detail of horn.

Pl. 88. Decorated bronze disc. Loughan Island, River Bann, Co. Derry.

Pl. 89. Decorated bronze ball. Walston, Lanarkshire, Scotland.

Pl. 90. Monasterevin-type discs.

Pl. 91. Monasterevin-type disc. Back. No prov.

Pl. 92. Monasterevin-type disc, detail. No prov.

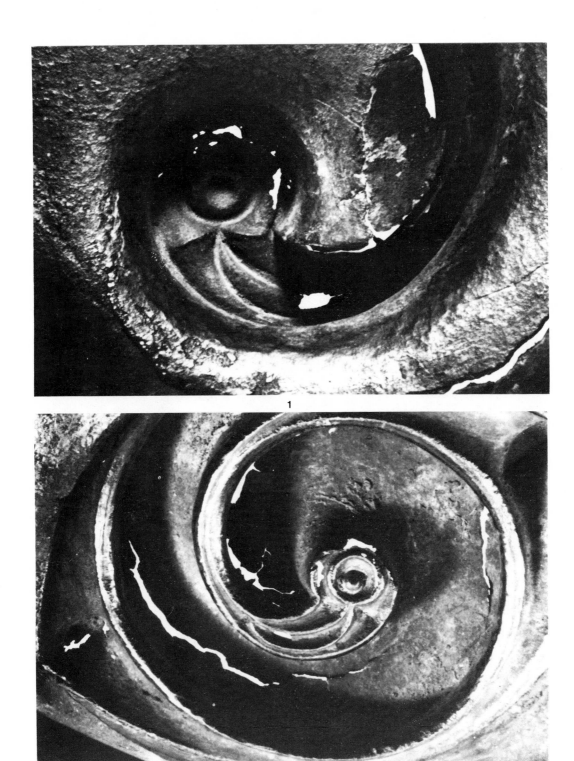

Pl. 93. Monasterevin-type disc, detail. 1 front, 2 back. No prov. (cf. Pl. 92).

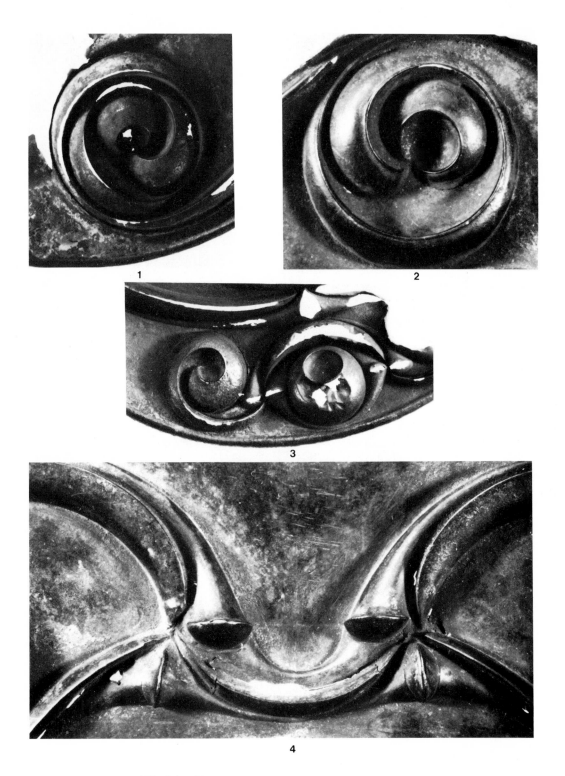

Pl. 94. Monasterevin-type discs. Details.

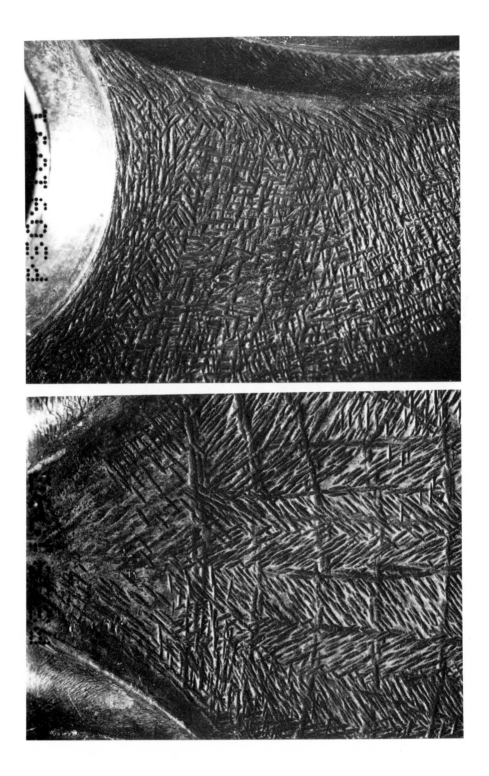

Pl. 95. Monasterevin-type disc. Details of toolmarks. No prov.

1

2

3

Pl. 96. Lambay, Co. Dublin. 1 circular disc. 2 details of central mount of
triangular disc.

1

2

Pl. 97. Somerset-type mounts. 1 Somerset, Co. Galway.
2 Ballycastle, Co. Antrim.

Pl. 98. Somerset-type mount. Somerset, Co. Galway.

Pl. 99. Somerset-type mounts. 1 Navan Fort, Co. Armagh.
2 Cornalaragh, Co. Monaghan.

Pl. 100. Bronze ring. Possibly North of Ireland.

Pl. 101. Bronze mount. No prov.

Pl. 102. Decorated stone. Turoe, Co. Galway.

Pl. 103. Decorated stone, Castlestrange, Co. Roscommon, showing base (Photo c.1920, from N.M.I. Archives).

Pl. 104. Decorated stone fragment. Killycluggin, Co. Cavan.

Pl. 105. Decorated stone, upper portion. Killycluggin, Co. Cavan.

Pl. 106. Decorated stone. Derrykeighan, Co. Antrim.

1

2

Pl. 107. Carved Breton stones. 1 Musée de Vannes. 2 Musée de Penmarc'h.

Pl. 108. Carved Breton stones. 1 Musée de Penmarc'h. 2 Audierne.

Pl. 109. Carved stone. "Lia Fáil", Tara, Co. Meath.

Pl. 110. Carved decoration on dolmen orthostat. Rathkenny, Co. Meath.

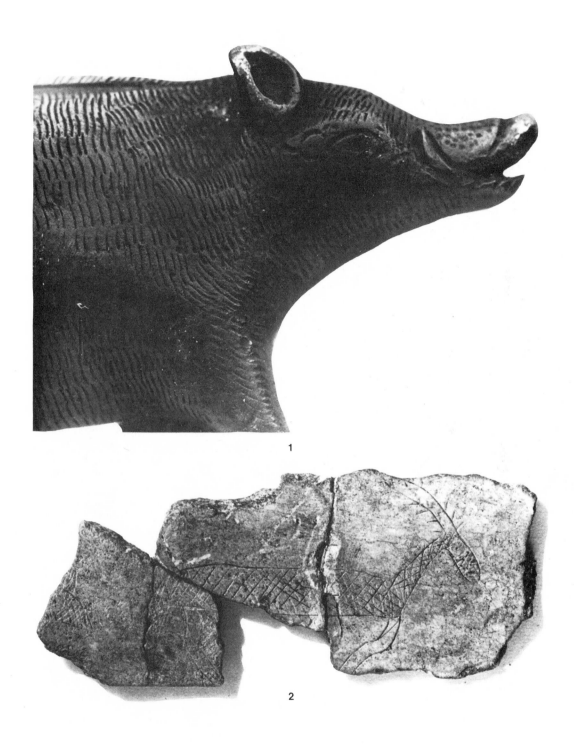

Pl. 111. 1 bronze boar, detail. 2 carved stags on bone flake.
Lough Crew, Co. Meath.

Pl. 112. 1 Wooden figure, Ralaghan, Co. Cavan. Detail. 2 bronze sword-
hilt, Ballyshannon, Co. Donegal. Detail.

Pl. 113. Carved stone heads. 1 Corleck, Co. Cavan.
2 Cavan town, Co. Cavan.